PHILIPPINE REPUBLIC

N

W   E

S

PACIFIC OCEAN

CELEBES

MOLUCCAS

NEW GUINEA (WEST IRIAN)

Kassar

TIMOR

AUSTRALIA

The Story of INDONESIA

The Story of
INDONESIA

by LOUIS FISCHER

Illustrated

Harper & Brothers · Publishers · New York

To George and Nell

Contents

PART II. THE PRESENT: PERSONS, PLACES, AND PROBLEMS

Illustrations

PART ONE

The Past: Romance, Gods, and Guilders

Chapter One

OF SHIPS, SPICES, AND WARS

BETWEEN THE Pacific and Indian oceans, between Asia and Australia, lie 7,900 islands. Once they were the Dutch East Indies. Today they are Indonesia. Three thousand of them are large, Java alone counting 57 million inhabitants. Some are no bigger than a peasant's farm. It is as though the gods that made the continents had a great deal of material left over and cast it helter-skelter into the equatorial waters.

A cluster of these islands called the Moluccas or Spice Islands was Columbus' goal when he accidentally discovered America. He knew the earth was round and that he could therefore reach the East Indies by heading west. But he made the mistake of thinking the earth was also small. "Dry land is six parts of it," he wrote King Ferdinand and Queen Isabella of Spain, his sponsors, on July 7, 1503; "the seventh only is covered with water." Since the seas were narrow, the voyage to Asia across the Atlantic would take less time than the route around Africa.

Columbus expected to reach Japan, China, and India. On November 12, 1492, a month after he first sighted American land, he reported to the King and Queen about "these islands of India." Until his death in Valladolid, Spain, on May 20, 1506, Christopher Columbus never suspected he had found a new continent. He believed he had come upon the Spice Islands, believed it so intensely that he sent home descriptions of spices which were not there.

While Columbus persisted in crossing and recrossing the Atlantic, Vasco da Gama, the intrepid Portuguese explorer, had, in 1498, discovered

3

the sea route from Western Europe to India by way of the South African Cape. Fellow countrymen followed in his wake. Ferdinand Magellan, for instance, sailed to India in 1505 and again in 1508. In July and August, 1511, the Portuguese commander Alfonso d'Albuquerque, with Magellan by his side, assaulted and took the seaport of Malacca on the Malay Peninsula, after which Magellan proceeded to the Spice Islands. In the next few years other Portuguese vessels anchored at Amboina, Banda, Ternate, and neighboring islands in the tiny Molucca archipelago and loaded precious nutmeg, cinnamon, mace, and cloves.

The Spaniards coveted Portugal's newly won position in Asia. Fortune smiled on them. When Magellan returned from the Moluccas in 1512 he quarreled with his king, moved to Spain, and renounced his Portuguese nationality. The Spanish monarchy thereupon outfitted five ships in which Magellan, hoping to succeed where Columbus had failed, proposed to seek a short westward route to the East Indies.

Magellan sailed from Seville, August 10, 1519. The little squadron arrived at Rio de Janeiro on December 13, 1519, and, hugging the South American shore, reached the Strait of Magellan on October 21, 1520. For thirty-eight days, amidst hardships, perils, losses, and doubts, they picked their way through the somber, chilly, mountain-fringed, 380-mile channel until finally they burst out on the broad ocean. Greeted by mild breezes and bright sunshine, Magellan gaily called it "The Pacific." Hopping from island to island, stopping at Guam too, Magellan sighted the Philippines on March 16, 1521.

In the Philippine island of Cebu, on April 27, 1521, Magellan fought a battle with hostile natives whom he was trying to convert to Christianity, and, wounded in the right arm by a javelin, in the face by a lance, in the left leg by a sword, he fell, and enemy warriors ran him through with scimitars until he died. He thus did not circumnavigate the globe. But one of his ships, the *Vittoria* (*Victoria*), continued to the Moluccas and took on spices; then, captained by Sebastian del Cano and manned by only eighteen surviving sailors (the others had died of scurvy, starvation, and wounds), it returned to Seville and dropped anchor on September 6, 1522—the first ship to sail around the earth. The voyage lasted just over three years.

Spain and Portugal competed furiously for the spice trade until, in 1529, they agreed on a division of territory: the Moluccas went to Portugal, the Philippines to Spain.

In those days of small boats, low speeds, and large casualties the monarchs and merchants who owned ships wanted them to carry compact cargo that brought high prices. Spices answered all the shipping requirements of the pre-steam age. They occupied little space and reaped rich profits. Spices were necessary for health, indeed for life. Food was heavy and monotonous, meats came to the kitchen in a semidecayed, putrid state, and appetites and digestion would have suffered but for the pepper, nutmeg, cloves, mace, ginger, and cinnamon added in liberal quantities to cooked and uncooked dishes. Spices served the physician too; for diseases of the blood, stomach, intestines, head, and chest, and for toothache, he often prescribed spices. The minuscule Moluccas produced what Asia, Europe, and Africa had to have. Apart from spices they yielded bird-of-paradise plumes, pearls, mother-of-pearl, and fragrant sandalwood. Sumatra also produced pepper.

In the circumstances, Portugal's monopoly in the Moluccas and elsewhere in Asia could not long remain undisputed. In 1580 Spain annexed Portugal and the Moluccas. Spain also owned part of Holland.

The defeat of the Spanish Armada in 1588 by England encouraged the Dutch to venture into the oceans in defiance of their imperial Iberian overlords. On April 2, 1595, almost a hundred years after Vasco da Gama's appearance at Calicut, India, four vessels, the first from the Netherlands, cannons mounted, pointed their prows toward Asia. Total manpower: 249. It took them 324 days to reach the East Indies. The expedition arrived back in Holland on August 14, 1597, after a homeward journey of 169 days, with only 89 men. The rest had died, 12 in fights with natives, 120 from scurvy, the remainder from other diseases. One ship was burned for want of crew. The nine Amsterdam businessmen who invested 290,000 florins in the venture earned 80,000 florins profit. This they deemed unsatisfactory. The income from the next expedition, which sailed in May, 1598, was four times the amount invested.

The race was on. Dutch fleet followed Dutch fleet, some by way of South Africa, others by way of South America in order to stop and prey on Spanish shipping before making the Strait of Magellan and the Indies. In 1602 the historic United Dutch East India Company was formed to trade with Asia, but equally, by the facts of life, to weaken Spain, against whom Holland was waging a protracted war for independence.

England and Holland likewise competed in spices. In 1603 the Dutch and British alone shipped 48,000 bags of pepper, each weighing 62 pounds—more than two and a half million pounds—to Europe. Demand continued to rise. Bigger business meant bigger headaches, for killing and commerce were partners and the overhead of the trade war was enormous. To drive out the British and achieve a monopoly of the valuable nutmeg trade, Jan Pieterszoon Coen, one of the first Dutch governor generals of the Indies, resolved on armed conquest of the Banda Islands in the Moluccas. "The Bandanese," writes Dutch historian Vlekke, "defended themselves with courage and skill, but their situation was hopeless. The islands were occupied after fierce fighting, and the population practically exterminated."

The British had sided with the islanders. "Whenever the Dutch got into trouble with the Indonesians," Vlekke comments sarcastically, "the British posed as well-meaning friends of the poor oppressed natives. . . . Nowhere was the competition fiercer than in the Banda Islands where the Dutch bluntly used their superiority in numbers and ships and maintained their 'rights of monopoly' by chasing the English out under a lavish display of gunfire."

Governor General Coen now needed a capital, a port, a single center for Dutch commerce in all Asia. He chose the ancient fortress of Jakarta on Java. The British desired it too. So did the King of Bantam in West Java. In 1619 Coen seized it, burned it, and began the construction of Batavia, which in time became the metropolis of the Dutch East Indies empire, a Dutch city on the edge of the tropical jungle with canals and short bridges and little houses to remind them of those they had left behind in Holland.

At Amboina in the Moluccas, ten Englishmen and their nine Asian bodyguards were executed by the Dutch in 1623. The "Amboina massacre" echoed down the decades in British polemical literature. A pamphlet published in London in 1712, and supplied with a gruesome frontispiece illustration of a Dutch execution chamber, carried the title *The History of the Barbarous Cruelties and Massacres Committed by the Dutch in the East Indies*. A second brochure, likewise dated 1712, by John Beaumont, bore the sneering and customarily lengthy name of *Dutch Alliances: or a plain proof of their observance of treaties; exemplified in the particulars of their inhuman treatment of their friends and confederates, the English, at Amboyna.*

The British were weaker and bitter. Denouncing the Amboina massacre, King James I said to the Dutch ambassador, "You are masters of the sea wide and large and do what you want." But historian Vlekke, coolly judging the event against the moral climate of the time and place, declares that it "was not even a massacre," and though it "kept its propaganda value for . . . 250 years" it was "only one of many bloody episodes in the history of ruthless commercial competition."

Spain, Holland's enemy and rival, was sinking. In 1640 Portugal regained her freedom from the Spaniards. At the battle of Rocroi, in 1643, France, an emerging military power, inflicted a notable military defeat on Spain. In 1648 the Spanish monarchy finally signed a peace with a united independent Holland.

Remained Portugal. The Dutch operation against her encompassed the globe. Holland drove the Portuguese from Brazil, from West Africa, from the Persian Gulf, from Ceylon, and in 1641, after a siege lasting several years, captured the Portuguese bastion of Malacca on the shallow, narrow Straits of Malacca between Malaya and Sumatra through which most trade from the West to the Indies had to pass. The Portuguese empire in Asia went into eclipse.

By 1650 Holland was the world's greatest power. She had a secure hold on the Malabar Coast in West India and the Coromandel Coast in East India. She held Formosa as well as Ceylon, South Africa as well as West Africa, parts of Brazil as well as islands in the Caribbean. The Dutch were feared and appreciated. When the Tokugawa shogunate in 1647 barred all foreigners from Japan, the Dutch alone were allowed to maintain an outpost on an island in the harbor of Nagasaki. Restlessly searching for new worlds, Abel Tasman, a Dutch explorer, discovered Tasmania to the south of Australia and two big islands which he christened New Zeeland (now New Zealand) after a province in Holland.

In Europe, Holland fished the North Sea and was mistress of the Baltic. Dutch bottoms carried most of Russia's export trade with the West. Dutch merchants had founded Archangel, the Russian arctic port, in 1584.

The Dutch were entrenched in North America too. In 1609 a group of Amsterdam merchants bought the services of the English explorer, Henry Hudson, and instructed him to find a shorter westbound route to the Indies—still that stubborn illusion that America was merely an unfortunate obstacle on the way to the wealth of the Far East. After four months spent traversing the Atlantic and nosing his ships into a number of inlets he reached what is now Sandy Hook, New Jersey, and then, in the *Half Moon,* touched at Manhattan, so named for the Indian tribe on the island. Later the good Dutch businessmen purchased the island for the equivalent of $24 and started to build New Amsterdam on it.

How did Holland, with fewer than two million inhabitants, achieve this eminence and might? She had money. Shipping, shipbuilding, and fishing constantly brought in profits much of which the thrifty Netherlanders saved and put at the disposal of Amsterdam bankers. Dutch shipwrights had commenced, in 1594, to construct a 300-ton monarch of the seas. Textiles flowed from Holland's factories and food from her farms. Her artisans were masters, her army good and brave, her seamen daring. In 1628, for instance, a Dutch captain captured a Spanish silver fleet carrying an enormous treasure of 11 million guilders. This was the golden age of Rembrandt, Frans Hals and Vermeer, of literary giants, and of notable scientists. Holland attracted foreign talent too. From 1629 to 1649 the French philosopher Descartes lived on her soil.

The Dutch used this period of world supremacy to reinforce their grip on the East Indies. The British retained a trading base at Benkulen, on the West Sumatran coast. Portugal to this day owns the eastern part of the island of Timor ("Timor" is Indonesian for east) as an inglorious reminder of her vanished imperial glory. But no European power now contested Holland's rule over the Indies.

The Dutch fall from the world pinnacle was as sudden and precipitous as the ascent. Amsterdam remained a great banking center: in 1782, John Adams, later George Washington's successor as president, went there to obtain a loan for the new, struggling United States. Dutch shipwrights excelled as before; in 1697, Tsar Peter I, disguised as plain "Peter Mikhailov," worked for four months in and near Amsterdam as a wage-earning ship carpenter to learn the art of shipbuilding and to hire shipbuilders for his country. Nevertheless, Holland could not maintain her number one world-power position. With a foothold in literally every continent, she was spread too thin and exposed to counterattack. In 1661 a Chinese leader, expelled from the mainland by the conquering Manchus —preview of the twentieth century?—escaped to Formosa and ousted the Dutch. (Later the Manchus ousted him.) From 1652 to 1654 England and Holland fought a sea war, and in September, 1664, despite the state of peace, the Duke of York, who later ruled as James II, captured New Amsterdam, ran up the British flag, and renamed the place New York. Peter Stuyvesant, the Dutch director general, hobbled out on his wooden leg.

England and France had put their houses in order and appeared on the world scene as dangerous competitors of Holland—and of each other. Britain, France, and Germany entered the industrial age. Having no raw materials, the Dutch lost many markets. Sweden and Russsia began to contest Dutch supremacy in the Baltic Sea. Holland likewise had to abandon Brazil. The Dutch empire overseas shriveled. But when, in 1671, rumors of the Netherlands' collapse encouraged Indonesian potentates to rebel, and England to contemplate conquest, the Dutch swept the British navy from the surrounding seas. The East Indies were a possession Holland meant to keep till the last breath. They saved her from being a poor little country by the chilly North Sea.

Chapter Two

GODS REMODELED

It MUST not be supposed that the Portuguese or Spaniards or Dutch discovered the East Indies in the sense that Columbus discovered America. Nor should anyone imagine those hardy sixteenth-century mariners climbing up the beaches of Banda, Ternate, and other spice islands and picking peppers, peeling cinnamon bark, or collecting clove buds while savages looked on in amazement. The Indonesians grew the trees, collected the spices, and sold them to the newcomers as they had sold them for centuries to traders and sailors from China, India, and Arabia. The Iberians' and Netherlands' only distinction was that they came from Europe.

Far from being "savages" like the people Columbus encountered in the New World, the East Indians had cities, temples, governments, irrigation systems, handicrafts, shipping, art, and literature.

The origins of the Indonesian people are not fully known. It has been established that man existed on Java about half a million years ago. The fossil creature, the upper part of whose skull, two molars, and a thigh bone were excavated in 1891 and 1892 by a Dutchman, Dr. Eugene Dubois, on the bank of the Solo River in Central Java, has been named Pithecanthropus erectus. This almost-human being, still strongly resembling an ape, presumably was a "missing link" between the simians and ourselves. (Another link has been exhumed near Peking.)

Dr. Bubois's Pithecanthropus erectus probably hunted tiger, tapir, and rhinoceros and heard the chatter of monkeys, for in his day Java formed part of the Asian continent. Alfred Russel Wallace, the great British naturalist, friend of Charles Darwin and author of a fascinating two-volume work published in 1869, entitled, *The Malay Archipelago, The Land of the Orang-Utan and the Bird of Paradise,* noted how shallow (300 to 600 feet) were the seas between Java, Sumatra, and Borneo and the Asian mainland. In contrast, the ocean reaches great depths (6,000 feet) farther east around the Moluccas and New Guinea but becomes shallow again between New Guinea and Australia. After years of research on the flora and fauna of the islands, Wallace concluded that the western parts of Indonesia, to a point somewhere near the Celebes, were once joined to the mainland and are therefore the natural habitat of the elephants, big cats, and apes native to Asia. But none of these animals is found in New Guinea, the home, like Australia and no other place on earth, of marsupials: the kangaroo, platypus, and so on. Wallace accordingly drew "the Wallace Line" between the Asian and Austronesian worlds.

However, tigers and rhinos do not ply boats; man does. The ethnographer Bronislaw Malinowski, in *Argonauts of the Western Pacific,* describes giant canoes, bearing as many as eighteen men, in which the primitive Papuans of New Guinea travel hundreds of miles over choppy seas. Water and distance never did block human adventure.

At his lunch table in Bogor one Sunday I remarked to President Sukarno on the resemblance I saw between some Indonesians and American Indians.

"Kon-Tiki," he commented.

"Kon-Tiki and Alaska," I said. "Asians must have crossed the Bering Strait, which is completely iced over in winter, to Alaska and trekked down to what is now the United States and beyond."

Indonesia's present population is the result of countless migrations grafted on the offspring of Pithecanthropus erectus. The first settlers, many millenniums ago, were Negritos from New Guinea or dark Dravidians who fled South India before the advancing Central Asian Aryans.

Before the dawn of history, and since, people from India and other regions of South Asia streamed into Indonesia. The Celebes has had an influx from the Philippines, 300 miles to the north. Countries as far apart as China and Arabia added their salt to the Indonesian mixture. Constant intermarriage produced a type basically Malay and Polynesian, yet enriched by the blood of a score of races and therefore showing endless variations.

Indonesian skin varies from brown to burnished-bronze reddish brown to glossy chocolate brown; the nearest Caucasian approach is a lifeguard's end-of-season tan. "When God," as an Austrian diplomat told the story, "wished to create man, He put the necessary materials into an oven and waited. The product came out black, overdone. On the next attempt the man was white, underdone. The third time everything was just right, a delightful brown, and He made many of them."

The Indonesians' hair is straight and a brilliant black. Beards are rare. A dozen isolated hairs on the chins of some men suggest that they never need shave. Noses are short; cheekbones usually high; eyes rounder than almond-shaped Chinese eyes.

Indonesian men and women are well-built with finely molded muscles, good carriage, quick nervous reactions, and manual dexterity. The average adult, however, is four or more inches shorter than in the United States, Western Europe, the Commonwealth, and Scandinavia. This is usually ascribed to climate, and that may indeed be a factor. It is as likely due to bad diet. In the Celebes, Bali, and Java I saw many children, who go naked till the age of six and older, with great distended "rice bellies," as the doctors diagnose them. Centuries of protein and vitamin insufficiency have stunted growth. Well-to-do Western-educated Indonesian parents declare that proper nourishment enables the new generation to shoot up two or three inches in stature.

Generalizations mislead. I met a Moluccan from Amboina who was six feet tall and almost white. Most Balinese are taller than the average Indonesian. Occasionally in Java one looks and wonders, "Is he Indonesian or Chinese?" The answer may depend on a slight difference in eye slant or skin tint. Just as mountains tend to create distinctions of race and dialect, so do islands, even more so—and Indonesia's islands are mountainous. Hence the myriad gradations in physical characteristics and cultural levels. There is the aboriginal Dayak in Borneo's swamp jungles and the sophisticated Javanese of Jakarta, the Stone Age New Guinea Papuan and the skilled Sumatran statesman.

Early data on or relics of Indonesian culture are rare. Hinduism, coming from India, apparently commenced as a trickle five centuries before our era and had struck roots by the time of Christ. The first authentic written report on a foreigner's visit to Indonesia is that of Fahien, or Fahian, a Chinese Buddhist pilgrim who went from China to India overland and, returning by boat in A.D. 414, stopped in Java, which he called "Yava-di" or Land of Millet. "In this country," he wrote in his book, *An Account of the Buddhist Countries,* "heretics and Brahmans flourish, but the law of Buddha scarcely deserves mentioning."

References to Indonesians as "heretics," "idolaters," and worshipers of many gods abound in the literature of the time. Actually they were animists. Animism is the belief that all living things, including animals and plants, are invested with a soul. Animistic beliefs still pervade Indonesia, and especially Java, home of 57 of the country's 87 million inhabitants. The waringin tree, for instance, known in India as the banyan, is sacred to many Indonesians. Its trunk grows to a great height and to a vast width—sometimes ten feet or more—for its branches bend downward and implant themselves into the earth only to take root and shoot up again as new trunks linked with the original one. Repeatedly renewing itself in this manner, and enduring for centuries, the waringin became a symbol of the vital essence. Holy images are occasionally housed in its foliage. Goat heads and chickens may be buried at its roots, in a form of animal sacrifice. Neither the whole tree nor any of its branches must ever be cut down. Even its mammoth creepers should remain inviolate. Once the gardener of Jakarta acquaintances removed a big vine from a waringin. The next day he died.

"If you want a girl to love you," the saying goes, "send her a packet of your hair." Hair has mana: the quality of magic. So has the kris, or short ceremonial dagger. A Jakarta university student, who spoke a fine English, read widely in Western literature, and was a complete rationalist in politics and ideology, told me that in his home in Central Java they used to burn incense every Friday, the Moslem Sabbath, before a case containing the family kris. One Friday they failed to do it and the kris danced in anger.

"How do you know this?" I asked.

"I saw it," he replied.

During a national crisis in 1946, President Sukarno sat and prayed before his kris all day and gave instructions not to be disturbed. The information was vouchsafed by a highly placed government official. I apologized for inquiring after the source of his knowledge. "I was there," he said. "I was then attached to the President's staff. The kris," he elaborated, "is a symbol of vitality. Sukarno prayed for strength. Prayer involved contemplation, self-analysis, and search."

Sukarno was no exception. Scratch an Indonesian and you will find an animist or mystic. Indonesia's population consists of about 2 million Hindus, most of them on Bali island, 5 million Christians, and 80 million Moslems. But the percentage of those wholly immune to animism cannot be great.

"The West," the permanent head of the Indonesian Foreign Office said to me, "combats and changes nature. We accept it." Nature is so sublimely beautiful, supremely mysterious, and intimate that they did not merely accept it. They made it their first god. Since then, over the ages, they have injected it into all imported religions.

A septuagenarian Sumatran of high culture told me that as a young man he was once walking by a stream with his grandmother when they spied a crocodile. "That," she exclaimed, "is my mother!" A departed parent's soul might choose to inhabit an animal or vegetation or to lead an independent existence in a wraith world. It may return as a specter to the scenes it knew, and since it could be present in the house or neighborhood at any given moment, it must be consulted, appeased, and fed. This is the basis of ancestor worship.

A split second after death, animists argue, the body is much like its living self. Yet it is totally different. The soul has escaped. The soul is life. Ancient Indonesians connected the soul with the shadow. The shadow is of a person yet intangible, now appearing, now vanishing. Is it like the soul which returns to God during sleep, like the spirit which inhabits human beings during a trance, like the special gift which enables the soothsayer to read the future?

The most popular art form in Moslem Indonesia today is the Hindu shadow play, or wayang. Especially on Java and Bali, audiences will watch it from dusk to dawn. The wayang, using leather puppets or human figures which cast shadows on a screen, depicts episodes from the Hindu classics, the *Mahabharata* and *Ramayana,* with endless Indonesian embellishments and modifications. It is Indonesian sacred drama: a king wrestles with demons; a holy man combats evil spirits. Addressing God, a wayang author says, "Your lamp irradiates me. This body is my shadow but I myself am in Your hands." The body is illusion, the shadow its reflections. The essence is the soul which is of and in God.

Subarda was the wife of Arjuna, the central figure of the Bhagavad-Gita, Hinduism's holy scripture. Summarizing a wayang about her, President Sukarno said, "Subarda fell ill and was unconscious for a long time. Her soul went wandering, looking for her body, searching for herself." Soul, shadow, spirit, ghost are one. Soul and God are one. Therefore, the argument runs, animism and theism are one.

Hinduism, Indonesia's first imported religion, meshed with the native animism. About the year A.D. 1000 a new immigrant wave from Burma, Siam, Cambodia, Laos, and Indo-China brought Buddhism to the Indies. But it did not compete with Hinduism or animism. They merged. Religion in Indonesia was dynamic rather than dogmatic. It made alliances. Hinduism and Buddhism assumed new shapes.

The Hindu God is a Trimurti, or trinity, of three faces: Brahma, the creator: Vishnu, the preserver; and Shiva or Siva, the destroyer. West Java worshiped Vishnu; Central Java, Shiva. Time passed, however, and Shiva softened. It became, as sculptures show, half female, thus less demonic, more humane, and not too different from the preserving Vishnu. Scholars continue to dispute whether a certain temple image is Shiva or Vishnu.

Subsequently, Shiva underwent a further transformation. Influenced by Buddhism, Shiva came to be represented as a benign, contemplative penitent. Statues of Shiva were now identical with Buddha's. A Shiva-Buddha cult arose which was a synthesis of opposites and thus a true mirror of Indonesian mentality. What is more, Shiva, according to Java mystics, went to Mecca and adopted Islam. That created a three-in-one oneness, the unity so desired by Indonesians.

The greatest relic in Indonesia is Borobudur, near the city of Jogjakarta in Central Java. A gigantic Buddhist stupa on a hill, built sometime between the ninth and twelfth centuries A.D., Borobudur has a rectangular base surmounted by a dome and contains nearly four hundred images of Buddha. The builders were Hindus probably born in India. Borobudur houses many sculptures which are Hindu, Hindu-Buddhist, and animist: Shiva in a horse-drawn chariot; Shiva's wife Durga, and their elephant-nosed offspring Ganesh; a god with wings and the spurs of a cock; a dog in the dress of a man; an elephant with four pairs of tusks; a bear with horns; a smiling warrior holding a kris; hunting and maritime scenes; West Indian Hindu faces with beards; a lion guarding a temple; a conventionalized lion head above the smiling Buddha; Shiva on a throne in the pose of Buddha; Buddha on a throne supported by tiny bearded lions; Buddha receiving offerings from human-looking angels on clouds; and so on.

Borobudur, therefore, is not purely Indian or Indonesian or Hindu or Buddhist. It is a unique manifestation of religious-artistic polygamy.

More than outward form changed. Under the smile of Buddha and the moderating impact of Java, Hinduism lost the rigidity—and the castes, taboos, and untouchability which mar it in India. It became a Hinduism without renunciation, penance, or fasts.

Just when the Hindu-Buddhist animism achieved its finest flower in the sculptures and reliefs of Borobudur, Islam appeared in Indonesia. Mohammedanism most probably first came to the East Indies in the ships of spice merchants from Gujerat, the home, then as now, of India's famed tradesmen, and from Persia. Arab sailors also helped convert Indonesia to Islam. Moslems from India and the Middle East visited Atjeh, the nearest Indonesian point of contact with the West, in the ninth century. From Atjeh, at the northern tip of Sumatra, Islam spread throughout the entire island, today still the Mohammedan fortress of Indonesia. In Java, however, the existence of native Hindu kingdoms checked the advance of the new religion. Nevertheless, Moslem merchants from India, Persia, and Arabia did settle in Javanese ports, where they waxed rich, married into influential Hindu families, and taught the Koran. After the decline of Hindu temporal power in the 1400's, Java too gradually accepted Islam, and so also did the rest of the Indies—except Bali, Hindu to this day.

In the lush, verdant, and well-watered East Indian isles, however, Islam could not remain the austere faith that sprang from the harsh sandy deserts and rocky wastes of the Middle East. It never, for instance, hid women behind purdah walls or the veil. Moslem women in Indonesia can take the initiative for a divorce. Indonesia mellowed Mohammedanism, lending it features of pantheistic Hinduism, atheistic Buddhism, and primitive animism.

An Indonesian peasant brought two goats to a temple as a sacrifice. "He, a Moslem," comments Dutch historian Vlekke, "was following an old Hindu rite practiced by his ancestors a thousand years ago." And the rite was animistic.

Islam settled, like new soil, on the underlying strata of Hinduism and Buddhism, and all three were interlaced with veins of the magic and mysticism of the animists.

Indonesia's civilization is like a marbled layer cake.

The Indonesian genius, in religion as in politics, runs to compromise and rejoices in the commingling of divergent elements. The Indonesian mind, particularly in Java, is tolerant. The people are too close to nature and too easy going to be doctrinaire, too emotional to be intellectually arrogant, abusive, or irascible, and too gentle to hate or segregate. Grudges do not endure, and the door is never closed against defeated opponents or repentant prodigals. This characteristic, to be sure, is subject to deviations. The Indonesian sometimes runs amuck and is capable of great cruelty. But normally he would rather absorb, ingest, and transform than reject or annihilate. Unpin-downability, or avoidance of inflexible classifications, is a strong trait. Partitions between ideas are perforated, and pigeonholing is therefore a trying task. Anybody left in one compartment in the evening may have vanished, reclassified himself, by morning.

Into this elusive Asian culture Europe, cold, commercial, and Christian, erupted in 1511.

Chapter Three

FROM MARCO POLO TO NAPOLEON

MARCO POLO is the first Christian and European known to have seen Indonesia. His father, Nicolo, and his uncle, Maffeo, left their Venice home in 1260 to transact business in Constantinople, and then traveled overland, via Bokhara and other Central Asian regions, to the court of the great Mongol ruler, Kublai Khan, conqueror of China. On a subsequent journey, Papa Polo took Marco along. Marco Polo loved to write and has left us accounts—revealing even when not quite accurate —of China and of trips between the Great Khan's ample realms and Venice.

In 1290, Marco Polo, homeward bound, visited Sumatra, which he called "Java the less" though it is almost four times the size of Java. His next stop was Java. "Experienced mariners," his diary entry reads, "say that it is the greatest island in the world [it is as large as England] and has a compass of 3000 miles. It is subject to a great king and tributary to no one else in the world. The people are idolaters. The island is of surpassing wealth, producing black pepper, nutmeg, spikenard, galingale, cubebs, cloves, and all other kinds of spices.

"This island is also frequented by a vast amount of shipping, and by merchants who buy and sell costly goods from which they reap great profit. Indeed the treasure of this island is so great as to be past telling. And I can assure that the Great Khan never could get possession of this Island, on account of its great distance, and the great expense of an expedition thither."

His data on spices were wrong; Java did not grow them, it sold them. But on military matters the conquering Kublai might have listened to the shrewd civilian Marco. For in 1292 the Khan sent an army against Java. It seems an ambassador of Kublai had had his face tattooed or otherwise mutilated by King Kertanagara of East Java, and disdaining to pocket the insult—as good an excuse as any for aggression—the Emperor resolved to subdue the island.

Until shortly before the invasion, Indonesian chronology is cloudy and dates are dim. History deals hazily with royalty born of gods and adept in magic. Thus King Kertanagara was a descendant of Angrok, who was conceived with the help of Brahma and became the embodiment of Vishnu after Shiva had adopted him. Kertanagara, though less auspiciously sponsored, expanded westward in Java, and conquered Bali, some of the Moluccas, and parts of Sumatra. This probably provoked the Great Khan's ire.

Kertanagara eluded Kublai's long avenging arm when a rival potentate murdered him before the enemy soldiers appeared. The son of late king, Prince Vijaya, thereupon offered his services to the invading Mongol army if it unseated his father's murderer. The Mongols obliged, and for their pains were subjected to hit-and-run guerrilla attacks. Unable to summon reinforcements from their remote homeland, the Mongols took to their boats in 1293 and sailed away to China.

Vijaya then founded the Madjapahit Empire, whose glory endured until 1389—almost a century. It was a Golden Age. The Madjapahit period is the brightest name in Indonesia's ancient era of independence and is proudly given today to social organizations, commercial wares, and streets. Its greatest leader was not a king but Gajah Mada, prime minister to the last Madjapahit ruler, whom Vlekke regards as "the most interesting figure in Javanese history" because "he was the first of all to succeed in unifying the whole archipelago under one rule." Gajah Mada achieved this goal by the only means available in those slow-motion days: he bribed lesser kings, princes, and rajahs into submissive satraps and, leaving them some rope and the symbols of power, exacted tribute through the agency of a fleet which moved among the outer islands to awe and if necessary destroy.

Prapanca, poet laureate of the Madjapahit Empire's heyday, glorifying his monarch, wrote: "Truly King Hayam Wuruk is a great potentate. He is without care or worries. He indulges in all pleasures. All beautiful maidens in Janggala and Kediri are selected for him, as many as possible, and of those captured in foreign countries, the prettiest girls are brought into his harem."

Paradise did not outlast Prime Minister Gajah Mada. Upon his death the hedonistic King refused the burdens of government and divided the empire among his four sons. Further splits occurred which gave the watching rulers of the Malay Peninsula, Siam, and China unlimited opportunities to nibble at the unity of the Indies. The empire lived but lost its vitality and vassals. The Moluccas and several Sumatran principalities began to pay tribute, or when possible only homage, to China. Other fragments achieved shadowy independence. Madjapahit splinters survived till about 1525.

At about this juncture Europe entered the Orient.

Vital and united, the East Indies might have resisted the white intruder. Divided, they fell and gave Europe the cue which brought it on the stage for more than four centuries.

Of the early Europeans in Indonesia, John Crawfurd, the British Resident in Java from 1811 to 1816, writes: "The plunder of the east, for it did not deserve the name of commerce, was their object. . . . To give an equitable price for the commodity they purchased, or to demand no more than a reasonable profit, never entered into their minds. They considered the natives of those countries as fair game."

Given British competition with Holland, this official could not be expected to spare the Dutch. "The first Dutch adventurers to the East," he charged, "were a set of rapacious traders, who found themselves unexpectedly called upon to exercise the functions of politicians and sovereigns."

In fairness, he tarred the British with the same brush. As between his own country and the Netherlands, he found it "difficult to say which party was *least* to blame, unless we pronounce in favor of that which had the smallest power of aggression. On both sides the mean and bad passions which were excited by avarice, and by commercial and national rivalry, were carried to an unexampled extent."

The Dutch East India Company, authorized by the Netherlands to conduct economic and political affairs in the Indies Archipelago, was "a state within a state," "a law unto itself," "a sovereign state with her own treasury, currency, executive, laws, army and navy," writes Professor Justus M. van der Kroef, a Dutch authority. "Company officials lived in Oriental splendor with all the attributes of princely power."

In *Colonial Policy,* a massive two-volume *magnum opus,* Dr. A. D. A. de Kat Angelino, a Dutch defender of the Dutch record in the Indies, agrees that "the small powers of resistance of the Eastern communities increased the temptation to exploit them, and generally to give way to baser instincts." The exploitation lasted two hundred years.

The Portuguese and the Spaniards were the worst offenders. They came for gold and God and no devilish act was too black for them. Their

policy was the Bible or the Sword, and as often, Spices or the Sword.
Eight thousand miles from the Mediterranean they continued the war
fought in Europe and the Holy Land against Moor and Saracen. By
doing so they brought Christianity into disrepute and fertilized the new
soil of Islam. "The Christian religion, in the countries of the Archipelago, and in those around," John Crawfurd wrote in 1820, "is justly
unpopular, because in every instance, it has been the instrument of
political intrigue, or been propagated by violence, when the consequence
of its introduction has been the inevitable loss of the most valuable political and civil rights."

The Europeans were not impelled by imperialism. Nobody thought of
dominion, only of getting rich quickly and, by ingrained habit, of saving
"pagan" souls. To the Iberians, says Netherlands Professor B. Schrieke
in *Indonesian Sociological Studies,* Mohammed was "the devil incarnate.
Whoever spared one of his followers failed in his duty, a duty which in
most cases was all the more zealously fulfilled because political and
commercial interests were benefitted by it."

By comparison the Dutch were mild. But they were not in the tropics
for their health. They found they needed a monopoly in order to make
more money. Little sultans in the puny Moluccas, petty kings in the
Celebes, in West Java, and in Central Java harbored the notion that they
could continue trading directly with China, Portugal, and Britain. The
Dutch East India Company stopped such activity and set a naval watch
for pirates and smugglers who tried to elude its orders. Native princes
who demurred succumbed to Dutch superiority in arms, martial valor,
and military organization. If the defeated ruler proved amenable he
kept his phantom throne. Elsewhere the Dutch company appointed puppets who were as compliant as they felt they had to be.

Thus a private firm geared to money-making found a loose empire
lying in its lap. Nevertheless, guilders remained the goal. The Dutch
East India Company's brain was a hungry purse and its heart a bookkeeper's account book. To raise prices a predetermined number of
nutmeg and clove trees were cut down in the Moluccas, to the consternation of the natives who fought for the living things but were brushed
aside by an armored arm. In 1707 coffee seedlings from India were first
planted experimentally in Java. They prospered beyond expectation.
Soon Java coffee won world renown. Guilders rolled into Amsterdam's
banks. The company now resorted to crop restriction by reducing the
price paid to the peasant grower. He responded by losing interest in
coffee culture altogether. The company counterresponded by introducing
compulsory deliveries enforced by native regents and district officers.
The peasant had to sow and sell.

The company, now the trader-ruler, exercised political power and economic control but had next to no contact with the people. There might be a Dutch Resident in some regions. But actual administration was left to hereditary regents and village headmen who collected export crops, dispensed blind justice, and maintained order under the ultimate sanction of Dutch force.

This seventeenth- and eighteenth-century social system was an Oriental despotism imposed by Occidentals and implemented by Orientals. The Dutch were one pinnacle of society. Though they had no rights, for the orders of the Governor General and his Amsterdam directors were undisputed law, they enjoyed un-European privileges. They worked hard, lived hard, drank hard, and died in masses from still-unnamed tropical diseases. The royal Indies families were the other social pinnacle. Their courts were centers of indolence, luxury, and profligacy. Their pageantry amused the white man and awed the brown. The evils of an aloof, foreign tyranny were compounded by an unfeeling Eastern feudalism. Native rulers, submissive to the company, in effect owned the land, the villagers who tilled it, and the produce. In the cellar of society dwelt the slaves and the host of unpaid and poorly paid servants. Since few women came out from Holland, female serfs and maids filled a special need in Dutch households. Mixed-blood children of course outnumbered the interracial marriages which ensued.

The Indonesian people, thanks to Dutch oppression, Islamic sterility, and no leadership, succumbed to a cultural coma, political paralysis, and economic decline. Dutch and immigrant Chinese business activities destroyed the once-important native class of merchants and mariners. The peasants had no power, the princes no courage or ambition. Salvation from within was unlikely.

Presently, a revolutionary tidal wave from America and France touched the Indies. Not that the ideas of Jefferson and Danton stirred a single Indonesian. It was merely that the far-off archipelago felt the shock when the volcanoes of freedom erupted in Philadelphia and Paris.

"All men are created equal," thundered the Declaration of Independence on July 4, 1776, in Philadelphia. This document, which could be renamed the Anticolonial Manifesto, proclaimed to subject peoples that "when a long train of abuses and usurpations, pursuing invariably the same object, evinces a design to reduce them under absolute despotism, it is their right, it is their duty, to throw off such government."

Often in history—today, for instance—ideology interlocks so tightly with the struggle of nations for supremacy that it is difficult to know where social aspirations end and the power lust begins. France smarted under her expulsion from Canada and India by Britain. Holland had lost wars, New York, and other territories to the British and knew that their ascendancy would menace the East Indies. When, accordingly, the thirteen American colonies rebelled against King George III, the reactionary, soon-to-totter Bourbon monarchy in Versailles and the conservative Dutch joined in the hostilities against Great Britain.

In Paris on July 14, 1789, a throng of the poor and underprivileged stormed the Bastille, symbol of injustice and the inaccessible power of kings, nobles, and feudals. The Bastille became a beacon of revolt to Europe.

The dust of the volcanoes failed to attain the Russian steppes. But the flame of the American Revolution and the fires of the Bastille warmed millions of hearts from Warsaw westward. Holland could not remain immune. The Dutch may have been fighting to keep their Indies colony when they linked arms with France to liberate the American colonies. Yet by so doing they opened the door to the ideas of the French Revolution—and to the boots of Napoleon's soldiers.

The Indies felt the effect.

Chapter Four

PRELUDE TO RAFFLES

In 1795 Napoleon's army invaded Holland. With it marched a Batavian Legion of patriotic Dutchmen who believed they were using the French to free their country from oligarchic despotism. One of the high officers of the Legion was a lawyer named Herman Willem Daendels. Experimenting in fiction and hoping to found an all-European Bonaparte dynasty, Napoleon crowned his 28-year-old brother Louis King of Holland in 1806. The next year Louis sent Marshal Daendels to the East Indies as governor general. He governed from 1808 to 1811, when England enthroned Raffles.

Dutch son of the French Revolution, Daendels went to the Indies to destroy feudalism and bestow freedom. Yet revolutionary dynamism made him a tyrant (as it did Napoleon and more modern exemplars); he in fact fell into the rut of the system he wished to bury. The past prevailed over his resolution.

An English diplomat who visited Java en route to China in June, 1816, and published a book in 1818, called Daendels "ferocious to an unparalleled degree." "An anecdote," the diplomat wrote, "is related of his arrival late at night at one of the regencies, and ordering some eggs to be prepared for his supper; the native chief unluckily had none in the house and had the temerity to inform the marshal, that no eggs were procurable at that late hour. Daendels seized one of his pistols, that were always placed near him, and discharged it at his head; the ball passed near his ear. The regent, a man of some humour, says that the whizzing of the bullet had a most wonderful effect, all the hens in the village beginning to lay their eggs immediately: the fact was, that a second search, under the fear of death, overcame the difficulty." No wonder Daendels regarded the Javanese regents as "timorous."

Like the anecdotes that circulate nowadays in totalitarian countries, this story is authentic even if apocryphal, for it reflects Daendels' contempt of the regents. He abolished the hereditary rights and regal pomp to which they, like feudal lords in all ages and continents, attached very great importance.

Daendels treated peasants with equal harshness. He did not abolish forced labor or compulsory crop deliveries, for he could not; the Dutch authorities at home expected him to earn profits out of export monopolies.

Yet how was it possible to wring gold from the ruin which Daendels inherited? Raffles painted a picture of that ruin in bookkeeper's figures. Nothing but thorough, the Englishman had the books of the Dutch East India Company examined on his arrival in Batavia. He reproduced the accounts in his giant-size two-volume *History of Java* published in 1817.

From 1613 to 1693, the Dutch company's net annual profits averaged 600,000 guilders, making a total income for the eighty years of 48 million guilders. From then the earnings sank and in 1724 the company turned the corner into a deficit. By 1779 the cumulative losses for the entire period beginning in 1613 amounted to 84,985,425 guilders. The descent continued until 1795, when the directors in Amsterdam resolved to close the enterprise and transfer the colony to the Dutch government. The company's machine had run down. The country was run down. Commercial cupidity culminated in self-destruction. The Dutch East India Company expired in 1799, leaving a debt of 134 million guilders.

Some Dutchmen knew what was wrong and one offered proposals for change. As early as 1791 Dirk van Hogendorp, Dutch governor of Northeast Java (later one of Napoleon's generals), had, under French revolutionary inspiration, sent a report to the company denouncing Indies' feudalism and declaring that "tyranny destroys itself." He urged basic reforms, but the Dutch government rejected this intelligent program and Raffles later noted the results:

"The system of contingents and of forced services," he wrote in the *Substance of a Minute,* dated February 11, 1814 (which filled 283 large printed pages), "reduced the people to the lowest state of vassalage and subjection." Dutch officials "universally employed the services of the people without regular hire."

The Indonesians reacted normally. They rebelled.

In this sick archipelago Daendels had to make money from exports, from coffee in particular. "Nearly the whole of the coffee gardens in the

Eastern Districts [of Java]," Raffles' *Substance of a Minute* stated, "were planted, during the administration of Marshal Daendels, by means of forced services, and in many instances, the gardens, and even the graves of the Javanese, were sacrificed to the general arrangement." For the construction of defense roads and forts he corralled additional forced labor. To supervise these commercial and military activities Daendels used the very regents whom he had humiliated. They remained in control of the native economy.

Daendels instituted administrative reforms. He purged the judiciary. He cleaned house. He broke with tradition. Vlekke relates that immediately after Daendels came to the Indies he shocked his subordinates by deciding to leave the "unhealthy and desolate city of Batavia" and reside in the town of Buitenzorg [Sans Souci]—now Bogor—35 miles due south where it rains 135 days a year. "High officials told him that in the prevailing rainy season he would need 30 teams of horses to get there. 'I shall use 31 teams,' said Daendels, and started."

But all the Governor General's horse teams and all the Governor General's men could not pull the Indies out of the muck. "The Indies' most active and energetic governor" Raffles called Daendels. "The thundering marshal," as everybody knew him, had to save the Indies from the brink of bankruptcy and the reality of revolt and at the same time convert this wreck and ruin into a bastion which could resist a British attack. For none doubted that in her world war against Napoleon England would not permit his Dutch province to retain such valuable strategic real estate in the Pacific.

Defense was therefore Daendels' chief preoccupation. "The recruiting of troops in Amboina and Madura and also the purchase of slaves in Bali and Makassar, who receive their liberty on entering the corps, have been ordered," Daendels wrote, in French, to King Louis of Holland on April 27, 1808, from Batavia.

The Governor General worked feverishly under the dangling British sword of Damocles. His letter of September 7, 1809, to King Louis reported that in March Admiral Drury of the British fleet had so disposed his ships that "neither Moors, Arabs, Armenians, nor North Americans can bring in the necessary goods for the colony or take away our produce."

The problems Daendels confronted were exhausting, but usually his stamina prevailed, and his correspondence with King Louis and Emperor Napoleon, all in French, reflects his impressive energy and determination. In March, 1810, an American blockade-running brig, felicitously named *The Goldsearcher,* put in at Batavia, and by it Daendels sent Louis a letter dated April 21, 1810, in which he expressed the hope that it would soon be possible to transport colonial goods "direct to the ports of France and Holland and to receive in return the commodities of which the colony is in urgent need." However, "Your Majesty will note that we were sent 5000 pairs of shoes although there are no Europeans here to wear them."

The British naval cordon, however, grew tighter daily. Things got so bad that on April 20, 1810, he brought them to the attention of Napoleon himself. "The oriental colonies of His Majesty, the King of Holland, my Master," Daendels wrote, "are in a critical and unhappy situation. Conditions prevent the Americans from coming for our colonial goods with the exception of some spices, and to bring us piastres and European articles such as wine, whisky, iron, cloth, etc.

"Our greatest need," he continued, "is more officers, noncommissioned officers, soldiers, and sailors, for since 1796 the colony has received no help except for one battalion." Many officers and noncommissioned officers in Java had fallen ill. He wanted 300 subalterns, 600 to 700 noncommissioned officers, 3,000 soldiers, as well as naval personnel, doctors, surgeons, "some distinguished superior officers," and a number of good and experienced administrators "with a reputation to lose."

Daendels assured Napoleon that "if we receive this aid, for which the colony will pay, I feel sure that these precious possessions, which I have the good fortune to govern, and to render useful to the King, my Master, and the motherland, will be in no danger and will even be able to assist in the early humiliation of the British in this part of the globe."

A little over a month later, however, the Governor General sadly informed Napoleon that the British had seized the Moluccan island of Amboina and were threatening others. He required officers and men experienced in battle. On the same day, May 26, 1810, he gave the King of Holland further information on the defeat: the British took Amboina with two frigates and one corvette, although the commandant of the island, a French colonel named Filz, had at his disposal a garrison of 1,500 "of our best troops. I have had him arrested." Later he had him shot.

Hinting at anti-French intrigues in the Indies and Holland, Daendels warned the King that "our worst enemies are not in London; the colony is in danger, but it shall be surrendered to the British only after my death. . . . I am trying to make *the impossible possible* so as to save this Colony and give the lie to those who would sell out the Colony and to preserve the reputation of loving my King, and my Fatherland and of detesting the British and their supporters."

In a letter dated July 5, 1810, addressed to Napoleon, Daendels described the situation as "painful" and requested military reinforcements. He had 16,000 troops on the island and was adding new recruits. To the King on August 20, 1810, he said fortifications were being built on Java and the iron foundry at Semarang had been enlarged to manufacture more munitions. He pleaded for officers, soldiers, and sailors. The colony would pay all costs. In a sad postscript he stated that now Banda in the Moluccas had fallen to the British. But the loss was not serious, he asserted.

The British were closing in. Frantically, in November, 1810, Daendels called for rifles, artillery, and shells, and pistols and sabers for the cavalry. By the ship which carried the letter, he wrote, he was sending a gift to the King and coffee for his own wife. She would pay the duty.

Fate gave Daendels only three years to make the impossible possible. He was doomed to fail. Even if Dutchmen in Java and Holland had not sabotaged his efforts (especially after their country had officially been brought into the French Empire in 1810), even if his health had been excellent instead of poor, and even if he had received the meager reinforcements which Napoleon, hard pressed himself, might have spared, England would have secured his downfall. At first intermittently, and then hermetically, the British navy in Asian waters blockaded the Dutch Indies while London and Calcutta weighed the wisdom of occupying them. Daendels could not get exports out or supplies in.

Finally the sword dropped. The British arrived. A fleet "consisting of upward of ninety sails" and carrying 10,000 fighting men—half of them Indians—and Lord Minto and Raffles, anchored off Batavia in August, 1811. The landing encountered negligible resistance.

Chapter Five

RAFFLES RULES THE INDIES

ON ARRIVING in Jakarta (which the Dutch called Batavia) one notices that wheeled traffic keeps to the left as it does in England and India. In Holland it keeps to the right. Who introduced the present system? Raffles—and it has endured for almost a century and a half.

Raffles aimed to make Indonesia "the other India." London considered the seizure of the Dutch-owned archipelago a war measure against Napoleon. Raffles saw it as a permanent extension of the British Empire. Born in 1781 (off Jamaica on a ship named *Ann* captained by his father), he was only thirty in 1811 when he became ruler of Indonesia with the title of lieutenant governor. But Sir Thomas Stamford Raffles knew what he wanted. In fact he, John Crawfurd, and other young Englishmen had been stationed at Penang and at Malacca, in Malaya, for several years studying the Malay language and Indies history, geography, and customs, and consciously preparing for the day when Great Britain would own the Indies as well as India.

In 1810 Raffles spent four months in Calcutta, then India's capital, planning with Governor General Lord Minto how to expel Holland from Indonesia and how to convince London that the expulsion was desirable. When the British government agreed, Raffles was chosen. He ruled the Indies for over four years.

Raffles had imagination, a touch of genius, and visions of a British Asia. The world being in flux, it was the hour of big dreams. Napoleon, facing

27

the Pyramids in 1798, already had one mental foot in India. When he realized, after Nelson's victory over the French on the Nile, that the great prize would elude him, he urged Tsar Alexander I, at their 1807 meeting in Tilsit, to send a Russian army across the Hindu Kush and into the valley of the Indus. There is in the Russian archives a letter from Napoleon to Alexander, dated February 2, 1808, in which the Corsican proposed the formation of a Russo-French army to conquer India. "England will be enslaved," Napoleon predicted. He offered the Tsar Stockholm as a reward for his anti-British efforts in Asia.

Everybody was playing for maximum stakes. Raffles too.

A somewhat Napoleonic streak ran through Raffles' personality. He was an imperialist and a reformer in the grand manner. Though his country fought the American colonies and the French Revolution, the spirit of both animated his acts. Napoleon fascinated him. During a trip to England in 1816 his ship, after rounding the Cape, stopped at St. Helena, where Raffles eagerly sought and obtained an interview with the ex-Emperor, the most distinguished prisoner in history. The Bonaparte fired a rapid cannonade of questions about East Asia, scarcely listened to the answers, and marched off.

A second incident is still more revealing. On June 26, 1823, long after Raffles had been relieved of his high post in Java, the vessel taking him from Sumatra to England halted at Batavia Roads, where Sophia, his second wife, far advanced in pregnancy, had to be moved to a hospital in the city. The gracious Dutch Governor sent word that he would allow Raffles to land but could not receive him because of his deeds against "the interests of my Sovereign." Raffles stayed on board the entire week. Hundreds of small craft came out into the harbor and circled the ship while their occupants tried to get a glimpse of their famous, fabulous former ruler. In a letter penned in his cabin he compared the commotion with what might have happened if Napoleon had suddenly appeared off the coast of England. "Had Napoleon returned to life," he wrote, "and anchored in the Downs, it would not have excited greater agitation in England, than my arrival has done here." But he added, "the sensation might have been very different."

To compare the effect of Napoleon's imaginary apparition with his own in the flesh and to feel that the Frenchman would have evoked hate whereas he evoked a contrary "sensation," reflects Raffles' Himalayan conceit. Yet he probably wrote the truth. The news that Raffles was in Javanese waters must have ripped through Batavia like a tornado and aroused endless curiosity and the fears of the Dutch and the inchoate expectations of natives throughout the land.

After Raffles' death his widow, Sophia, wrote a monumental, 723-large-page *Memoir on the Life and Services of Sir Thomas Stamford Raffles.* In it she referred to Java as the "Queen of the East." Raffles had an imperialist's love affair with that queen. His relationship to the whole archipelago was equally adoring. The islands aroused his tenderest affections. They presented, he said, "a fairy scene of enchantment deserving of a poet's pen to describe its beauties." Raffles loved the inhabitants too. "Few people attend more to the courtesies of society." They were "never rude or abrupt," ever "pliant and graceful, amiable and ingenuous." Though "they have been found capable of receiving a high state of intellectual improvement," "nothing is so easy as for an artful man to persuade the common Javan that he possesses supernatural powers," for Indonesians had "infantile credulity." He aspired to be their protecting father-possessor.

Despite normally bad health, Raffles traveled incessantly, first throughout Java and Bali, later in Sumatra and the other islands, conducting archaeological, economic, sociological, and cultural investigations. The Dutch, he complained, had left "no scientific map of Java," but he praised their road system which enabled him to go from Surabaya to Semarang, 200 miles "in only twenty-four hours" and thence to Buitenzorg in "only two and a half days and this without fatigue." On these arduous journeys he discovered ancient inscriptions, two on copper, which he had deciphered and translated.

The bizarre and barbarous also caught his attention. Of Bali he wrote: "The bodies of the deceased are invariably burned, and the wives and concubines of the higher classes perform the sacrifice of *Satia* [suttee]. A few days previous to my leaving Bali, nineteen young women, the wives and concubines of the young rajah, who was lately put to death, sacrificed themselves in this manner." Perpetual widowhood, he found, sometimes served as a substitute for this incineration of consorts on the funeral pyre of a dead husband. "We will not make a second marriage," the deprived wives vowed collectively, "for you alone knew the arts of love. We dread the thought of being subjected to another's authority."

In 1820 he reported to his friend, the Duchess of Somerset, on an extended sojourn among the Bataks, or Battas, of Sumatra. "They eat one another, and relish the flesh of a man better than that of an ox or a pig. . . . The Battas are not savages, for they write and read . . . they have also codes of law of great antiquity, and it is from a regard for these laws, and a veneration of the institutions of their ancestors, that they eat each other; the law declares that for certain crimes, four in number, the criminals should be eaten ALIVE." In cases of adultery, "relatives of the wife appear to partake of the feast." The criminal's brain is "carefully preserved in a bottle for purposes of witchcraft, etc." The culinary details of cannibalism, which he realized was ritual though brutal, interested him too: "In devouring flesh, it is sometimes eaten raw, and sometimes grilled, but it must be eaten on the spot. Limes, salt and pepper are always in readiness, and they sometimes eat rice with the flesh, but never drink toddy or spirits; many carry bamboos with them, and filling them with blood drink it off. The assembly consists of men alone, as the flesh of man is prohibited to females; it is said, however, that they get a bit by stealth now and then . . . the palm of the hands, and the soles of the feet, are the delicacies of epicures. . . . On expressing my surprise at the continuance of such extraordinary practices, I was informed that formerly it was usual for the people to eat their parents when too old for work." Nevertheless, he stressed, the Battas were gentle folk; they revered him and his companions, the first white men they had seen, as gods.

Though his father's indebtedness forced Raffles to leave boarding school at the age of fourteen and take a clerkship in the East India House in London, he became a self-taught man of learning. He revived the comatose Batavia Society of Arts and Sciences and read to it lectures several hours long, subsequently published, on anthropology, excavations, religion, linguistics, and sociology. He studied Javanese and attended and described wayangs based on the *Mahabharata,* the *Ramayana,* and the legends about Panji, "the most renowned Hero of Java story." He ordered a survey of Java from which it emerged that the island was 575 miles long and 117 to 48 miles wide. Owing to its volcanic origin and history, he explained, Java contained no metals or, at best, limited deposits of gold and red ocher. The census of Java and Madura—the two are always grouped together—which Raffles needed for his economic reforms, showed a population, nearly equally divided among males and females, of 4,615,-270, of whom 94,441 were Chinese and 27,142 were slaves owned by whites and Chinese. The average age of males at marriage was 16, of girls, 13 and 14. "An unmarried man past 20," Raffles commented, "is seldom to be met with, and an old maid is considered a curiosity." Divorce was frequent, connubial constancy rare.

Raffles' studies intensified his passion to revolutionize Indonesian society. Observation induced him to conclude that material conditions took precedence over, though they did not entirely nullify, the effects of racial traits, climate, and soil fertility. "Situated as the Javan peasantry are," he decided, "there is but little inducement to invest capital in agriculture, and much labour must be unprofitably wasted; as property is insecure, there can be no desire for accumulation." He knew "few examples," therefore, "of great affluence or abject distress among the peasantry."

This analysis was Raffles' warrant for the reforms which—more than his role as the founding father of Singapore—constitute his claim to a permanent place in the colonial hall of fame. In a sentence, he proposed to lift Indonesia out of feudalism into capitalism and, considering the state not only of Asian but of European society in the second decade of the nineteenth century, even the wish and attempt to do so must be accounted heroic and historic.

Under the feudal system no land was owned by the individual peasant. "A written lease, as far as I have heard," John Crawfurd, the British Resident, reported to Raffles, "is a thing altogether unknown." The cultivator tilled his plot of land, from which he might be reassigned to another the following year, and could pass it to his heirs for use. But the landlord was a sultan or regent who collected an arbitrary amount of taxes, usually one fourth to one half of the crop on irrigated soil and one third to one fifth on nonirrigated soil. In addition, the farmer was compelled to deliver to the village heads and their aristocratic superiors a portion, never specified in advance, of his harvest at prices fixed by them. Forced labor in the service of the landlord constituted a further vexatious feature of feudalism.

Moreover, taxes on internal trade, which might include the sale of commodities a peasant woman carried to market in a basket on her head and sometimes, it is said, the child she carried in her womb, "were levied," Raffles wrote, "by corrupt and extortionate agents, and in worst instances were farmed out to Chinese."

"It would have been unworthy of the British character," he declared grandly, "to have remained quiet spectators to abuses, and to have admitted the continuance of feudal barbarism." The Dutch, he charged, had perpetuated the Indies feudal system which antedated their arrival. They "looked for revenue only in their commercial monopoly" of spices, opium, coffee, and other produce, Raffles said, leaving the collection of taxes to native chiefs and Chinese. "The Javanese abhor the Chinese," Raffles asserted, "and yet these were the only class of people entrusted by the former Government in the collection of these revenues."

In 1811 Raffles ordered the abolition of forced labor and compulsory deliveries. Taxes would be collected by the government and land leased to each cultivator. The first leases had a three-year limit, but in 1814-1815, permanent tenure was introduced, and Raffles, in visits to the Bantam and Cheribon districts, liked the results: bigger crops, more work done, less crime, and waning influence of native chiefs.

"I have had the happiness," Raffles wrote in a self-congratulating letter to a friend in October, 1813, "to release several million of my fellow creatures from a state of bondage and arbitrary oppression."

The British government took in taxation "about two-fifths of the first rice crop, leaving the second crop, and the fruit trees and gardens attached to the villages, free from assessment, the cultivators free from personal taxes, and inland trade unrestricted and untaxed."

To prove that liberalism paid, Raffles' *History of Java* reproduced an audited statement, signed by Accountant J. G. Bauer, and dated Batavia, February 16, 1816, showing that the revenues of Java and dependencies had mounted steeply under the British administration. "What might have been expected," Raffles moaned, "had confidence once been established in the permanence of the Government, and the tide of British capital been once fairly turned into it?"

But what of the sultans, regents, and village heads whose fat incomes and feudal powers were doomed by the reforms? Raffles personally visited many districts and interviewed numerous nobles and hereditary native rulers. To compensate for the financial damages inflicted by the new system, Raffles engaged the chiefs "on fixed salaries." "In the month of July [1813]," Raffles wrote, "I had the satisfaction to conclude an agreement with the Sultans by which they were relieved of contingents and forced services and consented that the internal administration of the country should be exercised by the Government, in consideration of their being secured in their possession of certain tracts of land, with the continuation of the annual pension in money, which they had previously enjoyed." Raffles persuaded himself that "the Sultans entered into the views of the Government without hesitation," and since no choice was open to them they undoubtedly gave that impression. The Indies were now governed "without the intervention of native authority."

Nobody, of course, even considered self-government from below. The blow to feudalism was blessing enough. But Raffles did introduce a jury system and otherwise improved the judiciary. In fact, the first British proclamation in the Indies, on September 11, 1811, "ordained that torture and mutilation should no longer make part of a sentence to be pronounced against criminals." The chopping off of fingers or a foot had been common penalties, and many an offender was impaled on a sharpened stick driven up his back from seat to neck and left in the tropical sun to expire, days later, of thirst, hunger, and pain.

Raffles also hoped to free the slaves. As a follower of William Wilberforce (1759-1833), the British philanthropist, under whose influence England abolished slave trading in 1807 and ended slavery in 1833, Raffles proposed similar measures in the Indies. He actually freed some slaves. But headquarters in Bengal demurred and called emancipation "premature."

Raffles ran ahead of his times. Like radicals in every age he bred enemies and like all power men he spawned rivals. His most effective foe was Major General R. R. Gillespie, commander of the British armed forces on Java, who intrigued assiduously in Calcutta after he had been transferred there. Lord Minto, India's governor general, guarded the Little Napoleon of Batavia from harm, but on Minto's death in June, 1814, charges were preferred against Raffles and he was tried.

Unfortunately for the defendant, he had bought land at public auction in Java. Having legalized the sale of large estates to Europeans, he purchased one himself. Such, it seems, is the magnetic pull of material possessions that the official who ruled an empire wanted a fragment of it he could call his own. This act gave a cutting edge to vaguer accusations, and for several years Raffles, a sick man, lived under the strain of the pending judicial proceedings. The British East India Company's "Honourable Court of Directors to Bengal" finally judged on February 13, 1817, that "the charges, in so far as they went to impeach the moral character of that gentleman, have not only not been made good . . ." To be sure, his purchases of land were "unquestionably indiscreet" but "do not at all derogate from those principles of integrity by which we believe his public conduct to have been uniformly governed."

"Principles of integrity" apart, Raffles, the imperialist revolutionary, had evolved a modern concept of colonialism. The Dutch conservatives who remained in the Indies during the British occupation abhorred his land reform. Even the liberal Dutch administrators, whom Raffles wisely retained in his service (they were anti-French), could not swallow or stomach his philosophy of empire. One of the most progressive of these—he became a valuable, intimate adviser and collaborator of Raffles—was Henry W. Muntinghe. He feared, not without cause, that despite the legal abolition of feudalism, the conservative peasantry would remain in a feudal relationship to the village chiefs and that freedom for the farmer to sow what he wished would result in rice growing to the exclusion of export crops. It was one thing to introduce capitalism, yet another to give the peasant that awareness of money which is the essence of capitalism. The tiller's sole preoccupation was subsistence and a little extra which he could barter for his minimum requirements in raiment and implements.

Henry W. Muntinghe, moreover, argued in a memorandum submitted to Raffles that "The safest principle which can be adopted . . . is that every colony does or ought to exist for the benefit of the Mother-country."

Raffles disagreed. British self-interest could not be the sole criterion of colonial success. The bug of "the White Man's Burden" had already bitten him and he therefore told Muntinghe that revenue collection in a colony must not interfere with "an endeavor to civilize its population." Of course, if civilization marched with a full treasury, as Raffles' regime did, so much the better.

Events in Europe cut short the debate. The powers defeated Napoleon, banished him to Elba, and assembled at the summit Congress of Vienna. Raffles feared the worst: that Java would "be given up at a peace to a foreign power (which God forbid)." The worst did eventuate. At Vienna, on August 13, 1814, Lord Castlereagh, the British foreign secretary, signed away the Indies to Holland. He was actuated by a political motive: the wish to strengthen Holland against France and Prussia. Economic factors also played a role. The peasants of Java, unaccustomed to paying taxes, had fallen into arrears. Nor did they buy the cotton goods which the British East India Company shipped to the Indies. Raffles' failure to force the cultivation of export crops—except coffee—resulted in financial losses to the British company, which, therefore, recommended to the British government that Java and the Moluccas be abandoned to Holland. Such was still the primacy of commercial over imperialist considerations.

But Raffles' imperialistic hopes flared anew in those famous Hundred Days in 1815 when Napoleon escaped from Elba to gamble one last time with the fate of Europe. "The wonderful extraordinary change in the politics of Europe, by the reappearance of Bonaparte has, with all its horror," Raffles wrote from Batavia, "shed one consoling ray on this sacred Isle, and Java may yet be permanently English." Waterloo extinguished the ray.

On August 19, 1816, the Dutch returned to Batavia. Raffles left Java "with a heavy heart." But even in sadness and frustration his devotion to the people remained dominant. Referring to the return of King William I of Orange to his throne in the Netherlands after the dark Napoleonic years of exile at Kew, near London, Raffles wrote: "Holland is not only re-established, but I hope renovated; Her Prince has been educated in the best of all *schools*—adversity; and I hope the people of Java will be as happy, if not happier, under the Dutch than under the English. I say happier," he added, "because Java will, in importance, be more to Holland than she could ever be to England." The sun never set on Britain's far-flung dominions. But Java was all Holland had.

Having delivered this valedictory, Raffles did a strange thing for one so anti-Dutch: he went to Brussels to dine with William I and Count Gijsbert Karel van Hogendorf. "The King and his leading minister," he wrote to William Marsden, a British friend, on July 27, 1817, "seems to mean well." This faint praise was followed by criticism: "But," Raffles added, "they have too great a hankering after profit, and *immediate* profit, for any liberal system to thrive under them."

The King's gracious gesture of inviting the enemy to a meal in the palace failed to conciliate Raffles. He was resigned, perforce, to the return of the Dutch to Java. But he meant to deprive them of Sumatra. For he had no sooner taken up his consolation job at Benkulen, the British toehold in West Sumatra, on March 22, 1818, than his roving imperialist eye, boundless ambition, and bouncing energy made the Dutch squirm. He moved swiftly through the great island courting sultans and planting trouble for Holland. The Dutch "say," Raffles wrote, "I am a Spirit that will never allow the East to be quiet and that this second Elba in which I am placed is not half secure enough."

They were right. Soon after his arrival at Benkulen, Raffles took over several islands in the Sunda Strait between Sumatra and Java. The Dutch complained to Calcutta, and Raffles was ordered to withdraw. In June, 1818, Dupuy, who had been Raffles' Dutch secretary in Buitenzorg, came to Padang to protest his former chief's seizure of the Sumatran west coast. Raffles refused to yield. Again British authorities in India sided with the Dutch, and Raffles retreated.

Presently Raffles fixed his glance on a strange, jungle-covered object, 27 miles long and 14 miles wide, with a population of 150, most of them fishermen—the island of Singapore, just off the southern tip of the Malay Peninsula. The Netherlands claimed the island, which for Raffles was the best reason in the world for acquiring it. He took possession on January 29, 1819.

"Singapore is everything we could desire, and it will soon rise in importance," Raffles predicted at the time. "What Malta is in the West that Singapore may become in the East." He conceived of Singapore as a free port for trade between Europe and India, China, and Java. It became that—a great emporium with a population of a million and a half, as well as a great naval base, and stands today as a living monument to a man who could dream. "A child of my own," he called it.

For Raffles Singapore was a steppingstone to bigger goals. He must have regarded its purchase as a mate-in-seven-moves gambit in the great chess game with his Dutch adversaries. For having secured Singapore he demanded Bangka and Billiton, tin-rich islands to the south and southeast of Singapore; they control the approach to the important South Sumatran district of Palembang whose sultan waged intermittent war on the Dutch. Raffles likewise coveted Nias Island off the Sumatran west coast; it commands the northern sea approach to Padang, the strategic key to Central Sumatra.

Raffles used geography as generals use armies: to harass, encircle, and defeat. In addition he adopted the modern technique of subversion; he mobilized a fifth column of native rulers to undermine Dutch power.

Raffles' chief obstacle was not The Hague but London. The British government drove him to despair. "Almost all that I attempted in Sumatra," he wrote in a letter to the Duchess of Somerset in March, 1819, "has been destroyed from a delicacy to the Dutch. If this last effort [Singapore] for securing our interests also fails, I must be content to quit politics and turn philosopher."

He continued to worry. "It appears to me impossible," he said in a letter dated July 22, 1820, "that Singapore should be given up, and yet the indecisive manner in which ministers express themselves, and the unjust and harsh terms they use towards me, render it doubtful what course they will adopt."

Raffles lobbied in London and intrigued in Sumatra. A British Sumatra would be a counterpoise to Dutch Java and, conceivably, a means of some-day recovering Java, his first and greatest love.

The British ministers in London, however, were not thinking of making Sumatra their colony. They preferred an exchange with the Dutch: Sumatra went to Holland; the Malay Peninsula and Singapore, to England. Raffles had no part in this 1824 deal. The year before, failing health forced him to relinquish office and go home to Britain. On this, his last voyage, the ship caught fire, and his notes, manuscripts, sketches, and a large natural history collection were destroyed.

Raffles was happy to be in England at last and forever. Though consumption, recurrent headaches, and whooping cough racked his body, which had never been strong, the creative urge animated him as it always had. He founded London's present zoo in Regent's Park. He bought a farm, next to that of William Wilberforce, the emancipator of slaves, and re-equipped it with zest and imagination. London society lionized him.

The East was never far away. His first wife and the children he begot with her, as well as all his children except a little daughter, Ella, by his second wife, Sophia, had died of tropical diseases in the Indies. The East India Company dunned him for debts which he never knew existed.

The strain proved too great. At 6 A.M. on July 5, 1826, his forty-fifth birthday, Lady Raffles found him at the bottom of a flight of stairs. He was dead from an apoplectic attack.

Chapter Six

RUSSIAN REPORTS ON A REVOLUTION

It was one thing to hand Sumatra to Holland on a parchment platter and for Holland to say, above her red seal, that Malaya was British. It was an altogether different thing for the two governments to administer these territories. In many parts of the Indonesian-Malayan world scores of sultans, rajahs, and princes ruled large regions where the foot of a foreigner never trod and where neither British nor Dutch writ ran. Indeed, some vast territories were political vacuums without even native rule.

To make British rule a reality Raffles had reduced the native rulers to petty puppets shorn of power and living on his political alms. But Holland's return to the Indies in 1816 threatened this and all other Raffles reforms.

How do the Dutch regard Raffles? Dutch scholars, with few exceptions, try to shrink Raffles' self-portrait from king-size to man-size. They contend that he used a fine prose pen to magnify his own achievements and minimize Holland's. Some of the Englishman's innovations, they claim, were actually initiated by a Dutch predecessor, Marshal Daendels, and others did not work. While partially just, these are nevertheless mere snipings at the swollen head of a mammoth figure. The big fact, seen in objective perspective, is that Raffles undertook to bury the feudal past and give the Indies a modern system of capitalist imperialism. Britain returned the Indies to Holland "in better condition," writes Dutch historian de Kat Angelino, "than when she acquired them." That is the best possible tribute to Raffles' brief rule.

But now Holland faced an historic decision: to go on or go back?

Baron van der Capellan, the first post-Raffles governor general, believed in "Netherlands Liberalism." The Dutch King, he declared, intended "to promote the interests of all his subjects, without exception." This startling egalitarian pledge could not be implemented, however, by the riffraff, flotsam and jetsam, and social failures who had made a government job in the Indies their last haven. Van der Capellan asked the homeland to send out officials of the highest morality and ability. He ordered them to study native languages. He traveled into the interior to study the lives of plebs and nobles and introduce improvements.

The spirit was willing, but Holland was weak. A colony must be viewed in the mirror of the colonial power. The Napoleonic Wars hurt the little country. When the fighting ended, British and French industries drove Dutch goods out of many markets and British and French ships drove the Netherlands merchant marine from many seas. Paupers filled Holland's streets.

International entanglements made matters worse. In 1815 British Foreign Secretary Lord Castlereagh, with Russia's sanction, allowed Holland to incorporate Belgium into the Kingdom of the United Lowlands under William I. Later Luxembourg was brought into this involuntary union. The arrangement strained the treasury. The restive Belgians seethed helplessly until, by the elusive law of revolutions, a mere incident—the Brussels performance on August 25, 1830, of Daniel Auber's opera, *La Muette de Portici,* about a 1647 revolt in Naples—started an anti-Dutch riot. The riot became a revolt. The revolt led to an expensive war, to French armed intervention, and, after much delay, to the independence of Belgium in 1839.

These troubles cost money. Holland had to look to the Indies for funds to keep the kingdom afloat. So van der Capellan's "Netherlands Liberalism" retreated, step by step, before the mother country's need to stave off insolvency. He reinstated and farmed out the hated taxes on internal trade which Raffles had abolished. At toll barriers women were frisked intimately for hidden goods, usually by Chinese. Female ire spread like a prairie fire through the chivalrous countryside. The people became disaffected. Yet the Governor General was not their enemy. To protect them he prohibited rich Indonesians from selling land to Europeans, Chinese, and Arabs who, he feared, would exploit the peasantry. The rich repaid him with hostility.

Upper-class bitterness and mass anger combined to provoke a rebellion which lasted from 1825 to 1830. The Dutch call it the Java War.

In the center of Jakarta there is a broad thoroughfare called Djalan Diponegoro, or Diponegoro Street, which is a kind of political Park Avenue lined with the homes of high officials and ex-officials. It takes its name from Prince Diponegoro, the leader of the Javanese in the Java War.

Diponegoro was the son of the Sultan of Jogjakarta by a concubine. Under Javanese custom this was no disadvantage; he might have inherited the throne. Yet when the Sultan died, a minor son, Prince Jarot, became his heir and Diponegoro was bypassed. On Jarot's death, his infant son Manol succeeded him, and again all honors eluded Diponegoro. It is easy to conclude that Diponegoro grew envious and hence rebellious. That would be a quarter-truth. The dissolute life at court nauseated Diponegoro. He frequented religious schools, turned mystic, and read the Koran in solitude. Presently he heard "voices" which instructed him to rid the land of royal immorality, rural poverty, and Europeans. Joined by disgruntled landlords, dispossessed peasants, and disreputable adventurers, Diponegoro the ascetic went forth to war.

There was no telegraph, telephone, or airplane. Communication between Holland and the Indies was by letters carried in slow boats halfway around the earth. The first news about the Java War came to the Lowlands from England. It was relayed by the Tsarist Russian ambassador in Brussels to his foreign minister in St. Petersburg on January 16, 1826. "The rumors from England about a mass uprising on the island of Java provoked by fanaticism and hatred of Europeans," he wrote, "have, thus far, been neither confirmed nor denied in government newspapers. If the insurrection proved to be general, the numerical superiority of four million Javanese over 30,000 Europeans threatens the latter with the most serious peril."

A few hours later he added a postscript: "P.S. I reopen the envelope in order to have the honor to inform Your Excellency that an American ship, which sailed from Batavia on September 19 of last year, has delivered letters in Amsterdam which, while unofficial, are apparently worthy of credence." They told of a "decisive victory over the Java insurgents" on September 13. Nine days later, however, the same Russian ambassador, who signed himself N. D. Guriev, reported to K. V. Nesselrode, the General Secretary of the Tsarist Ministry of Foreign Affairs, that the "decisive victory" had not been decisive. Victory went now to the government forces under the command of General de Kock and General van Geen, now to the rebels commanded by Prince Diponegoro. Holland, accordingly, was sending out 2,000 volunteer soldiers. "The cost of transporting each volunteer will be 700 florins."

In a letter dated October 5, 1826, the Russian ambassador told his government that the seesaw war on Java continued. He described rebel strategy: "They avoid battles with the troops and have adopted a plan of undermining the strength of the Europeans with the help of the unhealthy climate and fatigue. Such a method of warfare may in the end give them superiority."

The Dutch generals in Java needed more soldiers. "The government," Ambassador Guriev informed his government on November 3, 1826, "is energetically equipping a unit of 3,000 men for its East Indies colonies." The envoy took a dim view. "When one thinks of the alarming growth of the insurgent mood," he wrote, "it is hard to say anything definite about the future of the colony." His letters, and those of his successors, penned in French, then the language of diplomacy even between Russian and Russian, have been preserved in the Tsarist archives and were published in Russian translation in the March-April, 1958, issue of an academic Soviet journal called *Istorischeskii Arkhiv* (*Historical Archive*). Everything they contain checks with authoritative Dutch sources.

The 3,000 additional recruits had been collected and loaded on ships. Suddenly tragedy struck. Not far from the Dutch coast two of the three ships sank. With the exception of forty on the *Wassenaar,* all men could be rescued. But the provisions and munitions went to the bottom and so did the money for pay and expenses.

The war strained Dutch resources. Not only did it take its toll in men and materials; trade suffered. The situation deteriorated steadily. On April 10, 1828, the Russian reported than an insurgent unit of 700 to 800 had routed a Dutch force commanded by Colonel Nahuys. "The moral effect . . . may raise the spirit and increase the intransigence of the Javanese rebels who, finally, have seen how low the prestige of the invincible Europeans has fallen." In October, 1828, the rebels won another victory.

Then, unexpectedly, the wheel turned. High Priest Kiyayi Maja, Diponegoro's closest adviser and the person most responsible for the fanatical spirit of the rebels, was taken prisoner in a hand-to-hand encounter. Depressed by this loss, realizing that his men were tired after five years of warfare, knowing too that though the enemy suffered he could not win, Diponegoro sent an emissary to the Dutch suggesting parleys. On March 28, 1830, the Prince appeared by appointment at the official residence of General de Kock in Magelang. But he proposed unacceptable terms. De Kock thereupon arrested Diponegoro and shipped him to Makassar in the Celebes where he lived in exile for twenty-five years, till his death in 1855 at the age of seventy.

No record exists of Javanese casualties in the long Diponegoro rebellion. But Dr. E. S. de Klerck, a former lieutenant colonel in the Dutch army, puts Holland's losses at 8,000 Europeans and 7,000 Indonesian mercenaries.

In his two-volume *History of the Netherlands East Indies* de Klerck fixes the financial outlay at 20 million florins.

The Java War also killed the policy of "Netherlands Liberalism." Now, more than ever, Holland needed money to promote her own welfare and to police the colony. In 1830, the year the war ended, Johannes van der Bosch, the new governor general of the Indies, accordingly introduced the so-called Culture System which, until its abolition forty-seven years later, turned Indonesia into a Dutch gold mine and a cauldron of native discontent.

The Netherlands historian de Kat Angelino describes the Culture System as the "compulsory cultivation of indigo, sugar, pepper, tobacco, cochineal, tea, cinnamon, and coffee." The forced labor and forced deliveries abolished by Raffles were restored. Every peasant could be drafted to work for the state on its terms. To carry out the Culture System regents and regional chiefs were re-employed as Dutch government agents. Van der Busch resurrected their privileges, pomp, and power. The antifeudal iconoclasm of Daendels and Raffles vanished.

The Culture System produced fantastic fruits. Between 1831 and 1877, writes Holland historian Vlekke, the Netherlands treasury received 823 million guilders from the Indies. The annual Dutch budget, he says, "did not exceed 60 million guilders in the years between 1840 and 1880." Of this, the Indies contributed 18 million, which he calls "very considerable," almost a third. "Once the System began to yield results," he explains, "the human tendency to profiteer as much as possible revealed itself in the Netherlands Ministry of Colonies, and for nearly 20 years government expenses in the Indies were pared to the bone, without regard for their educational and political needs, in order to raise the figure of the remittances from Batavia to Europe."

Not only did Holland cut expenditure on schools and other social benefits for Indonesians. She cut military expenses in the archipelago—outside Java. At the same time the Dutch were determined to establish themselves firmly in Sumatra and the other outer islands and reduce the independence of local potentates. Thus, a new Russian ambassador, F. Maltits, addressed K. V. Nesselrode in St. Petersburg on November 13, 1847, about a battle in Sumatra "which apparently cost much blood on both sides." Dutch troops, "notwithstanding the stubborn resistance of the natives," finally took the fortress of Bonjol.

Sporadic skirmishes continued on Sumatra. Meantime, fighting flared in Java. A nephew of Prince Diponegoro, Maltits said in a letter dated August 16, 1840, "was able to inflame the fanaticism of local inhabitants." The ambassador felt discouraged. "It is distressing to learn," he declared, "that discontent exists among the people, numbering 8 million, who were formerly regarded as completely loyal to the Dutch government and who, having understood the secret of their own strength, may succumb to the idea of achieving independence."

How premature!

Guerrilla fighters operated in Sumatra, Java, and other islands, but not till 1846 did the ambassador report "a rather serious revolt" in Bantam, West Java.

These short-lived geysers of native enmity faced the Netherlands with a dilemma: Holland could never organize a large, reliable native army as the British did in India where hundreds of thousands of Sikhs, Rajputs, Gurkhas, etc., forming famous regiments, fought under the Union Jack in many wars at home and abroad. These martial races of India saved British blood and money. But in Indonesia the martial races were hostile and the friendly races were not martial. Small Indonesian contingents did, to be sure, serve the Dutch when in the right mood, but for the most part Dutchmen had to wage the wars and put down the rebellions, and this, given the great distance from Holland, the rough terrain, and the tropical climate, meant heavy casualties in men, ships, and finances. To avoid them the Netherlands government often refrained from decisive action, with the result that defiance which might have been smashed in a season's hard-fought campaign sometimes dragged out for years.

The two outstanding examples are the beautiful island of Bali and the Atjeh region at the northern tip of mammoth Sumatra.

Ambassador Maltits' first dispatch about Bali was dated The Hague, July 18, 1846. It stated that the punitive expedition which should have been sent from Java was delayed by the nonarrival of ships from Europe. Crude, rickety cargo boats were therefore used to transport 2,000 soldiers and some artillery batteries from Batavia to Bali. Preliminary skirmishes with the rebels ended rather badly for the Dutch. Accordingly, the Governor General himself, accompanied by Major General Cochius, the commander in chief, traveled to Surabaya to be nearer the war theater. The outlook was grave because the rebel sultans "have succeeded in gathering 30,000 men and making a large purchase of arms in Singapore" whereas the Dutch attacking party numbered 3,000 "of whom only 400 are Europeans."

Pessimism in the Indies communicated itself to The Hague, where Admiral Rijk, the Minister of Colonies, frankly gave the Russian the key to the entire Indies situation: "The power we exercise in the Indonesian archipelago over the local population, numbering 12 million souls, is only a moral power. The Sultans of Java bear the European yoke out of fear, and the smallest victory over us by the Balinese insurgents could destroy our prestige in the eyes of the Javanese and resurrect the hopes which the native leaders of this people conceal only with difficulty." The ghost of Diponegoro and the specter of independence tormented the Dutch subconscious.

The course of battle in Bali followed a known pattern. The Dutch landed, captured an island fortress, and forced the sultans to sign a surrender pact which bound them to pay tribute and refrain from attacking ships flying the Dutch flag, but not other flags, which were wrecked off the coast. Then the Dutch army, which had business elsewhere, departed, leaving a garrison to compel the sultans to comply. But the garrison was small and the sultans fickle. Batavia accordingly sent two punitive expeditions to Bali in 1848. They won several victories. Then, "unexpectedly stranded without sufficient food and munitions," Maltits explained to St. Petersburg, "they were forced to retreat to the coast to seek the protection of the cannons of the fleet." This event, the ambassador correctly anticipated, would arouse Netherlands uncertainty about the future of the Indies where, he learned, the expanding population now numbered 16,-234,564, of whom fewer than 50,000 were whites.

During 1848, Admiral Rijk informed Maltits, reinforcements from Holland brought Dutch strength in the Indies to 22,000 men and 36 ships. This enabled the Netherlands to dispatch 7,000 troops and 18 men-of-war to Bali "to avenge last year's defeat inflicted by the rebels," the envoy wrote on May 17, 1849.

Nevertheless, Bali did not submit to Dutch rule until the twentieth century.

Intermittent anti-Dutch warfare raged in Java, Sumatra, Borneo, the Celebes, and other islands. The most murderous struggle occurred in Atjeh. This kingdom in North Sumatra gave Holland more trouble than all of Java, than all the rest of Indonesia. The war with Atjeh (population only 800,000) was the biggest, bloodiest, costliest military operation in Dutch colonial history. "The Sultan of Atjeh," a new Russian ambassador named N. A. Stolypin wrote to his government on February 17, 1873, "is completely independent of the Dutch protectorate. The people of the Sultanate are proud and martial." Of late relations with the Sultan, always strained, had grown ice-cold, and "an aide of the Indies Governor General, delegated to settle a number of questions with the Sultan, was sent back in far from diplomatic fashion."

At this juncture the Dutch received secret information that the Sultan of Atjeh had bought arms in British Singapore and that "one prince of his house," according to Stolypin's letter to the Tsar's minister, "had won the support of a foreign consul there." Now there was a telegraph line from Java to The Hague and the Governor General wired the disturbing news, and asked for warships and troops to bring the Sultan to his knees. Meanwhile he sent to Atjeh an extraordinary mission consisting of the commander in chief of the army, the commander of the navy, the vice-chairman of the Council of the Indies, and much personnel with a view to concluding a good-neighbor treaty with the Sultan. But if the mission failed, it "would," in the words of the Russian diplomat, "allow the armed forces to finish its work."

Dutch units moved up the long Sumatran coast into the sultanate of Atjeh. Soon enough a battle began in which General Koehler, the Dutch commander in chief, was killed and his army of 7,000 forced to retreat. The very next day, April 8, 1873, Stolypin forwarded another letter to his government with news of a catastrophe: "The expedition to Atjeh has failed and the army is being called back" to Java. Later that year another expedition, twice as large as the first, sailed for Atjeh. Fighting raged fiercely, but as late as November 17, 1874, the Sultan, according to Stolypin, "displays no desire to submit." The Sultan's men, he said, "were well-armed, made skilful use of trenches during attacks, and showed a complete contempt of death."

The Dutch troops were decimated by fighting and cholera. At home, the ambassador stated, Hollanders were saying it was no longer necessary to "speed toward the final and secure goal"—the subjugation of Atjeh.

The end did not come until 1908, after thirty-five years of war. J. S. Furnivall, the British authority, estimated that it cost 400 million florins. The dead and wounded were not counted.

Moslem Atjeh and Hindu Bali fought so fiercely out of loyalty to native rulers who governed by divine right, who were indeed of divine birth. This was Diponegoro's strength too; the Javanese knew him as a religious mystic of royal blood. War against the Christian intruder thus became a holy war for faith, prince, and fatherland. All three were one and hard to beat.

The entire period from the beginning of the Java War in 1825 to about 1877 can be viewed as a slow-burn Indonesian revolution against Dutch colonial expansion and commercial exploitation via the forced labor of the Culture System. It was time for reform.

Chapter Seven

INDONESIA CRAWLS INTO THE MODERN AGE

When a letter took four months from the Indies to Holland by sail mail, the Dutch people could not be expected to know much about the colony or to be very much interested. Besides, they had their own daily cares.

The first steamboat arrived in the Indies in 1830. Twenty years later two Dutch steamboats were making regular trips between the motherland and the possession. As communications improved concern increased.

But the Dutch King's power was absolute and, given his special personal interest in colonial affairs, public pressure, even if it had existed, would have availed little.

Came 1848, Europe's Year of Revolution. Holland got a new constitution limiting the monarch. Parliament won new rights. It banned slavery in the Indies in 1859. From 1867 it passed on the annual Indies budget.

In 1860 Dutch indignation, stoked by a novel on Indonesia, boiled over into politics. *Max Havelaar, Or the Coffee Auctions of the Dutch Trading Company,* makes little pretense at plot. It is a poorly disguised "I Accuse" sermon by Multatuli (I Have Suffered Much), a former Dutch official in the Indies named Eduard Douwes Dekker who resigned his post in order to shock the Dutch nation with the true tale of the crimes, corruption, and injustice practiced daily in its name. Max Havelaar, a good official, intervened to stop the cruel maltreatment of the peasantry by native chiefs. But his white superiors blocked him at every move. To eradicate an evil would prove that they had allowed it to exist. To enter-

45

tain a complaint would mean a black mark against them in the files. Village headmen and regents punished peasants for the "error" of making a complaint and forced them to withdraw it. Dutch officials condoned this practice, which made their life smoother. As a result "the system of abuse of power, of plunder and murder, under which the poor Javanese suffer" was wrapped in silence and perpetuated by inaction. "Will not the long suppressed discontent—suppressed in order to be able to deny it—" Multatuli cried, "be turned at last into fury, despair, and frenzy? Cannot you see the Jacquerie at the end of all this?"

Max Havelaar carried the anguish of the Indonesians and the guilt of the Dutch right into thousands of quaint little houses along the placid canals of Holland. The nation writhed as Multatuli hammered home his points. He frightened them. He shamed them. The press, Parliament, the government reacted. It was clear that the evil of forced labor and state monopolies, and the lies and hypocrisy which they bred, would no longer be tolerated by a country that took pride in its piety.

After a Dutch literary effort had thus altered Indies politics, French engineering made its contribution to reform. On November 11, 1869, the Suez Canal was opened. Before then the colony was seen solely as a source of profits from farm exports. Now reduced transportation time and costs meant that Dutch industries, which were erasing a century-old lag and becoming competitive, would regard Indonesia as a market. Dutch manufacturers knew they could sell more goods to wage-earning labor than to unpaid forced labor. The livelihood of Holland no longer depended on maximum extortions from the colonial peasantry. The canal, moreover, made Indonesia a place where Dutchmen might settle without submitting (sometimes succumbing) to the long round-the-Cape voyage and cutting themselves off, except for a rare trip, from family and country. Only officials had gone to the Indies. Now immigrants started going. Whereas in 1872 Europeans, a term always including Dutch citizens of Indo-Dutch ancestry, numbered a mere 36,467, the figure rose to 43,738 in 1882, to 58,806 in 1892, to 80,910 in 1905, to 168,000 in 1920, and to over 240,000 in 1930.

Most of the early arrivals planned to live the envied life of plantation owners. But how could they do so if the government remained the only landlord and the sole producer of profitable export crops?

Thus religious and liberal sentiment against forced labor, the hope of finding Indonesian customers for the output of Holland's expanding factories, and the desire of some Dutchmen to leave their chilly gray motherland for the sunny equatorial East combined to uproot the tyrannical Culture System of state feudalism on which the parasitic native feudal class fed. In 1870 it was decided to end the system. Gradually, state farm monopolies were abolished. The government withdrew from sugar growing in 1890. Coffee cultivation by forced labor held on till January 1, 1917. Therewith, the Culture System, born 1830, died, except for the government opium monopoly.

The withdrawal of the Dutch government from business created opportunities for Dutch businessmen.

The Culture System was iniquitous because it compelled the peasant to work for a foreigner while impoverishing himself. But it attacked a problem which is and may ever be the key to economic progress in Indonesia: the need of an export surplus. It might have mitigated the sin of the system had its profits been used for the economic development of the Indies. They were used in and for the Netherlands.

The Culture System was scrapped as a result of the victory of the liberals over the conservatives in the increasingly assertive Dutch Parliament. This set a pattern: from then until the Indies became an independent republic (and thereafter unto this day) the shape of Holland's policies toward Indonesia has been determined by the balance of power in Dutch politics.

In general, however, the evolution of Netherlands democracy after 1850 brought benefits to the Indies.

The Dutch conservatives would have perpetuated the feudal Culture System. The liberals advocated free enterprise and free labor. Some saw pitfalls in the new capitalism. Eduard Douwes Dekker, the creator of *Max Havelaar*, predicted in a pamphlet entitled *Once More Free Labor*, published in 1884, that with "the replacement of the Culture System by so-called free labor, the present advantages enjoyed by the State would pass into the hands of individuals . . . this change would result in an increase of abuses." He opposed "the hypocritical pretense that European profit-seeking has in mind the well-being of the Javanese." If rich Europeans and aristocratic natives were permitted to buy land and use "so-called free labor" on it, the peasants, he feared, would lose their farms and become a landless, land-hungry rural proletariat. Indeed, this prospect so disturbed him and the thought that his famous novel might have contributed to it so distressed him that he penned the saddest words that can come from an author. "I wished," he said in his pamphlet, "I had never written that book."

Having lived close to Indonesians, Dekker knew the one great danger inherent in the new free land-purchase scheme: "Serving his master is the *religion* of the Javanese." Indonesians have always been lord-fearing. This originated in the era when kings were believed to be gods. Regents as the agents of kings and village chieftains as the agents of the regents were entitled to similar veneration. Later, when chieftains and regents served the foreign master, the Dutch were able to build their empire on Indonesian lord-fearing.

Dekker, and others, opposed the free labor as well as Culture System because under both the peasantry would be submissive. They preferred independent peasants owning farms which no one could take from them. No lords; no lord-fearing. To the extent that legislation could achieve this objective the reformers got what they wanted. Agrarian laws, passed in 1875 and implemented over wider and wider areas till the end of Dutch rule, protected the native smallholder. A plot of ground held for generations by a family in usufruct but without ownership now became the personal property of the working peasant. He could lease it to Chinese or Europeans under official safeguards which prevented them from exploiting his economic weakness, but he was not allowed to sell it. If a peasant cleared new land in the jungle it became his private possession. Estates, on the other hand, could be leased from the government. As the government stepped out of farming, big planters took over.

The new arrangements had the virtue of defending the village, the heart of Indonesian life, from disintegrating factors. This is one reason why the Dutch won the reputation of being good colonizers. Holland strove to fulfill the Indonesian peasant's dream of being a proprietor. Individual ownership of land in Java rose from 47 per cent of the total farmed acreage in 1882 to 83 per cent in 1932. In the same period land held by the village as a whole, as a community, fell from 42 per cent to 13 per cent. Both processes reduced the village chieftain's power over the people. The Dutch Civil Service, now more conscientious, enlightened, and able than in earlier periods, frequently intervened to shield the small cultivator from unscrupulous native landlords, Dutch planters, and Chinese usurers.

Land reform in an underdeveloped country is not synonymous, however, with prosperity. In 1902 the Netherlands Queen ordered an investigation into "The Diminishing Welfare of the People of Java." The spreading impoverishment was due, in part, to income taxes which Indonesians paid whereas Dutchmen in the Indies, even wealthy Dutch plantation owners, did not—until 1908. Many peasants became debtors, borrowed money, thereby lost their farms, and became farm laborers or moved to the growing towns. The steeply rising birth rate likewise bred poverty and drove people away from the crowded countryside. The population of Java and Madura was 23,609,312 in 1890, and 40,891,093 in 1930. The other or Outer Islands had an estimated 10 million inhabitants in 1890 and 18,246,974 in 1930. No land reform can provide for so many added bodies. Oil production, tin mining, railroad construction (the first

Indonesian railway, a 160-mile line from Semarang to Jogjakarta was built in 1873), and other forms of urban industrialization created some employment. But compared to the pressure of population the relief was negligible.

The Indies had entered the modern age and were accordingly exposed to modern social and economic diseases.

The vast bulk of Indonesians were peasants who suffered in varying degree under the Culture System, under free labor, and under private ownership. The native middle class also had its troubles—chiefly, the influx of Chinese and Arabs. The number of Chinese in the Indies increased from 221,438 in 1860 to 1,233,214 in 1930. Immigration swelled the Arab population from 8,909 in 1860 to 71,335 in 1930. The Chinese came from China as laborers, but by industry, thrift, and talent quickly dominated domestic trade and moneylending. This left little room for the growth of an Indonesian middle class. The presence of the Chinese, however, was only partly to blame. Indonesian mentality remained feudal long after the feudal economy of the Culture System disappeared. (Feudal psychology still survives.) And feudals regard money-making as undignified. There are no castes in Indonesia, but the middle class felt it would lose caste by engaging in commerce. Some peasants saved money and moved up into private business. The middle class, regarding itself as aristocratic, feared that it would move down by doing the same thing.

Few members of the Indies middle class gained admission into the Dutch Civil Service. Few could obtain the education that would fit them for the professions: law, medicine, engineering, and so forth.

An unemployed, underemployed, disgruntled middle class is the best carrier of nationalism and revolution. Resentful itself, its indignation feeds on the unhappiness of the rest of the people. Finding no fitting economic role to play, the middle class becomes a frustrated intelligentsia which aspires to lead the country to prosperity and national independence.

Nationalist movements defy logic and consequently irritate the coldly legalistic colonial powers. From the dawn of the twentieth century Holland tried to make amends in the Indies. In 1901 Queen Wilhelmina announced "The Ethical Policy." The Netherlands, she declared, had "a moral duty to fulfill" toward the people of the Indies. Dutch businessmen in Indonesia had been sending considerable sums home, but not the Dutch administration. No longer did Batavia make contributions to the budget of Holland. On the contrary, in 1905 Holland contributed 40 million guilders (the guilder, or florin, was the equivalent of one shilling eight pence in gold or 40 U.S. gold cents) which were used for "the amelioration of economic conditions in Java and Madura," in the next fifteen years. The government also opened a chain of pawnshops designed to provide credits for the peasant and save him from economic strangulation by loan sharks. Yet it was precisely this period that saw the dawn of organized Indonesian nationalism. The Dutch thought they deserved praise for what they were doing. The nationalists condemned the foreign ruler for what he was not doing. The colonizer can never win. Whatever his acts, whatever his motives, he is always pursued by the anti-imperialist cry, "Too little, Too late."

Chapter Eight

SHADOWS OF THE FUTURE

THE INDIAN CONGRESS PARTY which, under the guidance of Mahatma Gandhi, Jawaharlal Nehru, Maulana Azad, and Vallabhbhai Patel, liberated India from England in 1947 was organized by an Englishman, Allan Octavian Hume. He launched the party, as early as 1885, with the blessing of Lord Dufferin, the British Viceroy, and served it as general secretary until 1907. The Congress President for 1888 was George Yule, an Englishman; for 1894, Alfred Webb, an Irish member of the British Parliament; for 1904, Sir Henry Cotton, a retired British official of the Indian Civil Service; and for 1910, Sir William Wedderburn, the former secretary of the governor of Bombay. Gandhi praised the devotion of Hume and Wedderburn to India.

The British, it would seem, showed farsighted wisdom in founding and fostering an Indian political body that might channel popular protest into legal moderation. But this too failed to stem the rising tide of nationalism. Slowly the Congress party outgrew its collaborationist boyhood, became a demanding youth, and finally an irresistible adult giant.

When I first went to India I was astonished at the frequency with which Indians mentioned the Russo-Japanese War of 1904-1905. I noted the same thing in Indonesia. Never before had an Asian nation defeated a European country. Japan's victory over Russia gave a fillip to the national movements of the Orient. It meant: We can win; the whites are not invincible; let's bury our inferiority complexes. "Japan's success," writes J. S. Furnivall, the British authority on Burma and Indonesia, "started an impulse which was to transform the peoples in Netherlands India, as in other tropical dependencies, from the extreme of acquiescence to the extreme of self-assertion." Each retreat, defeat, and humiliation of the West gave (gives) the still insecure Asians renewed confidence in the triumph and survival of their nationalism.

To be sure, misery fed the nationalist movements. But the essence was the elemental urge to oust the foreign master from one's own country and rule it instead, and the moment this possibility loomed the colonial government was in for trouble. Every argument, no matter how cogent, every improvement, no matter how real, melted in the rays of the rising sun of independence. Paint the rosiest picture of what the colonial authorities had done and intended soon to do; draw the blackest sketch of the hardships and horrors awaiting an infant nation. The answer would always be that self-government is better than the best outsider's government. This is pure emotion. But then all dependent peoples, especially Asians, are emotional. The West holds a comforting view of the Oriental as phlegmatic, resigned, passive. Brown skin is actually very thin skin and a skillful compatriot can, with the slightest touch, arouse the Asian to roaring passions that border on hysteria and burn practical considerations to ashes.

Early in the twentieth century the Dutch discerned the pale-green shoots of Indies nationalism and began to plan remedial action. They found, for instance, that Indonesians who went to Mecca on the annual *haj* (pilgrimage) returned with notions of a Pan-Islamic international unity which was not conducive to loyalty to Holland. In 1894 about 7,000 traveled to the Moslem holy city; in 1911, 20,000; in 1926, 52,000. Many stopped in Cairo, where they came in touch with Pan-Islamic militants.

The Netherlands government accordingly consulted Snouck Hurgronje, the famous scholar with a flair for adventure and politics. A professor of Islamic law and religion at the University of Leiden, speaking Arabic fluently, Snouck risked his life to enter Mecca, the forbidden city for non-Moslem infidels, and stayed six months, behind a disguise and an assumed name, studying Islamic lore and the sentiments of Indonesian pilgrims. His personality and academic standing gave him influence; at one time he held the post of counselor for native affairs to the Netherlands Ministry of Colonies.

What to do about hajis importing a subversive ideology from Arabia? Do something positive, Snouck replied: make them at home in Dutch culture and thus bind them spiritually to Holland. "The Indonesians," he said, "are imploring us to give them instruction; by granting their wish we shall secure their loyalty for an unlimited time." This was sober advice. But it was also dynamite. For middle-class Indonesians encoun-tered numerous discriminatory obstacles in getting an education, and once they had it the opportunities open to them were far fewer than those open to white men. It all fed anti-Dutch sentiment. Thus the positive became negative, and antisubversive measures nourished subversion. Most of the Indonesian nationalist leaders were Dutch-educated, either in Holland or in Dutch schools in Indonesia.

Because education was the gateway to enlightenment, professional status, perhaps a government post, and to the enticing, inviting West, large numbers knocked. A small percentage was admitted. In 1864, at the dawn of the liberal period of the Indies, the Dutch government removed the ceiling of 25,000 florins—a comical sum—on expenditures permitted annually for native education. In 1882 the budget for the schooling of Indonesians amounted to 1,190,000 florins; in 1887, to 999,000.

According to figures reproduced by Professor George McTurnan Kahin in his standard work, *Nationalism and Revolution in Indonesia,* the average number of Indonesians attending Western-type primary schools was 2,987 in 1900-1904; 61,425 in 1925, and 74,697 in 1928. The number attending high schools above the ninth grade in 1940 in all Indonesia was only 1,786, compared to 5,688 Europeans. These high schools graduated 374 Europeans, 204 Indonesians, and 124 Orientals (chiefly Chinese) in 1934-1935, and 457 Europeans, 204 Indonesians, and 116 Orientals in 1938-1939.

This narrow road to a diploma became a mountain footpath at the college level. The enrollment of the technical school, established in 1919, of the law school, established in 1924, and of the medical college, estab-lished in 1926, included 637 Indonesians in 1940. Thirty-seven were grad-uated in that year from all three institutions.

This was a gloomy picture. But it is not difficult to sympathize with the Dutch in their dilemma. A government commission reported in 1929 that "about twice as many pupils graduate with a Western education as can be found jobs for." Were they, then, to educate additional Indonesians for unemployment? Yet if education remained limited, more young people would become disgruntled and turn to revolutionary nationalism. Whatever it does or does not do, the colonial power is its own gravedigger.

I discussed Indies education with Dr. de Kat Angelino, author of the two-volume *Colonial Policy,* who in the 1930's was in charge of Indonesian schools. "We let it be known," he said in The Hague, "that if a village built a school the government would equip it, send a teacher, and pay all expenses." It was no problem for peasants to put up a school. The village and the jungle just outside it abound in bamboo trees of all calibers. Long strips of bamboo an inch or an inch and a half wide are torn off, plaited together at right angles, calked, and fitted into a yard-square frame. These frames become the "prefabricated" sections of walls. Several partly unattached frames will be the windows. Bamboo poles serve as supports for the walls and beams for a roof made of red clay tiles or thatch, which are readily available. The earth is the floor. A peasant group could construct a mosque or a church in a day. "Yet how few of them," Angelino remarked, "were ready to build a school."

Who does not know that peasants in underdeveloped countries must be educated to educate their children? "Why should we send our children to school," peasants in India and Spain, and in Russia in the 1920's, have said to me, "when so many educated people are out of work?"

West and East saw things from different angles and the twain did not meet.

But suppose the Dutch had provided enough primary schools, high schools, and colleges. To employ their graduates they would have had to replace Dutch government officials with Indonesians and fill Dutch business houses with Indonesians—in effect, ultimately abdicate state, trade, and industry to the native population, and go home.

The issue, therefore, was: Independence—yes or no? The Dutch answered in the negative.

The Indonesian movement for independence began late and timidly. The first organization with even faintly nationalist aspirations was Budi Utomo (High Endeavor), launched in 1908 by middle-class intellectuals to promote popular education. It soon counted 10,000 members. Since the law prohibited political organizations or political meetings, Budi Utomo eschewed politics. But politics were in the air. In 1908 the government authorized local councils of elected representatives. Elections stimulated political discussions.

In 1912 Moslem businessmen united to protect themselves against Chinese and Arab competitors. They called themselves the Sarekat Islam (Moslem Association) and among their goals were the cultivation of the good Islamic religious life and of the commercial spirit among Indonesians. Overtly, these purposes were not political. But any getting together of Indonesians to promote their interests was bound to make them conscious of all the forces, Dutch included, that worked against those interests. The authorities, therefore, did not permit the Sarekat Islam to function as a nationwide organization. It was to exist on a local basis. Yet its political and national character did not long remain hidden. By 1913 the branch representatives of the Sarekat Islam, led by Tjokro Aminoto, met in national congress in the city of Surabaya still disclaiming political motives but barely able to disguise them. A year later the truth came into the open. Raden Achmad, speaking for the organization in March, 1914, said, "The people have joined Sarekat Islam en masse because they seek their rights. . . . The people see their rights continually threatened. That is why there is a great cry for them to unite to defend themselves and to resist with more power those who rob them of their rights." In the same month, at Semarang, Tjokro Aminoto declared bluntly that "the progress which it [Sarekat Islam] wants is not going to be hampered by religion." Christians joined it, as did teachers, workers, peasants, aristocrats, and Indonesian civil servants. At its 1916 national congress the membership numbered 360,000. It was a formidable force, and had it remained, as the Indian Congress party remained because of Gandhi's influence, a cohesive whole uniting all classes and ideologies, the challenge to Dutch rule would have been more immediate.

But the Eurasians or Indo-Europeans, offspring of Dutch-Indonesian marriages, who were neither Dutch fish nor Indonesian fowl and had their own fish to fry, organized separately. More important, Marxism commenced to bore from within the Sarekat Islam. A Dutchman named Hendrik Sneevliet worked assiduously in Semarang, winning sympathy in the Sarekat for the Soviet Revolution of November 7, 1917, and for revolutionary methods rather than gradualism. He met with some success among Dutchmen but attracted few others until he was joined by Eduard F. E. Douwes Dekker, a remote relative of the author of *Max Havelaar*. This Dekker was of a mixed origin encountered often in Indonesia: his paternal grandfather was Dutch, his paternal grandmother French. His maternal grandfather was German, his maternal grandmother Javanese. He, therefore, was Eurasian, or an "Indo," as Indo-Europeans were called. Dekker coined the slogan "The Indies for Those Who Make Their Home Here"; that is, not for the Dutch who came and went.

This sort of exclusive nationalism found an ally in Marxism. For the nationalists were anti-Dutch and anti-Chinese, and the Marxists were anticapitalists, and the capitalists were Dutch or Chinese.

The Indonesians, with rare exceptions, had not yet entered the capitalist stage. Subsistence farmers, and the vast majority of peasants fell into that class, employed no labor, created little surplus, and had little to sell; they could not be called capitalists. The same applied to the intellectuals, the government officials, teachers, the few professional people, the nobility, the aristocrats. They had no capital, they were not in business. Not being capitalists the Indonesians easily lent themselves to anticapitalism. Anticapitalist sentiment was further stimulated by the advancing impoverishment of the Indonesian people. Indonesian anticapitalism was (is) a form of nationalism. (Robbed of its masks and misleading verbiage Soviet anticapitalism is too.)

The nationalist moat between Indonesians, on the one hand, and the Dutch and Chinese, on the other, grew wider, accordingly, as a result of Marxist anticapitalist infiltration. It came as no surprise, therefore, when the September, 1918, national congress of the Sarekat Islam resolved that "Considering that the majority of the population lives in a miserable condition, the Sarekat Islam will always oppose any predominance of sinful capitalism." In explanation of this cryptic phrase Tjokro Aminoto said "foreign capitalism is always sinful." In other words, Indonesian capitalism was not.

Coming events cast their shadows before. Sensitive to world trends toward self-determination and to the emergence of Indies nationalism, the Dutch government authorized the formation of a People's Council of Indonesia, which held its first session in May, 1918, in Batavia. At first the majority of the 39 Council members were Dutch. Half of the total were elected by local boards. After the election, the Governor General appointed the remaining half, it being understood that 50 per cent of the appointees would be Indonesians and the other 50 per cent Europeans and non-Indonesian Asians. In 1925 the Council was expanded to a membership of 60, of whom 30 were to be Dutchmen, 25 Indonesians, and 5 Chinese and Arabs. In 1928, however, Asians won a stronger position in the Council with 30 Indonesians, 5 Chinese and Arabs (whose sympathies were with the Dutch), and 25 Dutchmen.

The Council held two short sessions a year. Its members enjoyed parliamentary immunity but it was not a parliament. It had no legislative or executive functions. It could discuss and advise and thereby influence the Governor General. But it could decide nothing against his wishes. Many Indonesians consequently refused to collaborate with the Council.

Meanwhile the Marxists in the Sarekat Islam had openly embraced Communism and, in 1920, joined the Moscow-mothered Comintern or Third International. Friction followed in the Sarekat Islam between the antireligious Communists and the Moslem anti-Communists. They might have compromised and they would perhaps have co-operated but for the inherent power urge of Communists who saw co-operation merely as a steppingstone to control. Under the stern anti-Communist leadership of Tjokro Aminoto and Haji Agus Salim, the inevitable split ensued early in 1923. It weakened the Sarekat. It revealed the Communists as mirrors of Moscow's foreign policy and domestic conflicts.

In the mid-1920's (1925, 1926, and 1927) the struggle between Stalin and Trotsky for the succession to Lenin reached its greatest ferocity. Stalin seemed certain to win. But the Trotskyites carried influence in the army, among university students, and in the government apparatus. What was no less irritating to Stalin, the Trotskyites proved him wrong on a number of key issues, notably China, which was crucial to the entire Stalin-Trotsky feud. Trotsky argued that China was ripe for revolution and Moscow should therefore help the Chinese Communists form local and provincial soviets and in every other way undermine the position of Generalissimo Chiang Kai-shek. Stalin, nevertheless, supported Chiang. In 1926, in the midst of this debate, Chiang Kai-shek sent out executioners with swords to behead Communists in the streets of Shanghai. The Trotskyists quickly condemned Stalin as the archcollaborator of the anti-Communist counterrevolutionary Generalissimo. To erase the stain and demonstrate his devotion to revolution Stalin, in 1927, ordered a coup d'état in the South China city of Canton. It was a vain bloodbath in which hundreds of Chinese paid with their lives to give Stalin an argument, however flimsy, to hurl back at Trotsky.

The Communists of Indonesiá were likewise the unwitting victims of the clash of power in Moscow. Stalin knew that Indonesia was not ripe for a Communist revolution, and in May, 1925, he said so publicly, at the same time branding as "left deviationist" those impatient extremists who differed with him. He advocated a policy which the Indonesian Communists were practicing in the 1950's: the wearing of the fig leaf of nationalism so as to win the largest possible following. But a year later, under the verbal lashings of the Trotskyists, he was eager to refute the charge of sabotaging the world revolution by his conservative, restraining policy. Moreover, the counsels of the Third International were divided and its instructions, therefore, confusing. Sometime in the latter half of 1926 it ordered the Indonesian Communist party to make a revolution. To succeed the move would have had to expel the Dutch and then overcome the opposition of Indonesian religious nationalism. It was sheer madness even to think of undertaking such a doomed adventure. But Indonesia was merely a little pawn in the big fight for Soviet internal supremacy.

The revolution made in Moscow's divided brain broke out in the night of November 12, 1926. The big five leaders of the Indonesian Communist party were Semaun, Tan Malaka, Musso, Alimin, and Darsono. Of these Tan Malaka, the Comintern's representative in the Far East, firmly opposed the coup for the same reasons that Stalin had opposed it in 1925. He claimed it was premature and unprepared.

Thus the Indonesian Communist counsels were as divided as the Third International's. There are several versions of what happened. In Jakarta, in 1958, Darsono, now an anti-Communist employee of the Indonesian Foreign Office, gave me his version. Having told the Indonesian party to

stage the revolution, Darsono affirms, Moscow changed its mind and withdrew the order. This sounds plausible; the same thing took place in the
German revolution fomented by the Kremlin in 1923: the signal was
given, then Moscow sent a STOP signal.

But as in Germany, so in Indonesia, the outbreak occurred. According
to Darsono, Moscow's second instructions were kept secret by Musso, who
favored the revolution. Musso had visited Moscow late in 1926, yet he
never revealed what he was told. This lends verisimilitude to the interpretation that the Kremlin bosses told him not to proceed with the revolution. It is also conceivable that one of the Soviet leaders urged him to go
ahead. That is part of the story. A more decisive contribution to the failure
of the revolution was the action of the Dutch government. Intensified
Communist agitation and a series of strikes had indicated to the authorities
that trouble was brewing. They may have placed informers in the Red
organizations. Wholesale arrests followed and the Communist groups
were forbidden to assemble. Torn with dissension and harried by the
police, the Communist party could not function well. The chances of
success, always slim, fell to nil.

Blinded by formal discipline and fateful illusions, the Communists
launched the ill-fated enterprise. So great was their faith in the magic
of the revolution that they believed only one shot was necessary, one
victory, and the Dutch walls would come tumbling down. The first night
they attacked the Batavia prison and were thrown back with losses.
Fortune was no friendlier to their second effort: an assault on the telephone exchange. Nowhere, except to a small extent in Bantam, in West
Java, and Padang, in Central Sumatra, did the Communists win any
popular support for their sad venture. The government was never threatened. It crushed the coup in less than a fortnight, and then moved rapidly
to smash opposition elements. Thirteen thousand persons were arrested,
of whom 4,500 were sent to jail and 1,308 to concentration camps in remote regions of the colony. In subsequent years the Communists gave
some signs of life, usually in the form of vain violence. But in 1938 their
anti-Dutch activities ceased entirely. For Russia, frightened by the Hitler
menace, decided, in 1935, to mollify the West and try to strengthen it
against Germany. In accordance with this policy twist, the French
Communists, for instance, were told by Stalin in an official communiqué,
also signed by pro-Nazi-to-be Prime Minister Pierre Laval, to drop their
advocacy of disarmament and support France's rearmament. All Communist parties, moreover, were ordered by Moscow to form united fronts
with Socialists, Liberals, and anybody else who would join. To achieve this
end, and make themselves acceptable united-front partners of those who
favored imperialism, the Communists had to compromise, and the Dutch

Communist party went so far in the abandonment of principle as to stop advocating Indonesian independence. The Indonesian Communist party silently marched in step. This betrayal of the national cause at Moscow's behest, plus the aftereffects of the 1926 coup, eliminated the Indonesian party as a political force until after the end of the Second World War. The wonder is that it ever recuperated at all.

Chapter Nine

THE UNWILLING AND THE WEAK

QUEEN WILHELMINA's 1901 announcement of the Ethical Policy for the Indies had stated that "As a Christian Power the Netherlands is obligated in the East Indian archipelago to regulate better the legal position of native Christians" and "to lend support on a firm basis to Christian missions." This had to be Dutch policy, for the Dutch are very religious-minded, and several of their strongest political parties are founded on religion. The Dutch administration in Batavia, accordingly, financed Indies Protestant and Roman Catholic institutions which proselytized natives.

Nevertheless, the colonial government remembered that at least 90 per cent of Indonesians were Mohammedans. Loyal to the precepts of Professor Snouck Hurgronje, Batavia paid minute attention to Islamic sensibilities. Indeed, this was often exaggerated, for as Cornelis van Vollenhoven, the great Dutch expert on the Indies, taught, Indonesian life conformed more to pre-Islamic customary, or adat, law than to the precepts of the Koran. In the fervently Islamic Central Sumatran region inhabited by the remarkable Minangkabau race, for example, adat law sanctioned matriarchal rule, which conflicted sharply with the male supremacy of Islam, and throughout the archipelago female-initiated divorce, an Islamic heresy, was and is permitted by an agreement between spouses which is part of the marriage contract.

The Dutch authorities, however, solved the dilemma by respecting both adat and Koranic law, leaving the choice to the people and never forcing Dutch or Roman law on them.

This wise nonintervention policy paid good dividends. It blunted the edge of nationalist hostility to the foreign government. A similar result was achieved by interposition: between themselves and the Indonesians the Dutch interposed native sultans, regents, and other rulers. Professor Amry Vandenbosch, in his book *The Dutch East Indies,* describes the political system as "in essence a joint government of two autocrats, one European, the other Indonesian, with a clever [Dutch] Governor getting his way most of the time." The native rulers were simply too inefficient, indifferent, and backward to cope with the multifarious tasks facing the administration of millions of people in the modern age. The Indonesian autocrat, accordingly, paid little attention to practical matters and was an autocrat in name only and in fact a puppet who sanctioned Dutch orders. But what these fiction potentates lacked in power they sought to gild with pomp. Lord Linlithgow, the British Viceroy of India before and during part of World War II, once told me that no maharajah ever came to him without asking that he be allowed a salute of more guns. An equally weighty matter in the Indies was whether such-and-such a regent should be entitled to have a bright, big parasol held over his head during public ceremonies. More than fourscore regents and sultans were retained in Java in transparent impotence. In other islands native rulers sometimes exercised some power. But with few notable exceptions the regents and sultans served as a Dutch shield, for a large part of the peasantry still held them in a reverence reminiscent of the Middle Ages.

Nonintervention and interposition were high hurdles impeding the progress of the Indonesian nationalist movement. There was another. While keeping aloof from delicate matters like religion, social tradition, and legal customs, the Dutch governed by a method which involved knowing everything, being everywhere, and managing as much as possible. J. S. Furnivall, contrasting the British administration in India and Burma he knew from long personal participation with Dutch rule he had carefully studied played on a word, "babu," which in Indian languages means a clerk and in Malayan a nursemaid. The British registered what was done and punished offenders, the Dutch wanted to be a governess to a nation they considered childlike. "You," Furnivall said to the Dutch, "try to keep a man from doing wrong; we make it unpleasant for him if he does wrong. You believe in protection and welfare; we believe in law and liberty." I have heard Dutchmen explain the reason for this distinction. "We were a small country ruling a vast archipelago," they contend, "and it is better to anticipate troubles than let them germinate and grow." It goes deeper than that. Toughness with oneself and others and a dog-

matic demarcation between good and bad are basic to the national behavior of the Dutch. They are not exactly flexible. They feel duty-bound
to extirpate evil. Once they fix a goal not even their common sense, love
of tidiness, and obedience to regulations will stop them. This was their
approach to the nationalist movement during the late 1920's and all
the 1930's. Alerted and alarmed by the 1926 Communist coup, Batavia
fished with a fine net which brought in the guilty but also gathered up
innocent suspects for "protective custody."

The nationalist movement consequently ebbed. Many persons were
frightened away from it by the extremism of the Communists and their
loyalty to Russia. Moderates took refuge in Moslem welfare and cultural
organizations like the Mohammadiya. Others appreciated Dutch political
reforms that gave Indonesians experience in the legislative procedures.
In such periods of frustration, popular movements tend to splinter. This
happens, for instance, to émigré organizations which, banished from their
native lands and seeing little prospect of returning, split ideological hairs
and pursue personal jealousies until the parent body breaks into halves
and then the halves break in half, and so on to ruin. Similarly, the
fifteen years preceding the Second World War saw a proliferation of
groups and grouplets in Indonesia each avowing the goal of national
independence and each hampering the other. Since they could not effectively fight the Dutch they fought among themselves.

The need was unity. In an attempt to form an inclusive non-Communist,
pro-independence body, the Nationalist Party of Indonesia (PNI) was
launched on June 4, 1927. It elected as its chairman a recent graduate of
the technical school in the Javanese city of Bandung: Sukarno, the future
President of Indonesia. He was an engineer. More important, he was an
orator. "Neither an airplane from Moscow," he stated, "nor a caliph in
Istanbul" would bring them salvation. They had to help themselves.

Dr. E. S. de Klerck, a retired Netherlands military man and author of
the *History of the Netherlands East Indies,* gives the Dutch reaction. "It is
true," he writes, "that the mutual sympathy of the revolutionary nationalists and the Communists was not at all great, but the activities of both
of them were indeed directed towards the overthrow of foreign dominion. The tone struck in the meetings of the Indonesian Nationalist
Party grew more and more bold and reckless, in spite of the repeated
warnings of the police to restrain their utterances. Though authority
was ignored, the police refrained from taking strong action, in order
to avoid giving the impression that they wanted to interfere with the
rights of free speech and corporate life. The demagogues, far from ap-
preciating the long patience of the Government, only saw weakness in

this lenient attitude. At last the cup overflowed. In the beginning of August, 1929, after reports had come in indicating threatening disturbances, a final warning was given to the leaders of the party. Nevertheless when it appeared that an attempt on the Government was being planned towards New Year, the Governor General, at the instigation of the Attorney General decided to take action. On the 29th of December, Sukarno and some other leaders were arrested, and not a day too early, as appeared from a thorough investigation. The sentences were very liberal indeed. Neither capital punishment nor penal servitude, as were applied in French Tonkin the very same year, but only a four years' imprisonment for the chief offender and milder punishment for the three other leaders, whilst the party was dissolved as being dangerous to the public peace and safety."

A good commentary on Dr. de Klerck's account is his next two sentences. "Soon," he says, "another radical association arose from the latter's ashes, viz. the Pendidikan National Indonesia (Indonesian Educational Union), in short denoted by the very same initials PNI, not by way of defiance, but because of some mystic value being attached to the grouping of letters by Easterners." Maybe it was defiance—as well as mysticism. "The union," he continues, "was started by Dr. Mohammad Hatta, a revolutionary" who, with Sukarno, founded the Republic of Indonesia.

After waiting seven months for his trial, Sukarno received a three-year prison sentence, a very mild punishment for an alleged plotter to overthrow the government. Some Dutchmen in Indonesia felt that even this moderate verdict was unjustified and that Sukarno was not guilty as charged. Having reflected long on the trial, the editors, all Dutch, of a Batavia liberal fortnightly entitled *De Stuw* (*The Dam*), published an extensive unsigned article in their issue of June 15, 1931, criticizing the Sukarno sentence. Dr. H. J. van Mook, later acting governor of the Indies, then a civil servant and member of *De Stuw's* editorial board, now tells me that he wrote the article. "The top leaders of the P.N.I.," it said, "were people of such stature that they could have had no illusions over the results of violent conflict and must have fully understood that such a conflict would have played completely into the hands of the conservative diehards and could only have had as its results not only the destruction of the P.N.I. but also immeasurable injury to the whole Native movement. In spite of the judicial decisions handed down in two cases, we hereby declare our conviction—firm though without factual support—that Engineer Sukarno and his supporters by no means had force as their 'immediate goal,' they were on the contrary very much afraid of acts of violence on the part of their followers."

Apparently this view was shared by other officials and nonofficials, and the Dutch government released Sukarno in December, 1931, exactly two years after his arrest.

Restored to freedom, Sukarno continued his efforts to unite the nationalists. Despite his pacific behavior, he was again arrested in August, 1933, and exiled to the island of Flores. Later the Dutch shifted him to Benkulen, in Sumatra, where he stayed till the Japanese released him in 1942. Hatta and Sutan Sjahrir, a brilliant young intellectual, both of the Minangkabau race, both educated in Holland, were likewise interned, first in New Guinea, then in the Moluccas, and so too were many hundreds of nationalists.

Some contend that persecution is always useless. But ubiquitous surveillance and rigorous repressive measures did cripple the nationalist movement. The Dutch were never in any danger.

Since arrests made mass organizations impossible, temperate politicians tried diplomacy. In 1936 a resolution moved by Sutarjo and approved by a 26-20 vote of the People's Council, was submitted to the government in The Hague. It proposed an imperial round-table conference which would draft a plan for a ten-year transition period ending in Indonesian independence under Article One of the Dutch Constitution, that is, within the Federal Union of Holland. The government did not reply for more than two years. Finally, on November 16, 1938, Prime Minister Dr. Hendrik Colijn and Minister of Colonies Charles Welter rejected the Sutarjo petition for "lack of clarity" and because the suggested conference would conflict with the Constitution.

Holland was just as unyielding after the Nazis had driven the Queen and her government into exile in England. When the Atlantic Charter was signed by President Franklin D. Roosevelt and Prime Minister Winston S. Churchill on August 14, 1941, and by the Dutch government, among others, on September 29 of the same year, a member of the People's Council inquired whether the Charter's statement that its signatories "respect the right of all peoples to choose the form of government under which they will live," applied to Indonesia. He was told that "adherence to the Charter does not represent a special reason for new consideration regarding the aims of its [the Netherlands government's] policy, more especially as far as the Indonesian population is concerned." True, the Queen had, on July 30, 1941, promised an imperial conference after the war, but no word was said about self-determination. If self-determination was Holland's purpose, what prevented Her Majesty from announcing that Indonesia would select its own government in accordance with the Charter?

It is Indonesia's tragedy that none of this prepared either side for the future. The nationalists were sorrowfully aware of their inability to oust the foreign ruler. The colonial power knew the strength of its own intentions to stay. Holland rejected the idea of an agreed settlement with the independence seekers and they scarcely hoped to achieve it. This situation made understanding and trust, even contact, impossible. Holland lost the Indonesian friends who might have been her bridge to the people's heart.

The evolution of Hatta and Sjahrir illustrates what happened to numerous others. Hatta, later prime minister and vice-president of the free Republic of Indonesia, and Sjahrir, the Republic's first prime minister, were arrested and banished to Digul, in remote, Stone Age New Guinea, in January, 1935. Sjahrir was and is a Westerner. "Every young man and young woman in the East," he wrote in his book, *Out of Exile,* which is a series of letters from exile, "ought to look toward the West, for he or she can learn only from the West to regard himself or herself as a center of vitality capable of changing and bettering the world. . . . For me the West signifies forceful, dynamic, and active life," he declared approvingly. Though he wanted freedom for his country he was in no sense anti-Dutch when arrested at the age of twenty-six. But thoughts in exile changed his attitude and also that of Hatta, whose political psuedonym was Hafil. Hatta had refused to co-operate with the Dutch in the People's Council or in any other way, "yet in many respects" Sjahrir, who spent every day with him, wrote in March, 1938, "he still had faith in the conventional morality and humanity of colonial government. He never thought about secret police and the possibility of terrorist methods being used against political opponents, who, like himself, intentionally and consciously acted within legal limits . . . he still maintained a high opinion of the respectability and methods of the colonial rulers against whom he made a stand. Now he thinks differently about these things."

"The same is true in my case, as well," Sjahrir added. Before his arrest, he and his colleagues "propagated suspicion toward the government, but we did not realize that we ourselves regarded it with a measure of moral trust. At one time, Hafil [Hatta] did not believe that he would be banished. . . . The same was true to an even greater extent of the others in our party. Most of them, in fact, still don't understand how it is possible for them to be regarded as dangerous to the state for what they have done—or rather, haven't done. . . . It was really a revelation for Hafil, and he has learned more from it than during all his years of 'political life' in Europe."

Having arrived at this judgment of his own and Hatta's development away from faith in the Dutch, Sjahrir took a fresh look at those who were co-operating with the government and decided that they "co-operate because they do not think they will be safe against the methods of force that they deem the rulers capable of if they don't co-operate. In other words, they have such a low opinion of the humanity and morality of the rulers that they think it safer not to be opponents of the regime, or at least not openly."

Part of this is no doubt laced with the bitter taste of exile which robs a young man of many years of his life. That in itself is a condemnation of repression. But this does not devalue Sjahrir's analysis, for knowledge obtained subsequently from more rigorous authoritarian and totalitarian countries demonstrates that while dictators get relief by removing their domestic enemies from the scene, they also make cynics, sycophants, and timeserving, lip-service hypocrites of everybody else. Belief in decency or ideology vanishes, leaving only ugly materialism.

The wide and misty psychological gulf between Dutch and Indonesian still shapes policy. Dutch methods underlined the inferiority and weakness of the natives. Seeing only Netherlands intransigence, the Indonesians despaired. Their hopelessness in the face of Dutch stubbornness would help to explain much that happened in the Indies during and immediately after the Second World War.

Chapter Ten

JAPAN OVER THE INDIES

DURING THE decade before the war cheap Japanese goods had found an expanding market in the Indies. Ten thousand Japanese businessmen, classified by the Dutch as Europeans, competed with the Chinese—a fact that did not trouble Indonesian nationalists. The Japanese, moreover, curried favor with the Indonesians by giving them executive jobs in their enterprises, something the Chinese never and the Dutch seldom did.

Though thinking Indonesians had no ideological kinship with the Nipponese warlords or rising-sun imperialism, neither were they animated by the automatic antipathy that characterized politically conscious persons in independent nations. To the sensitive individual in a colony the paramount consideration is his country's lack of freedom. This is true even if, for private or other reasons, he consents to co-operate with the foreign ruler. His goal remains national liberation. The advent of the Japanese intensified the desire.

Japan defeated the Dutch in the Indies quickly. Holland's unprepared air force and fleet, supplemented by meager Australian, British, and American contingents, fought heroically but in vain. Holland's puny land army melted away before the mass Japanese onslaught. The Indonesians, inevitably, were impressed. A power that had held sway over them for more than three centuries vanished in three weeks at the touch of fellow Asians.

It would be wrong to suppose that a military conqueror, even one so competent and ruthlessly methodical as Japan (or Nazi Germany) can, during a war, administer every square mile of the countryside and every house and street of the teeming cities. He swoops down to seize crops, slave labor, and suspects. His secret police snoops assiduously, fills concentration camps, shoots and hangs, and guards buildings, bridges, roads, and top personnel. Vast areas and most minds nevertheless elude him. He cannot be sure of the intentions of those natives whom he must employ in his administration. He is often terrorized by this condition and becomes frantic, for he is not really master in the house he has occupied. The Japanese did not hold down only Indonesia. They had seized a huge fraction of Asia with several hundred million inhabitants. As the war wore on, they were increasingly harried and harassed by the American, British, and Allied armed forces. Their inflammable homeland cities were being bombed. Supplies ebbed. Communications were cut. Anti-Japanese activities flourished.

When Japan took over Siam in December, 1941, Prime Minister Pibul offered token resistance for twenty-four hours, then capitulated and collaborated. At the same time he flagrantly connived at the open support which Regent Pridi gave the Western Allies. Pridi organized the Free Thai movement which, throughout the war, maintained contact with the American Office of Strategic Services (OSS) and its British equivalent. In the first phase, the American and British agents landed in Siam by boat, but as the liaison was perfected they came and departed in their own airplanes, and Pibul's director of police facilitated their work.

The possibility of similar actions was apparent to many Asians. Under the Japanese occupation of the Philippines, José P. Laurel, a former justice of the Supreme Court, served as president of his country and was widely regarded as a Nippon puppet. But he was not. In Manila, in 1952, Admiral Raymond A. Spruance, the United States ambassador, told me that on leaving the Philippines after the fall of Bataan and Corregidor, General Douglas MacArthur and President Quezon requested Laurel to stay behind and do what he could for his people. Ambassador Spruance called Laurel a patriot.

In Indonesia, Hatta collaborated with Japan. He and Sjahrir came to an agreement. Hatta was too well known for underground activity. He, consequently, "would have to lead an open existence," Sjahrir affirms in *Out of Exile*, "and perhaps would be obliged to work with the Japanese up to a certain point, for the good of the movement. I would then lead our organization and direct our underground work."

They kept the agreement. "Hafil [Hatta]," Sjahrir wrote in retrospect, "never made common cause with those Indonesians who went to work for the Japanese because of either material designs or political sympathies. He always regarded himself as a democrat and nationalist who had been prevailed upon to accept a position by *force majeure*. Using this position, he tried to do what he could for our cause. Moreover, he accepted his position at the behest of our party. To him were delegated the tasks of securing funds for us and of facilitating the travel of our workers. Hafil acquitted himself of these tasks capably and faithfully. He also received our reports and warned us when he heard that something was brewing on the Japanese side. I heard from him everything that took place among the Japanese and among the collaborating Indonesians."

Sjahrir stayed in his sister's house at Tjipanas, among the lovely mountains southeast of Batavia and Bogor. There he tended her orange trees and rice fields and led the underground. Several PNI members set up a radio monitoring apparatus in the house which enabled Sjahrir to keep himself and his colleagues informed on world events. "Throughout the occupation," Sjahrir writes, "this listening service continued in operation."

In the early months of the Japanese presence many Indonesians were pro-Japanese. This impeded underground work. Nevertheless, Sjahrir traveled incessantly throughout Java gathering impressions and talking with trustworthy political friends. Gradually the atmosphere changed. The Japanese commanders had decreed that all male students were to shave the tops of their heads and that this exposed spot was to be smacked by schoolteachers in case of indiscipline or faulty scholarship. The students demonstrated against this gratuitous insult. Moreover, notices were posted requiring Indonesians to bow low to every passing Japanese, whether in or out of uniform. This too provoked resentment. Far worse, Moslems were expected to bow in the direction of the Emperor of Japan at public functions and during their prayers. But this bow resembled the obeisance every devout Moslem makes five times a day at prayertime in the direction of Mecca. The prostration before the Mikado in Tokyo accordingly aroused Indonesian religious leaders to fury. On one occasion Dr. Haji Abdul Karim Amrullah, a famous Moslem divine from Sumatra, was the only Indonesian invited to sit on the platform with Japanese officers at a 1943 meeting in Bandung. When the officers rose to bend worshipfully to the Emperor, Dr. Amrullah remained seated. This was an offense to their Shinto feelings, as offensive as refusing to stand when the national anthem is sung or a national banner is carried past—and in wartime. Yet nobody touched the brave doctor. In fact, the injunction to perform the Emperor bow was withdrawn shortly thereafter. Indonesians may not be as sternly Islamic as their brethren in the Middle East or other arid regions of the earth, but challenged by an alien faith they rally to their own.

The Japanese heaped injury on insult. Villages and city blocks were surrounded by Japanese troops and thousands of able-bodied Javanese carried away for manual labor in Burma, Siam, Indo-China, and other segments of the "Co-Prosperity Sphere." A large proportion never returned.

The accumulated ill feeling facilitated the work of Sjahrir and other secret nationalist resistance groups.

Sjahrir was living in Tjipanas ostensibly because of bad lungs. But he frequently descended, by two-hour autobus ride, into the dank air of low-lying Batavia to see Hatta and exchange information with him. Hatta had been put in charge of a Japanese advisory bureau on relations with nationalists. In this capacity he kept insisting that Sukarno be brought from Sumatra to Java. Finally the Japanese assented. On the very day of Sukarno's arrival in Batavia, Sjahrir met him in Hatta's home. "It appeared that Abdul Rachman [Sukarno's assumed name] had been strongly affected by Japanese successes," writes Sjahrir. "Evidently he had also been treated rather roughly in Sumatra by the Japanese. He regarded them as pure fascists, and felt that we must use the most subtle counter-methods to get around them, such as making an appearance of collaboration. He further considered the future to be far from promising, because he thought the war with Japan would last at least ten years."

Sjahrir, somewhat critical of Sukarno, was more optimistic and consequently urged drastic resistance as well as subtle collaboration. Sukarno and Hatta agreed. "For several months," Sjahrir says, "Abdul Rachman [Sukarno] kept me fully informed concerning the course of his discussions with the Japanese, and occasionally came to ask my advice."

Alone the formidable, unavoidable chaos of foreign occupation would scarcely explain the ease with which the Indonesian resistance leaders and official collaborators maintained contact. Nor is it conceivable that the Kempeitai (Japan's secret police) knew nothing at all about Sjahrir's activities. There must have been a running debate in Tokyo and at the highest Japanese level in Batavia on what to do about the Indonesian nationalist movement: suppress it or use it? To judge by the Japanese gyrations, vacillations, experiments, and reversals described in Professor Kahin's *Nationalism and Revolution in Indonesia,* no strategy for the duration was ever evolved. Policy depended on Japan's chances of victory. When Hitler invaded Russia he felt sure of quick success. His plans, accordingly, did not envisage courtship of the population. On the contrary, he preferred to exterminate or expel the inhabitants of the western and southern parts of the Soviet Union in order to create *Lebensraum* for settlers from Germany. Indonesia is no exact analogy. But if the Japanese believed they were going to win the war they would be less likely to grant independence to Indonesia; they would want the archipelago for themselves. If they thought victory less probable they would seek to earn the good will of the Indonesians and enlist their aid in the war effort by promising them self-government.

Now faith in the ultimate defeat of the Allies varied from group to group in Japan. The confidence of the navy, for instance, commenced to wane during the second year of the war and it, therefore, manifested considerable tolerance, indeed friendliness, toward Indonesian nationalism. Other Japanese power factors were not ready for such a course until 1944 or even 1945. This cleavage in Japanese councils was meat for the Indonesian politicians; one Japanese authority occasionally protected them from another.

Three main elements, none homogeneous, held the Indies wartime stage: the Japanese occupants; the Islamic spiritual leaders (kiyayi) and teachers (ulama), whom the Japanese considered otherworldly, hence less political yet Pan-Islamic and therefore opposed to Britain, France, and Holland which had ruled Moslem lands; and the nationalist politicians. The Japanese attempted to use the religious leaders against the nationalists. The nationalists tried to use the Japanese. The question often was: who would outfox whom?

The cautious play between opposing forces commenced from the very day of the Japanese conquest. Indonesians had been subject to Holland so long that they naturally, if naïvely, regarded the expulsion of the Dutch as equivalent to liberation. Great, therefore, was the jubilation which, almost automatically, became a festival of independence. Immediately Lieutenant General Imamura, the Japanese commander in chief, posted a decree forbidding "any discussion or organization . . . concerned with the political administration of the country." Talk of independence was taboo.

The Nipponese interpreted the joy of the population to mean, as professor Kahin states it, "that they could exploit the resources of Indonesia for the benefit of the war effort without having to make concessions to Indonesian nationalism." They accordingly launched the Triple A movement in April, 1942. Triple A signified: Japan the Leader of Asia, Japan the Protector of Asia, Japan the Light of Asia. Drunk with many victories and much self-love, the militarists apparently regarded the Indonesians as children who would welcome this kind of fairy-land Shintoism. The inhabitants of the Indies, however, had already suffered enough from the occupation. The Triple A movement, says Kahin, "was a complete fizzle."

Having failed to get anywhere by making no concessions to nationalism, the Japanese made concessions to it. In March, 1943, they organized the Center of People's Power, [Putera for short, in Indonesian] with Sukarno as chairman and Hatta as vice-chairman. The appearance of Putera reflected new Japanese doubts about the outcome of the war. In June, 1943, Japanese Prime Minister Tojo announced to the Diet that Indonesia was to enjoy a measure of self-government, and he repeated the assurance at a mass meeting in Gambir Park in Jakarta on July 7. In September, in fact, Putera acquired an advisory board which the occupation authorities promised to consult before adopting important measures. On November 10, 1943, Sukarno, Hatta, and Ki Bagus Hadikusuma, head of the Mohammadiya, were flown to Tokyo to thank the Emperor for this benefaction and receive decorations from him. However, when Sukarno took advantage of the visit to ask Premier Tojo to grant Indonesia independence he met with a rebuff.

Six months after it was born Putera had a child called Peta, or Volunteer Army of Defenders of the Fatherland. Peta was destined to play an important role under the occupation. Its officers and soldiers, all Indonesians, have also decisively influenced the affairs of the free Republic of Indonesia. The Japanese conceived and trained Peta for the purpose of aiding Japan in repelling an Allied invasion of the Indies; by mid-1945 they allowed it to reach a strength of 120,000. Indonesians streamed into it in masses and assiduously learned the art of war.

The Japanese saw Peta as the marriage of Islam and Japan. Peta's made-in-Japan flag showed the red rising sun on a green field, green traditionally standing for Islam. Within the sun were Islam's white crescent moon and a star. Brushing aside this naïve symbolism, Sukarno was able to convince the Japanese that before an army would fight for its country it had to be imbued with nationalist sentiments. He and Hatta, and others, accordingly, were often granted permission to address the recruits. "By 1944," says Kahin, "the average Peta member was consciously strongly nationalist, anti-Japanese, anti-Dutch, but for the most part favorably disposed toward the other Allies, particularly the United States."

By 1944 the volunteer army called Peta became a battlefield of contending forces. On the one hand, the Sukarno-Hatta nationalists had the inside track for Peta propaganda and hoped, at the propitious moment, to wrest independence peacefully from the Japanese. On the other hand, several Indonesian undergrounds believed that if their country was indeed invaded by the Allies Peta would do best to fight the Japanese and thereby win world recognition for Indonesia's right to be free.

All Indonesian attitudes reflected two factors which made the Japanese situation hopeless: the mounting hatred; the approaching Western Allies.

Almost thirteen years to the day after Japan's defeat and surrender, the *Times of Indonesia,* an English-language Jakarta daily, in a harsh verdict considering the lapse of time, declared in an editorial on August 13, 1958, that "As we who lived through the occupation can testify, the Japanese are probably the most stupid of all Asian peoples in their dealings with natives of other races for, with that compound of arrogance and idiocy which is the make-up of the average Japanese, they have a genius for getting themselves thoroughly detested. That Japan was bound to lose the war is one of those self-evident facts any schoolboy should have known: that Japan lost the friendship of the whole of Southeast Asia in a matter of some forty months is something of more than ordinary interest for the historian. What cost the Japanese the good will of the countries they raped was their brutality. . . ."

The hatred bore bitter berries in the shape of short, sporadic outbursts of anti-Japanese violence, one of which, involving Japanese soldiers in a West Java village on January 18, 1944, earned an official communiqué and a public explanation. In February, 1944, a detachment of Peta soldiers rebelled against its Japanese superiors at Blitar, an East Java town.

Indonesian hostility, however, and everything else, paled into insignificance as the Nemesis invoked by the foul folly of Pearl Harbor came closer and loomed larger by the hour. Island-hopping Western armies and bomb-dropping Western planes were slowly moving in for the kill. Yet it is known that the Allies did not expect an early victory, nor, presumably, were all Japanese completely downcast. In Indonesia, for instance, Japan continued to maneuver. Putera, founded in March, 1943, as a Japanese instrument, was disbanded in March, 1944, because it had become an Indonesian nationalist instrument. In its stead the occupation authorities set up the People's Loyalty Organization [Hokokai in Japanese], which they thought would be more amenable to their orders. The substitution registered another Japanese failure. Yet the new body likewise did not satisfy the distraught Nipponese and so they also created Angkatan Muda, or Youth Association, into which they dragooned elements thought to be pro-Japanese and others known to be anti-Japanese. They wanted everybody under one roof, the better to control them.

On September 7, 1944, General Koiso, who succeeded Tojo in June, promised Indonesia independence "in the very near future." But the November 1, 1944, issue of a Japanese-subsidized Indonesian magazine, tongue obviously in cheek, censured "people with little or insufficient knowledge" who complained because independence was being delayed. Most people apparently had "little or insufficient knowledge."

The Japanese military now played the best, perhaps the last, card in the deck: their own ideology. Independence, they saw, would be a moat rather than a bridge. A newly liberated country fights no battles but its own. Only a common political philosophy could serve as a bond. The militarists had one ready-to-wear, they thought, for Indonesia. Its component parts were: an authoritarian state that would get things done by dictatorial means; secret groups of elite who could, by drastic methods not excluding assassination, force the government to obey their wishes; a classless society of equals which eliminated poverty and aristocracy—except the aristocracy of self-sacrificing individuals who served the state.

Few, perhaps, accepted every feature of this philosophy. But some aspects would appeal to many, the Japanese believed. There were the kiyayi Islamic preceptors and ulama teachers in each village with their millions of peasant followers, who had been wrenched out of their century-old otherworldliness by the Japanese and dragged into politics. In their localities they were likely to practice the democracy inherent in Moslem mores which require prince to stand beside pauper in the mosque and pray in unison to Allah. But on a national scale parliamentary democracy meant zero to them, and if they had heard of it then only that it was something the Dutch performed at home but denied to the colony. As they acknowledged the all-wise religious Prophet who also ordered their secular lives, they might, at a lower level, defer to an unquestioned political leader. There were the urban sophisticates, impatient, intolerant of oldsters and talkers, patriotically idealistic or personally ambitious, who equated democracy with the West, capitalism, and imperialism, and felt the call to make big social, economic, and political changes in a hurry. There were the Communists, who, as the military Fascists saw it, grew on the same totalitarian tree as themselves, and, if they could only be weaned from Moscow, might join Nippon in combating the decadent, democratic, plutocratic white West.

The postwar life of the Republic of Indonesia suggests that some of these idea-seeds did grow into entangling mental weeds. But in 1945 they could not serve the rising-sun conquerors. The Allies were writing "You have been found wanting" in letters of fire on the wall of history.

Clearly now, nothing could bar Indonesian independence. The Indonesians were urgently demanding it. Why Japan did not grant it is a riddle. Nothing would have been lost; or rather, all would soon be lost: Japan was on the eve of surrender. Possibly Tokyo, seeing the encircling doom, simply paid no attention to what was now the minor problem of the Indies. However, on August 8, 1945, Sukarno, Hatta, and Rajiman received a summons to proceed to Saigon, Indo-China, where, on August 11, Marshal Terauchi, the Japanese regional commander in chief, promised them independence for August 24, on the assumption that the constituent assembly, already in session, would by then have drafted a constitution. August 11 was five days after the first atom bomb was dropped on Hiroshima, two days after the second atomic bomb fell on Nagasaki. Why did Japan still procrastinate? *In extremis,* any sympathy for Indonesian nationalism would have manifested itself in a quick, unconditional grant of independence.

Sjahrir and many other nationalists were unhappy about events. They did not wish to receive independence at the hands of the dying military leadership of Japan. They wanted to take it.

August 14, the day Sukarno and Hatto returned from Indo-China, Sjahrir saw Hatta and heard about the delays. Sjahrir commented that the Japanese plan was "a swindle." By August 24, they would have surrendered. "I suggested to him [Hatta]," Sjahrir wrote, "that our independence be proclaimed immediately. I was vehement because of my conviction that the moment to act had arrived, it was now or never."

Hatta went off to see Sukarno. At noon Hatta came to Sjahrir's dwelling and reported that Sukarno "was not convinced that things were really so bad for the Japanese." Disappointed, Sjahrir rushed off with Hatta to talk to Sukarno. Sukarno, says Sjahrir, "finally promised that the proclamation would be issued after five o'clock that afternoon."

Underground organization and secret resistance groups got busy. Word was passed to be ready for a mammoth public celebration. Indonesians in the Japanese press service were told to flash the proclamation to the thousands of isles of the archipelago and to foreign countries without waiting for Japanese permission.

Still Sukarno hesitated.

Japan surrendered on August 15. But Indonesia did not yet know this.

Meanwhile the patience of the students, some Indonesian military, and a section of the underground had run out, and at 3 A.M. on the 16th they kidnaped Sukarno, his wife and children, and Hatta, and carried them away, in secret, to a Peta garrison thirty miles from the city.

That afternoon the Japanese learned where Sukarno and Hatta were being held and sent Subarjo, the Indonesian chief of the Consulting Office of the Japanese navy in Java, and a Japanese, to parley with the captors. The young guards finally consented to release them, whereupon the two leaders were brought to the Jakarta home of Admiral Mayeda, director of Japanese Naval Intelligence in Indonesia. Mayeda had previously evinced sympathy with the more authoritarian Indies nationalists.

Far into the night consultations continued under Mayeda's roof. The turning point came when a highly placed Japanese privately informed

Hatta that by the terms of the surrender Japan had no jurisdiction or freedom of action, she could only act for the Allies and was therefore in no position to grant independence or sanction a declaration of independence. This eliminated all doubts. The Indonesians would have to do it themselves and assume the risks.

On August 17, 1945, before noon, Sukarno pronounced Indonesia a free republic.

Chapter Eleven

THE RETURN OF THE DUTCH

On a June morning in 1958 I taxied out to a green suburb of The Hague to interview Charles Joseph Ignace Marie Welter. He treated me to an aurora borealis of passion both grandiose and tragic. The magnificent display came from a man of seventy-eight, solid like a single block of granite, powerfully, compactly built, neckless, with a gray-haired bullet head, a voice that rang with emotion yet remained under perfect control, and gestures that reflected strength and sadness.

Charles Welter served as Dutch minister of colonies in 1925-1926, and again from 1937 to 1941. Prior to that he had held official positions in Indonesia for thirty years. Spiritually he still lived in the Indies and they lived in him. "I love that country as one can only love a woman," he said to me. "It is so beautiful and fertile. Now those priceless islands have fallen into the hands of revolutionaries, professional revolutionaries. Throughout the world Dutch colonial rule was regarded as the best on earth. But today that great country has succumbed to famine, disease, anarchy, and rebellion." He was speaking out of the pain that comes of a love forever lost.

"I will be frank," he continued. "We were ousted by the British and the Americans. The British knew what they were doing. They have been our rivals in Asia for centuries and they sought to benefit in trade and power from our loss. But the Americans acted from ignorance. Your generals and admirals I respect. They understand world affairs. But your State Department understood nothing.

"Now the country is ruined. We would have made it the greatest nation in Asia, greater than Japan because the country is richer and the people better and more intelligent. General Douglas MacArthur would have saved the Indies and given them back to us. He comprehended. He did a wonderful job in Japan, he is a great reformer. We are a small country but we still had a mission to perform for the world which has now been denied us."

Impressed by his fervor and not wishing to add to his misery I had remained silent. Now I suggested that someday Indonesia would have had to attain independence. "Yes," he replied, shaking his massive head in sorrow, "in every way we worked to make ourselves superfluous. That was our sole purpose."

"When?" I asked.

"In 35 or 50 years the Indies could have become a nation," he said. "But not under a demagogue like Sukarno. When we were forced to turn over the Indies there were only 400 natives with college training," and he threw up his arms to indicate despair.

I might have reminded him that education was a Dutch responsibility, but I was in no mood to argue. "India under Gandhi and Nehru," he went on, "was further advanced. The University of Benares began to function early in the nineteenth century. We didn't open the technical school in Bandung, the law school, and the medical school until the 1920's."

"That was rather late," I commented.

"Yes, we were late," he agreed. "We Dutch have the faults of our virtues. We are thorough. We wanted perfect schools in the Indies, as perfect as those in Holland. We were late in setting them up, but in my opinion the Indonesians had no need for them earlier."

I adverted to the feudal Culture System with its forced labor and forced deliveries. "Yes," he affirmed, "all that was wrong and we abolished it in 1870."

I mentioned Raffles and said his ideas were different, he would have introduced capitalism. "Thomas Stamford Raffles," Welter declaimed, as though wishing to give him full honors. "A great man. He was the enemy of my country, and he would have taken the Indies from us, but he loved the Indies, and he and I are united by our love of that beautiful land."

His head sank even deeper into his shoulders and he seemed to be lost in thought. I waited. "India," he resumed, "has made progress since independence. But even India would not have been lost to England but for your State Department. Washington put pressure on the Labor government and threatened to deny it credit."

I reminded him that the Labor government had received an American loan of 3.75 billion dollars in 1946. India was granted independence in 1947. "I know for certain," he declared, "that the United States threatened us with starvation. We had food in Holland for only a fortnight and your government told us that it would starve us if we did not liberate the Indies. I said to my government, 'Let us starve and the world will know what America is doing in the name of slogans.' We nevertheless fought back. Toward the end, in 1948, we brought the flower of American journalism, [H. R.] Knickerbocker, and others, to the Indies, and I am sure that had they returned and told the American public the truth it would have turned the tide. But their plane crashed. I have no proof but I believe the Indonesians were responsible."

Knickerbocker was my long-time friend and I have always been fond of his family. His plane crashed in bad weather on a low hill a few miles outside Bombay, India, while trying to land.

Sad Mr. Welter. He grabbed at this straw, this might-have-been, with which he hoped to dam the current of history.

Love of the Indies is widespread among Netherlanders who have lived there. The British went to India for centuries and performed their duty as they saw it, but they never, or rarely, loved India. They dreamt of green England to which they would retire when their work in the colony was done. But the Dutch grew deeply attached to Indonesia. Many married Indonesians. Many would have been happy to live out their lives on a mountain or plantation in Java or Bali or Sumatra or some other tropical isle.

When India won her freedom the British left with regrets, perhaps, but no personal heart pangs. The chapter had ended, the tie was cut. But the Dutch have never had a divorce from Indonesia. The Indies are still in their blood. They long for them. They suffer from the separation. They speak of the country with affection and emotion, of its people with warmth, of its government with bitterness. They have been deprived, spurned by a beloved. Their homes are full of batiks, Bali wood sculptures, wayang masks, and other Indies mementoes. Their hearts are full of nostalgia. It all hurts, and pain often turns love to hate. They hate the politicians who achieved independence from them.

The Dutch are a stiff-necked, unyielding people. The motto of the Netherlands state, worn on the shoulder patches of its defense forces, is "Je Maintiendrai," in French: I will hold fast; I shall stand my ground; I shall keep what I have. A people who turned seemingly uninhabitable salt marshes into a rich, comfortable country and converted sea bottoms into fertile farmlands would have to be stubborn, tenacious, wed to its possessions, conservative.

Dutch conservatism shows in the national anthem. Its first stanza reads, in the official translation:

> William of Nassau, scion
> Of a Dutch and ancient line,
> I dedicate undying
> Faith to this land of mine.
> A Prince I am undaunted,
> Of Orange, ever free.
> To the King of Spain I've granted
> A lifelong loyalty.

Holland fought the King of Spain and liberated herself from his rule in 1648. Yet more than three centuries later the people sing of lifelong loyalty to him. It is as though Americans today would pledge allegiance to King George III.

Progress is everywhere in Holland. But the Dutch like to retain the past, retain what they had in the past. They had no intention, when the war ended in the summer of 1945, to part with their beloved Indies. The newborn Republic of Indonesia? It was illegitimate. Only Holland could rule there.

This attitude ignored all the power factors: the British and American armed forces in the Pacific; the Japanese troops who had been allowed to keep their weapons; the Indonesian irregular armed units and officials who had been administering parts of the country. The Dutch had nothing, no soldiers, sailors, airmen, or officials. But they felt they had a title rooted in prolonged occupancy and meant to assert it. As they had defied the sea at home and built dikes against it they now proposed to defy everybody who questioned their right to the Indies. They would rebuild their crumbled position. It took more than four years of heartache, bloodshed, recrimination, and anger, which have left a bitter legacy, to convince them it was impossible to roll back the waves that brought Asia surcease from colonialism.

Before victory was yet in sight, Roosevelt and Churchill exchanged views on whether the reconquest of the Indies should be assigned to Lord Louis Mountbatten's Southeast Asia Command or to MacArthur's Far Eastern Command. The Dutch had no part in the decision, but the issue put them in a quandary. They felt that if the United States retook the Indies the American bias against imperialism would come into play and hurt their chances of returning. If, on the other hand, the British were the active element, England might want the Indies for herself. In the end, Indonesia was included in Mountbatten's zone, but Dutch fears proved unfounded. The Attlee Labor Cabinet had no intention of annexing the Indies.

Nevertheless, plenty of trouble soon developed. Dr. Hubertus J. van Mook, Dutch wartime minister of colonies, now lieutenant governor designate of the Indies, and Dr. Charles van der Plas, Holland's representative at Mountbatten's headquarters, met Lord Louis on September 1, 1945, in Kandy, Ceylon, and demanded that the Japanese in Indonesia be ordered to suppress the new Republican government. There were as yet no Allied troops in Indonesia. Mountbatten gave the instruction, but the Japanese parried it; the task, as events showed, would have been formidable. Already Indonesian nationalists were engaged in lively combat with Japanese troops in an attempt to acquire arms and strategic real estate.

The first Allied personnel, a few handfuls, parachuted on to Jakarta's airport at Kemajoran on September 8, and shortly thereafter reported that "Most Nationalist leaders draw their following from the intellectuals and semi-educated, and of these the intellectual are the worst. They are very anti-Japanese . . . most of them. . . . The Nationalists are undoubtedly organizing for [diplomatic] recognition" by other countries. The nationalists had 80,000 men under a varied assortment of arms and controlled the public utilities of Jakarta and many more cities. The Republican government had set up ministries, was operating radio stations and newspapers, and regarded itself as the nation's functioning authority.

An Allied military mission headed by British Rear Admiral Patterson, Mountbatten's deputy, and including Netherlander van der Plas, arrived in Jakarta on September 16 and ten days later one company of Seaforth Highlanders followed. The next day, Patterson announced that the troops were there "to maintain law and order until the time that the lawful government of the Netherlands East Indies is once again functioning."

Meanwhile, van Mook, still in Brisbane, Australia, cabled to the Dutch Minister of Colonies in The Hague that "it is of the utmost importance to imprison the leadership of the so-called Republic of Indonesia immediately, because apprehension of the leading persons and a show of force will strip the movement of its strength." Accordingly, van der Plas persuaded Admiral Patterson to order the Japanese command to arrest all "terrorist leaders" in Java. "Terrorist" in this context meant anybody whose strength diminished your own.

Soon, however, Patterson heard from his superiors that he was not to intervene in any forcible way in Indonesian internal politics. Indeed, Mountbatten advised van der Plas to negotiate with Sukarno's government. The Dutchman replied that Holland was resolutely determined to have no truck with the Indonesian nationalists. In that case, Mountbatten affirmed, he would hold discussions with the Republic. The Dutch were dismayed.

British and Australian troops had been landing in the Indies to strengthen Mountbatten's meager garrison; from time to time they were accompanied by small Dutch units. Former Dutch soldiers released from Japanese concentration camps were put into uniform to augment Holland's power still further. President Sukarno protested to Lieutenant General Sir Philip Christison, the British commander of the Allied forces in Indonesia. Street clashes between Dutch and Indonesians multiplied. At the beginning of the war many thousands of Netherlanders who might have tried to escape but preferred to stay in the Indies were interned for the duration, humiliated, and maltreated by the Japanese. Their Indonesian friends and servants brought them food whenever possible and tried to alleviate their lot. The Dutch received the same kind treatment after the Allies began releasing them from the horror camps. But no sooner did the Indonesians sense that Holland expected to revert to mastery than friendship froze to enmity and violence flared. The British became alarmed. Their presentiments were confirmed by a telegram which Lieutenant Governor van Mook sent to The Hague government on October 17, 1945, suggesting that Sukarno and his colleagues might "soon disappear from the scene" if Holland remained steadfast in rejecting the idea of negotiations with the Republic. Mountbatten's aides in the Indies saw the possibility of being caught in the middle, with an inadequate army, between the immovable Dutch and the irresistible Indonesians. They accordingly concocted the usual compromise which satisfied nobody and settled nothing: van Mook was to meet Sukarno and they did, in the presence of General Christison, on October 23; at this informal gathering the British declared that they recognized only the Netherlands government of the Indies; but shortly thereafter the landing of additional Dutch troops was sternly interdicted by the British commander.

In effect, this British policy (of recognizing a government that was not governing and refusing recognition to one that was) constituted a declaration of war on the Indonesian nationalists. Ironically, the only troops available to enforce the policy were Japanese, and the British accordingly desisted from disarming them and put them back into combat. Japanese soldiers wrested the city of Bandung from the Republicans. In November and December, 1945, the Japanese were in action against Republican formations in Java, Sumatra, and Bali. "The heaviest fighting," writes Professor Kahin in *Nationalism and Revolution in Indonesia,* "occurred during the first half of November in Surabaya," the biggest naval base and port in East Java, with a population of 330,000, "where several of the large armed Indonesian youth organizations . . . resisted a division and a half of British and Indian troops, suffering extremely heavy casualties."

The Battle of Surabaya produced important results. It was sanguinary and disgracefully savage. The trouble began when a Captain P. J. G. Huyer, of the Netherlands Royal Navy, arrived in Surabaya from Batavia on September 23 with a written order signed by British Admiral Patterson authorizing him "to inspect the harbour works and all Naval installations." After inspecting for several days, Captain Huyer returned to Batavia and reported to Patterson, who issued him with a new order to "prepare the reoccupation of Surabaya." He was given a staff. These documents are reproduced in full in *The Birth of Indonesia* by David Wehl, a British intelligence officer in Surabaya at the time.

On arriving in Surabaya for his second mission, Huyer found the city in a "nervous and disquieting state." Indonesian youth were preparing for future struggles by disarming Japanese soldiers who seemed reluctant to die for British policy, Dutch colonialism, or Indonesian nationalism.

Captain Huyer realized the futility of staying in Surabaya under these conditions, but when he tried to leave town Indonesians took him and his associates under "protective custody" on October 8. The situation remained unchanged, with Indonesian authority dominant, until October 25, when the Forty-ninth Indian Infantry Brigade (British) landed at Surabaya. "The operation," writes Idrus Nasir Djajadiningrat, a serious Indonesian student of the period, in one of Cornell University's justly valued White Books, "proceeded smoothly and without opposition from the population." "All went extremely well," David Wehl confirms, "the Indonesian leaders assured the Brigade of their full co-operation." Captain Huyer and his staff were liberated.

October 27 was the fatal day. That afternoon British planes dropped leaflets on Surabaya calling on all Indonesians to surrender their arms within twenty-four hours. The Indonesians, remembering the Huyer mission and suspecting that Dutch troops were waiting in the harbor to seize control, grew greatly agitated. Brigadier A. W. S. Mallaby, commander of the Forty-ninth, consulted headquarters in Batavia and obtained a four-day postponement of Operation Disarmament. But the Indonesians were nervous and suspicious and attacked the brigade on October 28. Dispersed in small guard groups throughout the city, the British and Indians were threatened with destruction. Twenty thousand Indonesians, armed with small arms and tanks, according to Wehl's estimate, supported by, he says, 120,000 civilians brandishing krises, clubs, and "poisoned spears," had surrounded the isolated foreign soldiers and a massacre seemed imminent. It had actually begun. British officers and men were being brutally hacked to pieces with knives or, literally, torn limb from limb and then decapitated. In 1947, at the time of the partition of India, Hindus, Moslems, and Sikhs, whipped to religious frenzy, engaged in mutual slaughter of a most inhuman kind. Wells were stuffed with living women left to die, children were sliced into shreds before the eyes of their parents, trains jammed with refugees were waylaid and assaulted until not a single rider remained alive. Hundreds of thousands, some say a million, human beings died. If this could happen in the land of the meek Hindu it could happen in the home of the mild Javanese. The city of Surabaya ran amuck collectively.

So grave was the situation that the British appealed to Sukarno in Batavia, 620 miles away, and he and Hatta arrived in Surabaya by plane on October 29. A 24-hour truce, immediately effective, was agreed upon by Sukarno and General Mallaby, but because of the fighting the Indonesian leaders could not enter the city or establish contact with any Indonesian exercising control. There probably was no such person. The truce remained an unheeded scrap of paper.

The next day Major General D. C. Hawthorn flew in from Batavia and after much difficulty, for hand-to-hand battles raged at numerous roadblocks, he, Sukarno, Hatta, and Brigadier Mallaby succeeded in getting together at the Indonesian government building in the center of Surabaya. They called in a number of supposedly representative Indonesians and again provision was made for a cease fire, joint Indonesian-British patrolling of the city, safe-conduct for the miserable Dutch women and children internees who suffered as many casualties as the fighting men, and permanent consultation between Indonesians and British. Sukarno, Hatta, and Hawthorn thereupon enplaned together for Batavia. Five hours later Mallaby was killed. Mass murder continued. Lieutenant General Christison accordingly proclaimed by poster and radio that unless the attacks ceased and the Indonesians who had committed crimes surrendered, "I intend to bring the whole weight of my sea, land, and air forces and all the weapons of modern war against them until they are crushed." After these words some Indonesian extremists sobered up or fled and fighting died down but did not stop.

On November 9 the Fifth Indian Division landed at Surabaya. It was greeted by Indonesian fire from rifles, machine guns, mortars, cannon, and tanks. Major General E. C. Mansergh, commander of the Allied land forces in East Java, then summoned support from British men-of-war lying in the harbor. Eight Thunderbolts and two Mosquitoes strafed and bombed from the air.

Indonesian resistance lasted till the end of November.

This disastrous display of fanaticism and heroism taught all three parties a number of lessons. The Indonesian Republican leaders saw that their own uncontrollable irresponsibles, too heavily armed with Japanese weapons and too deeply indoctrinated with Japanese ideas of authoritarianism and self-immolation, constituted a serious threat to the cause of independence. The British saw that the situation was fraught with infinite peril if the Dutch and Indonesians failed to come to terms. The Dutch decided to take stock of their position.

Van Mook informed his government, after consulting the Netherlands military in the Indies, that approximately 75,000 Dutch troops would be required to pacify the archipelago. But on December 31, 1945, Holland had only 15,000 soldiers and 5,000 sailors in Indonesia and did not expect to raise that strength by more than 10,000 before October, 1946. Furthermore, as Prime Minister Professor Willem Schermerhorn stated, all Dutch military equipment from "the first trouser button to the last bullet" had to be obtained from England. A compromise proposal that would leave the British occupying Java while Holland endeavored to reoccupy the rest of the islands found no favor in the Netherlands. Holland was in no mood for compromise. Every contact between van Mook or some other Dutch official with an Indonesian leader raised a storm of protest and cries of "treason" and "Japanese collaborator" in Holland. England was being asked for buttons and bullets.

The situation demanded a basic reorganization of Indonesian political life. The government, since its formation on August 31, 1945, consisted of President Sukarno, Vice-President Hatta, a Presidential Cabinet appointed by Sukarno, and an Advisory Central National Indonesian Committee (or KNIP) of 150 members selected by Sukarno and Hatta. There were no political parties.

The indiscipline and anarchy of Surabaya, manifested elsewhere too, convinced the leadership that their weak authoritarian government could not combat the strong authoritarian mood engendered by Japanese teachings. The prevailing confusion and the opportunities it provided for highhanded, violent action by groups operating on their own but persuaded of their patriotism could only conduce to some form of dictatorship. Clearly the government had to be more broadly based, more representative of healthy political trends and all social strata. Democracy was needed to combat antidemocracy. For the first time, but not the last, the Republic faced the problem of how to administer a newly born nation called upon to do a man's job while still in swaddling clothes.

The Republic's political deficiencies had been obvious from the beginning. Six weeks after its inauguration, therefore, the government, on October 16, consented to convert the hand-picked, advisory KNIP into a parliament which could pass laws if the President approved them. While KNIP was not sitting its functions would be exercised by a Working Committee of fifteen members. The new Parliament (KNIP) now elected Sutan Sjahrir and Amir Sjarifuddin, who had led anti-Japanese resistance movements, as chairman and deputy chairman of the Working Committee, and the two chose the additional thirteen.

Simultaneously—the end of October—Sjahrir published a pamphlet in Indonesian entitled *Our Struggle,* which stimulated thought, controversy, and hostility. In his brochure Sjahrir, the less-than-five-foot-tall, boyish-faced man with a giant brain and leonine heart, penetrated to the core of several fundamental and recurring problems of the Indonesian state. He warned that unless the country guarded and expanded its social and economic democracy it would succumb to Fascism, for he saw that Fascism (he might have added Communism) consisted of "feudalism and super-nationalism" which were abundantly present in Indonesia (as they are in Russia). He noted that, geographically, Indonesia lay in the Anglo-American power sphere and must act accordingly: that is, independence from Holland would not erase the reality of Indonesia's dependence on Western capital, techniques, and might. Therefore, and above all, "The revolutionary-democratic struggle must begin by purifying itself of all Japanese fascist stain and opposing all those whose spirit is still under the influence of Japanese propaganda and education." Because this was the kernel of his argument he elaborated: "Those who have sold themselves and their honor to Japanese fascism must be thrown out of the leadership of our revolution —that is, those who have worked for the Japanese propaganda organizations, the secret police, in general, everyone who has worked for the Japanese fifth column."

Nobody could mistake Sjahrir's meaning. He was attacking not his friend Hatta, or Sukarno, or others who in agreement with him acted as collaborators of Japan for the good of the country. His targets were those who copied Japanese dictatorial methods because they had absorbed Japanese political thought. Their terror activities placed the Republic in jeopardy.

On November 3, a few days after Sjahrir's publication appeared, Sukarno lifted the ban on political parties. On November 9 Sukarno commissioned Sjahrir to form a Cabinet responsible to Parliament (KNIP). Sjahrir accepted, appointed his ministers, and received an overwhelming vote of confidence (81 for, 8 against, with 15 abstentions) from KNIP on November 27.

From birth until this day the frail Indonesian ship of state has been tossed between the Scylla of an irresponsible Presidential Cabinet to the Charybdis of an irresolute Parliamentary Cabinet. The former is removed from, or relatively secure from, the control of the legislative branch, whereas the latter is its creature and servant, as in Britain. Neither meets the dual needs of a new nation: an effective, stable executive held in leash by a serious, representative parliament. Indonesia has yet to create this ideal combination. In November, 1945, when Sjahrir became Indonesia's first prime minister, his Parliamentary Cabinet was necessary to channel the violence of the street into the eloquence of the forum. Gangs with self-made mandates were taking the law and policy into their own hands and attacking British soldiers, Japanese soldiers, Dutch soldiers, Dutch civilians, and Indonesian opponents. At the summit they had their counterpart, ofttimes their inspiration, in intriguing, ambitious plotters like Tan Malaka, the Communist who, together with several Japanese-type Fascists, hatched a shrewd scheme to supplant Sukarno and set up a dictatorship. The greater the concentration of power at the apex of the political pyramid the fiercer the struggle for supreme power and the larger the number of top-rank victims. Safety lay in deconcentration.

In this first crisis of the Republic, Sukarno, Hatta, and Sjahrir acted to diffuse power by distributing it among parties and between the executive and Parliament. It was a victory, as yet inconclusive, for democracy. For further security against conspiracy, kidnaping, and foreign pressures, Sukarno moved to Jogjakarta in Central Java, capital of the ancient Kingdom of Mataram, now the seat of the influential pro-Republic Sultan of Jogjakarta. It lay in the middle of a vast region where the President had a mass following. For a time Sjahrir operated from Jakarta and Jogjakarta.

Apart from putting the Indonesian house in order, Sjahrir's primary preoccupation was a settlement with Holland by negotiation. The two were related. The Dutch constantly added to their armed forces in the archipelago; Indonesians felt provoked. Skirmishes multiplied. "It was unfortunate for the Dutch," writes David Wehl, a British eyewitness, "that some of their troops were not sufficiently restrained or disciplined in their conduct. They were in a difficult position; they had little work of importance to do, they were among hostile people, and some of their companions had been killed or kidnaped. Nevertheless, it was bad for the Dutch cause that shooting affrays were sometimes started by Dutch soldiers, and Sjahrir himself was shot at in his car." Shooting affrays were also started by Indonesian soldiers and civilian bands. The Indonesians regarded the Dutch presence as illegal; the Dutch considered the Indonesian government illegal. Early in 1946 Dutch troops occupied the island of Bangka off the east coast of Sumatra; shortly thereafter Bali was taken; then, under cover of the British occupation, the Dutch military executed a successful landing at Surabaya. Presently the Dutch authorities in Batavia issued new paper money, and British soldiers were encouraged to accept it in place of the Japanese currency still in circulation.

The Dutch were in a hurry. Nehru had protested against the use of

Indian soldiers to fight Indonesians. The Indian and the British troops were eager for demobilization after the long years of war. Sooner or later the British would go, and the Dutch would have to go with them unless, in the meantime, their armed forces had been built up to impressive strength. This Holland was doing day by day. In effect, Indonesia now had two governments, one in Jakarta, the other in Jogjakarta. The Dutch had returned and were challenging the Republic.

Chapter Twelve

AN HISTORIC BLUNDER

LATE IN the evening of April 16, 1917, Lenin arrived in Petrograd from Swiss exile after traversing Germany with a party of fellow Bolsheviks in partially sealed railway cars. Having looked around after his ten years' absence from Russia, Lenin made a shrewd assessment of the weaknesses of the provisional, or Kerensky, democratic government and formulated a policy: "All power to the soviets." Deliberately Lenin urged "dual government" for Russia. The soviets, or city and village councils, were to compete with the Kerensky regime in ruling Russia. The outcome was indeed two governments. That amounted to no government, or chaos, a condition which enabled the Communists to seize power from Kerensky on November 7, 1917.

A not dissimilar development would have followed logically from the formation of two governments in Indonesia in 1945. The two governments, to be sure, functioned in different territories. Yet their areas sometimes overlapped. And their ambitions did too. Objectively, the survival of one presupposed the demise of the other. The Dutch, however, lacked the strength, as yet, to overthrow the Indonesian Republic, and the Republic lacked the strength to expel the Dutch. Moreover, the British army was on stage. In case of a fight it would face the choice of joining the Dutch or the Republic. But the Attlee Labor government, committed to the restoration of Netherlands rule yet unwilling, because of its political principles, to suppress the national independence of Indonesia, could have joined neither. It could only try to keep the two belligerents apart. Far better, therefore, to bring them together in the conference chamber before the fighting commenced. The British, too, remembered the Battle of Surabaya, and while it did not dispose them to friendship for the Republic, neither did they relish repetitions of that horror.

Addressing himself to the situation on November 23, 1945, Ernest Bevin, the British Foreign Secretary, carried water on at least two shoulders. On the one hand, his government "had a definite agreement providing for the Netherlands East Indies Government to assume as rapidly as practicable the full responsibility for the administration of the Netherlands Indies territory." On the other hand, "We have no intention of being involved in any constitutional dispute between the Netherlands and the people of the Netherlands East Indies." He went on to "advise that negotiations should be opened." On the one hand, however, "the Netherlands government refused to negotiate with Dr. Sukarno." On the other hand, "our generals met him and had a talk with him." To smooth over any ruffled feelings this kick might arouse in the Dutch, Bevin told the Indonesians that "the quicker [they] stop fighting and begin talking with the Dutch government, aided by us, the better it will be for the country."

Refusal to negotiate with Dr. Sukarno, the Republic's President and prime leader, meant a refusal to negotiate with Indonesia. The advice then to "begin talking" might have been directed at Holland. But Bevin, exchanging the blunt language of his long trade-union career for the circumlocution of diplomacy, had in mind results rather than reporting. So intent, indeed, was he on results that he pressed Holland hard to enter into negotiations with the Indonesian nationalists, (the United States did likewise) and, having won The Hague's assent, appointed Sir Archibald Clark-Kerr as the British intermediary at the coming talks. The appointment reflected the importance which Great Britain attached to a peaceful settlement in the Indies. For Sir Archibald (later Lord Inverchapel) was a first-rank diplomat who had just relinquished his post as ambassador in Moscow to fill the even more consequential post of ambassador in Washington. His interim assignment in Jakarta would be a trying one.

The mother of foreign policy is domestic politics. For commercial reasons, for reasons of national prestige, and because so many Dutchmen lived in Indonesia, the Dutch were reluctant to lose or loosen their hold on the Indies. No political party of importance was ready to forfeit the votes which support of Indonesian independence would have cost it. Reluctant to negotiate, the Netherlands was loath to conciliate.

Some Indonesian nationalists also found negotiation distasteful. They had long regarded Holland as the enemy within their gates. The Japanese occupation authorities, though ruthless, encouraged the teaching and use of the Indonesian language, substituted some ancient Indonesian geographic names for Dutch names, and employed far more Indonesians in the administration than Holland ever did. Now the Republic had been proclaimed. Yet the Dutch were coming back. Apprehension and resentment flourished. In the mouths of demagogues, therefore, the slogan "Negotiate upon the basis of 100 per cent recognition [of the Republic], and only after foreign troops have left the shores and seas of Indonesia" found many attentive ears. It helped the Communist Tan Malaka, intriguing to seize power from President Sukarno and Prime Minister Sjahrir, to organize a formidable-looking National Front (Persatuan Perjuangan) which included Communists, kidnapers, jingo nationalists, anti-Westerners, and men who had unconsciously allowed their minds to be brainwashed by Japanese methods and propaganda. The Front advocated the abolition of political parties, confiscation of foreign property, and no talks with the Dutch. It enjoyed, writes Kahin, "the outspoken backing of General Sudirman, the Commander-in-Chief of the national army...." Its immediate aim was the overthrow of the pro-Western, pro-negotiations Sjahrir.

Sukarno, always a shrewd tactician in politics, saw that, though this Front would unitedly and happily knife Sjahrir, it was otherwise divided. The army preferred Sukarno to the unscrupulous Tan Malaka, whose eye was on the President's office; the anti-Marxist Moslems distrusted Tan Malaka for his Marxist views; the party leaders realized they would be suppressed if the Front won; the seekers-after-power knew they would have none with Tan Malaka on top. Sukarno accordingly invited the Front to form a Cabinet. As he expected, it failed to agree on a list of ministers. Sukarno then asked Sjahrir to return to the prime-ministership. Thereupon the Front called a meeting in the city of Madiun to plan the overthrow of the government. Government troops intervened on March 17, 1946, and arrested and jailed Tan Malaka, Chairul Saleh, Sukarni, Mohammad Yamin, and other Frontists.

Approved by Parliament, Prime Minister Sjahrir had a mandate to negotiate with the Dutch provided they recognized the Republic.

On the beautiful Greek island of Rhodes, in October, 1958, Sjahrir talked about his 1946 attitude. "I felt sure," he said to me, "that Dutch colonialism was on the way out and that our independence would endure. Sukarno shared this view. He was more self-assured in Jogjakarta than he had been in Jakarta. Together, we traveled through the country in December, 1945, and in 1946, and everywhere giant audiences reacted enthusiastically to him. The Republic, we concluded, would survive. Opposition to negotiations came from fear for the future of our state. The same fear explains the cruelty of some of the armed bands; they thought only physical annihilation would prevent the Dutch from prevailing. I was confident, and confidence dictated my conciliatory approach to the negotiations." But, while certain that the clock of history which had tolled the hour of independence could not be set back, he knew the Republic's economic, military, and political frailty. He would have to make enough concessions to bring Holland to an agreement, yet not enough to give his no-negotiation enemies a stick with which to beat and oust him.

In the conference room, therefore, the Indonesian as well as the Dutch negotiators would look behind them to gauge the mood of their constituencies. The British were bent on inducing them to look at one another.

As in an Oriental bazaar, the merchant began by naming his highest price and the customer countered with the lowest possible offer. On February 10, 1946, in the presence of Sir Archibald Clark-Kerr, who had arrived nine days earlier, Governor van Mook proposed to Sjahrir a "democratic partnership" between Holland and Indonesia which would last "for a given period" until the Indonesians were capable to decide freely on their political destiny. Sixteen days later the vague term "for a given period" was vaguely translated "within the period of the working capacity of the coming generation." Thirty years? Fifty?

Sjahrir replied on March 12, demanding immediate recognition of the Republic's sovereignty over the whole territory of the former Netherlands East Indies archipelago, no given period of transition, and no "democratic partnership."

Having handed his public this satisfactory morsel, Sjahrir retreated and made a fresh proposal: Holland to recognize the Republic's actual, *de facto,* control over Java, Madura, and Sumatra but not over the large remnant of Indonesia; Dutch *de jure* control, or sovereignty, for the entire country; the Republic would join the Netherlands, and the Netherlands' Latin-American possessions (Curaçao and Surinam) in a political union.

Van Mook tells me that when he received Sjahrir's proposal he was surprised and pleased. He showed it to Sir Archibald Clark-Kerr, who likewise felt gratified. Both saw a wide-open door to a settlement.

Van Mook, knowing the politics of Indonesia, realized that only the Sjahrir Cabinet could make such a soft offer. Any alternative government would be far less co-operative. It remained for van Mook, therefore, to convince his superiors in The Hague that this was so. The scene, accordingly, shifts to Holland. There, on April 14, 21, 22, and 24, 1946, Dutch and Indonesian conferees met on the Hoge Veluwe, near Arnheim.

Idrus Nasir Djajadiningrat has written the history of the Hoge Veluwe talks in a Cornell University White Book based on the official Dutch record and on verbal and written communication with his Indonesian compatriots who were the Minister of Justice, the Minister of Interior, and the Secretary of Sjahrir's Cabinet, Mr. A. K. Pringgodigdo. Holland was mightily represented by her Prime Minister Willem Schermerhorn, Foreign Minister J. H. van Royen, Governor van Mook, Minister of Overseas Territories J. H. Logemann, and Minister of Social Affairs W. Drees.

The talks failed.

Immediately after the talks, Dr. van Mook considered resigning as acting governor general of the Indies. Dr. Drees, Minister of Social Affairs and the key figure in the Labor party, had told him at Hoge Veluwe that a treaty with the Indonesian Republic was impossible, first, because the Republic was not a recognized state and therefore Holland could sign no treaty with it and, second, the Republic exercised authority in only a part of the archipelago. Dr. van Mook, on the contrary, considered Sjahrir's proposals the best practical basis for an agreement and the time the most propitious. In the perspective of 1958, he saw that the failure at Hoge Veluwe was the fateful beginning of the end. Resignation, however, far from contributing to a solution, would merely have strengthened its opponents.

Clearly, Sukarno's collaboration with the Japanese was not the real obstruction. Sjahrir had never collaborated. Sukarno supported Sjahrir's moderate stand. Yet Holland continued adamant, uncompromising, and unalterably opposed to an understanding with the Republic. A major difficulty was the permeation of Dutch politics by religious ideas. Many Dutchmen believed in the divine right of the Dutch to rule the Indies. ". . . all authority derives from God," said Mr. Max van Poll, leader of the big Roman Catholic party, ". . . therefore, Dutch authority in the Netherlands East Indies is willed by God." Similarly, Mr. J. Meijerink of the Anti-Revolutionary (Calvinist) party, declared, "To maintain God's authority, the [Dutch] government may consider itself in God's service. . . . It must not hesitate to wield the sword if necessary." Such fervid sentiments made war in the colony a possibility.

Van Mook therefore persisted in urging a resumption of the talks. England warned the Dutch that her army would withdraw from the Indies in November, 1946. The Hague grasped the significance of this heavy prod: minus the British forces and in the absence of an Indo-Netherlands agreement, the Dutch would have to fight the Indonesian army and suppress an angered populace.

The negotiations were in fact reopened in September, 1946, at Linggajati, a hill station inland from Cheribon, a coastal city in northeastern Java.

The Linggajati Conference, crucial in the history of Indonesia, and of Holland, took place against a backdrop of the Republic's battle to survive infantile internal diseases:

Though Tan Malaka and his National Front confederates were still in jail, their organization continued to oppose Sjahrir. Over and over again they proclaimed their principles: no truck with the Dutch; seizure of foreign assets. But these were a false face. They wanted power at the expense of those in power—policy and ideology were mere masquerade. In March the Front had directed its attack against Sjahrir, regarding him as the weakest link in the government's strength. Now, since Sukarno and Hatta backed Sjahrir, these two were likewise marked as victims.

The Front's chances of success would have been close to nil but for the friendly position of the military. General Sudirman, army commander in chief, a former officer of the made-by-Japan Peta, countenanced the pro-Front activity of his subordinates and could not have been ignorant of the far-reaching plot. It began to unfold when troops under Major General Sudarsono opened the jail in the city of Surakarta (usually called Solo) and released Tan Malaka and other Front leaders. That same evening, June 27, 1946, Sjahrir, ignorant of what had happened, stopped in Solo for the night en route to Jogjakarta from East Java. He had gone to bed in an apartment on the second floor of a bank building when a Major Yussuf burst in at two o'clock.

Sjahrir believes that Yussuf had orders to kill him. But Yussuf had once been a pupil of Sjahrir and could not bring himself to murder his teacher. Instead, he carried Sjahrir off to the palace of the Sultan of Solo, where the Prime Minister shared luxurious prison chambers with Sumitro, a Socialist economist, Charles Tambu, later editor of the English-language *Times of Indonesia,* and others. "This was more than a kidnaping," Sjahrir declares, "it was a *coup d'état.*" An army division had occupied the city. The Front planned to seize the government. General Sudarsono's troops had taken Jogjakarta.

On learning of Sjahrir's kidnaping, Sukarno broadcast an appeal urging citizens to report any clue to the Prime Minister's whereabouts. When Sjahrir's presence in the palace became known loyal army units advanced on Solo from Surabaya, dislodged the rebel forces, and liberated him. At the same time the celebrated Siliwangi Division, faithful to Sjahrir and Sukarno, dispatched a tank-tipped column to Jogjakarta to expel the Frontists.

Events, apparently, were shaping up to a civil war. On July 2 Sudarsono and Mohammad Yamin presented themselves to President Sukarno and demanded that he dismiss Sjahrir, put Tan Malaka in his stead, and transfer to General Sudirman his official responsibility as commander in chief. During this critical interview Sjahrir, just arrived from Solo, entered the room.

"How did you get in?" Sukarno exclaimed.

The Presidential Guard, he explained, was loyal to Sukarno.

Sukarno thereupon ordered the arrest of Sudarsono and Yamin.

Everything now depended on General Sudirman. He, however, shrank from precipitating a civil war just when Dutch military strength, waxing daily and dangerously, threatened to crush the infant Republic's life. Popular sentiment looked with disfavor on domestic strife in the shadow of the foreign menace. In this atmosphere, Sukarno was able to persuade Sudirman to throw his support to Sjahrir and again arrest Tan Malaka, Subarjo, Sukarni, and other Frontist firebrands. Sjahrir now strengthened his Cabinet by including in it the Moslem Masjumi party leaders Mohammad Rum as minister of interior and Mohammad Natsir as minister of information, the Socialist Amir Sjarifuddin as minister of defense, the influential Sultan of Jogjakarta, Hamengku Buwono IX, as minister of state, the much-respected Haji Agus Salim as deputy foreign minister (Sjahrir remained foreign minister), and the nonparty notables Mrs. Maria Ulfah Santoso as minister of social affairs and Dr. Djuanda as minister of communications.

Thus reinforced, and without wavering in his courageous determination to reach a peaceful settlement with Holland, Sjahrir moved to the conference table at Linggajati.

The Dutch negotiators at Linggajati were Professor Willem Schermerhorn, who had only recently relinquished the post of prime minister in Holland's first postwar (Labor) government, Mr. F. De Boer, a Liberal, Dr. Max van Poll, of the Roman Catholic party, and, ex officio, Dr. van Mook. Sir Miles Lampson, former British ambassador in Cairo (later Lord Killearn) served for the first day or two as bridge and defroster, but soon the Dutch delegates were getting on so well with Prime Minister Sjahrir, Defense Minister Amir Sjarifuddin, and Dr. Johannes Leimena, a Christian from the Moluccas, that they dispensed with the intermediary and, having signed a military truce on October 14, advanced, with relative rapidity, toward the text of a political agreement.

At the later stages of the discussions in Linggajati, President Sukarno and Vice-President Hatta lingered in a place eight miles away called Kuningam. Thither Sjahrir occasionally sent Sjarifuddin to keep the leaders informed and to consult them on policy. Thither also went Professor Schermerhorn and Governor van Mook. It was Sukarno and Hatta, according to Sjahrir and van Mook, who first agreed to Indonesia's unconditional membership in a Federal Union with the Netherlands. So receptive, indeed, were Sukarno and Hatta to the terms of the envisaged settlement that Schermerhorn asked Sir Miles Lampson to convene a plenary session to make the fact known.

Recalling the event in 1958, when I interviewed him in his aviation research institute in the quaint Dutch city of Delft, Professor Schermerhorn said, "At that plenary session dinner I announced Sukarno's and Hatta's concurrence, but in a moment I felt something was wrong, Sjahrir commenced to demur. So I kicked Sir Miles' leg and whispered to him to adjourn the meeting. My intimation that the acquiescence of Sukarno and Hatta had clinched the agreement offended Sjahrir, and I accordingly urged the Prime Minister to go to Kuningam and iron out the remaining controversial issues."

Sjahrir did indeed hold out for several concessions: arbitration between Holland and Indonesia by a citizen of neither in case of dispute inside the Federal Union. This was written into the Linggajati Agreement. He also pleaded for joint 50-50 ownership of the Dutch plantations and factories which were now in Indonesian hands. In this he did not succeed.

Holland and Indonesia initialed the Linggajati Agreement on November 15, 1946. It was a major victory for both sides. Under the agreement the two countries might now be co-operating inside a friendly commonwealth conferring economic and prestige benefits on the former, material and political benefits on the latter, and a boon on mankind. But . . .

Holland delayed signing the agreement until March 25, 1947. By that time all the good will had been dissipated and the treaty vitiated. The initials were hardly dry when the Netherlands began making a series of doubtful interpretations of the agreement which, says van Mook, "torpedoed the whole thing." The government "raised quasi-legal arguments" to prevent the implementation of the treaty. The Dutch Cabinet, van Mook continued, was guilty of major mistakes. He lays "at least 75 per cent" of the blame for the failure of the Linggajati Agreement at the door of the Dutch government.

"Why?" I asked.

Returning from exile in England to a land damaged by Nazi occupation and facing the task of reconstruction, the Dutch authorities, van Mook explained, "lacked the time to accustom themselves to the new postwar world of anticolonialism. They were not reconciled to the loss of the Indies. I myself was accused of treason for having a talk with Sukarno. Also, domestic politics interfered. The country could find no strong government. Always a coalition, in which the Right insisted on law and order in the colony and the Labor party wanted to remain in office—so it gave in to the Roman Catholics. The Antirevolutionary [Calvinist] party, moreover, resisted rapid change."

Many Dutchmen opposed negotiations with Indonesia, many more opposed the results as written into the Linggajati Agreement. The heart of the document is Article Two, authored by van Mook, in which the Netherlands and Indonesia undertook to "co-operate in the rapid formation of a sovereign democratic state on a federal basis to be called the United States of Indonesia," and comprising, says the following article, "the entire territory of the Netherlands Indies." Meanwhile, Holland recognized "the Republic of Indonesia as exercising *de facto* authority over Java, Sumatra, and Madura," with 85 per cent of the population of Indonesia. The Republic promised to enter a Netherlands-Indonesian Union headed by the Queen (or King).

Governor van Mook noted that soon after the initialing of the Linggajati text, Indonesian armed bands and army troops commenced going home; a sense of relaxation spread over the Republican territory. Had this atmosphere endured, Sjahrir's hand would have been strengthened against the violence-loving extremists. In Holland, however, tension rose in the four-and-a-half months' interval between initialing and signing. "Speed," says van Mook, "was more important than caution, friendly gestures would have served better than legalistic verbal hairsplitting."

But conservatism, concentration on illusory self-interest, and party politics created a hostile Dutch climate which nullified the Linggajati peace, unleashed two wars, and cost Holland the friendship and business of 87 million Indonesians. In perspective, this looms as one of the many major mistakes in postwar world history.

During the war the Dutch, whether in concentration camps, the Nazi underground, or exile, had no clocks. They could not hear the ticktock of history. At war's end they did not know what time it was. They thought it was still 1939. It was actually 1947, and humanity had lived a century since the war began. India, Pakistan, Burma, and Ceylon were on the eve of freedom. The hour of national liberation had struck. Indonesia heard the cheering chimes.

Chapter Thirteen

VICTORY WITHOUT SUCCESS

EARLY ON the morning of July 21, 1947, a little less than four months after the signing of the Linggajati Agreement, Dutch troops invaded Java, Madura, and Sumatra. Holland called the hostilities a "police action." But since the Linggajati Agreement recognized the Republic "as exercising *de facto* authority" over these territories, "police action" was a misnomer for war.

Dr. van Mook, who served as Indies governor during the police action, justifies it on the ground that the alternative would have been starvation in Java and Sumatra. Indonesians in the Dutch-occupied areas were indeed suffering from hunger, and the Dutch too faced privations.

Holland complained that the Republican failure to supply the Dutch-administered parts of Java with rice was deliberate. "Finally, on May 31, 1947," reads a contemporary official Netherlands pamphlet published in the United States, "the Dutch and the Republicans came to an agreement for the delivery of 70,000 tons of rice from the current harvest, in exchange for textiles. The rice never came." But the inefficiency of which Indonesians are capable in even the most normal circumstances probably contributed as much to the nondelivery as policy. The situation merely highlighted the difficulties resulting from the existence in Java and Sumatra of two antagonistic governments, neither of which had complete control of the population.

Dr. van Mook has given me the startling information that the police action commenced and was temporarily stopped in June. "On D day plus two," as he put it—that is, on June 26, when troops were already in motion and ships had been loaded for an expedition against Madura— United States Consul William Foote volunteered to mediate the dispute and supply food. Van Mook states that he immediately called in General Simon H. Spoor and Admiral Helfrich, the supreme Dutch army and naval commanders, and inquired whether the offensive could be halted. When they replied in the affirmative, it was halted. Van Mook consulted The Hague, where the U.S. intervention stirred passions and fretting. Nothing came of Mr. Foote's initiative, and the police action was resumed twenty-five days later. The postponement, van Mook declares, remained a well-kept secret.

Now, if the police action was originally scheduled for June 24, it must have been planned in May—before the signature of the May 31 agreement about the delivery of rice. Even if it was planned in the first or second or third week of June, too little time would have elapsed after the signing of the rice agreement to warrant punitive measures because of its non-fulfillment. More likely the police action was the result of Dutch Prime Minister Louis J. M. Beel's visit to Indonesia early in May when, according to Dr. van Mook, he decided that "military action might be necessary."

To justify the police action, the Netherlands likewise charged the Republic with seeking diplomatic recognition from foreign governments in contravention of the Linggajati Agreement. The Republic, fighting for survival, did indeed try to bolster its international position. In the end, this actually saved the Republic's life. Dutch ire is perfectly comprehensible.

Picking one's way by the candlelight of hindsight over the dusty debris of mutual recriminations, it would seem that the police action was due less to food scarcity than to Dutch vexation over the very existence of the Republic. A year before the police action Holland was already engaged in moves to destroy it. From July 15 to 25, 1946, van Mook had conducted a preliminary conference at Malino, near Makassar, in the Celebes, with a view to setting up the state of East Indonesia consisting of the Celebes, the tin islands of Bangka and Billiton, Bali, and neighboring islands. A further meeting at Den Pasar, in Bali, agreed with van Mook on December 18, 1946, to establish a Great East Indonesian state. Dr. van Mook also formed two autonomous regions in Borneo.

Van Mook assures me that he intended the three units to be constituent members of the future United States of Indonesia. The Linggajati text, however, stipulated that the Netherlands and the Republic "shall co-operate" in organizing the United States of Indonesia. When, therefore, the

Republic saw van Mook launching these three states without its co-operation or advice or advance knowledge, the suspicion grew that he was creating puppets.

The Den Pasar Conference for the establishment of East Indonesia took place after the initialing of the Linggajati Agreement but before its signing. The Dutch could therefore argue that the agreement still had no validity and, moreover, that the date of the conference had been fixed even before the initialing. This formal contention notwithstanding, the holding of the Den Pasar Conference did conflict with the spirit of "shall co-operate" and inevitably provoked hostility among Republicans.

It is unnecessary to dissect Dutch motives at this late date. Everybody knows how suspicious newly independent countries are of the former colonial power and how prone they are to discern sinister plots against their lives in all that it does. Holland gave the Republic solid grounds for such apprehension. The least that can be said, therefore, is that van Mook would have done better to "co-operate" under the Linggajati text instead of proceeding unilaterally in works which gave the impression of trying to divide Indonesia so as to rule it.

Fearing that Prime Minister Sjahrir's policy of conciliating Holland would merely help her to split Indonesia, political parties in the Republic turned against him. An influential extremist wing of his own party did likewise. He consequently resigned on June 27, 1947.

Defense Minister Amir Sjarifuddin became prime minister and defense minister. Though less moderate than Sjahrir (later, in fact, he openly joined the Communists), Sjarifuddin sensed that the Dutch were sharpening their bayonets. He accordingly made proposals on July 8 that were tantamount to surrender, certainly to retreat: the Republic would desist from sending diplomatic representatives abroad, permit Holland to post a high Dutch official inside the republican government, and agree that the future provisional government of the United States of Indonesia include Dutch officials.

This July 8 offer came during the 25-day postponement of the police action. Its acceptance might have led to conciliation. But The Hague remained obdurate, its mind fixed on punitive measures.

Former Prime Minister Schermerhorn, chief architect of the Linggajati Agreement, hoped to save the situation. He saw the necessity of military intervention. "Technically, logically," he said to me in Delft in 1958, "the police action was justified. In 1947 Jakarta was a starving city, and even in the Governor's palace we could not get an orange drink despite the tropical heat." Yet Schermerhorn realized that a military campaign would settle nothing. "I consequently looked for a way out," he affirms. "On learning that our warships were about to sail to Jakarta from Surabaya and that the infantry had received their marching orders I tried to stop the action by the only means available to me. I spoke to the British Consul General." The consul, Schermerhorn states, wired Foreign Secretary Bevin, who, he presumes, telephoned U.S. Secretary of State General George C. Marshall. This would explain Consul Foote's attempt to block the police action. But the Dutch government, Schermerhorn contends, stood firm because of its "subconscious motive of burying the Linggajati Agreement" —and thereby burying the Republic.

In the end Schermerhorn, on orders from Chairman J. K. Vorrink of the Dutch Labor party, to which he belonged, joined his Roman Catholic and Liberal fellow commissioners in recommending the police action. Having tried to stop it and failed, he approved it in the name of party discipline. For the government of Holland was a Catholic-Labor coalition; the large Catholic party favored military measures, and the smaller Labor party, or its delegate in the Indies, could not obstruct them without breaking up the coalition. In the Labor party, too, sentiment for drastic steps in the Indies was strong, and Mr. Vorrink, therefore, acted to preserve his party's advantages in the coalition as well as in response to grass-roots opinion. But Schermerhorn lost his position in Dutch politics because he had gone behind the back of his own government to consult foreign governments.

Convinced that it was doing right and conscious of popular support, the Dutch government sent forth its tanks and soldiers against the Indonesian Republic on July 21.

The British army had withdrawn from the Indies on November 29, 1946. There were 92,000 Dutch troops in Java, Sumatra, and Madura (though at Linggajati Holland had recognized the Republic as the *de facto* authority over those islands). No Republican units could stand against this formidable force. The police action rolled forward with little opposition. On the fifth day of the offensive, July 25, Dr. van Mook said in a radio broadcast, "After having marched for hundreds of miles and passed through countless defense works, our casualties do not yet run into three figures. And the losses of the dissolving Republican armies are not very much higher." The Republican military detachments melted into the forests and highlands. Within a fortnight, most urban centers had fallen to the Dutch. "Three or four weeks more," van Mook states, "and nothing would have been left of the Republic."

The United Nations Security Council, on August 1, called "upon both parties to cease hostilities forthwith" and "settle their disputes by arbitration or other peaceful means." On August 25 it asked the foreign consuls in Indonesia to report on progress and offered to set up a committee of three

Good Officers to help in a peaceful settlement. On August 26 the Security Council "reminds" the two parties that hostilities had not ceased.

The foreign consuls in Jakarta reported to the UN on October 3, 14, and 22 that the cease-fire order had been and was being disobeyed. The Dutch evaded the UN order by announcing the "van Mook Line," an imaginary dotted line connecting the farthest points reached by the Dutch tank-tipped columns. They then proceeded to "mop up" the towns and vast agricultural tracts which lay between the most advanced points. In all, they occupied almost two thirds of Java and large segments of Sumatra. In Madura the Dutch moved beyond the van Mook Line. Meanwhile they threw a tight blockade around the unoccupied Republican areas where starvation already threatened.

At this critical juncture the UN Committee of Good Offices came into being. Holland chose to be represented on it by Belgium, and the Belgian government selected Dr. Paul van Zeeland, a former prime minister, as its member; Indonesia chose Australia, and Mr. Justice Richard C. Kirby, of the Australian Court of Arbitration, joined the UN committee; these two picked the United States as the third country, and the State Department appointed Dr. Frank P. Graham, President of the University of North Carolina.

The committee's first task was to bring the Dutch and Indonesians together again. But where? The Dutch insisted that the meeting take place on Indonesian soil. The Indonesians objected that any conference in Indonesia would meet under the threatening shadow of Dutch guns. Instead, Sukarno suggested Manila, Singapore, Colombo, or New York. The Dutch opposed all. Then, independently of one another, the Dutch and Indonesians proposed meeting on an American battleship off an Indonesian island. But when this was conveyed to the State Department it declined firmly: the Communists would call it the beginning of the American naval conquest of the Indies. Somebody wondered whether Australia might place a battleship at the disposal of the UN committee. Australia was not ready to incur the expense. Weeks were wasted until Dean Rusk, U.S. Assistant Secretary of State, hit on the perfect compromise: they would convene on extraterritorial "ground" aboard the unarmed United States navy transport *Renville*, then in Philippine waters. Everybody agreed. The ship was brought to Jakarta and anchored in the harbor.

The Renville Conference began in the most unpromising atmosphere. The three states set up by van Mook in East Indonesia and Borneo had continued to function under Holland's wing. In fact, he hatched three more: in Madura, West Java, and Southeast Sumatra. Before long he owned a brood of thirteen. Indonesian nationalists cried havoc. They saw this as an unmistakable sign that Holland was about to take back the entire archipelago and convert it into a supine puppet—hardly an auspicious prelude to negotiations.

On the *Renville* the three Good Officers, plus the Dutch and Indonesians, wrangled, haggled, juggled groups of principles, and pored over military maps from December 8, 1947, to January 17, 1948, on which date, *mirabile dictu,* they signed the Renville Agreement. A supplementary instrument was negotiated two days later.

That the Renville Conference produced an agreement is one of the wonders of postwar diplomacy. It points to the wisdom of "Keep Talking" as a desirable policy despite recurrent frustrations. It also shows that a dull scrap of paper may hold dramatic surprises, for the Renville Agreement looked like a Netherlands victory, yet it rescued the Republic and ultimately led to the departure of the Dutch from the Indies.

The Renville Agreement called for a second truce, this time on the van Mook Line, thereby squeezing the Republic into narrower, hardly viable confines. The Netherlands representatives would accept nothing less.

Then the Dutch confronted the conference with a block of twelve principles. "Take it or leave it," Dutch Prime Minister Beel said, in English, to Mr. van Zeeland and Dr. Frank P. Graham. These twelve principles were Linggajati without the Republic. Unlike the Linggajati Agreement, the twelve principles did not mention the Republic. The text offered "independence for the Indonesian peoples" and a sovereign United States of Indonesia linked in union with Holland. But nothing in the twelve principles would have prevented the United States of Indonesia from becoming a satellite orbiting helplessly around The Hague. The Indonesian nationalists and Dr. Graham so interpreted them.

President Sukarno, Vice-President Hatta, Prime Minister Amir Sjarifuddin, and the moderate Sjahrir accordingly rejected the twelve principles. They were adamant, desperate, and perplexed. What could they do? They were faced with a five-day ultimatum: if the Indonesians did not accept the twelve principles unconditionally, "liberty of action would be resumed" by Holland. That implied another military attack on the weakened Republic. Dutch troops were already moving.

Sukarno invited Dr. Graham to speak to a meeting of the Cabinet at Kaliurang, a hill station above Jogjakarta. Graham analyzed the situation created by the Dutch twelve principles but showed, too, how it could be altered by three amendments: mention of the Republic, a plebiscite, and a continuing role for the United Nations in supervising events to come in Indonesia.

Now Professor Henry P. Brandis of the University of North Carolina, a member of Dr. Graham's Good Offices staff, put the three Graham additional proposals into six principles. They won the assent of the Good Officers. Remained the problem of presenting them to the Dutch. Prime Minister Beel had said he wanted no further proposals from the Committee of Good Offices and particularly not from Dr. Graham, whom he considered pro-Indonesian.

Graham telephoned from Jakarta to the State Department in Washington and conveyed to Secretary of State Marshall, through Assistant Secretary Rusk, that new violence was imminent unless the Dutch moderated their position. Marshall immediately decided to support the six principles in talks with the Dutch if the Indonesians could be persuaded to swallow the twelve Dutch principles. Theretofore Graham had had little cooperation from the State Department and must have felt quite alone at the end of a long limb.

Prime Minister Beel was going back to Holland and the three UN Good Officers were invited to a farewell reception. Graham hoped he could turn it into an opportunity of handing the six principles to Beel. Van Zeeland was skeptical; he thought Beel would spurn any new proposals. Thomas K. Critchley, the Australian who had succeeded Mr. Justice Kirby, left the matter to Graham. Dr. Graham, with faith born of desperation and encouraged by his telephone call to Washington, was determined to try.

While several hundred guests were sipping drinks and filling the tropical air with a hum of conversation, Graham approached Beel and asked for an appointment that evening. Beel, whose plane was leaving early the next morning, agreed. In the evening Graham produced the six principles. He was making no new formal suggestions, he explained; these had been written by one of his assistants, and would not the Prime Minister think them over in The Hague? Mr. van Vredenburgh, Beel's Foreign Office adviser, quickly perusing the Graham paper, reacted unfavorably. In van Mook's opinion, it was worth considering. "I'll take it with me," Beel announced.

Secretary of State Marshall frankly told the Dutch his views. According to Dean Rusk, who was then in the State Department as assistant secretary for United Nations affairs and worked closely with General Marshall on the Indonesian issue, Marshall's firm support of the UN made him a stanch proponent of Dr. Graham's six principles which envisaged continued UN participation in a peaceful Indies settlement. Marshall's response to the Indonesian crisis, expressed in his talks with Dutch representatives, reflected the view that Western nations could no longer pursue a policy of beating colonial peoples into submission and that any such attempt in Indonesia was beyond Holland's military capability and would only drive the Indonesians toward Communism.

In deference to Marshall, The Hague finally agreed to include Graham's six points in the Renville Agreement. The Renville truce and the Dutch twelve principles were accordingly accepted by the Indonesians on January 17 and the six principles by the Dutch on January 19. The six differed decisively from the twelve.

The first of the six principles read: "The status of the Republic will be that of a state within the United States of Indonesia" enjoying (Principle Two) "fair representation." The twelve granted the Republic no such status and no representation.

The Dutch principles stated that if one party asked the UN "to provide an agency to observe conditions . . . the other party will take this request into serious consideration." This gave each side a veto on UN participation. But Principle Three of Dr. Graham's six said, "either party may request the services" of the UN and "the other party will interpose no objection." That made UN participation a certainty, for the Republic would insist on it.

"Free elections," according to the Dutch principles, "will be held for self-determination by the people of their political relationship to the United States of Indonesia." What question would be put to the people in such elections? Perhaps, "Do you wish to join the United States of Indonesia?" An affirmative majority could signify sanction of a Dutch-manipulated United States of Indonesia. A negative vote could mean the desire to remain a colony of Holland. The Dutch principle, therefore, was tantamount to "Heads I Win; Tails You Lose." But under the six principles a plebiscite, supervised by the UN Committee of Good Offices, would determine "whether the population of the various territories of Java, Madura, and Sumatra wish their territory to form part of the Republic of Indonesia or of some other state within the United States of Indonesia." This guaranteed that at least part of the Republic and Indonesian nationalism would survive. In fact, the nationalists felt certain that if ever a plebiscite did take place the vote would be overwhelmingly pro-Republic.

Interestingly enough, the six principles did not replace the Dutch twelve, they were officially called "additional." The Renville Agreement was thus a patchwork. Would there, then, be "free elections" based on the twelve Dutch principles or a "plebiscite" based on the six? Nobody knew and nobody has ever discovered, for the referendum was scheduled to take place between July, 1948, and January, 1949, but a month before January, 1949, Holland ripped the Renville Agreement into shreds by a second "police action."

That being the case, what was the value of the Renville document and why did both countries agree to it? Dr. Johannes Leimena, a mild-mannered, mild-minded Republic leader, said the Indonesians agreed to it under "perceptible American pressure." Pressure was indeed exerted—intellectual pressure by Dr. Frank P. Graham. In conversations with high Indonesian politicians he contended, as he contends now, that Renville saved the Republic. Being an agreement sponsored by a UN organ, it gave the Republic international standing. If the Dutch broke it, the Republic could appeal to the UN, to world public opinion, and to the United States. Without Renville, Graham says, the Republic would have had nothing. The Dutch would attack, as they were preparing to do; Indonesia would be conquered; the freedom-fighters would conduct guerrilla warfare in the jungle depths and mountain heights for years. Holland would be exhausted.

The Netherlands may have accepted the six principles in the conviction that the Republic lacked sufficient control over its troops to honor the truce. This, and the discrepancies between the twelve Dutch principles and the six Good Officers' principles, left enough loopholes for freedom of action against the Republic if and when the Dutch desired it.

Renville gave the Republic a reprieve. Holland felt unhappy. The Republic stuck in her throat. Free elections might strengthen it. Post-Renville talks on the plebiscite and other issues found Indonesians and Dutch locked in a stubbornness competition. Months passed. Summer began. Still no progress.

A year after the easy success of the July, 1947, police action the situation was again stalemated. Diplomacy on the *Renville* had robbed Holland of the fruits of her military victory.

Chapter Fourteen

COLD WAR IN THE TROPICS

INDONESIANS ARE not distinguished for stamina. But they are capable of spurts of dynamism. The Madiun Communist insurrection evoked one of these.

The Madiun revolt of September, 1948, had two parents: Renville and the Kremlin.

The Renville Agreement left almost two thirds of Java in Dutch hands. This was the reality. The plebiscite, the UN's arbitration, were music of the future. In desperation, the Republic drank the Renville cup of gall. It then swallowed Dr. Graham's six principles as a chaser of hope. But that did not prevent a heavy Renville hangover.

After Dr. Graham returned home and became a senator from North Carolina he described some aspects of the Indonesian situation in a statement printed into the *Congressional Record* of April 5, 1949. The Dutch policy, he declared, was "delay and attrition" aimed, the Republic felt, at "economic strangulation." Thanks to the tight Dutch blockade, the city population in the Republic-held, food-deficit territories suffered hunger. Cornell's Professor Kahin, visiting the Republican zone, saw many people wearing rags and gunny sacks; sterilized banana leaves were used as poor substitutes for cotton bandages; Dr. Yap, a famous Chinese eye specialist, told Kahin that "scores of his patients were needlessly going blind" for lack of a few ounces of vitamin concentrate kept out by the Dutch starvation cordon. The rump Republic was also short of raw materials and fuel, and even of paper for the new currency necessary to cope with the ever-rising inflation spiral. The distress was aggravated by nearly a million refugees who, fleeing before Dutch troops, crossed the van Mook Line into the already overpacked Republican homeland. Cases of bubonic plague were reported.

Prime Minister Amir Sjarifuddin, weakened by the stigma of having negotiated the unpopular Renville Agreement, could not deal with the crisis. During his six months as prime minister and defense minister he had used government funds to build up a personal following among the military by appointing and promoting officers loyal to him. At the same time he leaned so much toward the Communists that in December, 1947, Sjahrir, the democratic Socialist, asked him, in a letter, whether his first allegiance was to Indonesian nationalism or to Soviet Communism.

Suspicions and conditions forced Sjarifuddin to resign. He was succeeded on January 29, 1948, by Dr. Mohammad Hatta. As prime minister, vice-president, and cofounder with Sukarno of the Republic, Hatta was in a strong position, and he needed all his strength, for the Republic faced threats from without by the Dutch and from within by the Communists. The Communists gained a wily ally in Sjarifuddin.

Sjarifuddin was a Batak from North Sumatra. Born a Moslem, he accepted Christianity and always kept a Bible near at hand. Walking the deck of the *Renville* late one night, Dr. Frank Graham saw a light in Sjarifuddin's cabin and, whispering a greeting, was invited in. Sjarifuddin had been reading the thirteenth chapter of I Corinthians: "And now abideth faith, hope, charity, these three; but the greatest of these is charity." During the Japanese occupation Sjarifuddin joined the Dutch underground, was captured by the Japanese, and tortured. After the war, he became minister of information in Sukarno's first Cabinet. His deputy minister was Dr. Ali Sastroamijojo. Dr. Ali also served as minister of education in Sjarifuddin's 1948 Cabinet. Dr. Ali is my authority for saying that Sjarifuddin was a secret member of the Communist party during his six months' term as prime minister and defense minister. He had this information from Sjarifuddin himself.

Ousted from the prime-ministership, Sjarifuddin denounced the Renville Agreement which he had negotiated, openly joined the Communists, and waited for Hatta, his successor, to fail.

Prime Minister Hatta proposed surgery on the national economy and the army. He would reduce the number of persons employed unproductively in factories, government offices, and public utilities and transfer them to farms and small industrial units. But the use of a scalpel on featherbeds is a difficult operation; at the least it creates enemies for the surgeon. In addition, Hatta undertook to reduce the strength of the army from 463,000 in mid-1947 to a regular force of 160,000, and ultimately of 57,000. Demobilized soldiers would be directed to villages.

The situation was hand-tailored for the Communists. Revulsion against the West ran high. The Dutch blockade hurt. Holland continued to nurture her puppets. At Bandung, representatives of the thirteen van Mook-made states met from May 27 to July 17, 1948, to establish a United States of Indonesia—without the Republic. The Renville Agreement looked worthless. The only Western poultices, for the moment, were Dr. Graham's promises, whereas Moscow denounced every Dutch act. The Kremlin, to be sure, offered words only, yet to the miserable, words they like to hear are balm and may be remembered longer than good deeds.

Hatta's necessary measures to reduce manpower in industry and the army gave the Communists additional antigovernment arguments. Grievances and privations bred human dissatisfaction which breeds political opposition. Communism is opposition. The millions of illiterate peasants in Indonesia and India and the millions of workers in France and Italy who have voted Communist did not do so after a careful comparative study of the virtues of Adam Smith, Ricardo, John Stuart Mill, and Thomas Jefferson, on the one hand, and Marx, Engels, and Lenin, on the other. Their concept of Communism was either nonexistent or fuzzy. They voted their unhappiness and hopelessness. Communist parties try to ride to power on the blocks of malcontents who see no alternative.

Discontent, already great as a result of unemployment and undernourishment in Republican territory, rose to fever altitude when Hatta actually began demobilizing entire army and militia units. Some of the unit commanders were Sjarifuddin's appointees. Their dismissal struck at the Red future. The Sjarifuddin-Communist bloc, disguising its dictatorial intent under the name of "People's Democratic Front," accordingly took advantage of the natural reluctance of officers and men to be demobilized into unemployment and advised them to resist violently. Division staffs simply refused to send their troops home as Hatta ordered. Simultaneously, SOBSI, the Communist-controlled trade unions, called for political strikes.

Sukarno broadcast repeated appeals to patriots not to strike with the Dutch poised to attack. The strikes failed. Hatta dispatched armed student battalions and loyal divisions to compel obedience to his demobilization decrees. Fighting ensued, blood was shed, but the recalcitrant units were disarmed and forced to abandon their barracks. In this tense period Tan Malaka and his motley totalitarian cohorts supported the government against the Sjarifuddin-Communist party alliance. The two Communist groups were competitors for power; ideology played a tertiary role. The government consequently opened the prison gates for Tan Malaka and his lieutenants who, in other circumstances, might happily have attempted to overthrow the government.

Foiled by the Sukarno-Hatta combination, the Communists plotted an armed insurrection. On August 11, 1948, Musso—or Muso—the leader of the futile 1926 Communist revolt, arrived secretly in Jogjakarta after an absence of twelve years in Russia. Immediately, on Moscow's instructions, the Communist party (PKI) appointed him its general secretary and leader.

Loyal to the source of his power, Musso advocated open, unequivocal identification with the Soviet Union. "Obviously," he told the Students Federation on September 5, "a nation like Indonesia, which is fighting imperialism, cannot side with an imperialist power. It must align itself with the forces fighting imperialism, and that means Russia." SOBSI, the PKI's trade-union arm, added a significant gloss by attacking Nehru. "Imperialist America," it proclaimed, "is the leader of the Imperialist Front. We cannot remain neutral. We must choose one of the two worlds. The talk about a 'Third Force' is nonsense. Nehru, who proposes to form a third force, is pursuing a pro-imperialist policy. . . . We must find our friends among the new Democratic states of Eastern Europe. . . . We must not only make friends with Russia, we must have a strong relationship with Russia."

These bellicose statements had sharp Cold War overtones. The Madiun Communist revolt in September, 1948, was in fact a major Moscow gambit in the Cold War. The Kremlin had carried into Asia its crusade against the West, and the West, to Stalin, meant representative government, public liberties, and national independence. He hungered for more satellites.

History records hot wars provoked by imperialist competition. The Second World War was born of Mussolini's, Hitler's, and Japan's imperialist expansion—and the democracies' appeasing acquiescence in it. The current Cold War—the remarkable substitute, in the nuclear age, for an impossible hot world war—sprang from, and its prolongation is due chiefly to, Soviet imperialism.

Since 1939 the Soviet Union has annexed 264,000 square miles of formerly independent territory inhabited by 24,396,000 persons. It has assumed effective control, by way of satellization, of an additional 394,000 square miles with a population of 89,347,000. In all, 113 million citizens of free countries were absorbed into the Soviet Empire.

At first the United States condoned this. "Far from opposing," Secretary of State James F. Byrnes stated on October 31, 1945, "we have sympathized with, for example, the effort of the Soviet Union to draw into closer and more friendly association with her Central and East European neighbors. We are fully aware of her special security interests in those countries." The words reflect Washington's postwar woolly thoughts and misty hopes. But when Stalin made public demands for a fortress in the Turkish Straits and the cession of two Turkish provinces, when, moreover, the Communists sought by civil war to take over Greece as well, America made her first Cold War move: the Truman Doctrine of February, 1947, designed to prevent Turkey and Greece from falling into Stalin's lap.

Before adopting further Cold War measures, the United States wished to know Russia's intentions. To find out, Secretary of State George C. Marshall talked with Stalin during the March 10-April 24, 1947, Foreign Ministers' Conference in Moscow. American Ambassador General Bedell Smith, who was present, gave me the substance of the conversation. It lasted forty minutes, which, minus translation, was only twenty minutes. Marshall listed America's grievances: broken agreements, forgotten pledges, unanswered complaints. "Don't take these matters so seriously," Stalin mocked. Marshall alluded to the interminable, fruitless negotiations with Russia. "Well," Stalin commented, "after diplomats exhaust themselves in dispute they are ready for compromise." The brief interview depressed Marshall yet proved abundantly creative. For on returning home the Secretary of State, reporting to the nation by radio, said that, instead of waiting for "compromise through exhaustion," America would take therapeutic action. Marshall's motto read: "The only way human beings can win a war is to prevent it."

It was 1947. Europe's facts of life were ruins, rubble, and hunger. They bred the despair on which Communists feast. Accordingly, General Marshall announced that the United States proposed to help in Europe's economic rehabilitation. "Our policy," he said at Harvard University on June 5, 1947, "is not directed against any country or doctrine but against hunger, desperation, and chaos." As proof, the Soviet Union and its satellites were invited to the organization meeting of the Marshall Plan in Paris. Czechoslovakia, whose Cabinet included Communists in key positions, accepted. But Stalin told Czech Foreign Minister Jan Masaryk not to attend. Soviet Foreign Minister Molotov did attend with ninety-one assistants and said no.

Molotov's "nyet" is the key to the Cold War. Why did he need a gigantic delegation to utter that monosyllabic negative? His assistants' briefcases bulged with bids for dollars. Moscow believed that Washington was ready to grant credits to Communist states. But it objected to the organization of Europe. It wanted no co-operation with the West. "There is no doubt," the Moscow *Pravda* wrote on June 12, just a week after

Marshall's Harvard address, "that for the rapid and successful fulfillment of the plans for the development of industry and agriculture in Poland, Yugoslavia, Czechoslovakia, Rumania, Bulgaria, Hungary, and other countries, foreign credits are required. . . . However, when it is a matter of receiving American credits, it is quite natural that the East European countries prefer to deal directly with the creditors, and not with intermediaries, such as the British and French governments aspire to be." As Molotov stressed in Paris, the European recipients should merely make available to Washington "applications for the American aid required."

Moscow thus made clear that the East European countries needed and would take U.S. credits, but they could not join in a Marshall Plan organization where Communist and non-Communist states would engage in collaboration. Such intimate contacts with the West might imperil the Soviet Empire.

This is not an outsider's deduction. Andrei A. Zhdanov, member of the Soviet Communist party's Politburo, said so at the conference near Warsaw in September, 1947, where the Cominform was launched. America, he charged, according to the text printed in *Pravda* of October 22, 1947, aimed to "restore the power of imperialism in the countries of the new democracies and compel them to repudiate their close economic and political collaboration with the Soviet Union." Therefore, "the Soviet Union will exert every effort to prevent the Marshall Plan from being realized."

To thwart Western Europe's and the satellites' rehabilitation via the Marshall Plan, Moscow established the Cominform, consisting of the East European, Russian, and French and Italian Communist parties. The Cominform was an iron ring with which Moscow would bind and lead the satellites. To prevent Czechoslovakia's escape, the Communists engineered the February, 1948, coup. When Tito saw the ring closing he had the political wisdom and strength to break out of the Soviet Empire in June, 1948, and assert Yugoslavia's national independence.

Probing for weak spots and seeking to restore Soviet prestige after Tito's defection, Moscow, at 6 A.M. on June 24, 1948, threw a blockade around West Berlin. A 312-day Anglo-American airlift saved the city from being sucked into the iron ring and behind the Iron Curtain. French and Italian Communist efforts to seize power also failed.

All this was the prelude to the Madiun revolt. Frustrated in Europe, Moscow turned to Asia in the hope of making gains there and striking at Europe from the rear. In February, 1948, two Asian Communist conferences convened in Calcutta, attended, among others, by Indonesian politicians and delegates from the Soviet Asian republics. Participants who subsequently turned anti-Communist and produced documents to support their revelations have disclosed that these conferences approved Moscow proposals to start Communist rebellions in Asia. Irrespective of their evidence, revolts did erupt in Burma, Malaya, and Indonesia in 1948 and in the Telangana district in Hyderabad, India, in 1949.

Indonesian delegates returned from the Calcutta conferences, and from the International Youth Congress and World Trade Union Federation meetings in Prague in the summer of 1948, in an exhilarated Cold War temper and imbued with the spirit of violence and intransigence. Compromise, co-operation, and neutralism were out. The counterpart of the Cold War between Russia and the West was to be war between Communists and non-Communists everywhere. "The world is divided into two fronts," SOBSI declaimed on September 3, 1948. The Indonesian Republic, Musso stated, has lived "for three years under the leadership of the national bourgeois class which has always been indecisive and vague in facing the imperialists in general and America in particular." Sukarno and Hatta, Musso charged, "at this very moment are going to sell out Indonesia and her people to the American imperialists."

These echoes of Moscow's shrill Cold War cries and Musso's descent from Russia into Indonesia were necessary preparations for the Madiun revolt. But they disclosed that something was brewing. Presumably, too, the government had spies inside the PKI. Yet that was hardly necessary, for Indonesians love to talk about secrets.

There is good reason for believing that the authorities knew a Red revolt was scheduled for March, 1949, and provoked it six months ahead of time to catch the Communists off balance. The insurrection actually broke out in the city of Madiun (population 150,000) and Surakarta or Solo (population 400,000) while the top PKI leaders were scattered throughout Java on speaking tours. At this juncture Sukarno and Hatta goaded the emotional, less-disciplined second-rank and third-rank party chiefs into premature action by pressing Hatta's scheme of demobilizing superfluous army commanders—especially those with blemished loyalty. The officers, their jobs, prestige, and power threatened, seized Madiun at 3 A.M. on September 18 and immediately fanned out into nearby East Java villages. Battles occurred in and around Solo.

The next day President Sukarno appealed to the country by radio. "Yesterday morning," he said, "the Communist party of Musso staged a coup in Madiun and formed a Soviet government under the leadership of Musso . . . it is obvious that the Solo and Madiun incidents are not isolated events but are . . . designed to overthrow the government of the Republic of Indonesia. . . . Brothers, consider carefully the meaning of this: Musso's Communist party is attempting to seize our beloved Republic of Indonesia. . . . I call on you . . . to choose between Musso and his Communist party, who will obstruct the attainment of an independent Indonesia, and Sukarno-Hatta who, with the Almighty's help, will lead our Republic of Indonesia to become an independent Indonesia which is not subject to any country whatsoever."

Talk was not enough. The government moved troops swiftly. Large-scale fighting continued until September 30, when the famous Siliwangi Division recaptured Madiun. Fierce though smaller encounters raged throughout October. On the last day of that month Musso was killed in a countryside skirmish. Sjarifuddin and several of his comrades were captured on December 1. The Hatta Cabinet decided to try Sjarifuddin publicly, but its wishes became known too late; he was executed by the military in the field. Before he died, the story goes, he asked for a Bible and read in it.

(In-again-out-again Tan Malaka, liberated shortly before the revolt, was placed under house arrest shortly after it fizzled. When the second Dutch "police action" commenced in December, 1948, he escaped. The Netherlands Information Bureau in New York reported on May 27, 1949, that the 54-year-old Tan Malaka had been killed by a Republican officer. The Republic of Indonesia office in New York confirmed that the dissident "Trotskyist-Titoist" Communist had fled from his house when the Dutch attacked the town of Nganjuk and was captured and executed on April 16, on orders from Colonel Sungkono, military commander of the East Java Republican forces, who presumably thought the mercurial Red too dangerous to have at large.)

In the suppression of the Communists the government neither flinched nor faltered. The bulk of the population supported Sukarno and Hatta. The Dutch, who might have taken advantage of the revolt to march in, quell it, and destroy the Republic in the bargain, did not make a move.

Inevitably, the 1948 Communist uprising weakened the Republic; civil strife always does. But it was a big factor in Indonesia's salvation. For now nobody could believe—though the Dutch would so charge—that the Sukarno-Hatta government was Communist. This influenced American and world opinion during the critical year of 1949 in which Holland withdrew from Indonesia and transferred sovereignty to the Republic.

Chapter Fifteen

THE DAY BEFORE TOMORROW

WHEN THE Madiun revolt began, Dr. van Mook was in Holland about to resign his post. He rushed back to the Indies lest the Dutch authorities there use the Communist insurrection as an excuse for a military campaign to crush the Republic. Not that he sympathized with Indonesian nationalism. He simply felt that a second "police action" would boomerang against Holland. (It did.) But on his arrival the revolt was sputtering, and he returned to The Hague.

Van Mook had governed the Indies since 1945. Officially, however, he was lieutenant governor on half the pay of a governor general. Riled by this slight, which reflected the Dutch government's differences with him on policy, conscious, moreover, of the blind alley in which Holland found herself in the Indies and haunted by a premonition that things would get worse, he decided to retire.

For three years van Mook had operated at the far end of a long telegraph line. Cables from The Hague were often garbled. Sometimes they never arrived, and he had to act without instructions, a course that exposed him to rebuke. Besides, he adds, "the Dutch government lacked a clear policy, I got sick of it all."

"Didn't The Hague want to destroy the Indonesian Republic?"

"In a way, yes," he replied, "in a way, no. They could never make up their minds. The government did not lead. At times they were scared to death of Welter." Charles Welter, the former minister of colonies, had organized a small parliamentary splinter group of Roman Catholics which brought pressure on the parent Catholic party, and thus on the government, not to conciliate Indonesian nationalism.

"I was more liberal than The Hague," Dr. van Mook states. "The reactionaries in Holland charged me with liquidating the empire." He became the victim of unscrupulous attacks. Critics in Holland said he was a half brother of Sjahrir or the brother-in-law of Sjahrir. No such relationship existed. Enemies accused him of being a Freemason. He had joined a lodge but quickly allowed his membership to lapse.

"What do you mean by liberal?" I asked.

"Some Dutchmen," he began, "hoped that the Indies would revert to their prewar colonial status."

"Weren't you building a United States of Indonesia which the Dutch would control?"

"For a time, yes," he affirmed. "But I did not think of the leaders of the United States of Indonesia as a bunch of puppets."

This, apparently, lay at the heart of the friction between him and The Hague. Three years as top man in Jakarta were an education in Asian nationalism. Van Mook considered the United States of Indonesia a slow transition to self-government if not to independence. Backward-oriented Dutchmen regarded it as the shield of colonialism. Their wartime isolation from world events, Dr. van Mook asserts, blurred their vision of the new Eastern horizon.

The future had already arrived. Not only the past, even the present was obsolete.

For decades van Mook had served as a tough-minded Indies administrator. The niceties of negotiations were not his dish. He calls the Renville Conference an "exercise in sparring." The post-Renville period, with its changing American plans for a peaceful settlement, bored him.

This attitude, plus his personal grievances and political dissents, would explain van Mook's decision to resign. He had had an intimation in 1947, moreover, that the government expected him to go. Now the new Dutch government, based on the July, 1948, national elections, represented a clear shift to the right, and the choice of Laborite Dr. Drees as prime minister did not brighten the outlook. Dr. Emmanuel M. J. A. Sassen, the new minister of overseas territories, formulated his Indies policy without consulting van Mook and then summoned the leaders of the United States of Indonesia to The Hague in the evident hope of eliciting a demonstration of loyalty from them and enhancing their puppetry. Shortly thereafter Sassen wrote van Mook a superficially polite letter suggesting his resignation. The gulf between van Mook and The Hague had grown too wide.

Van Mook resigned on October 11, 1948. Former Prime Minister Beel succeeded him as governor. He was inclined, in van Mook's opinion, to hasty decisions, and quickly fell under the influence of the Dutch military in Indonesia.

Holland's power was growing stronger; the Republic's weaker. Sporadic guerrilla warfare annoyed the Dutch army. The embers of the September-November Communist uprising were still warm; the Republic had scarcely caught its breath after the effort to suppress it. A second police action to finish off the Republic was obviously in the cards. It came at 5:30 A.M. on December 19, 1948. A Dutch ambassador described it to me as "madness." Van Mook calls it "foolish" and suspects that Beel might have initiated it without specific Hague approval. Beel and General Spoor worked closely together.

The action was in clear violation of the Renville agreements of January 17 and 19, 1948.

Dr. van Mook was at least partly justified in calling the Renville Agreement "an exercise in sparring," for it had no immediate appeasing effect. The enmity between Holland and the Indonesian Republic remained, skirmishes between their armed forces continued, the states of the United States of Indonesia danced to Dutch music, and the Dutch blockade of Republican territory was drawn more tightly. Consequently, further negotiations were necessary. The UN's Committee of Good Offices offered its good offices. But now the committee was split two to one. Mr. Coert du Bois, who succeeded Dr. Frank Graham as American chairman, and Thomas K. Critchley, who succeeded the Australian Justice Kirby, therefore submitted an informal proposal for a peaceful settlement without the concurrence of their Belgian colleagues. But the Dutch refused to consider it. This, according to J. Foster Collins, a UN Secretariat official assigned to the Good Offices, "raised a personal barrier between the United States delegation and the Netherlands officials. During August [1948] the new United States representative, Mr. Merle Cochran, a veteran foreign service officer, arrived with a new staff." He had a new plan.

The name "Cochran Plan," says Mr. Collins, "is a good indication of the political realities." The Australian and Belgian Good Officers now disagreed so completely with each other that they abandoned the field to their American colleague. The Australian bowed out because, in the words of Collins, "most observers agreed that in the existing circumstances, the influence of the United States Government behind Mr. Cochran was the most effective force available." Only the man from Washington could try to bridge the widening chasm between The Hague

and Jakarta (Batavia), on the one hand, and the republican capital of
Jogjakarta, on the other.

But Cochran's plan would not work. It provided for Indonesia-wide
elections to a federal legislature, which were impossible in the pervading
chaos. It provided for the transfer by the republican and Dutch governments of their executive powers to one federal government headed by a
Dutch high commissioner with dictatorial rights. He could veto the acts
of the legislature. He could "assume all authority of the state," as Collins
puts it, if the federal government or any state government "was unable to
maintain order." But to maintain order in this manner he would require
the approval of the Prime Minister of the Republic and the Republican
Cabinet, which they were unlikely to grant. Holland demanded that the
Dutch High Commissioner be authorized to send Dutch troops anywhere
in any island if he saw fit. This meant eliminating the Republican army.
"It is not at all certain," writes Professor Kahin in his *Nationalism and
Revolution in Indonesia,* that the Republican Government "could have
induced the Indonesian Army to carry out its terms."

The Cochran Plan thus produced a deadlock. Though it made
maximum concessions to the Dutch, they wanted more. On December
11, 1948, the Dutch authorities in Jakarta informed the UN Good Offices
Committee that further "negotiations under the auspices of the Committee at this stage are futile." Holland was pushing the UN off the
landscape. The existence of two armies, the Dutch added, was "incom-
patible" with Netherlands sovereignty over all of Indonesia. Such complete sovereignty, protected by one army—Dutch—meant an end to
nationalism and the re-enthronement of colonialism.

In an effort to stave off disaster, Prime Minister Hatta requested
Cochran to attempt a resumption of negotiations. On December 13 Hatta
made far-reaching, indeed humiliating, concessions. The Republic, he
declared, was "prepared to concede that the [Dutch] High Commissioner
be given emergency powers to act in a state of war, a state of siege, or a
state of emergency." Moreover, the Commissioner alone would "be the
ultimate judge of the necessity for the exercise of [these] extraordinary
powers." Hatta asked only that "definite standards be laid down to govern
the High Commissioner's decisions." The High Commissioner (or High
Representative) was former Prime Minister Beel.

Holland, however, was in no mood to parley or delay. Her representatives had found Indonesian negotiators elusive, irksome, irresponsible,
and unreliable. The Dutch, accordingly, informed Cochran, who was in
Jakarta, that within eighteen hours the Republic must agree to the unlimited powers for the Dutch High Commissioner and the unlimited
right of the Dutch army to go anywhere in the archipelago.

Rice paddy in Java

Village family in Java

Photo by James Marshall

A Bali lady

President Sukarno chatting with Louis Fischer during plane trip

President Sukarno; "my favorite Indonesian woman," Mrs. Tasning Madahera, wife of an Army major; and the author

"No birth control," President Sukarno tells the author. On right is the Turkish journalist, Humbarachi

Dr. H. Mohammad Hatta

Lieutenant General Abdul Haris
Nasution

Photo by Dorothy Norman

Fatmawati, mother of five of
Sukarno's children

President Sukarno and his mother

Agfo-Brovira

President Sukarno, his wife Hartini, Mrs. and Dr. Grunek

Indonesian women

Betjak and boy in Jakarta

Indonesian children

Religious procession in Bali

Procession spectators

Photo by K. A. Rochman

Sukarno talking to mother and child as author looks on

Louis Fischer with Ruslan Abdulgani and his two sons in Jakarta

This eighteen-hour ultimatum did not even allow time to transmit the Dutch terms to Jogjakarta, the assembling of the Republican Cabinet, the formulation of a reply, and the telegraphing of that reply to Jakarta.

Cochran told the Dutch he could not "press Dr. Hatta to reply summarily . . . [to] your telegram because it calls for a non-negotiated blanket assent." The American diplomat refused to lend himself to a Dutch demand for the Republic's surrender.

At 11:30 P.M. on December 18 the Netherlands representative in Jakarta informed Cochran that in thirty minutes it was terminating the Renville truce. The delegate of the Republic received the same information at 11:45. But neither of them could transmit the threat to Jogjakarta, because the Dutch had cut all wires.

So, when the bombs began falling on Jogjakarta (population one million) at 5:30 A.M. on December 19 the Republic had had no warning. In fact, Cochran had expressed to Indonesian leaders, says Kahin, "his conviction that the Netherlands would not resort to force." They trusted Cochran because they trusted the United States and the United Nations.

George Kahin, in Jogjakarta at the time, describes the Dutch attack: "After the small Indonesian force defending the airport had been eliminated by an hour of heavy bombing and rocket fire, some nine hundred Dutch parachutists were dropped. They quickly secured the area, and soon a steady stream of Dutch transports began funnelling troops and supplies from the Dutch airbase at Semarang, some eighty miles away. Thereupon, Dutch bombers (American Mitchells) and rocket-firing P-15's and Spitfires began softening up Jogjakarta. . . . Bombs and rockets were loosed at various objectives, mostly of military value, and planes strafed the streets both lengthwise and crosswise." Dutch troops captured Sukarno, Hatta, Sjahrir, Foreign Minister Haji Agus Salim, Education Minister Ali Sastroamijojo, Air Commodore Suryadarma, and other Republican officials and flew them first to Prapat in North Sumatra and then to the island of Bangka. The Dutch also occupied Bukittinggi, the capital of Sumatra. "I certainly hope," quoth Dutch Foreign Minister Dirk U. Stikker on December 19, "that the military action will not last more than a couple of days."

Holland behaved as though she and her beloved Indies existed in a vacuum. What happened suggests that there is a big world, even though it be two worlds, and that it can, on occasion, apply power politics wrapped in principle to achieve a good end.

The Dutch military action stung many to fury. On December 20, the *Manchester Guardian* said in an angry editorial, "For the second time the Dutch have repudiated a signed agreement"—the Renville Agreement— "and resorted to force in the hope of suppressing the Indonesian nationalist movement." But "Nationalism," the *Guardian* taught, "is not to be put down by force." (Apparently each colonial power must learn this lesson the hard way through direct experience.) The *Guardian* hoped that the UN Security Council would "save the Netherlands government from its own folly." The same day an anonymous spokesman stated that the British government was "damned annoyed" at Holland's action. The London *Times* called it "one of the biggest gambles in [Holland's] history."

America was even more agitated than England. Dr. Sumitro, Indonesian Minister of Foreign Trade and Finance, saw Acting Secretary of State Robert A. Lovett in Washington on December 20, and the next day the *New York Times* reported his views. "Money received from the United States, for the purpose of reconstruction in Holland," Sumitro declared, "has been diverted at the rate of one million dollars a day to maintain an army of 130,000 troops in Indonesia. . . . I predict," he added in his wisdom, "that the Dutch will find no peace in Indonesia no matter how many so-called victories they win. . . . The fact that the Dutch were able to capture Republican leaders was due to the fact that our government believed that negotiations were still going on. With unheard-of treachery, the Dutch launched a sneak attack."

Indonesians called it a second Pearl Harbor.

Walter Winchell of the American Broadcasting Company poured one of his staccato sensations into several million American ears on January 2. "Behind the scenes of World War Three," he galloped. "Amsterdam. The terribly stupid blunder of the Dutch over Indonesia is worth twenty-five divisions to the Communists." The redoubtable Chicago *Tribune,* not addicted to the use of oil on troubled waters, urged, on December 22, that Queen Juliana and top Netherlands officials be hanged. In measured tones, the staid *New York Times* also expressed criticism of Dutch deeds.

President Philip Murray of the Congress of Industrial Organizations (CIO) protested by letter to the State Department. Robert A. Lovett replied in writing that the United States will not "endorse or condone" the Dutch military action. Holland, he stated, had "abruptly terminated" the efforts of the UN Committee of Good Offices. "The Netherlands government is aware," Lovett assumed, "that peace will be impossible of attainment unless the trust and co-operation of the Indonesian people, including the Republican elements, which have been in the van of the nationalist movement, have been enlisted." He then pointedly praised the Sukarno-Hatta government for having eliminated "a Communist revolt against its authority engineered by a Moscow-trained and disciplined Communist agent." The Dutch had been saying that the Republic was dominated by Communists.

Condemnation of Holland took on avalanche proportions after the Committee of Good Offices unanimously reported to the UN on December 27 that "Netherlands forces crossed the status quo line and initiated hostile military action against the Republic while the obligations of the Truce Agreement were still fully operative" and before the committee's mediation efforts had been fully used.

Indonesian propaganda added a pinch of sarcasm and a touch of bile. Said the Republican office in New York, "Holland, home of Kris Kringle and good cheer, timed its murder for Christmas when the world's leaders had conveniently dispersed. The UN General Assembly had adjourned. So had the United States Congress."

There was a silver lining. Before the UN General Assembly adjourned it had been meeting in Paris, and Secretary of State George C. Marshall attended the sessions from October till Christmas. Every day he received the chief delegate of at least one country, and without exception the Asian ambassadors, both before and after the police action, spoke to him about Indonesia and expressed their concern. General Carlos P. Romulo of the Philippines pointed out that America's world reputation as an anti-imperialist power was at stake. He and other envoys urged the United States to save the Indies from restored colonialism. Impressed by the repeated pleas, Marshall committed himself to support the Indonesian case.

Support came from many sources. On January 8 the High Commissioners in London of Australia, New Zealand, India, Pakistan, and Ceylon interviewed Foreign Secretary Bevin and told him that a British hands-off policy on Indonesia would cause infinite harm in Asia and lower British world prestige.

Asia was aroused. Prime Minister Nehru, denouncing the Dutch for "naked and unabashed aggression," invited Turkey, Egypt, Siam, Burma, Kuomintang China, Syria, Lebanon, Saudi Arabia, Yemen, Iran, Iraq, Afghanistan, Siam, Nepal, the Philippines, as well as Australia and New Zealand, to a conference of protest in New Delhi. United States Ambassador Loy Henderson and Dutch Ambassador Arnold Lamping attended as observers.

Strange events occurred in East Indonesia. In that state of thirteen hundred islands (population 15 million) which was created to be a puppet, the Parliament of eighty Dutch-picked members assembled a day before the military action to discuss a motion condemning the use of force against the Republic. Two Dutch legislators and three Indo-Europeans abstained; the rest voted for the resolution. The day after the military action the Cabinet of the state resigned. "These East Indonesian leaders," the *Manchester Guardian* reported, "have had disagreements with the Republican leaders . . . but their object is essentially the same, a sovereign, independent United States of Indonesia, and they express sympathy and respect for Dr. Sukarno, Dr. Hatta and the others as symbols of the Indonesian struggle for freedom."

"Dutch Worried," read a *Christian Science Monitor* headline over a dispatch from The Hague by Daniel L. Schorr. Small wonder. In Java and Sumatra the Netherlands army swept forward as predicted. The *Manchester Guardian* reported from Batavia, on December 31, that "The Dutch casualties for the first ten days of the operations were only fourteen men killed and ninety-five wounded." But everywhere else Holland was on the defensive. Within four days of the second police action, the United States government suspended Marshall Plan aid to the Dutch in Indonesia, and while the sum was small—$14 million—it was a black portent, for a swelling chorus demanded suspension of Marshall Plan aid to Holland, and that might mean over three hundred million dollars. "We don't want to finance Holland's colonial war," Americans were saying.

Interesting news from The Hague: The *New York Times* correspondent, David Anderson, cabled (confirming van Mook's suspicion) that the Dutch High Commissioner in Jakarta "Dr. Beel is said to have been responsible for the actual timing of the military assault, for the order forbidding neutral military observers in the field, and for the removal of the Republican leaders from Jogjakarta. In each case, the decision was made without the knowledge of The Hague." This revelation—for it was more than a theory—reflected the internal political troubles brewing in Holland.

The Dutch propaganda mill, most active in America, ground out bluster, innuendo, and saccharine. Dr. Herman J. Friedericy, head of the Political Department of the Ministry of Overseas Territories, stated through the Netherlands Information Bureau in New York on December 24: "The Netherlands government also wants sincerely to keep the friendship of the Indonesian people. But the Dutch are firmly convinced that friendship alone is not enough. [Had it existed it would have been quite enough.] Holland has been patient, perhaps too patient . . . with a Republican army attack impending on January 1. [No proof, and it seems quite unlikely that a very weak army would attack a very strong one.] Holland felt compelled to restore order. . . . We Dutch cannot be too surprised that America does not understand Holland's policy in Indonesia. Holland's policy does not fit into the usual stereotypes because it is something entirely new in the world." (It was as old as empires.)

The gentleman apparently thought that nobody believed him, for just a week later he issued a second statement: "Tomorrow a new year begins. Tomorrow also begins a new era of relationship between Holland and Indonesia, a new era based on voluntary co-operation and close partnership. I know the world is skeptical, even cynical about this new idea of voluntary partnership between Holland and Indonesia. . . ."

The world naturally felt skeptical and cynical about "voluntary co-operation" enforced by bombers and an army. It is true, however, as Dr. Friedericy affirmed, that tomorrow began a new year—1949. Before the year was out Holland would be out of Indonesia.

Chapter Sixteen

THE SHACKLES DROP

It was the night before Christmas, 1948, and the UN Security Council, meeting in Paris, passed a resolution impartially calling on both sides in Indonesia "to cease hostilities forthwith" and "immediately release the President and other political prisoners."

Five days later Dutch representative Herman van Royen (the Dutch spelling is Roÿen) promised the Security Council that hostilities would cease on the last day of the year—but not in Sumatra—and "It will of course remain necessary to act against disturbing elements." In other words, hostilities would not cease.

On January 11, Philip Jessup, deputy representative of the United States, delivered an undiplomatic speech. "My government," he told the Security Council, "still can find no adequate justification for the military action taken by the Netherlands in Indonesia. . . . In our view, the Netherlands military action is in conflict with the Renville Agreement. . . . No excuses offered by the Netherlands government can conceal the fact that it has failed to comply with the Security Council's demands both in refusing to order a cease-fire immediately and in refusing to release the political prisoners immediately . . . the representative of the Netherlands has failed to relieve his government from the serious charge that it has violated the Charter of the United Nations."

The Dutch government paid no heed.

On January 28 Ambassador van Royen, speaking to the UN in Lake Success, New York, again promised to carry out the UN resolution of the night before Christmas "to the extent to which it is compatible with the responsibility of the Netherlands for the maintenance of real freedom and order in Indonesia." In other words, the resolution would not be carried out.

Consequently that same day the Security Council adopted another resolution ordering a truce and instructing Holland to release the Republican leaders, restore the Republican government in Jogjakarta, and transfer sovereignty to the United States of Indonesia by July 1, 1950. Dutch Foreign Minister Dirk U. Stikker immediately declared the resolution "unacceptable."

On March 9 Ambassador van Royen asserted at the UN headquarters that, having telephoned Dr. Stikker in The Hague, he could now say authoritatively it would be "unwise and impossible to restore the Indonesian government" to Jogjakarta.

Thus far, obviously, Netherlands policy had not changed. The first Dutch police action was in disregard of the Linggajati Agreement. The second police action was in breach of the Linggajati and Renville Agreements. Both were directed to one clear purpose: the destruction of the Republic and of Indonesian nationalism and the substitution of a puppet government. As late as March, 1949, The Hague was pursuing this aim with exemplary inflexibility.

Outside Holland, however, new attitudes were taking shape. The British Labor government, sensitive to the feelings of independent India, Pakistan, Burma, and Ceylon, and of rich, dollar-earning Malaya, racially related to Indonesia, urged a firm UN stand against Dutch acts in the Indies.

Washington seethed. Before the second police action in December, 1948, the American delegation to the UN was under State Department orders not to castigate Dutch conduct in Indonesia. Two souls struggled in the State Department's breast: the "Europeans," whose chief preoccupation was good relations with Holland; and the "UN team," as one of its former members calls it, who felt that the UN's authority and Asia's public opinion should not be flouted. Throughout the period of Linggajati, the first police action and Renville, the "Europeans" remained in the lead, and it was only because Secretary of State Marshall threw his personal support to Dr. Graham's six principles that they were incorporated into the Renville document. The State Department, however, continued divided.

Some persons in the department sensed before December 19, 1948, that a second police action impended. The apprehension communicated itself to Dr. Graham, who had returned from Indonesia, and he informally called on General George C. Marshall in Walter Reed Army Hospital. With Marshall at the moment was Madame Chiang Kai-shek. Marshall, hearing the conversation in the corridor between Graham and an attendant, asked Madame Chiang to wait in another room and received Dr. Graham.

Graham shared with the Secretary his alarm over the imminent crisis in Indonesia. Marshall thereupon wrote a note to Acting Secretary of State Robert A. Lovett and gave it to Dr. Graham to deliver. But the "Europeans" in the department stood their ground against the "UN team" until the Dutch military action of December, 1948, and the storm it aroused in America cut the ground from under their feet. One of the first signs that the "Europeans" were in retreat was Philip Jessup's speech to the UN on January 11. Nevertheless, the State Department split lingered a little longer. American diplomacy was ready to criticize but not yet to act, and harsh words alone were unlikely to sway the Dutch.

A revolt in the U.S. Senate helped resolve the State Department conflict.

Robert Trumbull reported from Batavia (Jakarta) to the *New York Times* of January 13, 1949, that the maintenance of the Dutch army and air force in the Indies in 1948 "has cost $436,297,874." This exact figure obviously stemmed from official sources. Holland was receiving approximately $400 million under the Marshall Plan. The embarrassing conclusion could not be escaped, therefore, that in effect America was financing the Dutch war on Indonesian nationalism. The U.S. press and public roared their protest. American support of Holland against independence-seeking colonies clashed with a tradition born in the freedom struggle of the Thirteen Colonies. The Netherlands effort in the Indies, moreover, would retard Dutch economic recovery, impede the workings of the Marshall Plan, and supply mighty ammunition to the Communist parties of France and Italy, which still were bidding for power.

Indignant and distressed, the Senate, reacting to public protest, proposed punitive measures. On February 7, 1949, Senator Owen Brewster of Maine and nine of his Republican colleagues offered a resolution urging that Marshall Plan aid to Holland be stopped "until the Royal Netherlands government ceases hostilities against the Indonesian Republic, withdraws her armed forces . . . releases all Indonesian Republican leaders . . . and opens bona fide negotiations."

Brewster appealed to Senator Graham, former chairman of the UN Good Offices Committee in the Indies, to back his resolution. Graham had been hoping to see such a measure adopted by the Senate. On the other hand, he did not wish to slap Holland in the face. Public rebuffs sometimes make the stubborn more so. One day Senator Arthur H. Vandenberg, outstanding Republican leader, asked Graham to sit down with him in one of the Senate back benches. "Talk to me about Indonesia," Vandenberg said.

In the course of the conversation Graham asked, "What are we going to do about the Brewster amendment?"

"We're going to defeat it," Vandenberg replied.

It was defeated on March 8.

Vandenberg now consulted Undersecretary of State James Webb and Assistant Secretary Ernest A. Gross, and they, together with Graham, drafted a compromise, approved by Dean Acheson, who had succeeded Marshall as secretary of state on January 21, 1949. By its terms aid to Holland would cease if the UN Security Council voted sanctions against her—an intimation to The Hague that the Truman administration might suggest such sanctions.

Senate and State Department worked in perfect harmony. Acheson received Dutch Foreign Minister Stikker on March 31, and expressed the hope, according to a *New York Times* report the next day, that "a compromise could be reached soon over Indonesia." The State Department, the dispatch continued, "has been opposing efforts on Capitol Hill [in the United States Congress] to eliminate European Recovery allocations pending a settlement of the Indonesian question."

What the report did not say was that Acheson, knowing the mood of Congress, went further. He told Dr. Stikker that the State Department had been opposing but now no longer opposed the cutting off of Marshall Plan aid to Holland. Dr. Stikker took the message home.

Vandenberg presented his compromise text to the Senate on April 3. Brewster sarcastically called it a "slap on the wrist" and an "obvious surrender." But Graham, transmitting his views from a hospital sickbed, supported Vandenberg vigorously. Vandenberg himself told the Senate he was "in complete agreement" with those who condemned Dutch acts in Indonesia. But he added the hope that the Senate would "invoke a moral authority before it ever may become necessary to invoke a physical authority." The warning was unmistakable.

Vandenberg's version was adopted on April 6 by a voice vote which included Brewster's "Aye." He said it was better than nothing. It was good. The Dutch understood.

The Dutch responded quickly. On April 22 Holland announced her readiness to permit the re-establishment of the Republic in Jogjakarta and to release the Republican leaders provided guerrilla warfare stopped. Weeks earlier, the ever-optimistic Sukarno had predicted such action in a talk on the island of Bangka with *Newsweek* reporter Harold Isaacs. "This is our Alcatraz," Sukarno said, "but I don't think they'll be able to keep us here much longer."

Holland next initiated negotiations in Jakarta between Dutch Ambassador Jan Herman van Royen and Dr. Mohammad Rum, officially representing Sukarno and Hatta. Van Royen and Rum, "tactfully but tirelessly prodded" by U.S. representative Merle Cochran, according to Stewart Alsop's column from Jakarta in the New York *Herald Tribune,* worked fast, and on May 7, van Royen accepted the terms of the UN's January 28 resolution which Foreign Minister Stikker had earlier called "unacceptable." There was to be a cease-fire. Holland would restore the Republican leaders to power in Jogjakarta. A Round Table Conference would convene in The Hague to transfer sovereignty to the Republic.

Two days later the State Department "expresses its wholehearted approval."

One week after the van Royen-Rum agreement former Prime Minister Beel resigned as Dutch high commissioner in Indonesia because he objected to the "form and extent of the restoration of the Republic." General Spoor, commander of the Dutch Indies forces, also resigned. Spoor succumbed to a heart attack in Jakarta on May 25, at the age of forty-seven.

The Beel-Spoor policy was dead. Dutch troops began leaving Jogjakarta on June 24; within five days Republican troops took over.

When the Dutch seized Jogjakarta on December 19, 1948, and arrested the Republican leaders, they did not touch the Sultan of Jogjakarta, Hamengku Buwono IX, minister of state in the Republican government. They knew his mystic-religious hold on the people of Central and East Java. Because he was a scion of an ancient royal family, Javanese tendered him a reverence reserved for mythological gods. Even the water in which he was bathed was considered holy. Left by the Dutch in the lonely splendor of his vast Kraton, or palace, the Sultan never emerged from it during the entire Dutch occupation. He refused to receive Dutch emissaries or anybody else. The dignified aloofness of one so influential impressed friend and foe and stiffened Republican morale during the difficult leaderless period following the second police action.

Now, as the Netherlands army marched out of his capital, the Sultan emerged from the Kraton and ordered an end to guerrilla warfare. On July 6 he received Sukarno and Hatta as his palace guests and political superiors.

For all practical purposes, the Republic of the United States of Indonesia had been born. The child was delivered by the joint efforts of Acheson and the U.S. Senate. Changes in Dutch domestic politics brought the maternity ward to the right temperature. That the fetus did not die from Dutch military suffocation should be credited to the resistance of

Indonesia's civilian and military freedom-fighters, animated, subconsciously, it would seem, by a sense of historic destiny and the certitude that in our era nationalism pitted against colonialism must win.

The UN probably hastened the process of Indonesian liberation. Britain and the United States had decided that Holland's departure from the Indies would serve European recovery, Asian tranquillity, Dutch stability, and their own national interests. They used UN machinery to achieve a national objective as well as international ends. It is in such circumstances that the UN functions best.

Free Indonesia, born through the combined efforts of the Indonesian people, the United States, the United Nations, and the United Kingdom, now needed a birth certificate, a deed to its rightful possessions, and a statement of its inherited indebtedness. These were signed at the Round Table Conference which convened in The Hague on August 23, 1949. Dr. Hatta led the Republic's delegation; Sultan Hamid of West Borneo led a delegation from the fifteen federal states set up by Governor van Mook. The Republic and the federalists worked in concert. For the puppet heads of the federal states included nationalists who had collaborated with the Dutch for reasons of expediency or material gain. When they realized the Republic's attraction for their own people, when they saw that the Dutch would pull up ancient stakes, they made common cause with Sukarno and Hatta. The spirit of federalism and states' rights, however, remained strong, and before the two delegations flew to The Hague conference it was agreed that the new independent Indonesian government would be federal in nature with a bicameral legislature consisting of a popularly elected House of Representatives and a Senate of thirty-two members: two from each of the fifteen federal states and two from the Republic.

The Indonesians departed for The Hague not on a silvery cloud but in a dark mist of suspicion. Many Republicans, including party chiefs and government ministers, found the prospect of freedom from Dutch rule too good to be true. Just as Nehru and Krishna Menon told me in India in 1946 that the British were not leaving, so Indonesians could not believe in 1949 that Holland would write "Finis" to a stay of three hundred and fifty years. The unjustified skepticism, a natural product of prolonged foreign domination, distorted policies in both countries.

However, it was the end. The Round Table Conference came to the historic conclusion that Holland would irrevocably and unconditionally transfer sovereignty by December 30, 1949, to the independent Republic of the United States of Indonesia. Voluntarily, the Republic consented to enter a loose Netherlands-Indonesian Union or commonwealth operating "on the basis of free will and equality in status . . ."; it committed neither side to anything. Further, the Republic accepted a debt of 3 billion 400 million guilders, or approximately 1 billion 130 million dollars, incurred by the Netherlands government of the East Indies.

A single issue defied settlement: New Guinea, or West Irian. The Indonesians, especially the federalists, wanted it. Holland insisted on retaining it, otherwise, her delegates contended, the entire agreement would fail of ratification by the Dutch Parliament. A compromise stipulated that the final disposition of the vast Guinea territory would be determined by negotiation within a year after the transfer of sovereignty.

The Round Table Conference ended on November 2 with the signing of a treaty embodying all these points. The Dutch and Indonesian parliaments quickly ratified The Hague agreement. But Moscow *Izvestia* of December 8, 1949, referred to Sukarno and Hatta as "traitors to the Indonesian people" who were "carrying out the will of the American imperialists," and on December 13 Soviet Delegate Semyon K. Tsarapkin told the UN Security Council that "The Hague agreements form a shameful page in the record of the UN . . . the shackles of colonial slavery have again been imposed on the Indonesian people . . . with the assistance of the Sukarno-Hatta clique." It was not the first time, or the last, that a Communist curtain of brittle dogma obscured hard facts. On December 27, 1949, Holland transferred sovereignty to Indonesia. The colonial shackles dropped. Indonesia was free. Another empire had died.

Chapter Seventeen

EMPIRES ARE OBSOLETE

In The Hague in 1956 I questioned a retired Dutch official about conditions in Holland since the withdrawal from Indonesia. "We are better off than ever before," he replied.

At the Royal Tropical Institute in Amsterdam a scientist who had served seventeen years in the Indies told me of a conversation with recent French visitors. "I see how prosperous Holland is despite the loss of empire," one of the Frenchmen said. "Perhaps we shouldn't fight for ours."

I asked a topmost British permanent official in London whether freedom for India had injured England. "I shouldn't think so," he answered.

An American expert on the Far East denied that imperialism was a necessity to prosperity. "Japan's disastrous prewar attempts to conquer China," he affirmed, "were prompted less by economics than by militarists yearning for glory, grandeur, and power."

Colonies are a burden rather than a blessing. Had the British remained in India it would have become worse than a thousand Cypruses or a hundred Algerias. To be sure, the raw materials of Asian and African countries are indispensable to the very life of Western nations. Oil is one example. But no country can own the sources of all its needs. Even the richest states (America and Russia) depend on imports. No nation is independent. The law of personal, corporate, and political life is interdependence. Unhampered trade provides a desirable substitute for colonial possessions. Producers must sell.

But is it possible that crowded little Holland with 11 million inhabi-

131

tants and negligible natural resources can be more stable economically than when she owned the Indies archipelago with over 80 million inhabitants and a vast treasure of oil, rubber, copra, tin, tobacco, tea, and coffee? I put this query to economists, statisticians, and businessmen in Holland in 1956 and again in 1958. They said yes.

Between 1925 and 1934, the Dutch East Indies accounted for 8.9 per cent of the Netherlands' national income; in 1938, 8.4 per cent. The Central Bureau of Statistics in The Hague informs me that from 1955 to 1957 the figure was down to between 1.5 per cent and 2 per cent per annum.

At the same time Dutch population increased. Holland has a high surplus of births over deaths: 13.8 per 1,000. In the six years from 1950 to 1955 the population rose 794,000—despite a net emigration of 106,206 persons.

Population up; colonial income down. How did Holland cope with the resulting difficulties?

Like war, the crisis tapped unsuspected human resources. Spurred by fear of reduced living standards, the Dutch roused themselves to a supreme effort of adaptation to life without empire. The people did not sit down by the ruins of a realm and weep. They remade themselves.

There is an old saying which the Netherlanders like to hear even though in their piety they hesitate to pronounce the words. "God created the world," it goes, "but the Dutch made the Netherlands." This refers to Holland's remarkable record of turning water into land and washing out the sea bottom till it produced beautiful bulbs and edible cheese. Since 1949 the Dutch have continued to perform that miracle and added a second.

Unemployment, steady at 400,000 in the years before the Second World War, was barely visible at 40,000 in 1955. Jobs went begging for applicants. Real income rose 15 per cent between 1939 and 1955. Gross national product mounted precipitately from 17.5 billion guilders in 1949 to over 27 billion in 1955. In the same period imports doubled; exports more than doubled. Always thrifty and money-wise, the Dutch, in the seven fat years from 1949 to 1955, invested 32 billion 360 million guilders in their economy —though they ate better, dressed better, built more homes, and bought more bicycles and cars.

These achievements, all the more impressive in view of the wreckage wrought by war, Nazi occupation, and the great 1953 flood, might not have taken place, in the judgment of Dutch economists and businessmen, had the East Indies been retained. In Indonesia, they said, the unavoidable period of diminishing colonial returns had set in. Netherlands plantations and investments were still paying good dividends and every year thousands of Dutchmen found profitable employment there. But the imperial position had commenced to deteriorate even before the Second World War. Dutch retention of Indonesia after 1949 would have entailed tremendous outlays: one, to suppress nationalist opposition; two, to renew equipment and industrialize. Both processes could have been carried out only at the expense of investments inside Holland.

Money that would have traveled to Indonesia was plowed into Dutch enterprises at home. Textile factories, which formerly made low-quality cloth for the Indies, retooled and now sell the world a variety of qualities which permits competition with the best from any country. Skillful re-equipment in other branches, clever investment policies, and labor-management co-operation helped Holland to ride out the crisis. In olden days Holland's cheese, flower bulbs, Frisian cattle, potatoes, and other farm commodities bulked large in her exports. But between 1939 and 1955 industrial exports climbed 139 per cent. Industry accounted for 65 per cent of Holland's exports, agriculture for only 15 per cent.

Industrial progress went hand in hand with a vigorous global merchandising drive. Curtailed sales opportunities in Indonesia, which took a mere 2 per cent of Dutch exports in 1955, and just above zero in 1958, were offset by new buyers in Peru, Australia, Iceland, Japan, Africa, the Middle East, and above all, Britain, Belgium, and West Germany. While Holland faced the empire her back was to her neighbors in Europe. Now the Dutch have discovered that it is better to be master producers of wanted goods for rich countries than unwanted masters of poor colonial customers.

Holland likewise learned that her emigrants were as universally welcome as her products. A Dutch rice miller left Indonesia when the atmosphere there became too uncongenial. Now he owns a dry-cleaning establishment in Perth, Australia. From the end of the war to the end of 1955, 77,338 Hollanders settled in Australia; of these about 20,000 were former residents of the Indies. "These sons of Holland are not lost to us," a white-haired Amsterdam professor said to me. "They eat Dutch cheese, drink Dutch beer, smoke Dutch cigars, read Dutch books—and nobody minds if they celebrate Queen Juliana's birthday as well as Queen Elizabeth's."

Netherlanders who in the past would have held white-collar jobs in Indonesia now settle in Canada and other Commonwealth countries. Canada takes Dutch peasants too. Ethiopia, Pakistan, Brazil, and South Africa also receive a steady flow of Dutchmen.

Dikes and bikes are the contrasting symbols of Holland—dikes for sturdy stability, bikes for agile mobility.

Holland and Switzerland are proof that neither colonial possessions nor even natural resources are the key to national prosperity, but rather the ability and desire to work and a talent for management. A country that has these can purchase anything it lacks, but all the natural wealth of the United States and the Soviet Union would be worthless without technical know-how.

Empires once brought power and profits. Today they spell trouble. Empires do not pay.

"The era of imperialism is ended," U. S. Undersecretary of State Sumner Welles declared at Arlington Cemetery on Memorial Day, 1942. This was policy and prophecy. The end began with the independence of the Philippines on July 4, 1946, the independence of India, Pakistan, and Ceylon in 1947, of Burma on January 4, 1948, and the Dutch exit from Indonesia in 1949. It continued with the liberation of Tunisia and Morocco and other French African territories and of Malaya and Ghana by the British in the 1950's. Dots of Western imperialism remain in Asia and splotches of it in Africa; the big new empire is Russia's in Eastern and Central Europe. These too will end, and then the end will come to an end. One wishes it as much for the sake of the motherlands as for the colonies. It is crude to say that those who favored Indian independence were anti-British, or that anybody who wishes Washington would stop embracing Latin-American dictators is anti-American, or that persons who congratulate Holland on withdrawing from Indonesia are anti-Dutch. Freedom from dependencies relieves the imperial power of moral taint, material disadvantages, political handicaps, and strategic diversions. "Great Britain," British Foreign Secretary Lord Castlereagh said in 1812, "has derived more commercial advantage from North America since the separation than when that country was . . . part of her colonial system." England gained by losing the Thirteen Colonies. She gained trade. She gained from private investments in American enterprises. She gained an ally in the two world wars and their aftermaths. Britain also gained by leaving India. The colonial power loses a colony and an enemy and, given wisdom, finds a friend and business.

Holland did not display the wisdom. Her four-year colonial war in the Indies drained Dutch blood and treasure in an effort doomed to fail. The Japanese occupation that preceded it gave the Indonesians a taste for violence and a hunger for freedom. Having had the Dutch *and* the Japanese, they wanted no more foreign masters. If it was not clear when the Dutch returned to the Indies in 1945, it should have been clear to them a few months later that their military victories would be temporary and empty. Only a political solution offered peace. In 1946 Sukarno, Hatta, Sjahrir, and other nationalists were surprised that they had a government and knew how much outside help it would need. A Netherlands-Indonesian commonwealth was then possible. Even in 1949 some connecting tissue remained between former colony and former ruler. At the least there was room for co-operation in trade, aid, and investment.

All prospects were dimmed and finally destroyed by the New Guinea issue.

The Dutch were warned but did not listen. Speaking in the Second Chamber of the Netherlands Parliament on August 17, 1949, the eve of the Round Table Conference, former Prime Minister Schermerhorn, a dissident Laborite, said: ". . . the interest of the Netherlands lies in co-operation with the United States of Indonesia. If we should sacrifice this for the maintenance of New Guinea, it probably—no one can see into the future—will be very dearly paid for." He did see into the future. But Schermerhorn's party, having eaten of the political fleshpots, had acquired an appetite for rich food and therefore went along with its Catholic coalition partner in insisting that New Guinea (West Irian) remain under Dutch rule. Indonesia and Holland have paid very dearly for it.

Governor Pieter J. Platteel of Netherlands New Guinea remarked in The Hague in January, 1959, that half of his 700,000 subjects "still live outside Dutch administration," a *New York Times* report stated. "Their country of towering mountains and vast swamps is hard to penetrate." The Stone Age Papuans, the Governor declared, "use stone axes, shells, and sticks as their tools, and bows and arrows as weapons. They wear little clothing." They move every year because the soil is poor. Women do the hard work and the men are warriors. "This Stone Age existence," he commented, "is hardship, illness, and constant fear for life. It is also cruelty." He described the Papuan custom of cutting off a piece of a woman's finger each time a relative died, so that by middle age her fingers were almost gone. "The hands of men are mutilated only once so that they can remain good fighters."

Dutch New Guinea, with an area of 151,000 square miles—about the size of California—has been called "the land of unlimited impossibilities." Dutch geologists have, over the years, drawn up a long list of the mineral resources the territory does not possess. "Since 1936, the Netherlands New Guinea Petroleum Company," writes Professor Robert C. Bone, Jr., in a Cornell University White Book, "has invested, through December 1955, more than $100 million with a return for the same period of approximately $25 million, while future prospects continue dubious."

For Holland to give up the luscious, emerald-green empire of the Indies and retain the huge dead stone of New Guinea is modern madness.

This albatross around Holland's neck costs the national exchequer 100 million guilders—approximately $37 million—each year and the chances of any income in even the remote future are nil.

"The entire Dutch business community," the Hollander in the best position to make such a statement said to me in 1958, "disagrees with the government policy of holding New Guinea."

"That is a refutation of Marxism," I suggested facetiously. "I thought the capitalists rule Holland."

"No," he retorted sadly. "Holland is ruled by her political parties and often by parts of parties."

The parties, in turn, are ruled by emotions and stubbornness.

Before the Round Table Conference a Dutch Foreign Ministry diplomat sent to Dr. van Mook, who had recently resigned as Indies governor, an official document outlining The Hague's proposed policy of keeping New Guinea and invited his opinion. Van Mook replied in a letter dated July 14, 1949, the English translation of which he was good enough to write out for me in longhand. ". . . we must consider," van Mook suggested prophetically, "whether the proposed policy will not again deprive us of a major part of the remaining good will in Indonesia for an objective that has only emotional value and will cause us endless trouble."

Van Mook had administered, visited, and read about New Guinea. It is a country, his letter said, "of few if any economic possibilities with the exception of perhaps some mining. All the plans for settlement that were made in the past years have in my view been stillborn; as a refuge for groups that may be expelled from Indonesia it will only provide a mass grave."

Dr. Joseph Luns, Netherlands foreign minister, told me in The Hague, on June 26, 1958, that Holland had a "duty" toward the Papuans; she was in New Guinea with "a mission." Van Mook answered that. "It might be contended," his 1949 letter read, "that we should maintain possession of New Guinea exclusively in the interest of the Papuan population. That would mean, however, a rather fundamental change in the way in which we have governed the area until now"—van Mook should know—"and also necessitate a change of methods for the corporations working there." The corporations, he said, had always used Indonesians from the Moluccas, Java, and Sumatra, not Papuans, "because we could not recruit employees at the intermediate level among the Papuans, nor a sufficient number of skilled laborers." If the corporations continued to import Indonesians "in a New Guinea wholly outside the authority of the United States of Indonesia," it would "lead to continuous unrest which could, as we know from experience, also affect the Papuans." The nationalists, he affirmed, "have much better means to make trouble than we have to allay it." (With no Indonesians and few trained Papuans, how can Holland develop even the meager resources that exist?)

"Militarily," van Mook asserted, "certain parts may have importance; this will largely depend on possible agreements with others"—the United States, Australia, Britain, and New Zealand. But, he cautioned, the Indonesians will see in this and in any economic activity "a continuation of colonialism, whatever we may say, and will consider a military garrison as a potential threat."

Holland's legal position, van Mook said in a final paragraph, "is weak . . . neither at Linggajati nor at Den Pasar," he asserted, "was the exclusion of New Guinea from the future U.S. of I. [United States of Indonesia] made a condition . . . only its status within the U.S. of I. was left undecided." But, the former Governor concluded, "the main point for me is that the suggested solutions outside the U.S. of I. have neither a future nor any attraction."

This statesmanlike paper, never before published, answers all the arguments in defense of Holland's retention of West Irian. No discernible self-interest or idealism dictates it.

Has Indonesia's claim any greater validity?

"Indonesia's demand to annex New Guinea is imperialism," a French journalist said to me in New York. "The Papuans are not Indonesians and Indonesia does not belong there."

"Does Holland?" I asked.

By an ironic twist, Indonesia's claim to West Irian is based on Dutch colonialism. Indonesia does not demand the Portuguese half of the Indonesian island of Timor. She insists on obtaining West Irian because she regards herself as the heir of all Holland's Indies territory.

This, however, is a fact which fails to explain. Neither is there any economic motivation in Indonesia's policy; the West Irian she covets would be a financial headache to her too. An element of resentment, compounded by fear, does exist. The Dutch government's efforts to destroy the Republic up to 1949 were repeated by individual Dutch adventurers after that date and even as late as 1958, Dr. J. H. van Royen, Netherlands ambassador in Washington, officially requested Secretary of State Dulles and Assistant Secretary Walter S. Robertson to forbid the sale of American arms to the Indonesian government. A people may forgive enmity in war and close the ledger. It cannot forget the prolongation of antagonism by a bad loser. Given this background of hostility, given, too, the absence of a logical, rational, practical reason for Holland's wish to remain in New Guinea, many Indonesians jump to the conclusion that the territory will someday be used as a springboard for a military attack by Holland on Indonesia. Nonsense, but real nevertheless.

The greater reality is emotional nationalism. Nobody can sit in judgment over psychology. Nationalism constitutes the major fact of modern political life. It is a mistake, however, to assume that every independent country is a nation. Some new states in Asia and Africa are old countries inhabited by ancient peoples which boast great cultures. Yet that does not make them nations. A nation, though divided, as all human aggregations must be, by divergent regional, linguistic, class, caste, tribal, racial, economic, religious, or political interests and loyalties, is united by powerful cementing influences that transcend the divisive tendencies. But sometimes the divisions are too deep to bridge. Thus India in 1947 broke in two on the rock of religion. The Hindu-Moslem antagonism, exploited by politicians, would not dissolve in the spirit of nationalism. Elsewhere the chasm between the sheik who owns a hundred thousand acres and his undernourished, diseased peasant bars the way to unity and therefore to nationhood. In Indonesia insular selfishness, economic backwardness, and religion militate against national feeling. Even old nations may split and sink like ships in a storm. That was France in 1941.

For Europe the cure lies not in nationalist separatism but in international economic and political unions (*E Pluribus Unum*). European cohesion is zigzagging forward against a hundred obsolete obstacles. The new Afro-Asian states, however, must experience their expensive period of nationalism before they ripen for internationalism. Irredenta like West Irian, and colonies and satellites, serve as fomenters of acrid nationalism. What Israel is to the Arabs, what Kashmir is to India and Pakistan, that West Irian is to Indonesia—a chemical hate-inducer designed to bind together that which would otherwise be less firmly joined. It is wrong to regard the West Irian agitation as President Sukarno's personal idiosyncrasy. He is the living father of Indonesian nationalism and is using West Irian to strengthen it.

Like the Kashmir issue, the West Irian problem has defied diplomacy. The conference to settle the question, convened in accordance with the Round Table Conference decision, on December 4, 1950, ended in total failure. Thereafter, relations deteriorated steadily.

Holland's hot war against Indonesian nationalism and the retention of West Irian have hurt Indonesia more than the Netherlands. An amicable separation, like England's from India, would have favored the archipelago's economic development and domestic tranquillity and, no less important, eliminated the bitter anti-Western additive of Indonesian nationalism. Nobody has benefited more from the West Irian agitation than the Communists, who ride it hard in the saddle of "supernationalism." Nobody has benefited less than Holland, the West, and the Indonesian people. West Irian, that sunken hull of a dead empire, has kept the past from being buried and casts black shadows over the newborn present. Dutch diplomats have said to me, "The coastline of New Guinea is very long and poorly guarded. Someday the Indonesian army may land, in several places; there will be skirmishes; a cease-fire appeal will be made to the United Nations, followed by endless debates and trouble for us." The possibility of an Indonesian attack seems remote yet not impossible. In any case it obsesses Holland and costs money in armaments. Would it not be the better part of wisdom to open bilateral negotiations or deposit the problem in the lap of the UN or submit it to the International Court, which sits in the very center of the capital of Holland? When the past is dead it is better to bury or burn it and be reconciled to the present.

PART TWO

The Present: Persons, Places, and Problems

Chapter Eighteen

LAND WITHOUT TENSION

I saw more teeth in Indonesia in any one month than in a year in Europe and the United States; Indonesians smile often, and their laughing point is low. The air has no tension. Bustle, busyness, and haste are considered in bad taste. To rush is undignified, to preserve one's calm and poise in all circumstances is the highest virtue. The standards of behavior of the old nobility—the sultans, regents, and country gentlemen, or priyayi—remain good form today. The nobility did not strain, neither did it strive, for practical success. Its ideal was gracious living: the proper use of leisure, the dance, games, conversation, fellowship, and the contemplation of esoteric subjects.

Climate must have something to do with this radiant disposition and penchant for the easy life. The sun shines for many hours every day, even during the half-year-long rainy season. But economic conditions also are part of the explanation. Industrial progress and the concomitant modern tempo would have rent the priyayi tradition into shreds. Indonesian industrialization, however, has been limited and its psychological impact negligible. Few Indonesians went into trade; that was for Chinese. Few possessed enough capital to build factories or buy ships. The Dutch held an actual, if not legal, monopoly in those fields. Indonesians in the professions—medicine, law, and so forth—were not numerous, about a thousand in the entire archipelago. Men like Sukarno, who studied engineering, often went into politics. The technical intelligentsia therefore stood at weak battalion strength. Ambitious go-getters could be counted on the

fingers of two hands. Certainly they included no Indonesian civil servants.
Hard work at a desk would have been frowned upon.

Today government offices remain open from 7 A.M. to 1 P.M., Fridays
from 7 to 11:30, Saturdays till 11 A.M., and no work Sundays. On the pavement outside the house where I lived in Jakarta men with portfolios,
the badge of the ministry clerk—though they contain nothing more than
a sandwich—would congregate at about 7:45 and be picked up at 8
by an official bus which took them to work. The pace in government
bureaus is unhurried. Pauses for coffee drinking and newspaper reading
enjoy the sanction of prolonged usage.

In this gently rolling river of human activity the priyayi pattern retains
its hold on nobles, little nobles, and little people. It sets the national style
of deference to the aged, soft-spokenness, smiles, and extreme politeness.
When maids and bungs (brothers) enter a room on bare feet they bow low
from the waist and in that posture approach the table where they kneel lest
their heads be higher than those whom they serve. They retire by step-
ping backward in the same crouched position. A little laugh indicates
that what the observer might regard as a discomfort is really a pleasure.

"Is the earth round like a lemon," the city schoolteacher asked, "or
flat like a pancake?"

"Round like a lemon," the clever little Javanese replied.

"Can you prove it?" the teacher inquired.

He proved it by reference to a ship's mast appearing above the horizon
as it approached and disappearing as it departed.

"But suppose," the teacher said, "you tell this to the old people in your
village who have never been to school and they refuse to believe it?"

"Well," came the pupil's answer, "when I'm back among my people I
won't believe it either."

It is un-priyayi to differ with elders.

In Indonesia friends cautioned me to "talk Javanese." Words, they
said, are never what they seem to be. When faced with a request the
refusal of which would cause pain you say yes. When met with an argument which you would like to reject you agree. To do otherwise would
affront, insult. Always give joy first. Later you might indicate ever so
mildly what you really think. Circumlocution is the best policy. Never put
a direct question or expect a direct response.

The priyayi indulge in indirection from long habit and with great skill.
Thus, recently, the postmaster's wife in a Javanese town set her heart on
marrying off her son to the beautiful daughter of a local priyayi family.
The mother of the girl heard of it, and instead of fuming invited the
postmistress at teatime. Now, afternoon teatime speaks a language all
its own: if no tea is served, you must stay only a moment; if it is served

immediately on the guest's arrival, the visit should be short. The priyayi lady did serve tea but with it came a banana, though the lowly banana, which grows at every wayside, does not normally go with a cup of tea. Neither does the beautiful daughter of a nobleman marry the son of a postmaster. Nobody mentioned the match. The suit was dropped.

The priyayi mentality and the languid tempo of life are vestiges of Indonesian feudalism. Feudalism itself, as an economic system, is dead, but capitalism, its successor, has not yet been born, and in this twilight postfeudal, precapitalist era the spirit of the past clings fast because its body is doomed. Industrialization is invading the Indies and will surely conquer them. Meanwhile, evidence of precapitalism fills the streets and country roads. Capital is scarce in a precapitalist country (that is why it is precapitalist), human labor is plentiful, so trucks, carts, horses, and oxen are few and men and women double as beasts of burden. One sees long chains of women carrying on their heads sheaves of rice plants from the fields to their homes. They walk beautifully erect, arms swaying rhythmically, and only the eyes roam to take in the passing world. One pushcart would replace scores of these female transportation coolies. But what would they do instead? And whence the rupias to buy a wheelbarrow? Why spend on a laborsaving device when labor has so little value and use? Women walk miles to market with bamboo baskets of fruits or vegetables on their heads and return with a handful of salt or a yard of cloth in the same baskets. Their feet never tire, nor do they seem to question the economic wisdom of spending from sunup to sundown on a two-way transaction which may total 23 cents.

In cities, because the capital for establishing restaurants is missing, people eat out under crude sheds, or at long wooden tables unshielded from sun, rain, and the smoke of the open-air kitchen, or, most frequently, on their haunches after having purchased a meal from a vendor who carries his restaurant on his shoulders. The most conspicuous of these itinerant cafeteria owners is the Indonesian "milkman." Suspended from the ends of his bent bamboo pole are two huge tin cans, perhaps two and a half feet in diameter and three feet high, looking like oversize milk cans. "They must love milk here," a newly arrived American remarked on first seeing one. The cans actually contain pretzellike cakes as big as a man's hand made of a mixture of rice dough and shrimp paste, a cold Indonesian delicacy with a delightful tang and taste. Other traveling lunch counters consist of tiered, orange-colored, glass-enclosed boxes full of shredded cabbage, warm boiled rice, jars of spices, ready-to-eat noodles, and white china spoons and bowls. Accost the owner and he will set down his burden on the pavement, settle on his stool, and make you any desired mixture of the ingredients; while you eat the repast, he shouts the virtues of his wares. One peripatetic snack bar sells dried fish morsels served on rectangular green "plates" cut out of banana leaves.

The shoe repairman, the florist, the fruit peddler, the fishmonger, and a host of their fellow businessmen operate from similar two-basket, bamboo-pole shops. Since the loads are heavy and must, moreover, be kept in balance, the human beasts of burden take short, quick dance steps, swinging one arm lustily and using the other to hold the shoulder pole in place. The brush salesman carries enough merchandise on his pole to fill a storeroom: brooms, wicker laundry baskets, tin tubs, long-handled brushes, shoebrushes, whisk brooms, hairbrushes, everything but tooth-brushes. He and his family have probably made his wares from raw material obtained free in the suburban jungle.

Many of these precapitalists have their specific cries. The trudging restaurateur gives forth a "yip" which sounds like a musical hiccough or, if his lunch counter is light, he knocks a hollow bamboo stick on a solid piece of wood to create a pleasant ringing note. The cobbler makes xylophone-like sounds by shaking a primitive contraption which consists of horizontal metal strips fastened to a small iron bar.

At noon the shoulder-suspension shopkeeper finds a shady spot on the grass by a canal and slumbers for several hours till his muscles recuperate and the sun begins to relent.

The most ubiquitous antique on Indonesian streets is the betjak (pronounced *bechá*). This mechanism consists of an upholstered seat for two, if the two are narrow-hipped enough to squeeze into it, mounted on a tricycle base. The driver, bareheaded, barelegged and barefooted, in shorts and a shirt usually torn and threadbare and wet with sweat or rain, pedals behind the passengers and engages in banter with them or hums a tune. On an ascent or after stopping while the train passes one of the several level crossings that mar the city of Jakarta, he dismounts from his leather perch and pushes. When it pours he fastens a rubber sheet over the front of his little vehicle and puts up its hood to protect the passengers. For his toil and pains he is paid, depending on the bargain struck before boarding, three cents a mile or less.

The betjak "boys" are Indonesians in their twenties or thirties who will probably die young. Chinese own the betjaks. Jakarta's Lord Mayor Sudiro, a former schoolteacher, says the city (population 3 million) has 30,000 betjaks, each with a conspicuous license number plate on which a monthly tax is levied. Because too many betjaks are already idle, no new license numbers are being issued. The Chinese evade this restriction by attaching the same number to two or more tricycles. Nostalgia for China is reflected in the badly painted scenes on the back of each betjak including, usually, a tiger or lion and a river and a mountaintop. The betjak chain names painted on the mudguards follow no pattern at all: "Shanghai," "Djakarta," "Merdeka," and so forth.

According to the Lord Mayor, Jakarta in mid-1958 boasted 70,000 cars, trucks and jeeps, compared with 35,000 in 1953; 35 government buses, 12 private buses, and some 100 taxis. He did not mention the three or four over-age trolleys that creep sporadically through the streets or the "Opelettes," which are German Opel cars with bus bodies built for six who sit, knees locked, facing one another in perspiring proximity. They proved most useful, for after the Opelette reached its terminus I would say to the driver, "23, Djalan Pintu Air," or "American Embassy," and he would indicate that this was his last stop, and I would keep repeating my destination until he smiled, then laughed, and, for an extra fee, took me in lonely comfort to the place named.

It is possible to go into the center of town and hire a taxi for the day, but if you make an appointment with the driver for the next morning he is sure not to appear. Having earned enough one day he takes the next day off. Telephone for a taxi at 4 P.M. and the reply is, "We'll have one at six." Time is not of the essence. A time-sense arrives with the machine age and precision instruments.

President Sukarno insists on punctuality to the second hand. But in most other things he is the easygoing priyayi. Revolts may erupt, hostile guerrillas may fill the jungles; the state treasury reserves may be going, going, almost gone; the President remains his relaxed, smiling self and behaves as though he had not a care in the world.

Chapter Nineteen

SUKARNO AMONG HIS PEOPLE

AT A SESSION of the new National Council, its deputy chairman Ruslan Abdulgani, a former foreign minister, passed a note to the chairman, President Sukarno, which read in Dutch, "Louis Fisher is here for two months." Then in Indonesian, "Purpose, to write a book. It would be desirable for Bung Karno to see him in," and now in English and in quotes, "a relaxed and leisure atmosphere."

Sukarno drew an ellipse around my misspelled name and an arrow to the bottom of the note and wrote, "In the hands of Mahatma Gandhi, The New Testament has become T.N.T." He was quoting from memory from my Gandhi biography. Below the quote he added, "Tri Nitro Toluol" for T.N.T., and finally in Dutch, "Springstof"—explosive.

This was Sukarno's manifestation of priyayi-ism; he did not say no, he did not say yes, he revealed knowledge and evinced interest but made no commitment. The commitment came later in the shape of an invitation to travel with him for six days through Java and to Makassar and Bali.

I had been introduced to Sukarno at a Soviet diplomatic reception in Moscow in the summer of 1956. I saw him again at Jakarta's Kemajoran Airport just before the take-off of our Convair. Taller than the average Indonesian, handsome in well-tailored uniform, his marshal's black baton under his arm, he inspected an honor guard, shook hands with each of the civilians arrayed abreast in soldierly fashion to bid him Godspeed, stood to attention as the band played the national anthem, and then entered the plane. He was seated in the rear of the cabin at a table, and wore a light overcoat, apparently expecting cold weather in the higher altitudes. The two double seats in front of him, the one behind, and the one across the aisle remained unoccupied. Our party included seventeen other Indonesians—Colonel Sugandhy and Major Sudarto, the President's adjutants; Dr. Lauw Ing Tjhong, his private physician (of Chinese origin but Indonesian citizenship); several members of Sukarno's staff; several security officers; several newsmen; and a photographer—plus two foreign journalists, a Turk and me.

As we were getting seated Sukarno called to me, "Louis, let's begin by shaking hands." We shook hands, he smiled and wished me a pleasant trip, I did likewise and returned to my place.

Stewardesses served cold citrus drinks and, later, a meal of Indonesian food too hotly spiced for me; I partook only of the rice. The flight to Malang in southeastern Java lasted two hours and twenty minutes. Major Sudarto, my neighbor, sang American folk songs and pointed out the peaks and active and extinct volcanoes below.

At the Malang airport, and at every other stop on our itinerary, the procedure was the same: Sukarno was the last out of the plane. As his feet touched the ground the band played "Indonesia Raya" (Great Indonesia), he reviewed the guard of honor, seized the extended hands of the civilians aligned in a row, walked through the air terminal, and entered his waiting, bronze-colored limousine which flew the large golden presidential standard.

From Malang the procession of cars and police jeeps drove to the nearby town of Blitar where Sukarno's mother lived. She was seated in a chair at the top of the five front steps of the house. The President mounted the steps and laid his head affectionately in her lap. She stroked his hair. Ninety, she looked like the universal mother. My mother would have looked like that had she lived, I thought.

When I met the mother I touched my palms together in front of me in the Hindu greeting, for she was a Hindu born in Bali, and everybody laughed congenially at the idea that I should have done something so Eastern. I also met the President's sister, who is in business. He was especially affectionate in introducing a beautiful niece. "He's not indifferent to feminine pulchritude," my notes read.

"Now I'll introduce you to a mother of three," the President said. "And here's a mother of five," he declared, turning me toward another very young relative. "We want more children."

I indicated disagreement.

"He doesn't agree," Sukarno guffawed. "We could feed two hundred fifty million."

"But you can't now. You're importing rice," I replied. (I had decided early in my stay that I did not know enough English to practice Javanese indirection.)

"You're not an ascetic," Sukarno said to me. The whole company joined him in the gaiety.

"No, but Indonesia needs family planning," I insisted.

"I had a letter from Nehru two years ago," he stated, "suggesting that we concern ourselves with birth control. But we could feed two hundred fifty million."

At this point his attention was diverted to several newly arrived guests. We sat together in the family dining room, Sukarno in tender proximity to his mother, and chatted for some ten minutes. Then the outsiders withdrew.

After the siesta, I met Sukarno on the porch. "Did you sleep?" I asked.

"No, I read magazines."

"*Time*?" I inquired. This was a reference to the *Time* magazine cover story of March 10, 1958, on Sukarno and Indonesia.

"I will not comment on the contents of their report, but why," he exclaimed with emphasis, "did they make me look like a monster?" and he held his hands to his head in a gesture of horror. Westerners, often in innocence, sometimes from blindness, cannot see others as others see themselves. The cover painting shows Sukarno's face care-lined and frowning, with an excess of green color and wrinkles against a background of demons, all of which must have hurt his vanity and carried unpleasant associations for one raised in a culture deeply animistic. The text itself was nowise so hostile as *Time* might have been. But the portrait meant more than the words and the magazine was banned from newsstands and its correspondent invited to leave the country.

Sukarno's mother had retired before dinner. The U-shaped table was laden with a sufficiency of dishes which were obviously delectable to everybody but me. I sat opposite Sukarno; and noticing that I ate only the rice and a hard-boiled egg, he sent his girl relatives repeatedly to the kitchen to bring me whatever was available in pristine, unspiced condition—chiefly raw vegetables. The President, speaking now Indonesian, now fluent English, now fine French, kept the conversation alive all the time, talking to his neighbors in a voice that would be overheard, addressing a diner at the far end of the table, or entertaining the entire company.

Between courses Sukarno passed around Indonesian cigarettes. American cigarettes, he said, contain some Indonesian tobacco; Russian visitors like Indonesian tobacco. "You know the Russians," he said to me.

"I lived in the Soviet Union for fourteen years."

"They are a great people," he declared, "but when I say that I'm called a Communist."

"They are undoubtedly a great people," I replied, "and they have done great things. One wonders what they might have achieved with freedom. Many countries of Europe, not to speak of the United States, have made more economic progress since the Second World War than Russia."

"I have been to Europe and Japan," he commented.

His Indonesian neighbors engaged him in conversation. "We are speaking Bahasa [Indonesian]," he explained to me. "I told Nehru this was our advantage. I can go anywhere in Indonesia and be understood when I speak Bahasa."

After dinner, the President, the Turk, two Indonesian journalists, and I sat on the porch. The journalists put some questions to me about America. "One Indonesian editor," a Jakarta news agency representative stated, "was arrested for insulting President Eisenhower."

"What was the insult?" I inquired.

"He called President Eisenhower a warmonger."

I said Eisenhower was not a warmonger, his mother was an absolute pacifist, the military are not necessarily militarists, the Second World War was started by civilians, Hitler and Stalin. "But," I added, "Eisenhower is in politics and he is attacked in the United States, and I see no reason why he should not be attacked whenever and wherever anybody pleases."

"We will not allow heads of states to be attacked in our country," Sukarno affirmed.

"Eisenhower is head of state," I said, "but he is also chief executive and top policy maker and if he were immune from criticism freedom of the press would be curbed."

"We will not allow heads of states to be attacked," Sukarno repeated.

He must have been thinking of himself. He was head of state, and officially he had no policy-making role. Actually Indonesian politics revolved around his personality and policy, yet because, on paper, he was only head of state, like the Queen of England, he felt he should be above criticism not only at home but abroad. The *Time* story and other personal attacks rankled.

Apropos of Eisenhower's "warmongering," the Turk thought America based her foreign policy too much on arms, too little on economic construction. "I agree with you," I said, "but if you inquire what most underdeveloped countries want first you'll find it's arms." The President withheld his opinion.

After a while Sukarno summoned us to a barnlike structure on the grounds. Walking across the open space we passed under a mango tree. "My father planted this tree," he reminisced.

A young woman would perform some dances. In fanciful make-up, heavy brocade costume, and a peaked hat over a towering, complicated hairdo, she looked so different from the girl who had waited on the dinner table that Sukarno felt he had to identify her. Before she appeared he walked up to the dancing space to unscrew the electric bulb which was shining in the eyes of the small audience. As he resumed his front-row seat, the gamelan, or native Indonesian percussion orchestra, began playing behind a latticed wooden screen. He went forward again and got them to move so we would see them. In dance performances—as in politics—Sukarno is the stage manager and impresario.

In the first number the girl represented a young man unhappy in love. She moved from one part of the floor to the other, but the real story and artistic effect were conveyed by the small subtle movements of eyes, mouth, neck, arms, and particularly by delicate use of the hands; each twist, turn, and bend of each long-nailed finger carried a meaning which the connoisseur would understand.

In the second dance the girl was Bhima, the giant warrior hero of the Hindu epic *Mahabharata*. Sukarno whispered the literary significance as the dance unfolded it.

Breakfast the next day at 6:30 sharp. There was no bread or milk, but I found sustenance in several sweet little bananas and stimulation in coffee. "Did you sleep well?" I asked Sukarno.

"Five hours," he reported.

"For a young man like you that's enough," I said.

"An older man like you needs eight hours," he countered.

His neighbor at the breakfast table was a recent bride. I inquired whether marriages were arranged by parents as they frequently are in India. "No, our women are freer, and more active," he explained. "That is because Islam in Indonesia strengthens individualism."

Taking leave of his mother (she died later in the year), the President reposed his head in her lap for a moment, then he invited each one of us to bid her farewell.

Returning to Malang, the party drove in cars with security jeeps in front and behind. At one spot a group of women had congregated on the road to cheer the President. He stopped the procession, alighted, talked to the women, and peered into their market baskets. One woman held a knotted handkerchief. He took it from her, untied the knot, and counted the money in it.

"I see you gave it back," I remarked. Sukarno and his aides laughed.

It was a three-hour, nonstop flight by Convair from Malang over land and then over the sea to the port city of Makassar, at the southern tip of the Celebes. "Celebes," of unknown origin, probably Portuguese, and of unknown meaning, is now, and has been since the Japanese occupation,

"Sulawesi," the name by which this island shaped like a mythical monster, or a Chinese character, was known to the ancient Indonesians.

At the Makassar airport, Sukarno pulled the visored cap of the one Indonesian woman photographer down to her nose and greeted each of a bevy of beauties assembled to please his eye. Nevertheless, one immediately sensed tremendous tension. Machine gunners were posted on the field. Just outside the air terminal stood two Bren-gun warriors, their weapons ready. The whole length of the presidential procession was escorted by military motorcycles, and the number of jeeps filled with carbine-armed sharpshooters was greater than on the Java legs of the trip. At frequent intervals along the road tanks and Bren-gun carriers stood guard. Every twenty feet a soldier with rifle pointed out into the rice fields, back to the cars, maintained an alert stance, and between the soldiers there were civilian volunteers pointing bamboo spears in the same direction. Guards also watched on irrigation-ditch ridges. An artillery battery could be seen as we drove past a bend in the highway. Where the road cut through villages the womenfolk leaned against the high, thick bamboo-pole stilts on which their rickety wooden houses rested or sat on their haunches holding babies between their knees, and never made a sound or moved a muscle. The men peered furtively from crude windows above. Naked children with huge distended "rice bellies" gaped. The silence was sullen and depressing.

Suddenly the line of cars stopped and a moment later, looking out, we saw Sukarno standing in an open jeep. Adjutants waved to the Turk and me to come forward and ride in the President's limousine. We were in the city. The pavements were packed thick with beautiful boys and girls, bright brown faces beaming, white teeth gleaming, arms waving, throats cheering, shouting "Merdeka" (Freedom) and "Hidup" (Long Life). The sensitive Sukarno must have been pained by that gloomy dash from the airport through the unresponsive countryside, but the second he entered the city he felt the changed atmosphere and jumped from his car into the jeep, waved, smiled, reveled, and wanted the foreigner journalists to notice it. Crowds grew; adults joined the youthful demonstrators the closer we came to the Governor's palace.

While we milled around in the palace reception hall, the military members of our party disappeared and returned wearing paratroop boots with diagonal zippers inside. One of them read the question in my look and said, "We must be ready for anything. This is a battlefield."

Kahar Muzakar, who had made the Makassar area a battlefield, fought against the Dutch for Indonesian independence and was an army officer until 1952, when he turned against the Republic. The explanation of this reversal depends on the person who gives it: some attribute his defection

to Celebes separatism and power lust; others think of him as a sort of
tropical Robin Hood who, disillusioned with the Republic for not expro-
priating the feudal rajahs, landed aristocrats, and collaborators of the
Dutch, made himself the champion of the oppressed peasantry. Whatever
the motive or motives, Kahar Muzakar, all agreed, holds sway over a
considerable territory outside the city of Makassar, where the residents
either fear him or willingly support him. Occasionally he makes forays
into the city itself to kidnap a schoolteacher or engineer or gas station
mechanic, and if these victims, who are free provided they remain in his
domain, need anything for their comfort or work, he sends armed men
into Makassar to steal it. Apart from these minor incursions, however, the
city was safe and many moneyed people as well as ordinary peasants from
upcountry had come into Makassar, swelling the city's population from
400,000 to 600,000.

Lately, according to several informants, Kahar Muzakar had joined
forces with the Darul Islam, whose militant members conduct serious
guerrilla warfare in West Java, parts of Sumatra, and the Celebes against
the Republic which they consider secular and therefore repugnant; they
want a theocratic state in strict conformity with the Koran as interpreted
by the scholars of old and the contemporary mullahs or religious teachers.

Thus Kahar would represent the forward striving of the reformers and
the backward yearning of the obscurantists. Nothing in Indonesia is
simple or unilinear; everyone's politics combine two strains or three unconnected layers or four conflicting interests or five discordant principles.
Sukarno himself thinks he is attracted toward opposite poles. "If I analyze
my personality," he said in a public address in April, 1958, "it is indeed
true that my character is between two points." Born January 8, under the
zodiacal sign of Gemini, he was, "according to astrology," a two-in-one
figure. As an engineer, he told his audience, he leaned toward exact
values, as an artist he liked the indefinable. "In the political field," he continued, "I am a follower of Karl Marx, but, on the other hand, I am also
a religious man, so I can grasp the entire gamut between Marxism and
theism." He warmed to the theme. He was a "receptive person," he said.
"I know all trends and understand them." Perhaps because of "my Gemini
star I have made myself the meeting place of all trends and ideologies. I
have blended, blended, and blended them until finally they became the
present Sukarno."

To a monolithic Soviet Communist this would be heretical nonsense,
to a Western monist, single-tracked in religion, philosophy, and politics,
it sounds incongruous. But to Sukarno, child of a Hindu mother and
Moslem father who found a name for his son in the Hindu *Mahabharata,*
dualism is natural and pluralism congenial, and his listeners did not find

it strange that the President should have spoken of himself as a Marxist at a nationwide congress of teachers' training schools held to commemorate *Nuzulu Qur'an* (The Revelation of the Koran), and that after the address he prayed for twenty minutes at the grave of one of his ancestors who introduced Islam into the Indies by making tactful use, Sukarno noted, of the Hindu gamelan orchestra and wayang dance.

Sukarno, who had never been abroad until 1943, grew up in a colonial world in which imperialism was sin and all imperialists were capitalists. To his generation anti-imperialism equalled anticapitalism and hence Marxism. But Marxism is a materialistic dogma and a man who believes in Gemeni and horoscopes is not materialistic. Nor can an animistic Hindu-Moslem who melds ideologies be dogmatic. Life and heritage prevent Sukarno from toeing anybody's line, not even the dotted ones he himself chalks from time to time. Emotions, imagination, intuition, and personal motivation—not doctrine—rule his mind. Maybe Marxism, to Sukarno, is nothing more than another, earthly, form of astrology—a second method of prognostication.

The best key to Sukarno is love. He is the great lover. He loves his country, he loves women, he loves to talk about women, he loves himself. The Dutch hated and hate him and therefore could establish no inner contact with him. The approach to Sukarno is through the heart. His approach is via the senses. Consequently, he cannot divide society into classes of workers, peasants, employers. For Sukarno there are only two classes: those he likes fondly and those he doesn't like. His commitment is not to principle but to people, to people as individuals and to his people as a nation.

The Republican troops stationed in and around Makassar had been fighting Kahar Muzakar and the Darul Islam, and Sukarno went to review them, inspect their barracks, and express his warm appreciation to them in a speech on the parade ground. On the return trip to the Governor's Palace, where he was staying, Sukarno stopped at a slum inhabited by the families of noncommissioned officers. It had rained; the square on which the homes faced was covered with puddles and filled with women and children. One woman, highly pregnant, extended her hand to Sukarno. He clasped it, patted her abdomen, and congratulated her. "She's in the eighth month," he said to me.

"That's all right," I remarked, "but ask her how many she has."

"Five," he translated.

I moved my head in disapproval.

I followed him into a bamboo shack consisting of three cubicles with earthen floors. Only he, the Turk, I, an adjutant, and the woman of the house could squeeze into the tiny kitchen. Sukarno looked into the pot on the primus stove, opened a bag of rice, and touched the vegetables in a basket. In the bedroom he raised the lid of a trunk and one by one lifted the neatly folded cotton batiks and soft pressed shirts. "Ask her how many children she has," I prodded.

Sukarno spoke to her. "Eight," he said.

I made a glum grimace. "Ask her why she has so many."

"She says it is God's will," he interpreted, and laughed.

The next three-cubicle hut housed six children and two parents.

As we now picked our way through the crowd and the mud from hut to hut a running debate developed between us. "We could feed two hundred fifty million," he said. "My problem is to improve housing."

"How can you provide adequate housing for all these big families?" I questioned. "How can you take care of their health when you graduate only twenty physicians a year?"

"We will," he said firmly.

At the President's elbow stood a beautiful woman who had sat next to him in the Governor's Palace. I inquired how many children she had. "Three," she replied. "Two boys, eight and five years old, and a girl of two, and that's enough."

"You're my ideal Indonesian woman," I declared.

Sukarno burst into a sunny laugh.

A woman spoke to me in English and volunteered the information that she had four children and would want more but cannot afford it. "We're all tired," she added.

I led her over to the President and urged her to tell it to him. She did. He laughed and said, "Now we're going to visit a woman who has thirteen children."

I lowered my head and arms in a gesture of despair. Inside, we interrogated the mother of thirteen. She was thirty-five, looked fifty, had married at fifteen, and gives birth to a child almost every year. There they stood, bunched together, a nine-month infant in the arms of a daughter of thirteen, a boy of two astride the hip of a boy of ten. "They all look healthy," Sukarno commented. "She looks healthy," he said, indicating the woman.

"They do," I agreed, "but how do we know? And what is their life expectancy? What does her husband, Sergeant Kowais, earn?"

She supplied the information and admitted that life was hard.

I suggested we inspect the quarters. One small room was filled with a double bed. Five children slept in it, the mother told us. In the next diminutive room there was a bed for three children and a narrow single bed for "Father," the woman declared.

"That means," I calculated aloud, "that five children and the mother sleep on the floor."

Sukarno asked her whether it was true and she said, "Yes, but sometimes I sleep with Father."

"I must concentrate on housing," Sukarno muttered.

"And birth control," I amended.

We stepped into the living room, which could not have been more than ten feet by ten feet, and Sukarno sat down on a chair and announced he was hungry. Somebody went in search of food and brought a hand of baby bananas that were delicious. "We have forty varieties of bananas in Indonesia and they are all excellent," the President boasted.

I brought the conversation back to birth control. "Maybe," the Turk suggested, "the thirteen children are the lady's contribution to the Indonesian revolution."

"Nonsense," I retorted. "These people live their simple, private lives."

Sukarno had the good sense to say nothing.

"I love children. They are wonderful," I began. "All I contend is that a woman, especially a woman in this poverty, must, for the sake of her health and the child's, know how to get a respite of two or three years between births so she can recuperate. We call that spacing. All I advocate is spacing."

Sukarno nodded affirmatively, a suggestion, I hoped, of dawning comprehension, perhaps of partial agreement. "Don't write that I favor birth control," he cautioned.

"Of course not," I assured him. "I'll write that you are a conservative and oppose it."

"I'm a revolutionary," he protested. "I want my people to enjoy a better life."

"Then you must educate them to have smaller families," I stressed.

The bananas had not stilled his hunger, so he asked for rice, and a housewife standing in the doorway went to fetch a potful. When she returned he requested a spice, and a bottle of ketchuplike substance was produced by a neighbor. He invited us to join him, but we were content to watch.

Chapter Twenty

ISLE OF THE GODS

On the 90-minute flight from Makassar to Bali I talked with Sukarno about Russia, Marxism, Indonesian foreign policy, and Indonesian domestic difficulties. "This is all off the record," he said at the beginning and end of the interview.

Bali is beautiful.

The Turk, two Jakarta journalists, and I were assigned bungalows in a beach hotel outside Den Pasar, the capital of the island. The moment I unpacked I went into the soft, cuddly, warm sea below the surrounding peaks. I swam again at midnight before going to bed. At that time I became aware of fires along the shore, fires that moved, and wondered what they might be until they came close and I discovered that they were burning bundles of palm fronds held by fishermen to draw fish to the surface.

Sukarno was living up in the mountains at a new government luxury guesthouse in Tampaksiring and we traveled there and back twice a day by car. On those trips of some 25 miles each way we passed from jungle to museum to rice field to villa. When the sun shines in Bali, and that is almost always, each flooded rice field becomes a golden mirror with its shimmering face to the blue sky; hundreds of them, as far as the eye can see, reach up, step by step, to the summits of the terraced hills. In the mirror a near-naked peasant, conical sunshade on his head, thigh-deep in black mud, guides a wooden plow drawn by two fawn-colored cows or one stupid-looking water buffalo. Most of the peasants are poor sharecroppers, gouged by landlords who sometimes take 75 per cent of the harvest and live in good houses close to the hovels of their servants. Bali is a small island, 2,000 square miles, about the size of Delaware, and its population, now two million, has doubled since 1940. Income from tourists and the sale of handicrafts does not make good the resultant drop in living standards.

But, though poverty is always poverty, though a half-empty stomach grumbles no matter what, Bali poverty seems to be gilded poverty, poverty at least partially anesthetized by an appreciation of the pervading beauty of a life literally out of this world and out of this age. A procession of some twenty men carrying curved poles two stories high surmounted by heraldic banners, and several hundred young women in single file, all of exquisite mien and gloriously thin figures, one group in pink blouses and ornate batiks, the second in purple, the third in green, the fourth in gold, all wearing small basketlike hats filled with fruits which will be deposited at the feet of a Hindu temple god, somehow lift human beings out of the rice-field mud, out of the pinched larder, into a realm where color, music, dances, games, and a daily coexistence with otherworldly creatures give additional dimension and a new value to life. If Moscow is drab, Bali is diadems. This aspect of Bali is museum for the outsider, living truth for the native.

Bali erects temples in the rice fields, in homes, on the road. The temples are Hindu but they are guarded by animist gnomes representing spirits which must be fed, and if the ubiquitous dogs eat the food set out in plates for the spirits, then they are the spirits and must not be chased away.

Spirits are everywhere; mostly they are ancestor spirits. Miguel Covarrubias, the late Mexican painter who spent a long time on Bali and wrote a big, scholarly, artistic book called *Island of Bali,* says, "The Balinese live with their forefathers in a great family of the dead." This sounds gruesome. Actually it robs death of terror and thereby makes life happier.

"Strange as it may seem," Covarrubias asserts, "it is in their cremation ceremonies that the Balinese have their greatest fun. A cremation is an occasion for gaiety and not for mourning, since it represents the accomplishment of this duty: the ceremonial burning of the corpse of the dead to liberate their souls so that they can attain the highest worlds and be free for reincarnation into better beings." Life with such dead is a holiday.

Hinduism means castes and there are castes in Bali. But the Balinese make life easy for themselves nevertheless. They eat beef and pork. In India, Hindu widows must not remarry; in Bali they do. Divorce is readily obtainable for women and men. Covarrubias (and other researchers) found that "the Balinese are naturally polygamous and it is common for men to have lovers and for women to take the extramarital relations of their husbands as natural." But female infidelity is considered a heinous crime. Men may have two wives, and if, as happens often, the first wife chooses the second, the relations between them are cordial. Second marriages, after the first wife has ceased to be childbearing, is one reason for the high birth rate.

Girls marry young—at sixteen or less. Foreigners romanticize about Bali, but the Bali approach to love is unmistakably carnal. A man's "direct solicitation," writes Covarrubias, "constitutes his declaration of love." All he says is, "Do you want?" The moon plays no part.

In this paradise of simplicity, marriage is by elopement. The method is sanctioned by tradition and rooted in the mores of the people. When a young Balinese decides that he has found his lady-love and wishes to marry, he does not ask her parents' permission, he runs away with her in the evening. He must not elope during the day. If he does he will be apprehended, arrested, tried, and imprisoned or fined. For daytime elopement might be kidnaping against the girl's will. The would-be husband could take her for a walk and carry her off despite her protests. But if she goes out with him after dark she knows what his intentions are. This signifies her readiness to marry.

The eloping bride is expected by Balinese conventions to take with her on her nuptial night a basket in which she has carefully folded an extra sarong, blouse, and scarf. When her parents note her nocturnal absence they look among her things and, on discovering that some are missing, know she is getting married.

The eloping couple spend their first night at the home of a friend. Custom requires any Balinese household to welcome a first-night bride and groom whether they know them or not. Usually, however, the elopers go to the home of an acquaintance, often a member of the same clan.

The groom must not take his bride on that first night to his parents' home. That would amount to a conspiracy between the young man and his family against the girl's parents. As she is leaving home, so must he.

On arriving at the house of their friend, the elopers send a messenger or, according to general practice, three messengers, to the girl's parents. Without revealing the whereabouts of the couple, they inform the girl's family that she is getting married of her own free will.

The newlyweds stay in hiding for three or four days. Then they present themselves to the bride's parents, who are expected to approve. The bride may be fourteen or fifteen, but it is too late for papa or mama to say no. Love on Bali brooks no opposition. The marriage having been consummated, the two families spread a wedding feast featured by singing and by those famous Balinese dances that combine delicate art and slapstick fun.

If Balinese fathers negotiate a marriage in advance and then inform their children, the young folks feel cheated of the adventure that is rightfully theirs. Marriage by elopement has resisted all modern pressures, and I was told that it is the preferred method of intellectuals, the rich, and the common folk.

Jungle, sun, sea, mountains, lush vegetation, freedom, and maybe, too, the nonfear of death, make for human beauty, and statistics, were they possible, would probably show more handsome men and delectable females per thousand on Bali than in most parts of the globe. Love on Bali finds an additional fomenter in the paucity of clothing inevitable in the tropics. Traditionally, Balinese women are bare above the waist. But foreign tourists have stared so much at Bali breasts and photographed so many, sometimes with white men in the pose of holding them, that the government now looks askance at uncovered bosoms, and not a few of those one still sees would benefit from brassières anyway.

Driving up from Den Pasar to Tampaksiring twice a day we stopped in temples, visited villages, photographed processions, and bought Bali wood carvings, hand-stamped and hand-painted batiks, and gruesome-looking wayang masks. We ate sometimes in the seaside hotel, sometimes in the guesthouse with the President. Covarrubias reported that he, a Mexican "raised on chilipeppers," would "cry and break out in beads of perspiration" when he ate spiced Bali food. I never touched it. Sukarno said I worried him, I wasn't eating enough. "Don't be troubled," I reassured him. "In 1942 I spent a week with Gandhi and the food was awful, but he let me look into his mind and I learned to love him."

"How is it," Sukarno asked, "that you who believe in Gandhi preach birth control?"

"Gandhi taught birth control by will control, but only the select can be celibate. I never," I explained, "accepted all of Gandhism. I consider family planning and limitation a practical urgent necessity, above all in a poor country like Indonesia—and India."

"I object to it because it conduces to moral laxity," he stated. "During my American tour I did what you have seen me do here at home: I looked closely at things, I asked women university students to open their handbags for me, and what did I see but foam tablets and rubber."

"Maybe," I said. "But this is the way people are made, and if they could not have contraceptives they would have babies. There are too many babies in Indonesia, and they weight you down economically. It shortens lives." I again put in a plea for spacing. This time he accepted it. (A physician told me weeks later that Sukarno's wife had been warned by her doctor after the delivery of her second child not to have another for three years.

"This," the physician suggested, "might explain the President's receptivity to spacing.")

Sukarno, quite debonair and without a visible care, was attending to serious business on the tour. A rebel government had been set up in Central Sumatra and another revolt raged in North Celebes (in addition to the guerrilla warfare around Makassar). These movements challenged the Republic; if they spread they would imperil it. The army in Java and Bali might have to be dispatched to cope with the insurgents. But army commanders, army officers, and even army units are as individualistically incalculable as most Indonesians. They like to make their own rules and do not always obey government orders. At every stop on this trip, therefore, Sukarno addressed meetings of army officers in intimate assembly halls and of noncommissioned officers on parade grounds with a view to reinforcing their loyalty by explaining to them what was at stake. Crucial in their attitude was his own popularity as leader.

Oratory is Sukarno's finest weapon. He infuses his speech with a delicately balanced proportion of dignity and folksiness, gravity and humor, artistry and showmanship, self-confidence, faith in the listener, censure of foreign nations, pride in Indonesia, easily digested generalizations, and specific calls to action. He told me he always speaks extemporaneously— except on August 17, when he makes the annual Independence Day Report to the Nation.

By the time we reached Bali I had heard him speak five or six times. It was never the same speech but the main argument did not vary, and, guided by the running translations which adjutants and Jakarta journalists had whispered into my ear and by the English words and phrases he liked to slip in, I could get the drift of what he was saying.

The meeting hall in Tampaksiring is a three-walled, roofed building open on one side to feed the eye with a large, breath-taking vista of nature's glory. Sukarno, in bush shirt with short sleeves, dark glasses, and the traditional Indonesian black-velveteen skullcap which fits down to the ears, sat facing the audience with several Balinese notables on either side. The first six rows of chairs were occupied by women who might have qualified for a beauty contest from sixty cities. Each wore the national costume: a form-hugging blouse, or kabaya, extending several inches below the waist; a tight, waist-to-ankle, hand-painted batik kain, or wrap-around, the ends of which are not sewn together; a gauzy scarf on the shoulders; and colored sandals on stockingless feet. The hair is pulled straight back with, perhaps, a coquettish curl on the forehead and a bun above the neck. The bun is a must and is purchased if it cannot be grown. This forward area was a painter's delight; the kabayas in all the hues of the rainbow and white; the kains repeating an endless yellow or blue or light-brown design on a darker brown base; the brilliant scarves; the jet-black hair; the smiling brown faces; the pearly-white teeth. They would have inspired any speaker, and particularly Sukarno, the lover, to his best effort. Behind the women were twenty-five rows of officers in tropical-green uniforms.

I was in the front row, a thorn among the ladies. Sukarno, sitting a few feet away on the other side of a low table, said to me, pointing, "See that woman on the chair before the last in your row? She is the mother of thirteen children." I gasped in wonder; she looked so young and beautiful. "This question on birth control seems to bother you more than it does me," I retorted. "I'd like to end the debate with one last word: in 1922 Margaret Sanger, the world champion of family planning, had difficulty entering Japan and was not permitted to lecture. In 1937 she returned to Japan and prophesied war if they did not curb their population. In 1952, after Japan had experienced three decades of imperialism and international strife not unconnected with her excess population, I saw Mrs. Sanger in Tokyo riding a sound-truck through the city streets shouting birth-control slogans." He asked the nearby women whether they wanted birth control and they shook their heads in the negative.

When he was ready, Sukarno rose, walked up the three steps of a small wooden rostrum, gazed intently at the audience, took out his white folded handkerchief, wiped his palms, returned it to his back pocket, uttered the words, "Ladies and Gentlemen," in a slow, low baritone, and began his speech while adjusting the three microphones (one an amplifier, the second attached to a tape recorder outside, the third connected with a local radio station). The tempo was deliberate, hesitant, as though he were groping for expressions. Now the pace quickens. He mentions India, Ceylon, Syria, Egypt. They are "nonaligned." He speaks the word in English, and adds, in English, "We are not sitting on the fence." "As between colonialism and Asians," he continues in Indonesian, "there can be no neutralism." He quotes George Washington's Farewell Address in support of Indonesian nonalignment. Every country has its own personality. "America is a state of mind." Her personality is embodied in the words " 'Life, liberty, and the pursuit of happiness.' We do not wish to pursue happiness. We wish to have and hold it." India has her own personality. It is "re-lig-i-os-ity." He pronounces it in English, syllable by syllable. He quotes Mahatma Gandhi. Italy too has her individuality: "Artisticity." Italians appreciate beauty in nature, in paintings, in women. When a beautiful woman passes, Italians whistle at her; and here he wet his lips, contracted them, and gave a wolf whistle, "hwit-hoo." He did not like the first result and tried again: "hwit-hoo." The hall rocked with laughter. When he was in Japan recently the press wrote that "President

Sukarno looks worried," but his motto was, in English, "Keep smiling." (More laughter from the audience.) Indonesia's personality expressed itself in joy, in the joy of new nationhood. "We are one, one in diversity, and let no outsiders seek to divide us. Indonesians never shall be slaves." Now he launched into an analysis of the Central Sumatran uprising whose headquarters was at Padang. "The Padang rebels advertise their anti-Communism, in the hope of receiving foreign support. They call themselves patriots. They are betraying the Republic. They aim to erase the achievement of August 17, 1945. Beware. The Dutch are still not far away, in West Irian," and he extended his arm to the east. "The rebels would break up the nation in the name of anti-Communism, then set up a dictatorship. If anti-Communism breeds dictatorship, how does it differ from Communism? I prefer democracy. [Applause] But democracy with social justice, not capitalism with exploitation." And so on. He held the audience in the palm of his hand, now increasing the tension, now melting it into laughter. He spoke for an hour and thirty-five minutes. Not a chair creaked. The women and men accorded him an ovation. His face beamed. He wiped his face and neck with the folded handkerchief.

"Have you ever heard a President whistle from the platform?" he said to me as he sat down.

"No, I haven't," I concurred. "That's a wolf whistle, a wolf trying to snare a lamb."

"I know," he said, and winked.

Presently the rain descended in torrents and the audience could not leave. Conversation hummed. Sukarno looked around, raised a finger for silence, and called on a man to sing. "He used to be a professional singer," Sukarno announced to those sitting near. The man took the rostrum, but before he sang he talked and it must have been hilariously funny, for every sentence evoked a gale of laughter. "Oh," Sukarno moaned, holding his sides and wiping away his tears. Now the President summoned the son of the man to the rostrum. "He's the father of the thirteen," Sukarno explained. He too joked, to the enjoyment of all, and then sang. The rain had not yet relented, so Sukarno invited a young woman to the platform. Laughter-making must be a Balinese gift; she likewise brought cheer with her introductory remarks and cheers for her songs. Sukarno's eyes were scanning the rows for more performers when the sun broke through and the meeting was adjourned.

Later that day we gathered to witness a performance of Bali dances. The government guesthouse where Sukarno stayed is built above a sacred pool in which only women bathe in as much or as little clothing as they choose. "Why don't you go for a swim?" I suggested to the President.

"I never learned to swim," he replied.

I failed to ask how it happened that a boy and a man who spent his life in these sea-girt emerald islands crisscrossed by rivers and dotted by ponds should not have mastered the simple skill of swimming. It may or may not be significant.

The first two dances were by young girls, scarcely nubile, said to be the best on Bali. They wore extremely heavy brocade costumes and trains which they kept kicking behind them. The action was of the body, neck, limbs, and fingers; their baby-faces remained immobile. Next, comedy entered. Men with stuffed clothing to give them outsize proportions and wearing fantastic masks, beards (in a beardless country), and lions' manes and wielding swords and daggers dueled, wrestled, and chased one another over the dance floor and outside the large tent where the performance was taking place. Guests within and uninvited spectators who ringed the marquee roared with laughter. Urchins inched into the tent and nestled at Sukarno's feet. There was no security.

During breakfast the next day Sukarno said to me, "You talked with Mrs. Oka."

Mrs. G. Bagoes Oka is the wife of the Deputy Governor of Bali. "Yes," I remarked. "I had a letter of introduction to her from Mrs. Mary Lord, of the United States Delegation to the United Nations."

"I know Mary Lord," the President said. "She's an idealist."

"Yes," I agreed.

"Mrs. Oka did not see eye to eye with you on birth control," Sukarno said.

"I met Mrs. Oka with her husband," I declared. "Mr. Oka informed me that the population of Bali had doubled in the past eighteen years. What will you do if it doubles again in the next eighteen years? On this Isle of the Gods there will soon be no room for human beings. According to Mr. Oka, Bali has only twelve physicians."

"We are encouraging transmigration," the President asserted.

"Mr. Oka," I replied, "told me that ten thousand had emigrated from Bali to the outer islands in the past three or four years. That's a drop in the sea. Raffles wrote that attachment to the tombs of ancestors kept people here from emigrating."

"What did Mrs. Oka say about spacing?" the President inquired.

"She sees the necessity of it," I replied.

"So do I," he affirmed, "but our people are unspoiled and we don't want them spoiled. Birth control in the West has conduced to loose morals. It introduces an element of fear which dilutes life's great pleasure."

"Without it the fear is greater," I suggested. "But you have agreed to spacing, and to space the woman must know how. That's my only contention."

"Even if we encourage family planning the economic problems remain," the President said.

This is a tragic truth. Neither in Indonesia, nor in India, nor in China, nor anywhere in the overpopulated countries of Asia, except perhaps Japan, could birth control, even if propagated with all the means at the disposal of governments, quickly flatten the rising population curve. It will take years, twenty-five years—unless a cheap, effective, harmless oral contraceptive is developed—before family planning takes effect. This is Asia's greatest dilemma and greatest danger, for overpopulation is an economic problem and therefore a supreme political problem. Nobody has the answer. No ism supplies the answer.

But Bali throws a soothing blanket of beauty over any feeling of crisis and tragedy. Bali beauty transcends natural beauty. Nature offers beautiful sights in many places. But in Bali natural beauty, unsullied by industry and the few easily overlooked towns, has created a cult of beauty which unites man with nature in a loving embrace. Here beauty is reality, all else transient illusion.

Chapter Twenty-one

THE RED AND THE GOLD

"I'm ONE of the few Indonesians with hair on his chest," a member of Sukarno's party said to me on the flight from Bali to Surabaya.

Later I changed my seat and talked with a presidential adjutant. "In a southern state of the United States," he declared, "the waiter refused me food. 'Only white men are served here,' he said. That was after I told him I was an Indonesian."

"The waiter probably never heard of Indonesia," I suggested. But my words were neither relevant nor comforting. We must remember, I thought, that brown skin is thin skin.

"Your embassy should give us weapons," the same adjutant urged. "Otherwise we will be forced to turn to the Soviets."

High above the Java jungle Major Sudarto, the President's personal aide, and I sang "Die Lorelei," and he rendered a solo medley of American, British and French folk tunes. He had never been outside Asia and ardently wished to visit the United States. "Russia?" I asked.

"No," he replied, "I want to study in an American military academy."

Surabaya is Indonesia's naval base, and the sailors paraded past Sukarno. For a reason that is opaque to me, sailors seem to march better than soldiers. I often had that impression in Moscow's Red Square and it was confirmed in Surabaya.

Sukarno spoke to the assembled defense forces on the parade ground.

I listened leaning against a wall with an Indonesian. "I am very fond of the President," he volunteered, "but . . ."

I waited. He remained silent, then indicated that he wanted to hear the address.

We had taken off from Bali at 7:50 A.M. and arrived in Surabaya at 9 A.M. We took off from Surabaya at noon and landed at Bandung two hours and fifteen minutes later; most of us slept.

They call Bandung "The Jewel of Java."

It boasts wide thoroughfares, parks, giant waringin trees, fine shops, cafés, no mosquito-breeding canals like Jakarta's, and—most important—altitude: 3,000 feet above sea level. This means less heat and less dampness than in low-lying Jakarta.

"Bandung should be the capital of Indonesia," I said to an army officer.

"It should be," he agreed, "but it can't." He paused, pondered, and proceeded: "Too many Darul Islam elements in this area," he explained. The city itself is safe from these guerrillas, who want a religious state as opposed to the Sukarno-secular state. But they harass the region. After almost a decade of military effort to crush them they are still vigorous, troublesome, and elusive.

The evening of our arrival I walked in the city. Cinemas were exhibiting American films with Spencer Tracy, Katharine Hepburn, Loretta Young, and so forth. Loud music drew me to a café. The owners were Chinese, the ice-cream-eating customers predominantly Indonesian with a few Chinese couples interspersed. A band of five young Indonesians played rock 'n' roll and sang the English words. But in deference to Moslem sensibilities, rock 'n' roll dancing is forbidden.

The next day was Sunday and our program called for Sukarno's appearance at a morning mass meeting. The official radio reported an audience of half a million in the meadow; I estimated 50,000 to 60,000. Swallows circled the tiered grandstand from which a trestled wooden bridge extended out some twenty yards to a speakers' platform. First, Mrs. Rasuna Said of Sumatra spoke and she emphasized that she was "a nationalist Moslem." Her seat was next to Sukarno's and mine was next to hers, so I could observe him closely during her address. His eyes were shut and his hands were folded in front of his chest; his lips moved. Perhaps he prayed. I had not seen him so intense. Then she made a slip of the tongue and gave August 17, 1975, instead of August 17, 1945, as the date of Indonesia's independence; a loud friendly laugh broke from the crowd, and Sukarno laughed and became his relaxed self again.

Sukarno told the audience that he was a Moslem *and* a nationalist. Apparently he, like Mrs. Said, felt Islam had to be stressed in Bandung.

But Sukarno underlined his nationalism more. He had seen the United States, he said, the Soviet Union, China, Canada, Central Asia, and Japan. No country was so beautiful, none so fertile as Indonesia, his best beloved. (He sent for his sun glasses.) The Republic came into existence on August 17, 1945, when imperialism was weakest; Dutch imperialism had been defeated by the Japanese and Japanese imperialism by the Allies. It could not have been born in the thirties, or at any other time. He had warned Holland in the late 1920's that if war came Indonesian independence would follow. For this he was arrested, right here in Bandung where he studied engineering.

One cannot just proclaim independence, Sukarno continued; nationalism requires certain conditions. The first condition is territory. "We have a big, rich country"—10,000 islands—"the most broken-up nation in the world," he quoted somebody as having called it.

People—the second condition of nationhood—can transform division into cohesion. In the 1920's he had proclaimed the slogan, "One nation, one flag, one language." This must become a living reality. "I am not Javanese or Sumatran, I am Indonesian." If one island has more it should give to that which has less. "I am teaching you like a father, like an older brother." We have territory, we need unity.

(The main grievance of the Padang rebels: Sumatran oil, rubber, pepper, tin, tobacco, etc., earned over 70 per cent of Indonesia's foreign trade income; Jakarta took all and doled out stepchild pittances to Sumatra. This just complaint aggravated the friction arising from geographic insularity and minor racial and religious differences between Java and Sumatra.)

The third condition of nationhood is one central government. "Not two governments, not three governments, but one!" Sukarno cried. Part of Indonesian territory, and some of Indonesia's people, were still under Dutch rule in West Irian (New Guinea). All must be united. The Padang rebels had set up a government in Central Sumatra. "They are traitors. They are not only against the central government, they are against you, against the soul of Indonesia."

I watched the audience while Sukarno was speaking, and my notes are interspersed with such parentheses as: People are beginning to leave . . . Inattention on the fringes of the crowd . . .

"The people can win against a thousand imperialisms," he continued, "if they are united under a single government." Indonesia's purpose is freedom from oppression. Social justice, not a capitalist state, is the goal. "I did not invent the principles on which our country is founded. I got them out of the soil and stones of our beautiful land."

But, Sukarno said, the Padang rebels are antidemocratic; their pockets are full of the people's money; they are spending it in night clubs; they are buying arms abroad to use against us; they want Indonesia to join one of the two great power blocs. "We must help keep the world from dividing into two antagonistic camps. Indonesia is not neutral; we are free and nonaligned. We are not sitting on the fence. We are opposed to colonialism whether it is in West Irian or Algeria or the Middle East." He praised Tito, Nehru, and Nasser. "We must be strong. To be strong we must work harder. Abroad recently, I was ashamed because Indonesia has been divided by traitors. We have had seventeen cabinets in twelve years. We have too many political parties. Our need is unity, unity, again unity."

He looked at his watch. "I have been speaking to you for forty-five minutes," Sukarno declared. "I can't believe it is so long. Let us sing 'Indonesia Raya.'" He conducted the singing, turning now to the grandstand, now to the right, now to the left, motioning with his arms for more volume. "No," he exclaimed, "that was not good enough," and he asked for a repeat performance. The singing improved.

Sukarno is a verbal virtuoso, an actor, and also a reactor. He senses his audience, and he could not help feeling that it was not with him. Sukarno is at his best in an environment of fondness and friendship. He closes up when he has to combat coldness. Sometimes, to be sure, he cannot distinguish between flattery and friendliness. He yearns so much for warmth that he may mistake sham for the true article. At the Bandung mass meeting the listener temperature was too low to be misinterpreted. The quality of the President's speech suffered.

When we returned to the Governor's palace there was the usual pause for coffee, cold citrus drinks, and cakes served by gaily adorned ladies. Sukarno sat alone on a sofa. I felt a compulsion to give him my impression of his speech—perhaps because I was sure nobody else would. I approached him and he beckoned me to sit down. "It must be difficult to rule a country like this," I began.

"Why do you say that?" he inquired.

"I thought the crowd did not respond to you this morning."

"I believe you are mistaken," Sukarno replied.

"I'm glad," I said, "but I had the impression that you did not lift the audience today. While you spoke people milled about and some left."

"No," he insisted, "my impression was different."

I had not expected him to agree. He changed the subject and we chatted amiably about his student life in Bandung.

Any person who has ever made a speech knows how painful it is to be told that one's effort has been unsuccessful. When we enplaned at Bandung for Jakarta on the last lap of the six-day journey I wondered whether his hurt vanity would spoil our relations. But as we reached cruising altitude Sukarno came over to my seat and asked how I liked "Indonesia Raya," the national anthem. I said I liked it very much, it had a lilt.

Sukarno turned to Major Sudarto and they began singing it. The Turk and several Indonesians joined. Then we all stood and sang the "Marseillaise." Below us the green carpet of Java unrolled.

"Now let's tease Louis," Sukarno suggested, "let's sing the 'International.'"

I smiled and said, "That's all right with me, but you know the Soviets have substituted a new nationalist hymn for it." They sang it; and I sang the Russian words.

"The State Department is going to cancel your passport," somebody joked.

I drew the green passport from my trouser pocket and figuratively ripped it in two. They laughed. "I sing what I please," I said.

Sukarno sat down on the arm of my seat and suggested we sing the Nazi "Horst Wessel Lied." "*Nieder!*" I exclaimed, and pointed thumbs down. He sang the first verse alone, rendering it in perfect German. The airplane concert concluded with a repetition of the "Marseillaise."

The President was in a contagiously buoyant mood. He apparently did not find it difficult to rule Indonesia. And he was not one to hide his feelings. He wore them on his short sleeves.

What with the ritual at the Jakarta airport on Sukarno's return to the capital, the drive to the government guesthouse, where most of the foreign journalists lived, and finding transportation to go into the center of town, I barely made the Presidential Palace in time.

Merdeka (Independence) Palace, formerly the Dutch Governor General's residence, is a huge, gleaming white rectangular structure fronted with fat white columns and deep porticoes. The porticoes were ablaze with color, for several score of most handsome young men and women, each in the brilliant and very different costume of his or her island or part of an island, had been assembled to illustrate the "Unity in Diversity" motto on Indonesia's official seal. When the parade started they formed a compact, picturesque group on the steps of the palace. Sukarno stood on the top step and shouted greetings through a microphone to the marchers as they passed. From time to time he sank into a chair. The sun glowed hot. It did not seem to diminish the vigor of the demonstrators. Each group had its favorite physical exhibition; as it came into view its members yelled slogans, shook their fists, sang, cavorted, danced, jumped, or cheered, or indulged in a combination of several of these. They carried banners, the red-and-white flag of Indonesia, but, more frequently, the red flag of Red China, the flag of the Soviet Union, red cloths marked with the sickle and the hammer, the red standards of the SOBSI trade unions, of the Communist Youth, of the Veterans (who wore red ties), and of the pro-Communist women's units (some in red skirts). On their red transparencies were written curses on the Western imperialists, American interventionists, SEATO, NATO, and the Central Sumatran rebels. This was a Communist manifestation against those insurgents, and the multitude mingled their throaty imprecations against the alleged foreign allies of the rebels with roars of "Bung Karno," "Long Live President Sukarno," and "Merdeka."

A few hours later, when the white Merdeka Palace was silhouetted against the black evening sky, the President entertained inside. Men in Western suits and black skullcaps and women in rich native dress filled the grand hall hung with huge crystal chandeliers. Sukarno, wearing a dove-blue marshal's uniform and black cap, stage-managed as usual: he first conferred with the director of the wayang, then he sent a senior officer to instruct the gamelan orchestra. The dances ranged from the funny fantastic to the classic.

On the wall behind the dancers was a map of Indonesia in gold (probably gold-plated tin) with nearby Malaya and the Philippines in outline. Superimposed on the United States, the Indies archipelago would reach from Oregon to North Carolina.

During the performance, barefoot waiters in white jackets and trousers served soft drinks and small packets of Java sweets wrapped in paper. Four of Sukarno's five children by Fatmawati occupied chairs in the third row. Sukarno refused, as was his right under Moslem law, to grant Fatmawati's request for a divorce when he married the young, beautiful Hartini, mother of his two youngest children. Many high-class Indonesian women, including the wife of at least one Cabinet minister, not only sympathized with Fatmawati, they refused to meet Hartini and sent letters to the ladies of the diplomatic corps in Jakarta to join them in the boycott. But no ambassador would miss an opportunity to entertain or be entertained by the President and the First Lady, so the attempted ostracism did not prevail.

The wayang, as usual, lasted far into the night and glued the delighted Indonesians to their chairs. I went home early thinking of the contrast between the plebs who marched in the afternoon and the gay upper-class gala of the evening. By usurping, or seeming to usurp, the streets, the Reds menaced the palace. All over the world the Communists were losing their intellectuals but recruiting asphalt trampers whose yells interfered with thought.

Chapter Twenty-two

SUKARNO AND THE COMMUNISTS

DIPA NUSANTARA AIDIT, secretary general of the Partai Kommunis Indonesia (PKI), is a square-set, flat-headed, black-haired young man born in 1923. I saw him once only at a lecture by Sukarno in Merdeka Palace. I never talked with him because he refuses to talk to non-Communist journalists. An interview with Aidit means submitting written questions and receiving written answers which he publishes in the Communist press. This affords the correspondent no opportunity of meeting him, sizing him up, or answering back. It enables the number one Communist of Indonesia to give long propaganda replies to brief inquiries and to show how cleverly he wards off foreign probings. Stalin and Khrushchev often did the same. In fact, Stalin used to interview himself and print the strange colloquy-soliloquy in the world's Communist newspapers. Non-Communist newspapers copied the contents.

However, what Aidit wants outsiders to know about his views and policies is communicated through published speeches. His July, 1956, report to the Politburo of the PKI declared that the party supports the "progressive" Cabinet of Prime Minister Dr. Ali Sastroamijojo and would like to participate in it. There was much to do. "The Indonesian economy has remained under the control, in particular, of Dutch capitalists" and "the condition of the majority of the Indonesian people continues as miserable as ever . . . the majority of the peasants are still without land and suffering under the exploitation of landlords . . ."

What did he advocate? "The PKI," he said, "does not demand the

173

seizure of lands belonging to the landlords and the division of those lands among the peasants. The policy of the PKI with regard to land is a reduction of rent."

What was his attitude to capitalists? "In the present stage of development, at least," Aidit stated, "the Communists do not regard nationalist capitalists as a danger. We not only do not oppose them, we even join with them in demanding that the government protect their economic interests . . . [so that they may] compete with foreign capitalists. . . . Indonesia's poverty has not been caused by national capitalism, but rather by the lack of national capital and the abundance of foreign capital. . . ."

The Moscowman was knocking twice: he bade Dr. Ali entrust several ministries to the Communist party. He reassured the landlords and capitalists that a government with Communist participation would do them no harm. What, other than unprincipled opportunism, was communistic about any of this?

On the other hand, Aidit fiercely denounced Indonesian leaders who barred his way to power. He linked "Hitler to Hatta to Sukiman." Hatta, he alleged, "wants to liquidate the Parliament chosen by the people." (Hatta's real crime was that as prime minister, in May, 1948, he rejected Moscow's offer to establish relations with Indonesia, and in September, 1948, he smashed the Madiun Red revolt.) Sukiman, the head of the Moslem Masjumi party, had, as prime minister, in 1951, ordered the arrest of several top Communists. Aidit would have forgiven them the past if they remained blind to the Communist fig-leaf camouflage of the present. But Hatta and Sukiman persisted in resisting the PKI's bid to enter the government.

At the sixth plenum of the PKI's Central Committee in April, 1958, the same Aidit, with Cold War black-and-white bluntness, assailed the West and praised the Soviets: U.S. imperialism ravaged Europe. A recession with millions of unemployed made America economically unreliable. Russian economy was blooming. Indonesia should therefore expand trade with Communist countries. Indonesia must avoid replacing Dutch investments with American, Japanese, and German investors; that would be like "driving a tiger away from the front door and letting a lion in through the back." A moment later the tiger was "the Dutch dwarf, arch enemy of the Indonesian people," egged on by the U.S.A. "The tradition of Indonesian foreign policy," Aidit suggested wishfully, "is not oriented to the West but to the East."

Turning to internal politics, Aidit demonstrably distorted truth in saying, "Hatta is on the side of the rebels." The widespread demand for a Sukarno-Hatta duumvirate to rule the country he called "demagogy." Hatta was anti-Communist, Aidit explained, because the Communists were anti-God, but "the question of believing or not believing in God is a personal matter." He charged Hatta again, as well as Sjahrir, with preventing the PKI's admission into the government. To be anti-Communist, he said, was to be antinationalist and antidemocratic. Suppose the Communists won a majority of the votes; would they still be kept out of office? Nasser was anti-imperialist, and that suited Aidit fine, but he sinned in suppressing Egypt's political parties. (Moscow was of course without sin in this regard.)

Aidit concentrated not on economic reform or social changes; he revealed the party's power lust. The ascent to power was carpeted with nationalism. He outnationalisted the nationalists. Dutch business must go. The Padang rebels, agents of Western, particularly American, imperialism, must be suppressed. West Irian must be wrested from Holland.

In the September-October, 1955, elections for Parliament, the total vote, cast for 29 parties, was 37,785,299. Of these, the PKI received 6,176,914 votes—more than 5 million in Java—which entitled them to 39 seats in a Parliament of 257. But in the regional elections in 1957 and 1958 the PKI electoral following grew by more than a million. In April, 1958, Aidit estimated that the party could now muster 8,264,300 votes. "Within approximately two years," he prophesied plausibly, "the PKI, which used to be fourth in strength, will be the number one party in Indonesia."

So much for Aidit's speeches. Communists, however, receive special elocution lessons in talking simultaneously out of both corners of their mouths. While Aidit said the party did not ask land redistribution, Communist electioneering in 1955 stressed it and Red orators in villages promised land to all who gave their ballots to the PKI. While Aidit emphasized the party's readiness to collaborate with bourgeois parties in the government, election propaganda condemned all other parties and glorified the PKI as the only "party of the poor."

"Why did you vote Communist?" I asked a peasant who admitted having done so.

"Because the Communists promise us a better life."

"And you?"

"They love this country," another villager replied.

The Communist vote-catching talent in Asia and perhaps Africa was born with the newly independent states. The day Burma became free, Rangoon rocked with festivities which included a *Zst Pwe* play whose final scene showed the people filling their pockets from a shower of gold and silver rain. The play was not the thing. Gandhi and Nehru realistically refused to paint a paradise on earth beyond Britain's exit door. But no matter. The eagerly sought elimination of a foreign government depicted as the source of evil was bound to arouse rosy hopes. When the expected gold and silver rain failed to follow freedom the Communists planted their seed in the soil of disenchantment.

No country is like another. Beautiful, bountiful nature and man's relaxed nature make the urge to material improvement less insistent in Indonesia than in India. On the other hand, by resisting the Sukarno-Hatta Republic for three and a half years and retaining West Irian, or New Guinea, Holland fomented Indonesian nationalism, the towering public emotion of the new state. The Communists, therefore, act like champions of the national interest. They give the impression of subordinating Communist economic and social goals to it. In India, Nehru has torn the nationalist mask from the Communist party. For years he was neutral toward it. But as their power waxed and their tactics grew more irksome he attacked them. The Indian Communist party, he said, "leans on, depends on, and looks to a foreign country." The Communist flag is a foreign flag, he declared. "The thinking apparatus of the Communist party of India lies outside this country. . . . Their body is in India but their mind is somewhere else." "They have been posing as if they were Russians." They were posing, he might have added, as if they were Indians. In a pamphlet Nehru condemned not only the Indian Communist party but Communism. "With its suppression of individual freedom," he wrote, "Communism calls forth violent resistance. . . . In its luckless association with violence it frees the evil tendencies latent in man."

Belatedly Nehru understood that in a new country nationalism is too valuable a weapon to lend to a disloyal opposition. In Indonesia this most potent political explosive was left lying around for the Communists to use against the nationalists and the government parties who, in March, 1958, had not yet made Nehru's discovery.

Communism in Indonesia was an importation with displaced loyalty which had tried, under Moscow guidance, to overthrow the Republic through violence in 1948. It should not have been difficult to keep the menace small by telling the people that the PKI was an immigrant Red wolf temporarily garbed in native sheep's clothing. But with true Javanese tolerance and indifference the marked victims smiled indulgently as the danger grew. It would have been simple to foresee that a powerful Communist party would drag the country toward the Soviet camp and thus vitiate the nonalignment or neutrality which Indonesia, in common with other Asian countries, purported to practice in international affairs. Eyes remained closed; tongues remained silent.

I spoke with Darsono, now decidedly anti-Communist, who, until 1929, when he recognized the complete divorce between the Kremlin's performance and Marx's theory, was a deputy member of the executive committee of the Moscow Third International. How, I inquired, did he view new developments in East Java, where Communists had won a majority in the Surabaya city council, and in Central Java, where they now governed several regencies or districts?

"It has its advantages," he answered softly. "Communists live on promises. When they begin to administer areas their promises will be tested and they will fail, as all others must fail, because of long-lasting material difficulties." Communists in office, he reasoned, would set back their movement.

"Does this apply to Communist acceptance into the national government?"

"That is different," he replied. "There they would infiltrate ministries and gain too much power."

However, Communist participation in the central government was the topic of the time and had been since the February 21, 1957, address of President Sukarno. That day he presented his Concept, which provided for Communist membership in the Cabinet. Wherever I traveled, in Jakarta, in other cities, on highways, in villages, ugly black scrawls painted on walls by Communists extolled the Concept as Indonesia's salvation. The new doctrine, labeled "Guided Democracy," reflected Sukarno's thinking and met Communist wishes. "Our state," he began, speaking to a select audience in the palace, "is in distress. . . . God willing, I will put before you this evening that which is called my Concept." The difficulties confronting the country were not of recent origin, "they have been of long standing, but have only recently reached their climax" in the Central Sumatran revolt. Therefore "he begged God to give us His guidance as to how to surmount them."

Sukarno admitted that "ever since we proclaimed the Republic of Indonesia on August 17, 1945, the Indonesian people, who formerly thought that the proclamation and the state would bring peace, happiness, and joy, have been for eleven years constantly—I almost said 'permanently' —disturbed."

For more than eleven years, he said, "we have never achieved stability in government. . . . Every Cabinet has lacked authority and has had to face strong opposition, so that no Cabinet has been able to hold out for quite a long time."

"This unsavory experience," reads the official English translation, brought Sukarno "to the conviction that we had used a wrong system, a wrong style of government, that is, the style which we call Western democracy." Later I was to argue with him and other leaders that they had never tried Western democracy. However . . . This Western democracy, or parliamentary democracy, Sukarno said in his lecture, "is an import democracy . . . not in harmony with our spirit," hence "all the excesses ensuing from the implementation of a democracy which is not in harmony with our [national] personality.

"Brethren," he continued, "in this Western democracy, in this Western parliamentary democracy, we come across the idea of opposition. It is this very idea, brethren, which has made us go through hardships for eleven years. Because we interpret this idea of opposition in a manner which does not agree with the Indonesian soul." It was opposition for opposition's sake; in the eyes of the opposition the government could do no good. The aim of the opposition was always the "overthrow of the existing government and its replacement by a government of the opposition itself . . . *coûte que coûte.*"

This system had to go. He did not wish merely to reshuffle the Cabinet or strengthen some of its pillars. "We should not only pull down all the pillars, the roof, the walls; we should pull down everything—not excluding the foundation—and lay a new foundation, erect a totally new building."

"My Concept," the President explained, "consists of two items . . . the Cabinet [and] . . . the National Council.

"My brethren, we should form a Gotong Rojong [Mutual Assistance] Cabinet. I expressly use the term 'Gotong Rojong' because this is an authentic Indonesian term which gives the purest reflection of the Indonesian soul." The key to the entire Concept is this: "The Cabinet should comprise all political parties and groups represented in Parliament which have attained a certain electoral quotient" or percentage of the vote.

"I do not violate Parliament," he assured. ". . . Parliament goes on." For this Parliament was the result of the 1955 elections.

But they should no longer discriminate against parties in Parliament. "We should no longer ask, Are you Masjumi, are you PKI, are you Nahdatul Ulama, are you Protestant, are you Catholic? . . . All parties in Parliament should be given the right to participate in the Cabinet. This is just, my brethren. Just, because it does not discriminate . . ."

Sukarno called it "the family principle, the Gotong Rojong principle . . . all members of the family at the dining table and at the worktable . . . the opposition, as we have interpreted it for eleven years, will disappear." Instead, "deliberation" (Musjawarah).

Gotong Rojong is deeply embedded in the Indonesian democratic traditions. "Paid labor," writes Mohammad Hatta in *The Co-operative Movement in Indonesia,* "was an unknown concept in the original Indonesian community. Whenever heavy work was to be done everybody helped . . . mutual assistance is practiced when building a house, working the ricefields, or carrying the dead to the graveyard."

Musjawarah, or discussion, is a natural outgrowth of mutual assistance

(Gotong Rojong). Co-operation presupposes agreement. Rather than have disagreement and conflict, tradition required that a project be dropped. Inaction was better than division. Therefore the village tried to achieve what is known in old Javanese culture as mufakat, or a consensus; if possible, unanimity. Voting was avoided; the rural community would talk endlessly, for days if necessary, to persuade dissenters to consent and co-operate.

In the mouth of the new Indonesian administrator, however, Musjawarah is a term of scorn for the national habit of endless committee consultations to escape individual responsibility and endless talk as a substitute for action. Sukarno's Concept, had it ever been translated into reality, would have made the big four parties—the PNI, the Masjumi, the Nahdatul Ulama, and the PKI—the chief elements in the new government. He called such a Cabinet "a four-legged horse."

"I never heard of four legs running a government," I said to Sukarno in March, 1958. "One brain would be better."

The President laughed. By that time he had heard plenty of criticism of his Concept, especially from opponents of the fourth leg, and this first feature of the scheme went silently to its grave.

The Concept's second feature, as outlined by Sukarno on February 21, 1957, was a National Council consisting of representatives of functional groups: labor, peasants, intellectuals, businessmen, Protestants, Catholics, Moslem theologians, women, youth, representatives of the islands, the chiefs of staff of the army, the navy, and the air force, the chief of the State Police, the attorney general, several key Cabinet ministers, "and, my brethren, God willing, this National Council will be led by me myself." The Council "is to assist the Cabinet with advice, whether such advice is required or not, because . . . I regard the Council as a reflection of our society, while the Cabinet is a reflection of Parliament."

The National Council functions, but its duties are not clearly demarcated from those of the minus-PKI Cabinet.

Sukarno's Concept address brought down upon him an avalanche of Western bricks, barks, and attacks. His "Guided Democracy" was interpreted as akin to Communism or a long lunge toward it. At the least, he wished to collaborate with Reds, critics said. Reading excerpts of the speech abroad I disliked it. He had been impressed, I decided, by the exaggerated glorification, lavish hospitality, and staged welcomes accorded him in Soviet Russia and China during 1956. Indonesians in the West and later in Indonesia told me that the Kremlin had met his every wish, including a beautiful young woman. Low gossip in high Jakarta circles spicily elaborated on the theme.

Such factors may have weighed in the emotional balance; we do not know. But since Sukarno unveiled his Concept on February 21, 1957, many things have happened to warrant its re-evaluation. The rise of a number of military dictatorships in the new states of Asia and Africa suggest that a common disease afflicts them. Its two symptoms are frivolous parliaments and unstable cabinets. In Indonesia, the disease was endemic. The political and economic results were devastating. Sukarno had correctly diagnosed the malady before any other Eastern statesman discerned it and offered a cure.

The cure would have been worse than the illness. Given the traditional Musjawarah, Communists in the Cabinet would have outtalked, outsat and tired out everybody else and either paralyzed the government or limited its actions to those they approved.

Why did Sukarno fail to see this? He believes in his ability to get people to agree with him through charm, eloquence, and faith in self. Franklin D. Roosevelt felt the same way and the feeling served him well throughout a successful career until he tried it on Stalin, when it failed and affected the peace settlement unfavorably. Sukarno must have been sure that he could manage the Communists inside the government. For were they not supporting him though they had been kept outside? And had they not shelved their Communist program for nationalism?

Except in the old Western democracies and the new Eastern satellites of Russia, Communism is not popularly viewed with horror or revulsion. Nor are Communists in much of Asia regarded as incorrigible and destined to remain beyond the pale forever. U Nu is probably the most ethical political leader in Asia. In his role of prime minister he addressed the congress of the ruling party of Burma for four and a half hours on January 29, 1958, dissecting and rejecting Communism, Marxism, and state capitalism. The speech reshaped Burmese politics. Several days later I met him by appointment at a garden party in Rangoon. He asked me what I thought of his speech. I said it was important and should be disseminated widely. "Some friends say it's childish," he commented. "There's one," and he beckoned gaily to a Burmese nearby.

U Nu introduced the man to me as a member of Parliament and a Communist. "Are you a member of the Communist party?" I asked.

"I'm a constitutional Communist," he replied to distinguish himself from the illegal Communists fighting U Nu's government in the jungle.

U Nu put one arm on the Communist's back and left shoulder and the other arm in the bend of the Communist's right arm. "That's all right," U Nu said, "I'm taking him away with me tomorrow." U Nu, a devout Buddhist, was leaving town the next morning for the four-day funeral of his religious guru, or mentor, and had arranged to have the Communist go and stay with him.

Temperamental tolerance and the predisposition of Afro-Asian nationalists to proclaim themselves Marxists are components of their soft attitude toward Communists. When they were college students and fledglings in the anti-imperialist struggle, the right thing to do, and the only alternative to being a reactionary, was to be a follower of Marx, usually without ever having read him. Nehru is still partly stuck in the London Left Book Club of the second half of the 1930's though of its three founders Victor Gollancz and John Strachey have moved beyond it and Harold J. Laski, alas, is dead. That triumvirate threw their ideological seeds into strong transcontinental winds, and the tares still sting and tear everywhere. U Nu, Kyaw Nein, and other Burmese, and other Asians and Africans too, have liberated themselves from the aberrations of their university days. Intellectually Sukarno, as I could judge from interviews yet to come, is traveling in the same direction. But he had to reckon with a Communist party which was indeed the largest in the land.

Must Sukarno, must leaders in the new Asia and Africa, also reckon with the infectious success of Communism in Russia and China? It has become a commonplace that India and China are engaged in social competition and that democracy in India is doomed if China proves that her totalitarian methods have yielded better material benefits than Indian democracy. I question this sweeping proposition.

The Soviet Union has built very many new cities, industries, and enterprises and has enormously increased its output, military power, and weight in world affairs. But no nation has responded by going Communist. The East European countries sovietized since 1939 were occupied and coerced by the Red army and the Russian secret police; they never chose or approved their present regimes. They are probably more anti-Communist today than ever—witness the East German zone-wide revolt in June, 1953, and the flight of three million East Germans, out of a total population of 18 million, to West Germany from 1949 to date; witness too the anti-Communist outbreaks and mood in Poland in 1956 and thereafter and the national uprising in Hungary in October-November, 1956. In Poland, Hungary, and Yugoslavia, all overwhelmingly agrarian, the peasantry has, by official admission, abandoned collective farming. These acts were, in effect, plebiscites against Communism.

The much-advertised Soviet economic achievements at home made few converts in East Europe. Rather the contrary; since these achievements, translated primarily into martial might, account for Russian territorial expansion, the East European peoples detest them.

Elsewhere the Soviet regime's influence on minds has waned as it gained in power. Moscow's ideological attraction was probably greatest in the 1930's, before its notable progress in industry and science and before its trials and purges, when Western economy was depressed and free Europe diminished by two Fascist states.

But the underdeveloped countries of Asia, it is said, are in a different position: the red shadow of China looms over them and her rapid forward strides inspire awe: there will be imitators; what does the emaciated Bombay worker or the Indian peasant who lives like an animal care about freedom if he can have another bowl of rice? Freedom is not an abstraction even to the hungriest. It means the right to organize in trade unions and win wage rises—a right denied in Communist countries. It means individual possession of a strip of land and of work animals instead of being dispossessed and regimented in collectives and militarized communes. If leaders and intellectuals in non-Communist Asia and Africa stressed these truths instead of digging their own graves by touting China's alleged economic victories; if they read Chinese and Russian statistics with some scientific skepticism—Khrushchev has admitted that Malenkov falsified production figures, and how do we know that his successor will not make similar charges against him?—if they cared to grasp the full significance of the Hungarian horror, Pasternak's persecution, and the flight of the Dalai Lama, China and Russia would become object lessons in what to avoid. To the Indian and Indonesian masses China is a million miles away unless brought near by a deluded intelligentsia which does not appreciate the benefits it enjoys.

"Will Indonesia go Communist?" has been a frequent question.

"If the future were certain there would be no need for policy" is my first response. What happens in Indonesia or anywhere depends on what the government does and on what other governments do. I suspect that the threat of Communist dictatorship, economic collapse, or internal rebellion would invite a military dictatorship.

Aidit once declared that it would take fifty years to convert Indonesia to Communism. This may be sand in the eyes of the unwary. It may also be his belief. It may be true. The half century is an opportunity.

Chapter Twenty-three

THE ASIAN MIND

ARSLAN HUMBARACHI, the Turkish journalist who accompanied Sukarno on the trip through Java and to the Celebes and Bali, was my neighbor across the ground-floor corridor and came to visit me the day I arrived in Indonesia and took residence in the new house assigned by the government to foreign journalists. Bernard Kalb, *New York Times,* John Roderick, Associated Press, and two newspapermen from India lived upstairs. Foreign journalists, especially in a remote capital, are a friendly fraternity.

The house has two beautiful, intimate assembly rooms, decorated with native masks and Indonesian oil paintings, for conferences of officials, army officers, writers, etc. The laughter which punctuated their deliberations rolled out at frequent intervals into my apartment.

I occupied two living rooms and a bathroom with a cement tub, cold-water shower, and toilet bowl without seat. The Dutch believed seats to be unsanitary, and their liberated colonial subjects have not yet overcome the superstition.

A playful lizard made his home in my bathroom. Its body was an inch long; the tail 1½ inches long. It had four legs, each with five stubby fingers which clung to the white tiles and whitewashed walls. When I sprinkled water on it from my shower it stopped and blinked its black little eyes. The next splash sent it scurrying into the hole from which a water pipe protruded. I hoped it fed on mosquitoes, but when I returned from the six-day trip it had not grown. Larger specimens raced on the corridor ceilings and the walls and ceilings outside. They never bothered anybody.

The mosquitoes hid in the two clothes closets and angrily resented my intrusion. Flit-gun volleys drove them off for a few moments, but they quickly renewed the attack. Their favorite targets were my ankles, which bore the wounds of battle for months thereafter.

Evenings when I returned to the apartment and put on the lights, at least a dozen two-inch-long cockroaches fled across the floor. Before I could even try to sleep I got in under the rectangular netting canopy suspended over my double bed to kill the mosquitoes that always managed to get in and to banish the cockroaches. They were flying cockroaches. They flew away.

Every morning I called "Bung" through the mosquito wiring of a window and in a few moments he would appear, bending low from the waist, carrying a tray with a Thermos bottle of hot boiled water, a whole pineapple (market price—5 cents) cut into triangles, eight small slices of toast roasted over a fire, condensed milk, and margarine. I had my own instant coffee. Having deposited the breakfast on my table, smiled, taken my laundry—which was returned immaculate and ironed in the evening —he bowed himself out with a broad smile. Five bungs served us, and they were quick and kind and spoke no language but Indonesian. Two read avidly at every opportunity.

I cleaned my teeth with cooled boiled water left in the Thermos from breakfast. But there was never enough for rinsing the toothbrush, so I rinsed it under the faucet. After that it did not make much sense to be germ-minded and I brushed my teeth with tap water and used it to wash down the daily vitamins. No harm came to me.

Outside the house, betjak drivers relieved themselves in the canal that ran through the street. Where else could they go? They were out all day trying to earn a meager living. The wider canals in the central streets are used for the same purpose as well as for bathing and laundering. Passing by, the eye took in all processes at a glance. Even poor houses are connected with a central water supply which,.the Lord Mayor swore, was adequately filtered and purified by a French-installed system. But the water runs through a meter and costs money. The canals are free. The Indonesian word for water is "air" (pronounced *ayer*) and it is as indispensable to life. I took at least four showers a day and typing made it six or seven. Yet I was always wet with sweat. Sea level at the equator makes torrid heat and heavy humidity man's inseparable companions. To dry out my bones I walked in shorts and sandals in the broiling sun every day. I began the practice after I noticed that the two infants in the house, one fathered by a bung, the other by the manager, were given regular sun baths by their nurses.

The blue suit in my closet showed white streaks. I thought I had accidentally brushed it against the whitewash. But the streaks defied rubbing. They were soft molds grown by the dampness and yielded only to ironing. A pair of doeskin bedroom slippers were so encrusted with mushroomlike molds that I threw them away.

Every hotel and even the middle-class home in India has electric ceiling fans which also chase away mosquitoes. But Indonesians fear fans as unhealthy, and except in foreign dwellings none, if I remember correctly, is to be seen. It may be due to the shortage of electricity. Upper-class private houses have their own small diesels to supply expensive but reliable current. Some ambassadorial residences and a few apartments in the nineteenth-century, run-down monstrosity called the Hotel des Indes enjoy air conditioning. But Indonesians abhor it.

On my first day in Jakarta an attempted telephone call from the house to the Foreign Ministry cost forty perspiring minutes and ended in my mounting a betjak and going there. That evening I learned to count from one to nine and zero in Indonesian: satu, dua, tiga, empat, lima, enam, tudjuh, delapan, sembilan, and nol. Some numbers could be dialed, most had to be communicated to the operator.

Journalists came to live in the house and went. Jolly, ruddy Richard Hughes, an Australian writing for the London *Sunday Times* and the *New York Times* Sunday magazine section, appeared, entertained with monologues at parties, betjaked around town, got his story, and returned to Hong Kong. T. Yamashita of Radio Tokyo, smiling yet grave, paid us a visit. The two Indians left. They, like Indian officials and nonofficials, discovered in Indonesia the virtues of British rule in India. "At least the British trained many Indians for our civil service. They left us with industries and an educated class," the refrain ran. "The Dutch left the people here with next to nothing."

Nevertheless, Jakarta is a city with broad, paved avenues, rows of good houses, a business district, a fair port, some block-sized parks, and a Western look. The center of Jakarta is crowded with vehicular traffic, pedestrians, hawkers, who spread their wares on the pavements, and beggars, who operate at traffic lights and the level railway crossings. It is a sprawling, well-nigh characterless town with not more than two or three distinctive buildings and little to please or impress the eye. Whole new residential quarters for the well-to-do have been erected since liberation and thousands of shanties for squatter-refugees from Darul Islam-infested areas in West Java, but no outstanding structure and **no** hotel, though **the** shortage of accommodations for foreigners and visiting Indonesians is woeful.

Foreigners lunched and dined at Chez Mario's, where Mario painted primitives and Vicky, his charming wife, supervised the good cooking and made the guests feel at home; they were an Italian couple who came on an operatic tour, fell in love with Indonesia, and stayed—come Dutch, Japanese, independence, and high water—for twenty-eight years. Second choices were the Capitol, with flies and dirty tablecloths, by the side of a tumbling canal, and the new air-conditioned Ambassador managed for the government by an overweight Dutchman. In any of these restaurants a journalist was sure to be invited to join the table of colleagues, embassy employees, or Indonesian acquaintances.

Indonesians like to entertain foreigners. At dinner parties one might meet members of Parliament, ministers, a deputy prime minister, literary folk, and so on. Once I broke through the copper-wire telephone curtain, interviews were easy to arrange. The Foreign Ministry helped. Some days I took three, even four interviews, which, what with transportation difficulties and notes, was as much as the body could bear.

Five workdays in steaming Jakarta created a physical need of thinner, cooler air for the lungs and scenery for the eye. Luckily, I had an invitation from Bill Palmer to spend my first weekend in Indonesia at his mountain retreat, and the invitation was repeated every week during my sojourn in the country. Seldom did I allow the pressure of work to interfere with the pleasure.

The roads that lead out of Jakarta were thick with traffic: cars, trucks, scooters, bicycles, betjaks. On the tailboard of one truck somebody had painted, in neat lettering, "Rock-and-Roll, I Love You." I hoped it was a government truck. Not that I fancy rock 'n' roll, but neither do I like governments to decide how its citizens should dance.

We took the road south and uphill to Bogor, which the Dutch called Buitenzorg (Without-a-Care). Outside the urban area nature is bountiful. Everything is green, every shade of green, and there are reds and yellows too. Fruits and vegetables grow to giant size. All vegetation is rich and tall. Man alone is thin and small. The houses close to the two-lane road are either made of stone or, the vast majority, of bamboo, and a single story high. They are surrounded by trees: fat stumpy banana trees; palm trees, some low, some rising to fifty feet, clean and straight as a telegraph pole, with a solitary crown of outstretched branches; bamboo trees of varying heights and widths either standing alone or in clumps three yards in diameter, and mimosa bushes hung with golden balls.

At Bogor the way is barred by the President's Palace, built for the Dutch Governor General, and the encircling park which merges into the world-famous, perhaps the world's most famous, tropical Botanical Gardens. The automobile makes a detour into the busy town—870 feet above sea level and therefore enjoying an equable climate with an average annual temperature of 77.7 degrees Fahrenheit (25.4 Centigrade). Snaking through pony carts, diminutive buses, pedestrians, and cars, we finally reach the open road. Presently rain descends in sheets. The windshield wiper cannot cope with this; the driver has no visibility and stops. Then he creeps forward. A boy walks along under a banana leaf which looks like an elongated, magnified elephant ear. A little farther on, two boys, arms entangled, use a banana leaf as their umbrella. Though most men are barefoot and barelegged and wear only one garment, which will dry in the sun the moment the cloudburst ends, they seek to hide from it. Only the slate-gray water buffaloes, wallowing in the ditches beside the road, relish the rain. Women raise their sarongs, displaying shapely legs. Passing cars hurl water cascades at one another and inundate windows and windshields. Peasants in Japanese-type straw sunshades lead buffaloes home. Most houses have red-tile roofs, else they would be flooded in downpours like this which occur two days out of every three in the year.

The bamboo trading shacks along the road are lit by hanging kerosene lamps; they still linger in the pre-electricity era of the precapitalist age. Beyond the strip of houses and shops lie the ricefields in irregular rectangles covered with pale-green plant clusters. The rice grows on terraces about two feet high, and each terrace is now a waterfall. The entire countryside, in fact, has become a landscape of flowing, splashing, falling water. Ferns, palms, trees, plants, and people drip with rain.

The sun appears; the rain relents. The poster on a restaurant front shows a charging bull, smoke issuing from his nostrils, and "PNI" and "Front Marhein." The animal is the electoral symbol of the Nationalist party of Indonesia. To vote PNI the voter uses a pencil to stab a hole through the bull on the ballot.

"Be Bop Dancing School" in English on a wayside hut. "Permanent Wave" on another. The culture of the West invades the East. The twain do meet.

Thick rain returns. Tall, thin rubber trees stand in military-square formation. As we ascend, dark, glossy-green tea takes over from pale-green rice. Up to 10,000 and 12,000 feet, as far as the eye can see, not a square cubit is bare of vegetation. In places the red soil is fifteen feet deep and endlessly fruitful, yet it has been worked so many thousands of years and washed by so much rain that it needs enriching fertilizer—which it does not get.

Bill Palmer's house stands on a shoulder where the mountain rests before rising to the Puntjak Pass and higher still. Tea shrubs cover the horizon. Clouds ring the peaks and as they lift the heart goes with them from ridge to ridge to the clear blue sky. The one-story house begins with a kitchen, then a spacious dining room which leads to a broad, roofed terrace flanked on one side by bedrooms, each with its bathroom. Beyond the bedrooms is a great pavilion open to the elements and in the pavilion a giant fireplace flames bright. After roasting in Jakarta one is happy to roast close to the fire. I slept under blankets, two blankets! Yet the sun, on its intermittent appearances through the rain-laden clouds, scorches. Two steps down from the terrace is a lawn graced with deck chairs and umbrellas and a level croquet court; farther down—a swimming pool fed by icy mountain water. Here red poinsettia grows to tree height and orchids bloom. Beyond Bill Palmer's is a smaller villa rented by an officer of the United States embassy and next to it the United States ambassador's bungalow. The residents and guests of all three houses merge and mingle for meals, entertainment, and conversation—invariably in Bill Palmer's pavilion. I have seen as many as fifty persons there for lunch. Visitors with a baby will find a crib ready. Books and magazines are supplied for bedtime reading. Bill possesses what the Russians call "a broad nature," a natural generosity, an unostentatious hospitality. Jakarta knows him as "the Second American Ambassador."

Bill Palmer has no official position. He is Eric Johnston's Indonesian representative and distributes American films. His parents were missionaries in Siam, where he grew up. He went to Indonesia in 1950 and has worked there ever since. He loves the people. Asia is in his blood. Asia is his cause. He wants the United States to do more in Asia, to be Asia-minded. A proud, patriotic American who resents the slightest slur on his country, he nevertheless criticizes State Department astigmatism which prevents Asia from coming into sharp focus.

Bill has six or more mature bungs who wear good suits, black skullcaps and no shoes. Every Saturday evening one of them sets up a screen on the lawn and a projector on the terrace. By that time the villagers have gathered. Young men observe eagerly as the bung threads the film through the machine and turns the switches. Spectators sit or stand on the terraces and on the lawn. A documentary or a newsreel is followed by the feature. On my first Saturday night it was *Casablanca,* with Ingrid Bergman and Humphrey Bogart and the original English sound. Many, perhaps most, of the hundred or more peasants who come to the free show had never even seen Jakarta. The picture portrayed an unimaginable world in an unknown language, and I often wondered what part of it reached them. Yet they sat and gaped, wide-eyed and fascinated. At times, however, some were just as interested in Bill's foreign visitors who might be playing bridge or scrabble or following the film, and if one nodded and winked at them they broke into joyous, shy smiles. Friends warned Bill Palmer not to do this. "They will steal everything that's loose," they predicted. But over the years nothing has ever been touched or taken away. The door to my room was not locked, and if, during an evening, I had to go into the room I would thread my way through the crowd and bid those standing against the door to let me enter. Yet the objects in the room were completely safe.

What hurts the West most in Asia is the arrogant confidence that it has a monopoly on virtue. The white man's political supremacy is gone but his feeling of superiority remains and the brown man senses it and closes up. The West in its generosity and sagacity gives to the East, as it must in expanding volume. Yet it never takes and this is what creates the gulf. The not-taking means Asia has nothing to give, and that offends. The Westerners who have been accepted by the East are those who took: among others, T. E. Lawrence became an Arab, and the Arabs followed him; Mrs. Annie Besant, an Englishwoman, identified herself with India, believed in theosophy, and was elected to lead the home-rule movement. Indians revere her memory. A statue of her is prominent in Madras. It is not necessary to "go" Chinese or "go" Japanese. It is merely necessary to discard the conviction that the Oriental is, in Nazi terminology, an *Untermensch,* an inherently inferior being who begs but has nothing to render in return. Asia gave the West all its religions. The teachings of Mahatma Gandhi are intimately relevant to most of the world's social, political, and international problems. Asian subtlety, tolerance, gentleness, and pluralism might be imitated with benefit.

Asians are sensitive. They resent being called Asiatics, a term which has the ring, to them, of colonialism, rejection, and contempt. They do not like the word "help." An Indian ambassador once requested his American audience to use "co-operation" instead. Nor do Asians, or Europeans for that matter, relish the concept of American leadership. Leadership means that somebody is being led. The poorer, weaker nations prefer partnership, which implies equality of status if not necessarily of strength.

The truth should not be denied. Asia is economically and techno-logically backward, and, in the first place, she has herself to blame. Sir Mohammad Iqbal, the spiritual father of Pakistan, encompassing the whole Moslem world in his poetic-philosophic vision, decided that, "During the last five hundred years religious thought in Islam has been prac-tically stationary," and he spoke of "the centuries of our intellectual stupor." India's castes and religious rigidity, China's despotism and ancestor worship, and in general Asia's domination by native sybaritic upper classes which enjoyed unhealthy luxury and remained indifferent to the misery of the mass and therefore to the technological progress which could eliminate it—all these are responsible for the great continent's poverty, sloth, sluggishness, and backwardness. They opened the door to Western imperialism.

This does not prove, however, that there is anything congenitally inferior in the brown or yellow man. "In their mastery of the material world," writes J. S. Furnivall, British authority on Burma and Indonesia, "India and Europe in the sixteenth century were far closer together than modern Europe and the modern tropics." Asia stagnated; Europe forged ahead. In part the fault was the West's. For without the intervention of Western imperialism Asia might have lifted herself out of the stupor just as Europe did after the Dark Ages. Instead, the West sat heavily on Asia for centuries and inhibited change.

Suppose—it requires a stretched imagination—China had conquered Europe in the thirteenth century and held it in bondage until 1947. Foreign rule would have lain like a thick glacier on Europe, freezing social processes and preventing the evolution from feudalism to capitalism to the welfare state and from petty principalities to nations which has actually taken place. Today, less than two decades after liberation from Chinese sway, Europe would be chasing the lost centuries. The departure of the Chinese would have released all the dormant strivings and divergent aspirations of various clans, tribes, geographic regions, linguistic groups, religious communities, privileged families, and frustrated persons. Issues which should have been adjusted long ago by the normal play of antagonistic forces in a free society would be creating explosive situations, perhaps revolts and civil wars, and obstructing national unity and material advance. A visitor from the outside—perhaps a Chinese—would deplore these conditions and point to the law and order that prevailed under the colonial government.

There is a need, therefore, for an objective division of the responsibility for Asia's backwardness, but no room for Western arrogance or Eastern humiliation. In their philosophy, religion, manners, love of nature, and capacity to enjoy life Asians may indeed be superior. The West, which includes Russia, is merely more advanced in its materialism and someday, when it catches up with Asia, it could realize how secondary material culture is.

Some Asians have repaid the white man's arrogance with an arrogance of their own and the white man's superiority illusion with a stance of superiority. These ugly phenomena I did not notice among Indonesians.

They consider themselves neither superior nor inferior as a people, and I encountered no arrogance. They have an exaggerated fear of foreign domination and interference. Otherwise their friendly attitude toward the outside world remains uninhibited, and it appeared to me that, despite slogans about Asian solidarity, they were actually cooler to Asians who thought of leading them than to Westerners who, for whatever reasons—contrition and conscience, perhaps—offered understanding and trust.

Bill Palmer showed not only his film. He showed trust. The reward was friendship.

Chapter Twenty-four

ALL WOMEN ARE CREATED EQUAL

A FACTOR in Indonesia's attractiveness is the treatment of women. In India the stranger who comes to a village hut or even a city home may descry the womenfolk of the household peeping shyly from behind the kitchen curtain while he interviews the men. But Indonesian women are always right out in front with their spouses and occasionally without their spouses.

Indonesian women are equal, and some are unequal—that is, superior.

The equality of women is rooted in the remote myths of the archipelago. According to the mythology of the Toba Bataks in North Sumatra, the world was created by the god Batara Guru and his daughter Parujar. She descended from heaven and, after a victorious struggle with a serpent named Naga Padoha, fashioned the earth out of a lump she brought with her. Then she married a god and gave birth to the first Batak.

Borneo's Adam and Eve were called Batang Timong and Uniang. One day Batang went hunting and Uniang stayed home to sew. When the husband returned he found that Uniang had stuck her finger with a needle and bled to death. Her blood fructified the earth; rice sprouts shot up immediately. Banana trees and other vegetation grew from her body. Variations of this genesis tale are heard on other islands. "In nearly all known Indonesian histories," writes Minister of Education Professor Prijono, "it is a woman who gives man food, in the first place rice. . . . But to give man his indispensable food, she has to die first. From her death comes life."

It was Eve's sin of listening to the snake and eating the apple that brought on the expulsion from the Garden of Eden. In Indonesian mythology, man is the first sinner. In the Minahasa region of North Celebes the man pulled a hair from his wife's head and she vanished. King Mohammad Sjah of Atjeh, says Professor Prijono, killed his wife by drawing out a hair in her chin. His brother, Mahmud Sjah, drove away his wife, who was a celestial nymph, by breaking his promise not to scold their children. Sorrow comes from the male's whims and wickedness, but "woman," Prijono concludes, "is imagined as the creator or co-creator, as disinterested wife, as adviser, as resource of power, as giver of life," who sacrifices herself to endow the earth with fertility.

Myths on Java tell how fire first came to man. It flashed from the body of a goddess. Woman likewise taught mankind to cook. King Siliwangi of Java, the story goes, had a wife who could put one ear of rice into a pot which soon filled with delicious white rice. The Queen gave the secret recipe to the women of the island but extracted a pledge from the King never to look into the pot. Once, however, curiosity overcame him and he lifted the lid. The Queen lost her magical cooking talent.

Queens were more than the authors of miraculous recipes. History, even nineteenth-century history, tells of queens who ruled. Minangkabau women still rule.

The Central Sumatran region around Padang and Bukittinggi is the home of a remarkable race, called Minangkabau, numbering no more than two million, which has given Indonesia some of its great leaders, among them Hatta, Sjahrir, Mohammad Natsir, the head of the Masjumi party, Haji Agus Salim, the late foreign minister, and many of the country's best modern writers.

The Minangkabau (the last syllable rhymes with *cow*) live under a matriarchate. Women own the fields, houses, shops, and so forth. Their children, for the most part their daughters, inherit the property and wherever possible keep it undivided as family capital which is worked collectively. When daughters marry they and their offspring remain under the mother's roof, and the roofs expand with the family. Minangkabau houses are high-walled and surmounted by a gracefully curved roof which rises to a sharp peak like some Chinese hats. As the family grows the house is extended and one can tell from the number of extension seams in the roof how many times the family has expanded.

The Minangkabau mother, aided by a brother, arranges her children's marriages and runs the farm or the business. The father has no part in this. But he helps arrange the marriages of his sister's children and assists in his sister's business. Husbands live with their mothers. When work is done the husband goes to his wife's house, sits on the doorstep, and clears his throat, or coughs, or hums a tune till he is admitted into the house to spend the night. In the morning he goes off to his mother's.

A rich Minangkabau woman told me that her father had four wives before he married her mother. "He was an old man," she said, "and I scarcely knew him. He came in the evening and went before we woke." Her mother married four husbands in succession and begat seventeen children from them.

Minangkabau women, and men, are excellent merchants. Throughout Indonesia, Chinese conduct much of the trade. But they have not been able to penetrate into the Minangkabau region. In fact, Minangkabau business people compete successfully with the Chinese in Jakarta.

A Minangkabau young man worthy of his salt leaves the ancestral village for another island to win laurels away from the womenfolk. In the Dutch period, if his mother or the community treasury could afford it, he went to Holland. Sometimes he then imported a wife from his clan in Minangkabau territory. That made him the master, at least the equal, of his lady. Voluntary exile from the matriarchate put man on his mettle and may explain the rich supply of male Minangkabau talent in Indonesia.

The Minangkabau race or folk is divided into hundreds, some say thousands, of clans and subclans. Subclans are really enlarged families. Marriages must therefore be exogenous—outside the clan. This is given as the reason why mothers must select their children's spouses. If love were permitted free rein, boy and girl might belong to the same subclan.

Thirty-two persons, invited by the Pakistan ambassador, sat sipping drinks in a circle in his garden before going into the house for their buffet dinner. The evening was still and not uncomfortably hot. A glowing ring of mist brightened the half-moon. Two gently curving papaya trees, about twenty feet tall and three inches thick, their green fruit hanging high, stood guard over us. I was fortunate to be placed next to a tall, sturdy Minangkabau woman, age forty-eight, as she told me without wincing, mother of five, of whom the oldest is twenty. Unlike Javanese women whose kabaya blouse reaches only a few inches below the waist, her embroidered kabaya fell to her ankles, and she wore not the form-fitting kain of Java that permits only short dance steps but a sarong which gives ample room for movement. She is in the import-export business with her husband, who is shorter than she. "I first met my husband on our nuptial night," she replied in answer to a question. Her mother and uncle arranged the marriage and informed her father. "Now it is different," she said. "Our children will choose their own spouses. But inheritance is still through the maternal line." Obviously, however, girls who marry at thirteen or fifteen—and that is not unusual—will still get their husbands via mama.

These adolescent wives have a long reproductive period, and, what with polygamy, which sanctions a second or third simultaneous marriage, and custom, which tolerates marriages between old men and nubile girls, the birth rate is bound to be high not only in Minangkabau but in all Indonesia. "What are you doing about it?" I asked the Minangkabau lady.

She retorted with astounding frankness for a first conversation with a stranger. "I saw in the newspaper," she began, "that you had a discussion with President Sukarno about birth control. I believe in it. In Hamburg recently I bought foam tablets. What do American women use?"

Indonesian women are not prudes in their talk, nor are their men puritans in their acts. Freedom rules. Some women resented Sukarno's casting off Fatmawati for the younger Hartini. But what really outraged them, especially those who had been campaigning for the right to obtain a divorce if the husband takes a second wife, was the President's refusal to give Fatmawati a divorce. In the diplomatic corps in Jakarta one heard much about the beautiful Russian girl who had found favor in Sukarno's eyes. But many Indonesian men commented, "A pretty woman? Why not?" They envied him his prowess.

There exists an ancient Indonesian custom called "Nikah-mut-ah," or temporary marriage, which is actually steady, one-woman prostitution. The eminent Moslem theologian, Dr. Haji Karim Amrullah, when asked during the war whether Islam could condone such short-term relationships for pay to console Indonesians in the Japan-sponsored Peta army, replied in the negative on the ground that the Japanese were "idolaters" (because they worshiped the Emperor) but "once we have a real Indonesian army," he added, "we can carefully reconsider the question of mut-ah." Ordinary prostitution is common.

Sex is neither a taboo topic nor an urge to be denied. A factory owner in Java, pure Dutch by birth, said women employees were more reliable and trustworthy than men, but women and men agree that the night was not made for anything but love. Result: he could not get workers for the late third shift. Women work in field and factory and, what with their responsibility for home and children, and because it costs money, they usually avoid extramural sex. Men do not.

Don Juans, however, must beware. "Angry Mob Takes Law in Hand and Beats Helpless Don Juan to Death," an English-language daily in Jakarta announced one day. "Enraged villagers of Genitri, Genteng sub-district," read the subtitle of the report, "recently manhandled to death a local Casanova before the powerless village officials and a policeman." The villagers were all men. Apparently Ramelan, their victim, had engaged in successful courtship of the womenfolk. Women are not immune. Neither are men tolerant of their own sin in others.

Whether as a result of early marriage, or nonlove marriage, or general laxity, the number of divorces, separations, and desertions is extremely high. Figures are available only for the Moslem community which, however, constitutes almost 90 per cent of Indonesia's population. According to government statistics, the number of Moslem marriages in Indonesia in 1950 was 1,276,000 and repudiations of marriage 629,000. Of the repudiated marriages 43,000 were subsequently reconciled and reunited. But that still leaves a ratio of 47 repudiations to 100 marriages. In 1951 the number rose from 47 to 54. In 1952 it was 57; in 1953 it was 49; in 1954, 51; in 1955, 55; in 1956, 52. Perhaps this has always been so. Perhaps it reflects the turmoil and emotional upheavals which follow a revolution. It is undoubtedly related to the strong trend from village to city as a result of unsettled conditions in some rural areas and the better possibilities of remunerative employment in towns. Compared to 1930, the population of Greater Jakarta has increased more than 3½ times, of Bandung more than 5 times, Medan more than 4 times, Makassar more than 4 times, Bukittinggi more than 3½ times; Jogjakarta's has doubled; Surabaya's, almost tripled. Part of the increase is due to births, but a larger part to huge migrations in which men often leave their village wives behind.

Moslem custom allows men to have four wives simultaneously. But this doubtful pleasure is reserved for the few. In 1930 only 2.5 per cent of Indonesian marriages were polygamous, and of these 95 per cent, or nearly all, were bigamous. Who but a sultan or a rupiah millionaire can afford four wives nowadays?

A village chief in the Jakarta region showed me his two houses—a wife in each—and "you notice they are at opposite ends of the village," he said with a smile. Such an arrangement places extra duties on the woman and, since the man must divide his time and energy between two families, each wife is forced into greater independence. She cares for her children and is jealous of her husband's relation to the second wife's children. Logically, each wife would wish to supervise the property which sustains her offspring and which they will inherit. Matriarchy, therefore, should go together with polygamy. Islam's original antifeminism probably militated against this combination. The wonder is that in profeminist Indonesia, where even the Creator needed feminine assistance, only the Minangkabau evolved a matrilinear society.

Life is change. All matter is in constant change. That is true, too, of all units of society, even of those like Indonesia's where the pace of change has been slow. Polygamy and matriarchy are vestiges of despotism or feudalism or both. Just as the joint family in India is disintegrating, so the big estate and the big house of the Minangkabau motherland are breaking up into smaller units containing one papa and one mama and their children and therefore beginning to resemble the man's world of most of the world. Since favored Java had better educational facilities than neglected Sumatra, many Minangkabau youths attend university in Jakarta, Bandung, or Surabaya, and they tend to stay in Java, where matriarchal rule does not flourish.

More and more Indonesian students are postponing marriage till they finish their studies. This raises the marriage age, at least in the cities, and is an unconscious, highly desirable form of birth control. A physician whose practice is in a university area stated that women students usually avoid premarital sexual intercourse for three reasons: custom, religion, and fear of pregnancy and disease, in that order.

Dress is changing too. At Sukarno's lecture to students in the palace, I estimated two hundred girls in an audience of two thousand, and not one of them wore a kain or sarong. "Why?" I asked several.

"Dresses are more comfortable" came the reply. Most of the dresses are pink. It goes nicely with brown skin.

Indonesia faces enormous, difficult problems. She will not meet them with one hand tied behind her back. Women will play an important part in the solutions. In view of the limited educational and employment opportunities, and because women have special domestic duties and bio-logical functions, men dominate the economic and bureaucratic scene in Indonesia as they do everywhere else. A surprising number of women, however, occupy key positions. If and when large-scale development begins, women are sure to contribute their share of the labor which, in a back-ward, capital-poor country, is the greatest capital asset. But where, as in In-donesia, women are free and equal they make an even more essential contribution. One of the reasons why Western nations are rich is that women enjoy rights and a strong social status. They therefore have an effective economic demand. A wife or a daughter can say, "I need a new dress" ... "We need a better house" ... "I must have my own car" ... "We should go on a trip" ... "We ought to give a party." This stimulates man's drive and initiative and raises material standards. But in many countries of Asia and Africa women are second-class human beings who cannot make demands to which the man listens. In part, of course, this is due to poverty. There is no use the woman making demands when the man cannot fulfill them. In part, however, that very poverty results from masculine indifference to the condition of women. The necessity of satisfying his wife's craving for things does not act as a spur. On the level above poverty men entertain alone and go visiting alone. This is an economic factor of underestimated significance.

Indonesia suffers from no such handicap. Women have rights—in village as in city. The moment economic progress begins, the social status of women should accelerate it.

Chapter Twenty-five

DJAMU, DUKUNS, AND MYSTICS

THE MINANGKABAU businesswoman whom I met at the Pakistan ambassador's dinner said she takes djamu during one week in every lunar month. I noticed that Indonesian women do not develop the "middle-age spread" and stay remarkably young-looking. Wrinkles are rare in a woman of forty or slightly more. When I asked how they retained their youth and beauty, they one and all answered, "Djamu." Mothers drink djamu for forty days after the delivery of a baby. Mrs. Hartini Sukarno told me she did. Repeated replies of "Djamu" started me on a long research road.

I asked Sarwono to help me. Sarwono, an English-speaking student of the Jakarta university, is the nephew of former Prime Minister Wilopo. He came to see me after I had interviewed his uncle, and asked endless questions about world affairs. He brought me some brilliant friends who were well-informed on Indonesian politics. I enjoyed this contact throughout my stay in the capital. Sarwono had the use of his brother's automobile and drove me around often. Given the transportation problem, this was a great benefaction.

Sarwono knew about djamu. It was dispensed by dukuns, or native medicine men. "That's a dukun," he said once as we passed a crowd in a small city square. The dukun, a gaunt orator, had made his sales talk and was now trying to sell his wares to the listeners.

"Sar," I queried, "have you ever gone to a dukun?"

"As a high school senior," he replied, "I went to one before an examina-

199

tion. He gave me a glass of water with a piece of paper in it and I drank the water."

"Did you swallow the paper?"

"No. It was a plain piece of paper with a red line ruled on it."

"Did the water help?" I asked.

"Well, I passed the exam," Sarwono answered, with a smile. He smiled perpetually.

"Many Indonesian intellectuals go to dukuns either for water to drink or for fortunetelling," Sarwono volunteered. "A high Foreign Ministry official got a piece of paper from a dukun inscribed with the Arabic letter 'alif' which he has pasted on the door of his study. It's for protection and inspiration."

I laughed.

The *Times of Indonesia* of July 8, 1958, recorded a case of religious-animist faith. A little girl disappeared from the village of Sekadau in the wilds of Borneo. A search party of Dayaks, only recently weaned from headhunting, found one of the girl's earrings on the bank of a nearby jungle stream and presumed that she had been devoured by a crocodile. They sought out a native Roman Catholic priest, who told the story to a reporter:

The priest removed his sarong, waded into the river up to his waist, slapped the water, and prayed. On returning to dry land, he said to the villagers, "Make a cross of ironwood. Tie it to a chicken and suspend it by a rattan vine over the water. At six this evening the crocodile will eat the chicken and be caught on the cross."

Everything happened as the priest had predicted. The crocodile was hooked on the cross. In the evening, the priest again waded into the stream, slapped the water, prayed, and tied the mouth of the crocodile with another rattan vine by which the villagers pulled the beast ashore. "The priest noticed a strange thing," the newspaper account read. "The crocodile did not resist."

"Don't be angry with us," the villagers said, patting the crocodile. "You are wrong. You must be punished."

There and then the crocodile was tried by a jury of elders, who decided it must die and be cut into equal-sized pieces for all present to eat.

When the animal was opened, the priest's miracle stood revealed: with his prayers and the cross he had caught the guilty crocodile. Inside its stomach the awe-struck villagers saw the little girl's second earring.

Ready credulity, in varying degree, characterizes aborigines, statesmen, and many between. "Few are the older politicians," Sarwono said, "who would think of accepting office or resigning before they consult a soothsayer." He named names. President Sukarno is reported to have had a soothsayer.

"My uncle" (former Prime Minister Dr. Wilopo, now chairman of the Constituent Assembly), Sarwono related, "suffered a severe asthma attack recently. We went to Western-trained M.D.s but got no relief. Then he visited a dukun, who gave him a glass of tap water with a piece of paper in it and bade him pronounce some mystic Arabic words after him. He became well in two days."

Sarwono and I argued the matter. "We Javanese," he explained, "believe that mind rules over matter." I agreed partially. If there are psychosomatic illnesses, there must be psychosomatic cures.

"Some dukuns," Sarwono declared, "are charlatans and mere peddlers of fake patent medicines. Others are decent people who practice Indonesian medicine based on the use of herbs, roots, and so forth. Our country has so few physicians I don't know where we would be without dukuns."

On April 1, 1957, according to the official 1957 statistical yearbook, Indonesia, with approximately 85 million inhabitants, had 852 physicians, or one doctor to 100,000 persons; 104 dentists; 13 pharmacists and 309 assistant pharmacists; and 1 orthopedic technician. Small wonder dukuns and midwives thrive.

I interviewed an Indonesian doctor who was graduated from a Dutch university. "Of course I believe that dukuns can produce cures," he said. "Faith healing has its dangers, but in a way it is an extension of medical therapeutics. Some dukuns are quacks. Others deserve the greatest praise."

"What about djamu?" I inquired.

"That is nature cure," he replied. "My wife takes djamu."

The more I heard about djamu the more I wished to talk to a dukun. Finally Sarwono made the arrangements and took me to Mrs. Duteri Retna Salehan Notohatmodjo, at 29, Djalan Sumenep, in Jakarta. She was seventy-one, and had been a dukun for forty years. Her son, a physician, sometimes sent her his patients, she said. So does a palace physician. On the other hand, she was undergoing treatment by an eye specialist for a slight eye tic. "I cannot reject Western medicine," she declared, "neither have I complete faith in the water cure or spiritual healing."

Mrs. Salehan, daughter of a South Sumatran father and a Jogjakarta mother, long ago learned about djamu from a sister of her grandmother, from a Chinese dukun, who was a native of Shansi province in China, and from dukuns in Sumatra and Solo. They gave her written instructions which she still follows. Her voice was gentle and she had a calm bedside manner. Patients visit her; she rarely goes out except to buy djamu. Some djamu is sent to her from Semarang; occasionally patients give her gifts of djamu.

Djamu is made from bark, leaves, grasses, herbs, buds, and the roots of trees and plants. As we sat and talked with the dukun, while I took copious notes, she showed us a large number of specimens. Some, wrapped in paper packets, were in the form of powder. Others looked like tea. There were also jars filled with djamu in the shape of beans, peas, flat buttons, and marbles.

The varieties were endless and though I returned with Sarwono for a second visit I did not list them all. Tjekok Temu, from a root which grows in Java, is given to a one-year-old baby for strength. At the beginning of puberty, girls take Kodok after menstruation; it cleanses the blood, enhances femininity, and lends brightness to the eyes and face.

Teen-agers, the dukun said, must retain their fat in order not to be too weak in old age. After fifty, a woman should drink a special djamu to prevent her from getting thin. But between twenty and fifty, women drink Sari Galian to enable them to keep their slim figures.

Lulur paste, made from rice mixed with pulverized bark and flowers, prevents wrinkles. It is applied twice a month, or once a week by a girl who wants to get married, for fifteen minutes. During the three months following childbirth, lulur should be used with greater intensity; in the first month, for fifteen minutes every day; the second month, fifteen minutes every other day; the third month, every day from Monday to Thursday.

New mothers take ten djamus, six of which are for internal use and four for external, during the first forty days after the delivery of a child. They are (1) Peluntur, to remove any blood left in the body. This looks like mustard powder and is combined with Java sugar and coconut sugar. Dosage: one tablespoon every morning during the first four or five days. (2) Djamu Parem Taon, a powder in envelopes, to contract the abdominal muscles. One tablespoon, mornings and afternoons, with salt and citrus juice added, but no sugar, for the first six days. (3) Parem Sawan, for eight days. (4) Galian for slimming, for ten days. (5) Galian Pentagen, mornings and afternoons for twelve days, to restore vigor. (6) Kelowas, to enhance beauty, reinforce sex appeal, and give the face brightness. (7) Tapal, one teaspoon for forty days, to beautify. (9) Pilis powder on the forehead to prevent headaches. (10) Param powder, made from a bean and mixed with water, to cover the entire body except the breasts.

All ten after-childbirth djamus cost 250 rupiahs, say $10, and must be ordered one month in advance. The dukun receives no fee. Her income is from the sale of djamu. Mrs. Salehan said many Dutchwomen would come to her for these djamus and now she has American and other western clients. The amounts of djamu to be taken and the combinations depend on the age of the mother, the number of previous births, and whether delivery was easy or difficult.

"Do men take djamu?" I asked.

"Yes," the dukun replied, "for men there is obat," which simply means medicine. "We have Obat Kurang Sjahwat for male potency. It is taken as a warm drink. The man under treatment must never use ice or eat cold food. That chills the body. He should have beer, warm dishes, and some spices."

She told of an Australian patient who was too fat to dance. She gave him Sinsat, a tea which dissolves in very hot water, to be drunk three times a day, "and no ice ever." He returned after a week and complained that he could not live in the tropics without ice and that he found Sinsat too bitter. She could not alter the taste, but if he took ice the fat would harden and the cure would be delayed.

For rheumatism in men and women Mrs. Salehan prescribed a powder for the body during the night to be washed off in the morning, and a drink three times a day called Obat Godokentjok.

"Asthma?" I asked.

"Asthma is too difficult," she admitted. "Its nature varies. I send the patient to a physician."

"Heart?"

"That too resists djamu and obat," the dukun said. "I have Obat Djantung which may help if the organ is not damaged and if the person has not suffered too long. I tell the patients to keep cool and be tolerant and loving."

"Once a young boy was brought to me with an inflamed appendix," she volunteered. "I gave him Obat Gindjal and no operation was necessary."

The leaf of the papaya yields a djamu called Godong Kates that cures malaria. The bark of the cinchona tree, which grows plentifully in Central Java, has been used for centuries, perhaps millennia, against malaria.

Leaving the vegetable for the animal world one discovers that the horn of the giant rhinoceros, ground to powder, is valued as an aphrodisiac. It is recorded that a Chinese merchant in Sumatra offered to exchange a new American automobile for a rhinoceros. The belief in the sex-inducing qualities of the rhino horn was leading to the total extermination of the rhinoceros in Borneo, Sumatra, and Java until the Republican government took some more or less effective measures for the mammal's survival.

Elsewhere in Indonesia, langur monkeys are killed by the hundreds because it became known centuries ago that they suffer from gallstones which, swallowed by human beings, supposedly cure fever. How these superstitions arose, whether they have any scientific basis, and how early man managed to learn that certain plants cure certain maladies remains a mystery. That herbs have medicinal qualities is nothing new. The Bible mentions mandrakes as an aid to female fertility. Nature healing seemed a miracle to the primitive mind and was often interpreted as the hand of God. Thus native medicine, magic, mysticism, animism, and soothsaying became associated, and they permeated psychology, daily life, religion, and politics in all of Indonesia but especially in Java.

Sujatmoko, a Central Javanese writer, publisher, and student of culture, told me that his father, a noted surgeon, was a mystic and had visions. In 1948, before the second Dutch police action, the father, who was remote from politics, told his family of a vision in which he saw himself attacked, in Jogjakarta, by Dutch troops. Presently two non-Dutch foreign soldiers appeared and crossed their rifles to stop the Dutch. When, later, the United Nations intervened to block the Dutch action, the father's vision was interpreted as prophetic.

In conversation after conversation, the prediction of the twelfth-century East Java soothsaying King of Kediri was quoted to me. "A white buffalo will come and rule over us for three hundred fifty years," the prophecy went. "Then a yellow monkey will rule for three and a half years. That will be followed by chaos."

"Do you believe it?" I asked.

"It has happened just like that," friends said in effect. "The buffalo was the Dutch, the monkey Japan, and now . . ."

In his prison cell Sukarno once had a daytime vision, a fellow prisoner recounted. Sukarno's outstretched arm reached out of the cell window and covered the entire country.

The third Congress of Indonesian Mystics convened in Jakarta in July, 1958. The third item on its agenda read: "The activities of 'black' and 'white' magic." President Sukarno addressed one of the sessions.

Dr. Grunek, an Austrian born in 1900, practiced medicine in Vienna until a visiting Chinese physician from Surabaya persuaded him to come to Indonesia in 1925. He has lived in Indonesia ever since, married a beautiful Javanese who is the mother of his two children (eight and seven years old in 1958), and in 1940 became a Moslem and changed his name to Dr. Grunek Mohammad Abdul Hadi. Having gone to Mecca in 1953, he is now Haji Mohammad Abdul Hadi.

I spent two evenings in the Bandung home of Dr. Grunek. From 1925 to 1934 he practiced Western medicine as he had in Vienna. Then, he does not know how or why, he felt the call to heal by mystic formulas. A woman brought him a girl of nine who was paralyzed and could only creep on her hands and knees. He visited her home once a week and concentrated on her at a distance of thirty feet. After several months of such treatment, he arrived one day and was greeted by the mother who said, "She's outside hopping around on crutches." He had healed her. . . . A man called at Dr. Grunek's office with a bottle of tap water. The physician concentrated on the bottle; the water cured the man of asthma. . . . "A friend of mine suffered from recurrent headaches," Dr. Grunek said. "I held my hands several inches from his ears. The headaches disappeared."

"I treat most patients as any Western physician would," Dr. Grunek said, speaking German. "But sometimes I am prompted to apply a mystic cure. It usually works."

We rambled through the world of Indonesian politics. "Java is the heart of Indonesia and Java is different," Dr. Grunek stated. "There is no understanding of Java without a consideration of the occult. Unless you fast and deliberately deny the body sleep you cannot understand magic and the occult."

A number of Javanese expressed similar sentiments. I was not ready to give up food or sleep.

Chapter Twenty-six

THE ARMY IN POLITICS

I HAVE NEVER known another country where geography counted for so much in politics. Indonesians do not like foreigners to mention this, and an official's wife, who had imbibed a drop too much at a dinner party, cautioned me "not to meddle and muddle" when I alluded to it, suggesting that I was an imperialist who sought to divide. But "geography," a covering term for the economics, history, demography, language, and social customs of a geographic area, plays a role everywhere. One has only to think of the southern states of the United States; Bavaria, Prussia, the Rhineland in Germany; the ethnic regions of the Soviet Union; and the provincial and linguistic loyalties which diminish the national unity of India. Indonesia's geographic divisions are simply more distinct because of the insular nature of the country. For political identification it is helpful to know whether one is speaking to a Sumatran or a Javanese and whether the Javanese is from Central and Eastern or Western Java. Geographic origin is not the only criterion. Many rise above it. For many it is decisive.

I was photographing itinerant food vendors outside my house in Jakarta when five young men, immaculate in white, who had been sitting on the benches of an open-air restaurant down the street, approached and asked to have their pictures taken. They were high school and university students, aged sixteen to twenty-five, spoke intelligible English, and told me, amid smiles, that they were Protestant Christian Bataks from Tapanuli in the Lake Toba region of North Sumatra. Their hero was Colonel Simbolon, a Protestant Batak from Tapanuli and leading figure in the Central Sumatran rebel group at Padang. They approved of all the rebel chiefs except former Prime Minister Mohammad Natsir, head of the Masjumi party, who, they alleged, wanted an Islamic theocratic state. "Does this mean," I asked, "that you are for Sukarno, who opposes a theocratic state?" They avoided an answer. They preferred Third Deputy Prime Minister Leimena, a Christian.

To extend my stay in Indonesia from one month to three I had to fill out forms at the immigration headquarters, buy a special stamp at the Jakarta central post office, and return with it to the immigration authorities who would affix it to my permit. I encountered trouble in the post office and went to the foreign mail desk, where the two young men spoke English. I explained my problem and they inquired who I was.

"Why aren't you in Padang?" they asked.

"Are you from Padang?"

"Yes," they said.

"And you sympathize with the rebels?"

"Of course," they asserted.

The Indonesian government began its military operations against the Padang rebels with the bombing of two radio stations in Padang and one in Bukittinggi on February 21, 1958. All three were hit and temporarily silenced, Tillman Durdin reported to the *New York Times* from Padang. The raiding planes, an American B-25 Mitchell bomber and two U.S. P-51 Mustangs, caused no casualties. Two days later, a day after the news of the bombing became known, Professor Bahder Djohan, a native of Bukittinggi and a Minangkabau, resigned as president of the government University of Indonesia in Jakarta. In April I went to see him in his home. "I warned my government in January," he said, "that if it used violence against the rebels I would resign. In my letter of resignation I urged the government to use the expedient of discussion—Musjawarah—the Indonesian way." The former President insisted he was an Indonesian nationalist, not a Sumatran separatist or a Central Sumatran patriot. Nevertheless, the Central Sumatrans I met either sympathized with the rebels or, like Professor Bahder Djohan, Dr. Hatta, and Sjahrir, tried to prevent hostilities by advising the rebels to make peace. It was clear that Dr. Hatta, whom Sukarno had asked to join the government, would not do so while it was fighting the insurgents. None doubted Hatta's fervent nationalism, yet a sentimental attachment to his Minangkabau homeland inevitably had some influence on his stand. It would not be otherwise in any other country. Emotions are at the heart of all politics.

The civil war put a strain not only on Sumatrans but on the loyal, progovernment military whatever their island origin. For the loyalist army, air army, and navy were being asked to use force against their war-of-independence buddies who, to make matters worse, held the same views on crucial issues in the dispute that precipitated the revolt.

Colonel Ahmed Hussein, the top rebel commander, told *New York Times* correspondent Bernard Kalb on April 2, 1957, he wanted a presidential, instead of a parliamentary, Cabinet to be headed by Sukarno and Hatta. If Sukarno would not agree, he favored a "benevolent dictatorship" to replace the present "unworkable" party system.

Brigadier General Djatikusumo, field commander of the government troops opposing Colonel Hussein, spoke in similar terms to Associated Press man Murray Fromson on April 21, 1958. Calling the rebel officers "my friends," he too advocated the re-establishment of the old Sukarno-Hatta partnership (which ended when Vice-President Hatta resigned on December 1, 1956), a five- to six-year suspension of elections, and the formation of a nonparty government backed by the army. "Basically," he said, "I sympathize with the rebels' political principles." He could not, however, condone the separate government at Padang.

Thus the vocal leaders of the rebel military as well as of the loyalist military were skeptical of parliamentary democracy and supported a mild dictatorship either by the Sukarno-Hatta duumvirate in conjunction with the army or by the army alone.

The rebel and loyalist military likewise saw eye to eye on the question of Communism; both proved that they opposed it on religious, political, and power grounds. The rebels, however, made the most of their anti-Communism because they were angling for United States aid and, knowing the official American mind, played that note for more than it was worth. Many Western newspapers and radio systems, finding it difficult to explain a civil war between two sides that had so much in common, seized on the reportorial life raft of "Communism" to explain in that one simplified term something that was manifold and complicated. The hoax worked, wrought confusion, and distorted American policy until it was saved from a perilously wrong turn by the beneficent intervention of events and Howard P. Jones, a new, clear-eyed American ambassador. Unintentionally, Sukarno facilitated the rebels' gambit by launching the "Guided Democracy" concept in his February 21, 1957, speech which called for Communist participation in the government. It lent plausibility to their anti-Communist crusade.

The rebels in Sumatra, as well as those in North Celebes, had legitimate grievances which should have been, and could have been, redressed by wise, providential leadership. The basic complaint was that they gave more than they received. Sumatra's exports, Sumatrans never tire of repeating, bring in 71 per cent of Indonesia's foreign earnings. The money, however, goes to the central government in Jakarta and most of it is spent in Java. Sumatra, about the size of California or Japan, is 24.9 per cent of the total area of Indonesia, but with only 13 million inhabitants it contained (in 1956) 16.5 per cent of the entire country's population, whereas Java, plus the small nearby island of Madura, is 7 per cent of the total area yet harbors 64.9 per cent of the national population. Though largely agrarian, Java is the most densely populated region on earth. It would die without Sumatra's income. Sumatrans, however, find no consolation in this nor in the fact that Java has better roads, railways, schools, and public utilities, and sends its castoff rolling stock to Sumatra.

Confronted with this roster of woe, leaders in Jakarta said, "Sumatra could have put its case to Parliament." But the one-chamber Indonesian Parliament is elected by proportional representation, and Java therefore has far more representatives than Sumatra. What Indonesia needs is a Senate. The same problem confronted the thirteen American colonies when the smaller ones, like Vermont, Delaware, and Rhode Island, feared that they would be submerged by populous New York, Pennsylvania, and Virginia. The answer was the Senate, in which each state, no matter how big or how little, has two members. When this parallel was suggested to Indonesians they exclaimed, "Yes, yes, we have been contemplating just that." But Indonesians have a way of contemplating and contemplating and discussing and discussing and doing nothing.

The Sumatran and Celebes revolts were what one might facetiously call extraparliamentary lobbying. Since they could not get their grievances redressed by Parliament or in any other legal way, the rebels rebelled and set up their own government, never intending to secede and trusting that the insurrection would be talked out of existence by Musjawarah and result in some satisfactory adjustment of the imbalance between Sumatra and Java and between the Celebes and Java.

This was not the first armed uprising. Free Indonesia has been punished with rich experience in army revolts, military coups, and guerrilla warfare. A month had not elapsed after the Dutch transfer of sovereignty when Raymond Paul P. ("Turk") Westerling, a former Dutch army captain, rallying Dutch deserters, captured part of the city of Bandung on January 23, 1950. A few days later he led an assault on the Parliament Building in Jakarta. The Dutch government denounced him publicly and in February, 1950, he fled from Indonesia by plane, and later returned to Holland to sing in the opera. Indonesian authorities saw in his exploits the hidden hand of The Hague. Sultan Hamid II of West Borneo, minister without portfolio in the Indonesian government, was arrested on April 5, 1950, as an alleged Westerling conspirator.

In the same month a revolt started by an Indonesian army captain named Abdul Aziz, who captured Makassar in the Celebes, was quickly quelled, and the Amboinese of the South Moluccan Islands set up an independent republic. President Sukarno blamed Holland. Amboina, the capital city, fell to central government troops in November, 1950, but sporadic fighting continued till 1952. Thousands of rebels, most of them former native soldiers in the Dutch army, were evacuated to Holland, whence expensive glazed-paper literature in the name of the dead Republic of the South Moluccas was still being circulated in English in 1955.

Dr. P. S. Gerbrandy, wartime prime minister of Holland, wrote a letter published in the March 28, 1951, issue of the London *Times,* calling attention to disturbances in Java. "A state of affairs has been reached," he declared, "when the greater Powers who are in large measure responsible for the removal of the historic authority of the Netherlands from the East Indies should . . . exert pressure on the government of Indonesia," which "seems unable to settle down," to "maintain law and order." The communication reflected a backward-oriented politician's bitterness over the loss of the Indies and his impotent, last-ray hope of Western intervention. It fed anti-Dutch emotions and suspicions in Indonesia, nothing else.

Indonesia, obviously, would brook no further foreign intervention. But her leaders knew, before Gerbrandy wrote, that their country had to settle down. However, they adopted the wrong means of doing so. Irritated by unrest in the Moluccas, Borneo, and the Celebes, suspecting that Holland, which fathered puppet states on those islands from 1946 to 1948, supported the dissident groups, President Sukarno and Prime Minister and Vice-President Hatta decided to transform the federal state into a unitary state. On August 17, 1950, the Republic of the United States of Indonesia accordingly became the Republic of Indonesia. The Senate representing the states was abolished, and Jakarta took over the centralized rule of the entire country.

Federalism in Indonesia suffers from its Dutch birthmark. To most Indonesian nationalists any Dutch principle or method of government is automatically wrong. But if your enemy says it is Monday and it is Monday you cannot call it Friday. Federalism is the natural and best form of organization for an archipelago of islands at different stages of economic, political, and cultural development, each with a certain amount of insular pride, local patriotism, and wish for partial autonomy. Intelligent concessions to this condition would, by gradually building stronger connecting tissue between loosely held segments, do more for national unity than the imposition of a unitary central government on refractory provinces.

The new nonfederal, Senate-less system did not stop the spate of army coups, military insurrections, and provincial eruptions. In the Celebes, Kahar Muzakar celebrated the sixth anniversary of the founding of the Republic on August 17, 1945, by going off into the mountains with 4,000 men whom he had tried unsuccessfully to enroll in the regular army's reserve corps. Even more troublesome was the upsurge in 1950 of the Darul Islam guerrilla movement in West Java under the command of Kartosuwirio. In 1952 Defense Minister Sultan Hamengku Buwono IX estimated Kartosuwirio's manpower at 10,000, a formidable force when operating in intricate mountain fastnesses and dark jungles. Most of the 10,000 were unemployed demobilized soldiers, landless peasants, disillusioned nationalists, Islamic fanatics, and plain looters and bandits, the uprooted children of an unfinished revolution.

Popular discontent, openly admitted a little later, was already in evidence. It infected the army: officers became emotionally restive and politically active. Under the strong Hatta Cabinet, during which the Dutch departed, and under his successor, Prime Minister Natsir of the Masjumi party, the army refrained from public pressure on the government. But in June, 1951, the commanders forced the resignation of the Minister of Justice in the Sukiman Cabinet because he refused to sanction the arrest of some guerrilla leaders. Friction also developed between the military and Mr. R. T. A. Sewaka, Sukiman's defense minister. It is not surprising, therefore, to learn from the carefully judicious, authoritative Cornell University White Book on the Wilopo Cabinet (1952-1953) by Herbert Feith, an Australian, that "the army leadership, representing an enormous center of political power, played a role of importance in ousting the Cabinet" of Sukiman on February 23, 1952.

This date marks the emergence of the army as a primary political factor. The weaker the civilian government the greater the influence of the military. In countries where representative government is new and fragile the army usually craves power. Military commanders regard themselves as patriots who cannot sit idly by while party bosses in the togas of ministers make a mess. The professional guardians of the nation against a foreign enemy, officers easily see themselves in the same role against a domestic menace in the shape of a shaky hand on the rudder of the ship of state. Underpaid themselves, the corruption of self-enriching politicians goads them to cleansing action and they thus appear to the public as champions of purity as well as of stability. This has happened in many less-developed countries and it happened in Indonesia.

Prime Minister Wilopo, a former attorney and schoolteacher, took office in succession to Sukiman on April 4, 1952. The 40-year-old Sultan Hamengku Buwono IX of Jogjakarta became his defense minister. The Sultan, as the country knows him, was the army's candidate. The officers respected his royal ancestry, ability, modesty, modern outlook, patriotism, and nonpartisanship. He is, after Sukarno, Indonesia's most charismatic personality.

On assuming the prime-ministership, Wilopo lifted the state of war and siege decreed by the Dutch in 1939. He released thousands of political prisoners—most of them captured guerrillas—and attacked the economic "decline the end of which one cannot yet see." The export boom caused by the Korean War had tapered off, giving a fillip to discontented elements and to the Communists, who now, for the first time, in accordance with a decision taken in May, began to act like nationalists, patriots, and lovers of landlords and domestic capitalists.

Amid squabbling parties, enfeebled ministries, and economic crisis, another power factor emerged: Sukarno. He had always been the biggest fact in the Republic. But, whereas Prime Ministers Hatta and Natsir restricted him to the role of head of state, their less-secure successors drew him into the arena of political jousts. Six and a half months after the Wilopo Cabinet was born, there occurred a major event in Sukarno's life and in the history of the Indonesian army and of the Republic, which is recorded in the chronicles as "The October 17 Affair."

On October 17, 1952, the army made its first attempt to seize power. The events of that day were the prelude to the 1956 revolts in Sumatra and the Celebes.

In 1952 the army was seven years old, the same age as the Republic. Some officers were Dutch-trained, more were Japanese-trained. Almost all, and many of the rank and file, had fought the Dutch in the 1946-1949 war of independence. The liberation of India was the work of civilians. The military did not fight to achieve it. The postindependence Indian army therefore remained a "British" army in that it would rather play polo than politics and did not interfere in the job of governing. But Indonesia's army commanders felt that having contributed to the birth of the state they had a duty to preserve it from party leaders who played politics to the country's disadvantage. The colonels intended to enter politics for the common good. This sincere purpose was buttressed by a will to serve their own good, or the army's good.

A money matter put the match to the fuse that led to the October 17 explosion. "By the middle of 1952," writes M.I.T. Professor Benjamin Higgins, "it was clear to the fiscal authorities in Indonesia that the country was facing a first-class financial crisis." The new Wilopo Cabinet decreed austerity. Since austerity, to appeal, must begin at home, the government restricted the use of automobiles by officials, reduced the size of diplomatic missions abroad, and otherwise tightened its belt. The main cut, however, was in personnel. According to Higgins, then the UN adviser of the

Ministry of Finance, the 1953 plan called for the dismissal of 60,000 civil servants, 60,000 soldiers, and 30,000 policemen.

The proposed demobilization was only one knotty factor in a knotty maze of knotty factors. The Sultan, as defense minister, Ali Budiarjo, secretary general of the Defense Ministry, Major General T. B. Simatupang, chief of staff of the armed services, and Colonel Abdul Haris Nasution, army chief of staff, intended to curtail military personnel in such a way as to alter the very nature of the forces. Borrowing from the Japanese and from the lord-fearing Javanese, the defense forces had been organized on a loyalty-to-the commander basis. The commander was a little father, an autocrat, a regional warlord. That might have been desirable in disjointed guerrilla combats with the Dutch when the government was far away or nonexistent and each officer and his men were a law unto themselves living off the land and finding weapons where they could. But now, with technical training, centralized leadership, and loyalty to the state the prime requisites, "pap-ism" had to go. The papas did not like it. Many were due for retirement under the latest scheme which provided for an army of 120,000.

President Sukarno, by virtue of his office, was commander in chief of the defense forces. Orders for important appointments or reassignments were signed by him. Early in 1952 Army Chief of Staff Nasution decided to transfer Colonel Simbolon, territorial commander of North Sumatra and a North Sumatran, to the East Java command. This was perhaps a measure against provincial warlordism which gave high officers an undesirably firm hold on the areas where they were born and enjoyed a large personal following. Simbolon would have replaced Colonel Bambang Sugeng. Sukarno refused to sign the order for the replacement.

Intrigue and personal vendettas began to rage in the army. A Colonel Bambang Supeno, remote relative of Sukarno, had urged the President to discharge Nasution. Supeno now traveled through the country collecting army officers' signatures to a petition urging Nasution's dismissal. "To counteract this development," writes Herbert Feith in his scholarly White Book, "the Armed Forces' Chief of Staff Major General Simatupang called a meeting of territorial commanders and other high officers at his home on July 12. At this meeting, at which Colonel Nasution was not present, Major General Simatupang asked Colonel Bambang Supeno to give an account of his activities. Tempers were aroused and before long Colonel Supeno walked out.

"On the following day," continues Feith, who at the time was employed by the Ministry of Information in Jakarta, "Colonel Bambang Supeno wrote a letter to the Defense Minister, the Prime Minister, and the Defense Section of Parliament, declaring he no longer had faith in his superiors. . . . Four days later, he was suspended from all duties" by Nasution.

The Sultan, Simatupang, and Nasution then went to the President to discuss the tangle. They could not help mentioning Sukarno's attitude to Supeno. "The conversation," says Feith, "became heated, particularly between Sukarno and Simatupang, and the meeting finally ended without any agreement. . . ."

The Sultan relieved Bambang Supeno on July 29.

For ten weeks, from the end of July till October 16, Parliament spent much of its time debating the military crisis. The point of departure was demobilization and the behavior of Colonel Bambang Supeno. But speakers ranged free and far into high politics and low recrimination. Dirty parliamentary and military linen was washed in public morning, noon, and night. Personalities spiced the discussions. Major General Simatupang was Ali Budiarjo's brother-in-law; Ali Budiarjo is Sjahrir's brother-in-law, and Sjahrir is the leader of the Socialist party, a nationalist but not vituperatively anti-Dutch. Above all, Sjahrir is a Westerner with a coldly analytical mind, a proponent of modernization, an intellectual, an adamantine anti-Communist with a closer affinity for Hatta than Sukarno. Members of Parliament and editors charged that the army was under Socialist influence. It was the Socialists, they said, who wanted a Westernized, depersonalized army, trained by the 900-man strong Dutch Military Mission then still in Indonesia. Communists joined in the cry.

The Sultan threatened to resign as minister of defense. Several colleagues in the Cabinet said they would go out with him. The Wilopo Ministry tottered. Some party leaders wanted to bring it down. Some sought a major political realignment. On about every issue several of the big parties were split two or three ways, some insisting that Wilopo stay, others that he go, still others that Parliament be dissolved and elections take place.

The situation grew more tense by the day. On October 10 "a large meeting of colonels and lieutenant colonels was held," writes Feith, "in an effort to close the divisions inside the army in the face of what was thought of as insults and threats from outside"—from Parliament and parties. The next day all seven of Indonesia's territorial commanders, the regional warlords in command of divisions, gathered in Jakarta and remained in the city in readiness for any development. Heavy army guards surrounded the Parliament Building. Jakarta, where prophecy travels by jet rather than betjak, hummed with the rumored dispersal of Parliament by the military, the kidnaping of Sukarno, an army government, or, on the contrary, the disgrace of Nasution, Simatupang, and the Sultan.

Parliament voted on a series of vague and confused resolutions on the morning of October 16. The strongest anti-army censure motion was opposed by the Moslem Masjumi, the Socialist party, the Catholic and Protestant parties and several smaller groups but passed by a tally of 91 to 54, with some abstentions, thanks to the PNI (Indonesian Nationalist party), which had split during the debate but, under Sukarno's pressure, voted solidly for the motion as did the Communists and several lesser, conservative parties.

When the balloting was finished, Masjumi leader Mohammad Natsir said, "I don't know what will happen now." The Sultan was expected to resign. Inescapably, Prime Minister Wilopo would have to resign. There would be no government. Would the army grab power?

To avoid a crisis the Sultan patriotically postponed his resignation.

Early in the morning of October 17, before the tropical sun had heated Jakarta's streets, 5,000 demonstrators congregated around the Parliament Building. Some looked like workingmen, some like peasants, some like soldiers in mufti. They carried, says Feith, "well-painted banners and placards." Among the slogans were "Dissolve Parliament"; "Elections Immediately"; "Purge the Corruptors"; et cetera.

Nobody knew who organized the demonstration. Though the matter was subsequently investigated, nobody knows. Suspicion fell on the army, and particularly on an army dentist named Colonel Mustopo. Whoever the sponsors, their product grew and soon numbered 30,000. A few of them broke into the building and smashed some cheap chairs and the delegates' cafeteria. Then the mass moved, as though directed, to the Presidential Palace.

Blocked by the fence, they called for Sukarno. He came out to the white-marble palace steps, looked around, and walked across the front lawn to the fence, where he chatted amiably with those nearby. The crowd cheered him for his priyayi nonchalance. Then he returned, mounted to the highest step, and began to address the multitude. Though I harassed secretaries and adjutants and badgered ministries, though I obtained all of Sukarno's speeches from 1945 to date, I could not, during my 1958 visit, obtain the text of that historic extemporaneous speech on October 17, 1952, which turned back a revolution. It had not been recorded. Earwitnesses say it was a masterpiece of sinuous oratory. The President promised early elections. But did they want him to dissolve Parliament like a dictator? Had they not fought for freedom? Did they wish to lose it and the democratic franchise which independence had brought them? "He both rebuked and soothed them," writes Feith, who was present.

As Sukarno spoke, two army tanks, four armored cars, and four cannons rumbled to the palace grounds. Looking at his audience, Sukarno could also look into the mouths of the cannons and at the muzzles of machine guns. He became furious. He lashed at those who would crush democracy with guns. He believed in liberty for demonstrators, not in monopoly power for militarists, himself, a political party, or anybody. The mass cheered. He sent them home cheering. Once more his magic tongue and charismatic personality had prevailed.

In a mingled mood of anger and satisfaction he went back into the palace, only to be confronted, at 10:15 a.m., with seventeen topmost army officers, including Simatupang, Nasution, Simbolon, Colonel Alex Kawilarang, territorial commander of West Java which embraced Jakarta, and Colonel G. P. H. Djatikusumo—in all, five of the seven territorial warlords of Indonesia and most of the brightest brass. No political tyro, Sukarno refused to be one against the military. Quickly he summoned Vice-President Hatta, Prime Minister Wilopo, the Acting Speaker of Parliament, and the chief presidential aide, Mr. A. K. Pringgodigdo. This now ceased to be army vs. president. It was a showdown between civilian authority and military power.

They talked for an hour and a half. "The officers' chief aim," writes Feith, "was to have the President dissolve parliament." They contended that the unrepresentative parliament made stable government impossible. Colonel Simbolon, scheduled for transfer from the North Sumatran Command to East Java, complained of politics in army assignments. Colonel Kawilarang reported on the stormy temper of his troops. The upshot was: dissolve Parliament and call a national election.

Sukarno refused.

Outside the palace troops were gathering. At 11 a.m., while the brass was pressing the President, the military cut all telephone and telegraph communications. Public meetings were prohibited by army decree. An 8 p.m. to 5 a.m. curfew was declared. Six prominent members of Parliament were arrested. Two major dailies were suppressed.

The stage seemed set for a quick coup.

But Sukarno was neither awed nor cowed.

Did Sukarno block an army attempt to seize the government? When I interviewed Nasution in his Jakarta home on May 18, 1958, he, now a major general, said October 17 was "half a coup." Nothing is ever the whole in Indonesia. It was a coup and a noncoup. Nasution had discussed his intentions with Sukarno several times before October 17. He had also mentioned them to Prime Minister Wilopo. The heart of his plan, apparently, was the use of the famous Siliwangi Division, under Colonel Alex Kawilarang, to establish a new government with more power in the hands of Sukarno and less parliamentary interference. Thus, Nasution's coup would have been directed not against the President but toward the enhancement of the President's and the army's position. However, the Sultan and Armed Forces Chief of Staff Major General Simatupang opposed the Nasution maneuver. For them he went too far. For a group of younger officers, more imbued with the spirit of the secret Japanese clubs which made policy in prewar Tokyo by means of silent dagger assassination, he did not go far enough. They wanted not only the dissolution of Parliament but also the arrest of a large group of anti-army parliamentarians. Only the President, however, could dissolve Parliament or sanction the arrests, but his oratorical triumph in front of the palace earlier that morning and his wrath at being threatened with tanks and cannon while he spoke put him in no mood to yield to anyone. He had himself enhanced his power and if he resisted the army high command he would be more powerful still. He accordingly sent the officers away with nothing. The commanders were divided, he was firm and euphoric. He was chief of state and father of the Republic. Surrender to intimidation or a league with naked armed force would have been beneath the dignity of his office and status. He stood his ground that day and it became a towering pinnacle.

Shrewd politician that he is, Sukarno saw nevertheless that no problem had been solved. There would be unhappiness in the army owing to thwarted ambitions and burning jealousies. To keep the reins and stabilize his eminence at the fulcrum he needed a balance against the army. In Parliament on October 16 the motion he favored had won by the combined ballots of the PNI and the Communists. Such an alliance under his guidance could give him control of Parliament. He fostered it. The PNI was part priyayi and part peasant. He wanted the support of both elements. If the army could corral a street demonstration against him, the Communists could mobilize one for him and also hold popular discontent in check.

The army upstarts had been whipped. The Socialists and the Masjumi scowled. Sukarno was in the driver's seat, his chariot drawn by two horses: PNI and the Communists. His popularity increased. So did his headaches. A really clairvoyant palace fortuneteller would have predicted that from the cold victory of October 17, 1952, a civil war would sprout in 1956.

Chapter Twenty-seven

MILITARY MERRY-GO-ROUND

WHEN AN ARMY plays politics and the politicians play with the army the final score is indiscipline.

Among the October 17, 1952, group of territorial commanders who put pressure on Sukarno was Lieutenant Colonel Dr. Suwondo. On returning to East Java headquarters in Surabaya he was arrested and superseded by a subordinate, Lieutenant Colonel Sudirman.

Another participant in the interview with Sukarno was Lieutenant Colonel Kosasih, commander of South Sumatra. When he arrived at his base in Palembang, he was deposed by Lieutenant Colonel Kretarto, a subordinate enjoying officer and government support.

On November 12, 1952, Colonel Gatot Subroto, territorial chief of East Indonesia, was ejected from his Makassar headquarters by his chief of staff, Lieutenant Colonel Joop F. Warouw, a native of North Celebes, who proclaimed loyalty to Sukarno but warned that he would not allow Defense Minister Sultan Hamengku Buwono IX or Army Chief of Staff Nasution to land in the Celebes.

Sukarno dismissed Nasution on December 18—"because of the October 17 affair" reads Nasution's official biographical sketch—and appointed in his place Colonel Bambang Sugeng, an opponent of Nasution and of the Sultan.

The Sultan thereupon resigned.

This was the first, but only the first, turn of the Indonesian military merry-go-round.

Reeling under the dizzying blows, Prime Minister Wilopo enunciated a favorite Indonesian unity formula: "All Under One Roof," like Sukarno's "All members of the family at the dining table." But the roof leaked and the rains were heavy. Though internal peace and the economic situation improved slightly, the taste for political feuding did not flag. In May, 1953, a simmering quarrel between top air force leaders boiled over. Vice-Commodore Sujono had charged that Commodore Suryadarma, air force chief of staff, was exceeding his authority and should be investigated. Suryadarma placed Sujono under arrest. In protest, pilot friends of Sujono hopped into their planes and cavorted over Jakarta.

This was a brief tropical cloudburst compared with the gathering political storm. Steadily, in the aftermath of October 17, the rift between the Masjumi-Socialist bloc, which opposed Sukarno, and the PNI-Communist alignment, which supported him, grew wider. Socialist popularity waned. The Masjumi party split, and a powerful fragment organized the Nahdatul Ulama (NU), or Moslem Teachers' party. With the anti-Sukarno forces thus weakened, Sukarno emerged as the man against whom no government could stand. Already chief of state, he became in addition the real, though not titular, head of every Cabinet.

A new government was needed to reflect this changed situation. Wilopo accordingly resigned on June 2, 1953, and was succeeded by Dr. Ali Sastroamijojo, a Dutch-trained lawyer and PNI stalwart.

Prime Minister Ali's Cabinet lasted from August 1, 1953, to August 12, 1955—a long life in Indonesia's political climate. I asked Dr. Ali why his Cabinet finally fell. He answered, "Lubis."

Colonel Zulkifli Lubis is the mystery man of Indonesia. One expert described him as "the only man who ever said No to Sukarno." Zulkifli Lubis and Nasution are cousins and natives of the Tapanuli area of North Sumatra, homeland of devout Moslems. As assistant chief of staff, Lubis secretly pulled strings in the October 17 affair, for Sukarno and against the demonstrating colonels. Sjahrir says "Lubis saved Sukarno." He consequently stayed in when Nasution went out. Lubis directed the quick coups which ousted the territorial commanders in East Java, East Indonesia, and South Sumatra immediately after October 17.

But when Sukarno overlooked him in appointing Nasution's successor and named Colonel Bambang Sugeng, Lubis gave Sugeng so much trouble that Sugeng resigned on January 16, 1955. Ironically, he who had intrigued against Nasution felt "unable," he said, "to cope with the political intrigues inside the army." The chief intriguer was Lubis.

Sukarno, however, refused to accept Sugeng's resignation.

The failure of the October 17 affair and Sukarno's personal success in quelling the coup gave him an advantage over the military. The army felt

the need of union. After preliminary talks in December and January between the coup men and the anticoup men, a military hands-across-the-
split conference was convened in Jogjakarta. It sat from February 17 to 25,
1955. According to an unpublished Cornell University essay by John R. W.
Smail, "270 officers, including the 7 territorial commanders and the leading
figures of Army headquarters," attended. Among them, in good Indonesian fashion, were Lubis and the commanders he had deposed after
October 17.

The conference adopted a "Charter of Unity" and urged the "Duumvirate," as it called Sukarno and Hatta, to facilitate this by appropriate
appointments; in other words, by restoring the officers dismissed in the
wake of October 17.

The last day of the Jogjakarta conference all was amity not only within
the army but between it and the government. To symbolize the peace,
Sukarno, Hatta, Prime Minister Ali, and other notables arrived for the
closing, and in their presence, in a great hall dimly lit by two candles and
amid the solemn roll of drums and a trumpet call, the Charter of Unity
was signed for the entire army by one person: Chief of Staff Sugeng,
whom Lubis had wished to remove.

Even this, however, could not save Sugeng, and he resigned as army
chief of staff on May 11, 1955. Colonel Lubis became acting chief of staff.
He naturally expected to be permanent chief of staff. Defense Minister
Iwa Kusumasumantri disappointed him. The new designated chief of
staff was Colonel Utoyo. On June 25 Lubis told Sukarno that he would
boycott Utoyo. Nevertheless, Sukarno fixed June 27 as the day when he
personally would install Utoyo. Lubis refused to attend. All high army
commanders absented themselves. Lubis ordered the army band not to
be there, and it was the Jakarta Fire Department band that played the
national anthem.

Defense Minister Iwa, on instructions from Sukarno, discharged the
31-year-old Lubis. Lubis, backed by most territorial commanders, refused
to be discharged. Indeed he insisted that he remain and Utoyo go. Lubis
openly justified this defiance. "Islam teaches me," he told the press in an
aggressive interview, "that I must obey my leaders, but also that I must
serve the general welfare." Having thus distinguished between the government and the good of the people, he said he might have allowed "a certain
group"—obviously Sukarno, Ali, and their associates—to use the army for
political ends. "A man of responsibility," however, "cannot do that. I
therefore decided to act according to the dictates of my conscience." In
politics, great ambition plus a conscience equals danger.

Dr. Ali, attempting to rescue his Cabinet, offered to dismiss Defense

Minister Iwa and Chief of Staff Utoyo and reinstate Lubis. Lubis rejected the compromise. Ali resigned as prime minister.

This was defeat for Sukarno. He had been planning to go on a holy pilgrimage to Mecca but postponed his departure to save Ali. When that proved hopeless, he left on July 18, assigning to Hatta the task of presiding over the formation of a new Cabinet.

Hatta's first conversation about the new Cabinet was with stormy-petrel Lubis. Masjumi man Burnhanuddin Harahap succeeded Ali on August 12, and thanks to Masjumi, NU, Socialist, and army support, stayed in office seven months. On October 27, 1955, Harahap restored Nasution as army chief of staff with the rank of major general. Colonel Lubis remained assistant in charge of intelligence work, a field in which his penchant for secrecy, labyrinthine connections, and pervasive influence found ample scope.

The Harahap Cabinet pursued moderate policies and courted the military by trying to curb corruption. Yet the army continued to harbor numerous unredressed grievances, the foremost being that it had to fight Darul Islam guerrillas in West Java, North Sumatra, and South Celebes with obsolete weapons and empty coffers. Frequently commanders could not find the funds to feed or pay their men.

These prolonged deprivations made the rampant official corruption more difficult to bear.

In one form or another, corruption lurks in the shadow of all governments in all countries, rich or poor, democratic or dictatorial. Nobody may cast the first stone. Yet corruption in retarded lands fresh out of feudalism and colonialism develops special features. Those who sacrificed, suffered, and perhaps went to jail in the battle with the imperial power feel they deserve compensation: government jobs or favors. Since employment openings are limited, political office or a civil service job is particularly attractive, not the least because it obviates the necessity of earning a living in business or industry, which the feudal mind still finds undignified and non-priyayi.

Government office confers a status the mere shopkeeper or manufacturer cannot hope to attain. The officeholder can rise still higher in status if he rides in a big car, lives in a big house, and has a big retinue of servants. His conscience and the situation permitting, he gets the necessary money illegally in return for a license, a tax loophole, a junket, a job, a promotion, an honor, et cetera. Where the civil service has neither experience nor ethical tradition and the officials are greedy, opportunities for graft are great.

The rising tide of corruption vexed the military. But the commanders could not bid the dirty tide recede, and gradually some succumbed to it. Beginning about 1953 and to an ever-increasing extent thereafter until the 1956 revolts, the army commanders in Sumatra and the Celebes augmented their official funds by selling island products direct to Singapore, Penang, and other foreign trading centers instead of through the central Indonesian government. Sumatra in this wise sold tea, tobacco, rubber, pepper, and coffee; the Celebes, north and south, sold copra, the dried coconut meat used for cooking oil, and palm oil for the manufacture of soap. In mid-1956 the chairman of the Parliamentary Defense Affairs Committee stated that with the proceeds of its smuggling operations the army command in North Celebes had purchased 5,000 tons of rice, 69 motor vehicles, and 400 bales of white cloth for distribution among soldiers and civilians. In the same area a Chinese rubber exporter kicked back to the army half of his receipts from the sale of rubber to Hong Kong and Malaya; some of the income went to barracks building. The warlords were achieving economic independence. The papas were taking care of their uniformed children. Smuggling in mounting crescendo put a premium on illegality, depleted the federal exchequer, and became a major, unconcealed, unsettling fact of Indonesian life. In 1956 Attorney General Suprato admitted that one third of Indonesia's rubber was being smuggled out annually to the tune of $125 million U.S. At 25 cents a pound, this meant half a billion pounds. It was a national scandal involving commanders who self-righteously justified their deeds.

Indonesia was heading for a crisis.

The country's first national election took place on September 29, 1955. In a very impressive demonstration of free democratic voting, 37,875,299 citizens cast their ballots for members of Parliament. At the head of the poll stood the PNI with 8,434,653 votes (22.3 per cent of the total), which entitled it to 57 seats compared to 42 in the previous, temporary House. The Masjumi, with 7,903,886 votes, also won 57 seats, an increase of 13 over its previous representation. The big surprise was the Nahdatul Ulama (NU), or Moslem Teachers' party, a splinter from the Masjumi, which piled up 6,955,141 votes, and 45 seats. The Communist party (PKI) likewise achieved a victory with 6,176,914 votes and 39 seats, a high jump from its earlier 17. But the Socialists dropped from 14 to 5 seats. In all, 29 parties elected 257 members of Parliament.

The new Parliament was installed on March 26, 1956, and the same month PNI leader Dr. Ali Sastroamijojo formed his second Cabinet. Shortly thereafter President Sukarno left for the United States and Western Europe, taking with him Colonel Joop F. Warouw, who had usurped the East Indonesia command from Gatot Subroto after the October 17, 1952, affair and was now involved in Celebes copra smuggling. Sukarno persuaded Warouw to accept the position of Indonesian military attaché in Peking.

Sukarno apparently had decided to uproot the warlords. In August, 1956, Colonel Alex Kawilarang, politically powerful territorial commander of West Java, received an appointment as military attaché in Washington. It amounted to golden exile. He was to surrender his command on August 15. At 6:15 A.M. on August 13, Kawilarang arrested Foreign Minister Ruslan Abdulgani, due to leave that very morning for the London conference on the Suez Canal.

When Prime Minister Ali and Army Chief of Staff Nasution learned of the arrest they took speedy action and secured Abdulgani's release in time to proceed to his plane—under heavy protective guard.

The excuse for the arrest was that he had been involved in corrupt practices with Chinese printers. But a special Cabinet commission, chaired by Deputy Prime Minister Mohammad Rum, investigated and found Abdulgani blameless. Kawilarang had arrested him on orders from Assistant Chief of Staff Lubis. The arrest was designed as the first move in a coup. Eight days after the arrest Colonel Gatot Subroto, ousted by Lubis in 1952, succeeded Lubis as deputy chief of staff. In October and November Lubis attempted two army insurrections against the government. On November 16 Nasution summoned Lubis. Lubis failed to appear. Nasution ordered his arrest. Lubis vanished but remained either in Jakarta or the vicinity playing tag with the police, even going to the cinema, and writing letters postmarked Jakarta to newspapers and politicians saying he would support a government of Sukarno, Hatta, and the Sultan but not of Dr. Ali.

In the midst of these disquieting developments Dr. Hatta announced on July 20, 1956, that he would resign as vice-president when the Constituent Assembly convened on December 1. Ever since the unitary state had abolished the federal Senate, the vice-president, who formerly presided over its sessions as in the United States, was a superfluous functionary and political anachronism. This formal objection apart, Hatta, as Mr. Indonesia Number Two, felt he could not accept responsibility for current policies and coming events that were casting their black shadows before. He had become estranged from Sukarno. The gulf between the central government and the outer islands troubled him. He attributed it to "Jakartaism." The country was cracking up, not from any basic division between Java and Sumatra and the Celebes but as a result of Jakarta's blunders, bungling, callousness, and corruption. The economic stagnation reinforced Hatta's wish to retire.

Nasution, who had tried to overthrow Sukarno on October 17, 1952, now ruled the army and backed Sukarno.

Lubis, who had supported Sukarno against Nasution on October 17, 1952, opposed Sukarno from his lair in Java.

Kawilarang, a Lubis man, went to Washington.

Hatta was on the way out; Sukarno was alone.

Sukarno, just back from a triumphal tour through the United States, Europe, the Soviet Union, and Red China, said on October 29, 1956, "I dream of a meeting of all the leaders of the political parties in this country at which they will decide to bury all the present political parties."

Sukarno did not acquire his aversion to parties in Russia or China. When the Republic was proclaimed in 1945, he showed a preference for no parties, or at best, one party, the PNI, his child. It was Hatta who introduced the multi-party system. Hatta, educated in Holland, is a strict, legalistic constitutionalist. Sukarno's primary preoccupation has always been unity. Bhinneka Tunggal Ika, Unity in Diversity, is the legend on Indonesia's coat of arms. Inscribed on a ribbon held in the claws of the defiant spread-wing Garuda eagle of Indonesian mythology, the motto expresses the longing to bring together that which equatorial waters and volcanic explosions have sundered. In separate fields on the Garuda's breastplate are depicted the symbols that bind: the gold star in the center field representing belief in God; the long-horned banteng, or wild buffalo, for the sovereignty of the people; a waringin tree for national consciousness; an elliptical gold chain of alternating round links for women and square links for men; and sprays of rice and cotton, which give food and raiment to the people and stand for welfare and justice.

Before Indonesia became a state, and while the Japanese were still in occupation, Sukarno delivered a speech, extemporaneous as usual, on June 1, 1945, enunciating the Five Principles (Pantjasila) on which a free Indonesia would rest. Pantjasila is the Republic's official credo. The first principle, in Sukarno's words, is "All for all," or nationalism. He called nationalism "the will to unite" on a united territory.

Even that unity was incomplete. "Let us not say," Sukarno urged, "that the Indonesian nation is the noblest and most perfect, whilst belittling other peoples. We should aim at the unity and brotherhood of the whole world." He called this second principle "Internationalism"—not "cosmopolitanism," which erases, but internationalism, which embraces nations.

Sukarno's third principle is "Representative government" in a House of Representatives operating on "the principle of conferring" to remove differences and achieve consent.

Sukarno sought not "merely political democracy" as in the West where "there is no social justice and no economic democracy." His fourth principle is "Social Democracy." Parliament, "the body for consultation," would promote common prosperity and individual equality. In all matters, he declared, "I want a settlement through negotiation," in the Indonesian tradition of Musjawarah. The House of Representatives would not be the arena of conflicting parties but a forum for consultation leading to agreement.

Finally, the fifth principle: "Faith in God the Almighty." Moslems, Christians, Buddhists, "would discharge their religious rites according to their own books. But let us all have belief in God." It unifies.

Sukarno saw symbolism in the five principles: five fingers on each hand; the five senses. But perhaps, he mused, some did not like five. He could compress them into three: "socio-nationalism," "socio-democracy," and "belief in God." Are even three too many? he asked. "All right, I make them one, I gather them again to become one. What is that one?"

"Gotong Rojong," he replied. "Mutual co-operation." "Come-on-pull-together for the interest of all. That is Gotong Rojong."

This June 1, 1945, speech contains every single thought and idea in Sukarno's February 21, 1957, Guided Democracy address which did not, therefore, bear the imprint of Russia or China. In the latter pronouncement, however, he did invite the Communist party to join "all members of the family at the dining table"—as naïve as it was unwise. The Communists, hate-ridden and power-hungry, are political cannibals. Given their passion for devouring others and one another, they would have devoured everything on the table and everybody at the table. Sukarno himself, fattened by the flattery they had fed him, would have made their tastiest meal. Gotong Rojong with Communists would be not co-operation but extermination. The proposal to bring the Communist party into a mythical "four-legged" Cabinet was authentic Sukarno and authentic old-Indonesia, but it just did not suit mid-twentieth-century Indonesia and the modern world.

Friction between the second Ali Cabinet and Sumatra had mounted even before the Guided Democracy speech. Increased smuggling became the thin wedge of revolt. Territorial commanders, trading independently and against the interests of the central government, soon took the next step: open defiance. On December 16, 1956, forty-eight senior Sumatran army officers met and signed a manifesto urging firm measures by Jakarta to check discontent. Then they drank to success and smashed their glasses to indicate a break with the past. Four days later, translating this ominous symbolism into deeds, Colonel Ahmed Hussein, age thirty-one, announced his seizure of the Central Sumatran administration. Colonel Simbolon made a similar statement for North Sumatra. However, 27 of the 48 manifesto signatories felt this went too far. The army itself was divided.

Sukarno dismissed Simbolon. Simbolon, a 37-year-old former school-teacher, retorted that he intended to stay, and appealed to Sukarno to replace Ali with Hatta.

To mollify the rebels, Sukarno declared on January 17 that "There is no escape for Indonesia from the system of local autonomy for the various regions." Ali, on February 7, admitted "a widening of the feeling of dissatisfaction among the armed forces." He too promised autonomy. The English-language daily *Times of Indonesia* urged Jakarta to negotiate with the rebels.

The year 1957 was the Year of Musjawarah, of secret talks, clandestine peace missions, and cat-and-mouse maneuvering—word wars, but no fighting. As soon as Simbolon defied Sukarno, the central government sent Lieutenant Colonel Djamin Ginting to replace him. Simbolon yielded and disappeared into the jungles of his native Tapanuli with the parting verbal gesture that, though he had the power to do so, "I will not give the order to attack or disturb anybody, as this would mean bloodshed."

Colonel Barlian, the territorial commander of South Sumatra, the rich oil and rubber province, stated in public that he hoped a Sukarno-Hatta regime would save the nation from disintegration. Meanwhile he would keep the revenues earned by his area and normally forwarded to Jakarta. As between the central government and the rebels, Barlian remained neutral.

Toward the end of January, 1957, Army Chief of Staff Major General Nasution called a conference of Sumatran military chiefs at Palembang, Barlian's headquarters. They met in a golf club built by an American oil company. Ahmed Hussein, the rebel, attended. During the conference, Simbolon emerged from the jungle and appeared at the golf club with ten armed bodyguards. He had a talk with Nasution and left unmolested.

On March 5, 1957, Lieutenant Colonel Ventje Sumual of the East Indonesia command, a former personal aide of Sukarno, demanded co-operation between Sukarno and Hatta, and a five-year military government under Sukarno. He expressed nonconfidence in Dr. Ali.

Hemmed in by revolts and disobedience, Prime Minister Ali resigned on March 14.

Sukarno proclaimed a state of war and siege, flew to Medan in the North Sumatra revolt region for a series of speeches, and returned refreshed to supervise the choice of the new Cabinet. Normally, the president appoints a *formateur,* who forms the Cabinet and becomes prime minister. This time, after an interval, President Sukarno appointed "Citizen Sukarno" as the *formateur* and summoned potential ministerial candidates to the palace. They collected in the Merdeka Room where Sukarno sat with a mass of military brass facing the seventy civilians, each of whom was handed an envelope and paper and asked to state whether he would serve. The entire procedure took ten minutes. Only Sukarno spoke. One of the few who indignantly wrote "No" on the questionnaire was Mohammad Natsir, chairman of the mighty Masjumi party.

Sukarno could not pick Hatta as prime minister, for, since Hatta would govern, Sukarno would merely rule as chief of state. With the best man thus eliminated, Sukarno chose the best of the rest—Djuanda.

Djuanda, who became prime minister on April 9, 1957, is modest, honest, serious, without party affiliations or political ambitions. He told me he would gladly yield the prime minister's office to Hatta and work under him. He was graduated in 1933 as a civil engineer from the Bandung technical institute, later studied economics and irrigation, takes a deep interest in economic affairs—unusual for Jakarta—and had served as minister of state for planning and as minister of communications. The new Prime Minister also took the Defense portfolio and collaborated smoothly with Nasution as well as with Sukarno, although, as he said to me, "I never accepted the President's Concept" of including Communists in the government. Sukarno knew that on this and other issues Djuanda differed with him. Djuanda is no yes man.

While Djuanda tried to patch up the national economy, the rebels remained rebels, secret peace emissaries moved between Jakarta and Sumatra, smuggling continued to grow, the treasury reserves continued to drop, Sukarno spoke, Hatta sat, rumors flew. The rivers of Indonesia race to the sea but the stream of life is placid. Babies are born, the rains fall, the sun shines, the rice ripens, the people smile. Politics affect every man, woman, and child, but few have a daily awareness of it. The political world is small and apart.

Someday, no doubt, something had to happen to resolve the conflict between government and rebels. Meanwhile the only thing that happened was Musjawarah—talk.

Suddenly a fateful act occurred. On November 30, 1957, Sukarno attended a ceremony at the Tjikini Grammar School in Jakarta, where Guntur, his eldest son, and Megawati, his eldest daughter, were enrolled. Sukarno left the school building at 8:55 P.M., greeted by the usual crowd of waving children, parents, teachers, and onlookers. The President had walked halfway between the school and the road on which his car stood and the driver had already opened the door of the car when a sharp explosion was heard. Immediately, a second hand grenade, thrown from a distance of only thirteen feet, burst close to Sukarno. He and two bodyguards threw themselves on the ground. A moment later they jumped up, and Major Sudarto, the President's devoted aide, put his hands on Sukarno's back and the two helmeted bodyguards pulled the President by his arms. Together they ran toward the car. "By the will of God," Sudarto said in describing the attempted assassination and drawing a diagram of it for me, "we rushed past the car. That saved the President's life, because just then a third grenade hit the car, shattered the windshield, and tore the interior apart." This grenade struck Sudarto's foot and he was later hospitalized. A fourth grenade exploded. A fifth came so near that it ripped open the left thigh of Oding Suhendar, one of the two bodyguards.

"Ding, hold on," Sukarno called to Suhendar, and gripping one another they sped across the road toward a house and were about to enter it when they mistakenly took it for a Dutch house, and in that moment of mortal peril, with a split second separating them from possible death, they turned away from it, lest the President of the Republic be saved in a Netherlands home, and dashed to the next dwelling of an Indonesian.

The grenades killed six children, one pregnant woman, and two presidential bodyguards, and wounded 150 persons, some of them crippled for life. Sukarno was unscathed.

Such a hairbreadth escape from death or injury at the hands of assassins motivated, the public trial showed, by political hostility, would unnerve the calmest man. Sukarno almost always appears relaxed and is always affable, yet something in him gave me the impression of a latent volcano. I once questioned him about it. I had learned the meanings of the names of his children by Fatmawati: Guntur, thunder; Megawati, clouds; Rachmawati (a girl), blessing; Sukamawati (a girl), soul; Guruh (a boy), thunder; and by Hartini, two little boys named Tofan, typhoon; and Bayu, wind. "These names," I said to Sukarno, "suggest that deep inside there is a turbulence in you."

He puckered his lips and rocked his head. "No," he replied, "they mean that I am close to nature."

But nature has quieter manifestations than thunder, clouds, storms, and winds.

Turbulence filled the political air. At the Tjikini murder trial, which received full coverage from the Indonesian press and radio, Tasrif bin Hussein, one of the four apprehended assailants, a gaunt young man in his early twenties with piercing eyes, long face, and a small black beard under his chin, denounced Sukarno as "a mere orator" of little use to the reconstruction of the country and especially of the outer islands, who therefore had "to be eliminated." He wanted the Constitution adjusted to Islamic law and called Sukarno a "kafir," or nonbeliever. "Bung Karno's Concept," he added, "is harmful." All this was printed verbatim in the newspapers and broadcast by loudspeakers to the huge crowd outside the courthouse. He also criticized "Sukarno's marriage with Hartini."

Did he feel any remorse? the judge asked.

"For the many victims," he replied, "but not if Bung Karno had been hit."

A second defendant, Jusuf Ismail, condemned the government as anti-Moslem and Sukarno as "chief protector of the Communists." A third, Saadon bin Mohammad, eighteen years old, exclaimed from the witness box that, "As an Islamic youth charged with calling Islamic laws into being in Indonesia I do not regret what I have done."

"What is really the Communist ideology?" the judge asked.

Saadon remained silent.

"Do you hate the President?" the prosecuting attorney inquired.

"The main thing that motivated me," he replied, "was the teachings given by my friends. I do not hate the President."

"Is there no other way of changing the administration?" the judge pressed. "Don't you know what the function of Parliament is?"

"I know a parliament exists," he asserted. "But I think it would be better to use force in order to achieve quicker results. I got my political and religious teachings from Saleh Ibrahim and Colonel Zulkifli Lubis."

Several defendants mentioned Lubis. From his Java hideout Colonel Lubis denied complicity. "I," he boasted, "would have succeeded." Shortly thereafter he joined the rebels in Sumatra.

Sukarno had gone to his children's Tjikini Grammar School in an agitated state of mind. The day before, the United Nations General Assembly refused to instruct Holland to negotiate a settlement of the West Irian issue. Sukarno had made West Irian (New Guinea) the keystone of Indonesian nationalism. Defeat at the UN pained him. But he apparently regarded it as an opportunity. He would stir nationalist passions and thus wipe out the division of the country.

On December 1, the day after his escape from assassination, two days after the adverse vote at the UN, Sukarno ordered a far-flung anti-Dutch action. Dutchmen would depart, Dutch properties would be confiscated, nationalism would be avenged, and the national economy liberated from the Netherlands stranglehold, thus providing the Indonesian middle class with new business opportunities and the working people with a demonstration of anticapitalism and anti-imperialism. Communists, taking advantage of the opportunity, went into action. Estates producing farm products for export were seized. Factories were taken over. Ships, the blood vessels of the archipelago, were confiscated. KLM's flying franchise was canceled. Result? Chaos, loss of capital, loss of skills, unemployment, and personal tragedy.

Slowly the Dutch had been losing their positions in the Indonesian economy. Twenty thousand emigrated in 1955; 16,000 in 1956; 13,000 from January 1 to December 1, 1957. Between December 1, 1957, and May 31, 1958, 33,000 Dutch citizens fled. In many cases they had to pull up deep roots. The forebears of my Hague doctor first went to the Indies in 1785 and he, born like his ancestors before him in Java, remained there till the 1950's. In many cases the Dutch citizens were Indonesians by marriage who had never been outside Indonesia. A Jakarta diplomat's driver, Netherlander by virtue of being his father's son, Indonesian on his mother's side, was counting down the days—ten, nine, eight, seven. On Zero day he would have to leave with his wife and children for Holland, a country where they would be total strangers.

A scene repeatedly recurs to my mind. I was standing on the chilly, damp, wind-swept Hague railway station platform in midsummer waiting for the Amsterdam train. A woman, obviously Indonesian, sat on a bench. Huddling close to her were two boys dressed alike in zipped-up leather jackets, shorts, and high woolen socks. One boy was tall, white-skinned, with golden hair. His brother was shorter, brown-skinned, with straight black hair and all the facial features of a Javanese.

The anti-Dutch campaign which began in December, 1957, hurt the Indonesian economy and applied no healing plaster to Indonesia's politics. On the contrary, it widened rifts and irritated responsible people. "The anti-Dutch campaign," Prime Minister Djuanda said to me in his office on March 21, 1958, "was badly timed because we are in difficulties of the gravest character. We will get West Irian," he added in his wisdom, "when we solve our internal problems and the Western powers have more confidence in us." He did not agree, however, that the Dutch should have been faced with the alternative of giving up West Irian or losing their business in Indonesia. It would not have helped, he thought. Ultimately, they had to be expelled. But the expulsion came at an "untimely moment."

The country raged. The Communists raced through the countryside with firebrands. They exploited every opportunity to inflame passions against the Dutch, against the rebels, and against their political enemies. Anybody who doubted the desirability of expelling Dutch enterprises was condemned. Vile innuendoes of complicity in the attempt on Sukarno's life were circulated. The merchants of hate had a field day. On December 27 Masjumi Party Chairman Natsir wrote a letter to Sukarno alluding to the "insinuation, provocation, and false charges which are set afloat in a whispering way" following the Tjikini grenade shower. He himself received anonymous threats. His house was defiled. Another Masjumi leader, Sjafruddin Prawiranegara, governor of the Bank of Indonesia, likewise felt the stings of insult and offense. Both Natsir and Sjafruddin thought their lives in danger and fled to rebel territory in Sumatra, Natsir to play a passive role, Sjafruddin to become president of the insurgent government. Former Masjumi Prime Minister Harahap likewise decided to escape to the rebels.

In the middle of the churning crisis Sukarno went abroad on January 6, 1958, for a "recuperation tour" of Japan, India, and other Asian lands. He probably wished to calm his nerves and let others calm the situation.

Speculation swirled. Sukarno had been "ousted," "deposed," "forced into exile." The London *Daily Telegraph* of December 23, 1957, learned from its Jakarta correspondent about "a persistent rumor," which is journalese for "my friends and I think," or, more often, "I think," that "President Sukarno, realizing that his popularity is now confined to the Communists, Left-wing Nationalists, and illiterate peasants, will never return to Indonesia from his 'holiday.' " Western newsmen in Tokyo wired that Sukarno "looks worried." On February 16, however, he was back in his capital, genial and self-assured. His power, prestige, and popularity had been underestimated in foreign countries. The rebel leaders made the same mistake. From Padang Prime Minister Sjafruddin (not to be confused with the dead Communist Sjarifuddin) broadcast a speech calling Sukarno a "coward and liar" and "unscrupulous." On February 10 Colonel Ahmed Hussein, rebel commander of Central Sumatra, went to the ludicrous length of issuing a five-day ultimatum to the Djuanda government to resign; otherwise he would take punitive action.

President Sukarno formally, smilingly, resumed his office on February 21 and stated that "we must face" the Padang "deviation" firmly and "with all the means at our disposal." The same day he ordered the bombing of Padang and Bukittinggi in Central Sumatra.

Civil strife had commenced. The radio recriminations were unfortunate and fateful. Without them the worst might have been avoided. Yet the Indonesian tolerance, which expresses itself, for instance, in the burial side by side in the same cemetery of Moslems and Christians, persisted. Colonel Joop F. Warouw, who had traveled with Sukarno in the United States, left his post as military attaché in Peking to join the rebels, but before doing so he called on Sukarno in Tokyo. Later Colonel Alex Kawilarang, Indonesian military attaché in Washington, left his post to join the rebels. "Why does he do it," I asked Premier Djuanda, "when the Sumatran insurrectionists are going down to defeat?"

Instead of excoriating him as a traitor as I had expected, Djuanda said, "Kawilarang is an idealist. He wishes to help his colleagues."

A messenger from General Nasution intercepted Kawilarang in Manila with a letter in which the Army Chief of Staff appealed to him not to throw his considerable influence to the enemies of national union. Nasution likewise invited Colonel Ahmed Hussein to a bury-the-hatchet conference of military commanders in Bandung and offered the rebel leader a safe return to Padang. Hussein refused to come. Even after the fighting had commenced, peace emissaries from Hatta, Sjahrir, and others plied between Jakarta and Sumatra. Indonesian Ambassador L. N. Palar, a Celebes Protestant, was brought from his post in Ottawa, briefed in Jakarta, and sent, in the company of several other Christians, to plead with their coreligionists among the North Celebes rebels for peace.

The Indonesian respects an opponent. "How did you feel," I said to Major Sudarto, "when you testified in court and saw opposite you the four men who tried to kill your beloved president? Did you hate them?"

"No," he answered, "I did not hate them. They acted out of loyalty to their principles."

In San Francisco in February, 1958, the Sultan of Jogjakarta told an interviewer that "there are good men on both sides" of the Indonesian dispute.

Civil war clashes with every ingrained Indonesian habit of action and thought. Herein may lie the basic reason why the rebels, when attacked, did not fight. They eschewed battles to escape annihilation and live another day for guerrilla warfare which, they hoped, would induce Jakarta to compromise with them.

Five British and American journalists were seated at a table in Jakarta's Capitol restaurant discussing the situation. "Nasution is going to drop several hundred paratroopers on the Pakanbaru airfield (in Central Sumatra). They will secure the airfield; more men will be dropped; other troops will arrive via the Straits of Malacca and move up the rivers toward Pakanbaru. From there it is a hundred fifty miles, northeast across the mountains, to Padang. That's the plan," the American explained, and his colleagues brought out scrap paper to draw circles and arrows like professional strategists.

"How do you know?" I queried.

"It's around town," he replied.

A Dutch businessman, in tropical white, approached the journalists' table. "What's the news?" one of them asked.

"The army is about to take Pakanbaru with paratroopers," he said. "They will move from there across the mountains to Bukittinggi and Padang."

"How do you know?" I queried.

"An army major told me," the Dutchman volunteered. An army officer told a Dutchman? I was skeptical. But in a few days that is just the way Pakanbaru was taken.

Arslan Humbarachi, a Turkish journalist, had won consent from the military to accompany the expedition which would make an amphibious landing near Padang. Before his departure he wrote two articles in the English-language *Indonesian Observer,* announcing the approaching move, its military objectives, and what forces and ships would participate.

These facts could have reached the rebels by a dozen channels. Yet when the assaults on Pakanbaru, Padang, and Bukittinggi occurred exactly as the journalists and the Dutchman and the Turk had foretold, the insurgents withdrew and their cities fell.

It was that kind of "war." Either the rebel colonels never intended to fight their opposite numbers among the loyalist military, who, they knew, were not very different politically, or the Sumatran and Celebes insurgents overestimated their armed and popular support and underestimated Sukarno and Nasution's determination to impose national discipline.

The rebels miscalculated and went too far by indulging in emotional radio outbursts and establishing a government in defiance of Jakarta. To tolerate that meant inviting chaos and sanctioning insubordination. Not even an easygoing, live-and-let-live Indonesian authority could afford to do that.

Chapter Twenty-eight

HATTA AND SUKARNO

On March 3, 1958, Sukarno went to Dr. Hatta's house on Djalan Diponegoro to try and induce him to re-enter the government. In civil war or peace, in office or out, Hatta remained a mountainous figure on the Indonesian landscape. Why? "Can you be objective about yourself," I said to him during an interview, "and explain what is Hatta, what is the secret of his influence?" He had been a private citizen for one and a half years, yet the question of a Sukarno-Hatta reconciliation was on every political tongue.

"It's irrational," Hatta replied. "You are in the East. People are irrational. They think Sukarno and Hatta can solve their problems. What I did for independence remains in the popular memory. Sukarno and I carry more weight than any party. We are symbols, forever linked in the national mind."

"Cult of personality," I interjected.

"Yes, but you cannot change it," he said, with a smile. "Even intellectuals think this."

Hatta was standing, when I arrived, dressed in a neat, uncreased white summer-material suit with thin stripes, a white shirt, and sober tie. His hair, black despite his five and a half decades, was carefully combed. He wore heavy, black-rimmed glasses. Small of stature, Hatta is nevertheless compactly built and impressive; not impressively handsome and charming like Sukarno, but impressively strong and composed. Temperamentally he and Sukarno are poles apart. Sukarno is the artist, Hatta the engineer.

Sukarno soars on the wings of his imagination. Hatta's feet are firmly implanted in the earth. Sukarno's one book, entitled *Sarinah* (a common feminine name in villages), deals with the rights of women; Hatta's book is entitled *The Co-operative Movement of Indonesia*. Sukarno loves the palace game of politics, Hatta prefers the university lecture hall. Sukarno is the mystic magician, Hatta the hardheaded diagnostician. Sukarno is carefree and flexible, Hatta has the stubbornness of a Dutchman. Sukarno is Java, Hatta is Sumatra. The Republic needs both. Indonesia, craving the oneness vital to an island empire open for centuries to mariners, merchants, administrators, and immigrants bearing diverse religions and cultures, ached to rejoin Sukarno with Hatta. Politics, which are persons, blocked the effort.

Avoiding circumlocution, Hatta talked with arrowlike straightness and sharpness. His is a search for the substance beneath the surface, not for the brilliant phrase. The country's basic problem? "Our people," he replied, "are strongly democratic. Even under rajah rule the village was governed democratically. But we have failed to translate democracy below into democracy at the top. An election with twenty-nine parties, each with its own symbol, is a farce."

When he was vice-president, he recalled, his guards persuaded the cook to vote for a certain party and taught her how to do it: punch a hole with a pencil through the party's symbol on the ballot. But in the polling booth she became confused and perforated the wrong symbol. He laughed.

"Our parties," Hatta continued, "are dominated by oligarchies. Personal influence in the parties is greater than in any other country. As a result, lesser leaders who crave power break away from the larger party and form parties of their own which they can manipulate."

The party chiefs draw up the lists of candidates for Parliament. Except in exceptional circumstances, Indonesians vote for a party, not for individuals: X votes elect the top person on the list, 2X votes elect the first two, 3X votes elect the first three, and so on. If the twenty at the bottom of a party's list of candidates feel they have no chance of election they form a new party and put themselves at the top of its list. In a big constituency of many millions, even a weak party can manage to elect the top two or three candidates. The one-chamber Parliament elected in 1955, consequently, included fifteen parties with five members or less. This fosters parliamentary irrresponsibility. The smaller parties, in combination with two larger ones, can always bring about a Cabinet's fall. The Cabinet must therefore bribe the small parties with jobs or other benefits.

"I favor the British or American system of small constituencies," Hatta declared. "Big constituencies prevent contact between the member of Parliament and the voters." The member must curry favor with his party boss, not with his electors.

"Couldn't the four big parties [the Masjumi, PNI, NU, and PKI] eliminate the small parties?" I asked. "Together they have a majority in Parliament."

"Yes," he answered, "but in politics you must have courage. The leaders of the big parties are afraid to alienate the small ones."

Indonesia had seventeen governments between 1945 and 1958. This averages less than a year per Cabinet, and each change of Cabinet entails political horse trading, buying and selling support, and so forth, apart from making it impossible for a government to gain self-confidence and begin carrying out its campaign promises.

"Our big mistake," Hatta affirmed, "was to abandon presidential government. Our first [1945] constitution provided for Presidential Cabinets. We achieved independence under a Presidential Cabinet. That was democratic. But the parties insisted that Cabinets be subject to Parliament," subject to the changing moods of party leaders who might combine any day, even though opposed to one another, to bring down a government.

"You have a Presidential Cabinet today," I said provokingly.

"No," Hatta stated. "We have a Parliamentary Cabinet, but the President has the power. Yet he is responsible to no one. Eisenhower is responsible. Sukarno, as chief of state, can do no wrong. In reality he does many things, right and wrong, but the law says he can do no wrong."

"Could you get Parliament to surrender its power to a Presidential Cabinet?"

"The Masjumi, the Catholics, and others want it," Hatta asserted. "The PNI, the PKI, and the NU are opposed. That is our dramatic difficulty."

"What you are urging, then, is a Sukarno-Hatta dictatorship."

"No," he objected, "we would not rule without law or against the law. In 1948, in Jogjakarta, my Cabinet was perfectly legal. We felt a heavy responsibility to democracy. Now Sukarno prefers a Parliamentary Cabinet because it enables him to wield power without responsibility."

(I took notes, first, because it was too hot in Jakarta to type out a record of each interview when I got back to my room; second, to show that I would quote.)

"Then the likelihood of your becoming vice-president again is very small."

"Very small," he agreed.

"Despite the fact that so many want you back."

"The PNI," he explained, "wants me back as vice-president but without power or function. Sukarno asked me urgently to return to office. He does not think I am indispensable to the governing of the country, yet he cannot find a way without me. He has created the National [Advisory] Council for himself. In effect, it is a supergovernment. Now he wants to create a National Planning Board for me. President Sukarno has good ideas, he thinks in large terms; he is weak on implementation. He sees things broadly, not in detail. He has a conceptual, not an analytical, mind. He generates idealistic ideas which turn out badly. The idea of the National Council is good. He did not make it representative. For instance, the Murba party is too strongly represented in it because he likes young, active people. The National Council is a supergovernment because it is headed by Sukarno. The Planning Board he wishes me to head would be a second supergovernment. But the two would conflict with one another and with Parliament."

I said, "Doesn't the fact that Sukarno favored the Murba party, which is considered Titoist or Trotskyite, contradict a widespread assumption that he has a preference for the Communist party [PKI]?"

"Sukarno is not under Communist influence," Hatta stated. "Many of the PKI leaders are his former pupils, and in his self-assurance he believes he can control them. He forgets that the PKI exploits his good will. Sukarno is a man of unity. He thinks in terms of a national unity that embraces all parties."

"You do not want the PKI in the government?"

"I do not."

"What about the army?"

"Our army," he asserted, "is anti-Communist. Here and there some Communists might have infiltrated it, but not many."

"What happens after the capture of Padang and Bukittinggi?"

"Force cannot solve our problem," Hatta replied. "Force will endanger national unity. For me, unity is the essence."

"Didn't you, on March 3, come very near to an understanding with Sukarno? What prevented the agreement?"

"We disagreed because the government was using force."

"What would be your solution?"

"My solution," he replied, "is: The rebels withdraw their February 10 ultimatum to the central government; the rebel government disbands; Jakarta lifts its blockade of Sumatra and the Celebes; the insurgent colonels are taken back into the army. Sjafruddin has stated that the rebel government would dissolve itself as soon as a strong government was formed in Jakarta."

"Is this possible?" I wondered.

"No."

"Then your return to the government is unlikely?"

"Unlikely."

It was Ramadan, the 30-day fast in which good Moslems eat and drink only between sunset and sunrise. "I will go now," I said. "You must be tired from fasting."

"No," he protested with a smile. "I feel fit. In fact, I get more work done these days because I don't eat lunch and so don't have to take an afternoon siesta."

I asked whether he would see me again. "Any time," he promised, shaking hands.

Exactly a month after this interview I drove from Jakarta to Bandung for the opening of a swimming pool by Sukarno and Hatta. At the Puntjak Pass (1,439 meters or just under 4,500 feet) we closed the car windows to keep out the cold. The ride between the Puntjak and Bandung offers the most exciting scenery in beautiful Java. At frequent intervals the roadbank dissolves to afford a grandiose view of great natural amphitheaters rimmed with mountain ranges and descending by green, water-covered rice-field terraces to fertile valleys far below.

"Here," the driver said as the road narrowed to a defile, "Darul Islam bandits held up an official automobile last week and killed two occupants." Farther on, he reported a similar incident.

Friday evening Sukarno addressed a Bandung mass meeting of university faculty and students in a cinema. He spoke in anger. "I say to the Western powers," he exclaimed, "don't play with fire." He warned against foreign intervention in Indonesia's internal quarrel. It might lead to a third world war. "I'm glad to see," he added, "that the journalists are writing this down."

Saturday morning Sukarno and Hatta arrived together at the Karang Setra Pool. The entrance ribbon was cut; hundreds of colored balloons were released; the guests snaked around the pool, shaped like two mammoth kidneys, to the clubhouse. The pool was built to attract the next Asian Olympic swimming events and looked, to my ignorant eye, like the biggest in the world.

Squatting on the floor of an anteroom, a native gamelan orchestra made gentle music with tinkling xylophones and long drums. But it was quickly drowned out by a band of Westerners from Bandung's luxury Hotel Savoy Homann occupying a raised platform in the ample clubhouse dining hall. Sukarno and Hatta, with Djuanda between them, sat in the front row tapping time to the latest American dance hits. After a while, Sukarno crooked his finger, the orchestra conductor approached, and returned to lead his players in the "Blue Danube." The President's next request was "Que Sera Sera," the popular American song.

Later, during an intermission between speeches, I talked with Prime Minister Djuanda. Two American journalists joined us and asked him whether Sukarno would be having talks today with Hatta about his re-entry into the government. Djuanda's intricate reply mingled evasion with a wish that he would, and for an hour thereafter the two and I debated about just what Djuanda had said. Sukarno and Hatta did exchange brief, whispered comments and smiles, and were in a relaxed, festive mood. Hatta delivered a three-minute unpolitical speech in a conversational manner. The swimming pool obviously did not provide a proper setting for high-level discussions, and it later emerged that there had been none.

Swimming and diving exhibitions followed the speeches. Plummeting females and twirling muscular males were outshone by a platoon of soldiers in full uniform and laden with guns and ammunition who jumped feet first from the highest diving board, made water wings out of their shirts, tied their heavy shoes around their necks, and then swam fifty yards. One man had to be rescued.

After dinner with Sukarno at the Governor's Palace (Hatta had left), we returned to the Karang Setra clubhouse for a fashion show. An orchestra of Indonesians (or were they Filipinos or Hawaiians?) wearing white-and-pink blouses with puffed-up, ruffled sleeves, strummed dance music and crooned the English texts while a woman announced on the microphone that "Miss Baby" would exhibit a bathing suit designed by So-and-so, and "Miss Baby" duly appeared in bare feet and much else bare, gyrated on the dance floor before the honored guests and tiptoed out, only to be succeeded by "Clara," "Miss Joyce," "Betty," and equal beauties in swim suits never meant to get wet. "Miss Baby" now reappeared in a ravishing, hand-painted batik dress, gyrated, exited. Ditto for all her brown sisters. They re-enacted the parade in evening dress. "Miss Joyce" also exhibited herself in native costume.

Passing the vitamins to me at seven-o'clock breakfast the next morning, Sukarno said, "Louis, last night's show seemed to bore you."

"I lost interest after the same girls came out again and again."

"I hope I shall never lose interest in women, not even in the grave," Sukarno exclaimed, to the amusement of the fourteen guests at the table.

I asked him whether Bandung had changed since his student days.

"Yes," he replied with a smile, "the women have changed."

"They've grown older," I suggested.

More laughter and more jokes.

Presently Colonel Sugandhy entered the room, clicked his heels, saluted, and shouted, "All ready for departure, sir." It was just too formal and military, and the breakfasters, Sukarno included, guffawed in unison. After a second's consternation, Sugandhy unbent and joined in the fun, thus starting another round of laughs.

The main highway from Bandung to Bogor had to be guarded against a possible Darul Islam suicide attack or kidnap attempt. Yet the long dash of the automobile procession through a cordon of Bren-gun carriers and truckloads of soldiers under cover of a helicopter which searched the mountains for any approaching bandit band, did not seem to depress the President, and when we stopped for cold drinks at his house on the palace grounds and occupied chairs in a circle under a giant waringin tree with small speckled deer grazing nearby, he was his happy, buoyant self. Sukarno's glands endow him with an almost constant *joie de vivre* that dispels the grimness of politics. The man conquers the statesman.

Chapter Twenty-nine

MEN AND MONEY

Two JAKARTA news items appeared next to each other in the *New York Times* on the 1958 anniversary of the founding of the Republic. One quoted a newspaper article by Dr. Hatta warning that Indonesia was heading toward the "valley of total bankruptcy." Economic problems, aggravated by rebellion, he wrote, made "the poverty and suffering of the people . . . more intense day by day. The limit has come." The second report said: "Carnival crowds thronged Jakarta tonight to begin three days of celebrations, including dancing, fireworks, and palace receptions."

The government had expelled the rebels from all cities and shrunk the insurrections to the dimensions of a vexatious, expensive guerrilla war. Here 700 shabbily dressed, oddly armed men emerged from a ravine to attack a garrison, there a squad blew up a bridge or ambushed a truck convoy. Nobody knew the whereabouts of the prominent insurgents: Prime Minister Sjafruddin, Finance Minister Sumitro, Masjumi chairman Mohammad Natsir, and the many colonels. It was a peace that was not peace.

Even in the most peaceful circumstances it will be difficult for Indonesia, and indeed for other underdeveloped, overpopulated countries of Asia, Africa, and Latin America to climb from the valley of bankruptcy to a plateau of prosperity. Gunnar Myrdal, the Swedish economist, concludes in his *Rich Lands and Poor* that the earth's rich countries are growing richer while the poor countries struggle, often vainly, not to grow

poorer. Karl Marx's faith in the victory of Communism in his time fed
on the assumption that capitalism made the rich richer and the poor
poorer. Actually the poor in Western industrialized nations have grown
richer. They therefore reject Marx and Communism. Russia may follow
the same pattern when her poor are richer. But what Marx falsely
prophesied about persons could prove true of countries. The result might
be Communism, Fascism, military dictatorship, religious obscurantism, or
chaos. In any event, the world's division into rich lands and poor, cor-
responding roughly to the division between white and colored peoples,
constitutes a major menace to international tranquillity and ethical man's
peace of mind.

"In the highly developed countries," Myrdal writes, "all indices point
steadily upward . . . business slumps and big depressions and even severe
setbacks due to wars appear only as short-term waverings of the firmly
rising long-term trend." But the progress of less developed countries "is
smaller," and many of them "are in constant danger . . . of losing ground."
In general, therefore, "the economic inequalities between developed and
underdeveloped countries have been increasing."

Inequality compounds the evil of poverty. Poverty creates suffering;
poverty in the shadow of the landlord's villa creates social unrest.
Similarly, the unequal development of countries disrupts international
life. The poor blame others. They envy and can be taught to hate. The
rich are unloved when they do not help and maligned when they help
too little. The adjustment of this imbalance between wealthy and impov-
erished nations is probably the most important task facing the remainder
of the twentieth century. The problem should be solved with love and
money.

Poor countries are poor because they are poor. This, though so obvious,
is the essential truth about the less-developed countries. They produce too
little and consume all of it. Unable to save, they cannot lay aside capital
for economic development.

I asked Dr. P. S. Lokanathan, an Indian economist and former director
of the United Nations Economic Commission for Asia and the Far East
(ECAFE), whether and how India could increase her rate of progress if
she went Communist. "Chiefly by reducing consumption," he replied.

But the consumption of at least 370 million Indians is already so low
as to stunt biological growth and reduce the capacity to work. The population of India, and the same goes for Egypt, is, with the exception of a
small upper and somewhat larger upper-middle class, literally too emaciated to permit of any further weight reducing. The totalitarian solution,
therefore, cannot be applied to advantage.

Writing from India about India in the *New York Times* of March 8, 1959, former Governor W. Averell Harriman said, "Capital is hard to raise in a country where fewer than 500,000 families have taxable incomes above $600 a year." Indonesia has even fewer families earning that much.

The Soviet Union accumulated capital by underpaying for work and overcharging for goods. Stalin locked the peasants in collective farms and compelled them to sell the government considerable portions of their crops at below-market prices. Such direct exploitation was supplemented by inflation, which curtailed consumption. All its concomitant cruelty notwithstanding, some underdeveloped planners and politicians propose to imitate this Soviet example. But Tsarist Russia was far more advanced economically than today's India or Indonesia. The Russian rate of economic progress from 1890 to 1900 was impressive: over 8 per cent a year. Russia produced four million tons of steel in 1914, which is more than any non-Communist Afro-Asian country did in 1958. She also exported huge quantities of oil and grain, and built industries with part of the proceeds.

War and revolution inflicted much damage on Russia, yet a solid industrial and agrarian base remained. Nevertheless, Stalin did not launch collectivization and the first Five-Year Plan of intense industrialization until October, 1928, after seven years of the New Economic Policy (NEP) which allowed the peasant bulk of the population and the trading class to enrich themselves by private capitalistic endeavor. The Soviet state then sliced off the newly acquired fat to lubricate the apparatus of economic development.

Most underdeveloped countries lack the fat. Nor will their people permit the slicing-off. "It is highly doubtful," wrote British Laborite Aneurin Bevan, "whether the achievements of the Industrial Revolution would have been permitted if the franchise had been universal. It is very doubtful because a great deal of the capital aggregations that we are at present enjoying are the result of wages our fathers went without." Had the fathers, or really the grandfathers, won the right to vote and organize effective trade unions they would not have submitted to the exploitation necessary for capital accumulation.

This is the dilemma of Afro-Asia.

Almost all Western countries achieved nationhood and industrialization before they became as democratic as they were at the end of the nineteenth century. But the newly independent countries must become nations and achieve prosperity in conditions of democracy. To cure the capital anemia somebody, either the state or private entrepreneur, would have to squeeze the people thin and dry. The people are likely to resist with their votes, their trade unions, and other democratic rights.

Intellectuals and colonels accordingly scan the horizon for a Kemal Pasha Atatürk or a Nasser possessing the force, glamour, dedication, and unscrupulousness to drive upward and onward over the prostrate body of crushed opposition and then, they hope, abdicate or die and bequeath the dictatorship to a freedom-loving heir. Atatürk did salvage a nation from the wreck of an empire, but whether his country achieved much economic progress during his regime is moot. Who can guarantee that the blood of the slaughtered goddess of liberty will fructify the land? Experience teaches that groceries and amenities come with liberties, whereas dictatorship conduces to the power of the state and the enrichment of a new upper class. In the regiment the pay envelope remains thin.

Many young states of Asia and Africa still hope to eat their cake and have it, attain material advancement and retain personal freedom. It may be difficult. One thing seems certain: citizens are more likely to make sacrifices to capital accumulation by the state, in the proclaimed interest of all, than to accumulation by private business. The future of Asia and Africa points, therefore, to government planning, government participation in industry, and government control of private industry.

This has been called Socialism. State capitalism is a more accurate description. For even in a democracy, and certainly in a dictatorship, the state or government should be differentiated from society or the nation. The waxing power of governments makes such differentiation more necessary than ever. Socialism, on the other hand, implies ownership and management by society, by a society voluntarily organized in guilds or co-operatives or communes to run factories and farms. Such a system, at present nonexistent, would permit the diffusion of economic and hence of political power and would not, therefore, curb liberty. But state capitalism is an economy totally controlled and operated without popular consent by a dictatorship which causes the state to flower rather than wither. Or, as in some countries of Europe and Asia and even in the United States, it is state management or supervision of only a part of the largely private economy with a view to accumulating capital, reviving derelict industries, rehabilitating neglected farm regions, creating giant public utilities, providing for defense, and avoiding mighty monopolies. This mixture of state and private economic systems offers a viable, sometimes profitable, alternative to pure private capitalism which the new Afro-Asian states will not accept and to Communist-run total state capitalism which in self-interest they should not accept.

In the matter of capital accumulation, so crucial to the prospects of representative government and civil liberties, Indonesia enjoys advantages over many Afro-Asian countries. The sources from which the Dutch extracted huge fortunes are, with few exceptions, still there. More sources may be there, for vast areas have never been explored. Sixty-nine per cent of the area of the outer islands (outside Java) are covered with forest and nobody knows what lies beneath. Borneo, the archipelago's largest island—bigger than Japan—is terra incognita except for the coastal rim. "Indonesia is among the world's richest nations," writes Bernard Kalb in the *New York Times,* "yet most of her people walk barefooted on untapped wealth." The green island empire awaits the geologist, surveyor, engineer, laborer, and capital.

Indonesia is fortunate, too, in being a multicrop and multiproduct country. Dr. Hatta wrote in 1956 that Indonesia was producing 40 per cent of the world's rubber supply, 30 per cent of its pepper, 33 per cent of its copra, 24 per cent of its palm oil, 8 per cent of its tea, 6 per cent of its sisal fibers, 2 per cent of its sugar, 2.5 per cent of its coffee, 6 per cent of its tobacco, 1.5 per cent of its petroleum, and 20 per cent of its tin, and also has coal, bauxite, manganese, copper, nickel, gold, and silver. In natural resources, he declared, Indonesia is "surpassed only by the United States and the U.S.S.R."

Rich land but poor.

Poverty in the midst of wealth is a tragedy and a challenge to Indonesia's government and people as well as to the friendly outside world. No social system will long endure if it fails to use the opportunities that lie so abundantly underfoot.

Indonesia's export trade, the best source of capital, held up fairly well until smuggling and revolts undermined it. Although shipments abroad of live animals and animal products, tobacco, tapioca, tea, coffee, sugar, pepper, copra, quinine, and fibers have fallen sharply since the end of the Dutch period, petroleum and rubber sales to foreign countries in 1956 were almost double the Dutch figures.

On the other hand, rice, the staple food of Indonesia, had to be imported in tremendous quantities. Under the Dutch the country grew enough rice to feed itself. In 1950, owing to population growth and war, Indonesia imported 334,000 tons of rice; in 1956, 763,000 tons; in the first five months of 1958, 700,000 tons at a cost of $100 million American. "With the present position of our foreign currency reserves," wrote Charles Tambu, the hard-hitting editor of the *Times of Indonesia,* "this is a luxury we can ill afford." Imports of textiles and machinery also increased. As a result, imports and exports were evenly balanced at $800 million in 1956. The situation leaves no capital surplus for investment.

Investment and development are further hampered by the high cost of government. The numerical strength of the Indonesian defense and police forces is probably six times that of the Dutch, and the army of officeholders has multiplied even more. The number of state employees in 1930 was 144,974; in 1952, 571,243, and going up. Government jobs are not only the major industry, they are, in view of slack effort, the major national charity.

Indonesia cries out for an economic tsar and a technological revolution. Rice offers one example. Rice yields vary widely: 3,100 pounds per acre in Italy, 2,350 in Japan, 2,060 in Egypt, 1,500 in China, but only 1,030 in Indonesia despite her rich soil and ample rain, and a mere 750 in India. If India and Indonesia tripled their rice harvests by better seeding, weeding, transplanting, and fertilizing, major economic and political problems would be solved. In India, moreover, man competes for his food with marauding monkeys, wild cattle, crows, parrots, and peacocks. In Indonesia the robbers of the human larder are the rat and the pig. Experts in Jakarta say pest suppression could cut food imports to zero. Improved seed would achieve the same end.

Dr. Hatta stresses a serious discrepancy between Java and the outer islands which could, if eliminated, change the face of Indonesia. In Java, he points out, there are 1,058 persons to the square mile (compared to 309.3 in New York State, according to the 1950 census; 714 in Belgium; and 321 in India). But the outer islands have only about 52 persons to the square mile. As a result, crowded Java can afford a maximum of half an acre for the typical farmer, whereas Sumatra, the Celebes, Borneo, and numerous other islands are underpopulated and underdeveloped. One obvious answer would be transmigration from Java (and Bali) to the outer islands. But government statistics show a total of some 25,000 transmigrants in 1956, and 125,000 from 1950 to 1956 inclusive. This is a mere drop in the human sea of 57 million which is Java. A perceptible thinning out of Java and Bali by transmigration would require an enormous capital expenditure on industrialization, irrigation, flood control, and resettlement. The task is really the same as that of finding the money and trained men for developing all of Indonesia. Java, though congested, is itself underdeveloped. Everywhere on the great island one sees wasted water power, wasted soil, and wasted labor. Transmigration, therefore, is merely one aspect of Indonesia's central economic problem: economic growth to match population growth.

Birth control is increasingly necessary because the birth rate is higher than the death rate. Indonesian statistics are inadequate. Dr. A. Saleh, Minister of Health, admitted in April, 1958, that "statistical records are incomplete" and that even in Central and East Java, which have the best health records, they "are not very reliable." He estimated the death rate for Indonesia at "10 to 15 per thousand." But this did not include infant mortality. The 1957 United Nations *Demographic Yearbook* estimated that of 1,000 infants born in Indonesia, 150 die before they are one year old; 7 to 16 mothers die for every 1,000 births. The official *Statistical Pocketbook of Indonesia, 1957,* had demographic data for only 15 regencies or districts in Java, and in these, in 1956, the death rate varied between 9.5 per thousand in Bogor to 23.3 in Pekalongan. Worse still, in 8 of the 15 districts the death rate had risen sharply above the 1952 and 1953 levels. The main killers are malaria and tuberculosis. Thirty million Indonesians suffer from malaria.

Despite the high death rate due to poor sanitation, malnutrition, and inadequate health services, Indonesia's population is increasing an estimated 2 per cent a year; in India 1.75 per cent. These are relatively small. In the United States the increase from July 1, 1957, to July 1, 1958, was 1.68 per cent; in England (not the United Kingdom) the excess of births over deaths between 1951 and 1956 averaged 2.2 per cent per annum. But a 2 per cent increase for Indonesia means 1.7 million additional persons each year to feed, clothe, house, educate, entertain, transport, and govern; 1.7 million additional persons to compete for the insufficient food supply and the already overloaded facilities.

Karl Marx never proclaimed that a Socialist country could, while in the process of development, provide adequately for all its inhabitants. He merely contended that capitalist economies suffered from unemployment because of laborsaving machinery and faulty distribution. Laborsaving devices through rapid mechanization are a characteristic of all so-called Socialist societies, notably the Soviet Union where some of the resulting unemployment is concealed in factory featherbedding, overmanned collective farms, and overstaffed government offices. Russia also suffers from faulty distribution, most obvious in housing and clothes, which leads to strong pressure from below for birth control, although the U.S.S.R. is underpopulated. The Kremlin was therefore forced in 1955 to relegalize abortions, which it had banned in 1936. There is even greater need for birth control in overpopulated China.

Clearly, then, the population problems is a fact of life which no ism, system, or facile theory can efface. For some decades at least, a rising population in Asia and Africa will retard progress. Each time an enormous push-and-pull effort succeeds in lifting the great weight of 87 million Indonesians one small notch, the 1.7 million annually added persons will drag it down again. And in India the 7 million yearly increase will nullify the climb of the more than 400 million. A development program in these conditions comes close to being a labor of Sisyphus.

But without economic expansion Afro-Asia would drown in its human sea. Family planning or no, therefore, development must go on.

Economic development has two interlinked aspects: men and money. Skilled workers, farmers, and managers are indispensable to the efficient use of capital. Without capital, skill would be wasted. Between men and money there is no priority. Both are necessary simultaneously.

In most constructive fields, the Republic of Indonesia has achieved little. Education is the important exception. In all cities, towns, and villages one sees new schools. Old universities have been vastly expanded and new technical institutes founded. With conscious care the authorities are striving to build a literate, educated nation equipped with the knowledge required for economic progress and a cultured life.

Millions of adults attend schools for illiterates. Those who complete the course receive much-prized government certificates. In recent years, between one and two million testimonials have been issued annually. By the middle of 1956—Indonesian statistics lag miserably—the total was 7,380,494. It has mounted steeply since. In 1948, the last full year of Dutch rule, according to the Indonesian Ministry of Education, 7 per cent of the population was literate; in 1958, an estimated 57 per cent.

The Education Ministry gives the following enrollment figures for 1956-57: over 7 million children in primary schools compared to 2 million in 1939-40; junior secondary school students 608,834, compared to 21,875 in 1939-40; senior secondary school (including vocational) students 128,121, compared to 4,460 in 1939-40; and 32,501 in higher education compared to 637 in 1939-40.

I visited university faculties in Jakarta and Bogor, and talked to students in my apartment and elsewhere. I found them intelligent, avid, quick, clean. Some of their textbooks are mimeographed. Laboratory equipment leaves much to be desired. But the desire to learn is keen, and classroom discipline, judging by what I saw and heard from teachers, excellent.

Higher education, however, suffers from one serious drawback: the love of clean hands. Of the 1,200 students at the Bogor agricultural school of the University of Indonesia, more than 99 per cent were not farmers' children, and only one student, so I was told, wanted to be a farmer. The ambition of the rest is to serve as government officials or to teach in vocational schools or extension courses.

Employment in a government office is regarded, with good reason, as the closest thing to leisure in the priyayi, or gentry, tradition. Manual labor, in the eyes of the upper and middle classes, lacks dignity. Work was for slaves, now for the masses, not for anybody who can push a pen. This "clean hands" disease afflicts India even more than Indonesia and is a major obstacle to economic development in other less-developed coun-tries. Often the most vivid impression carried away from America and Europe by Asian visitors is the love and respect for hard work. Without these, material advancement becomes impossible.

In Calcutta once I lifted a chair to carry it into another room. "No, no, no," a rich Indian visitor exclaimed in horror, and took the chair from me and handed it to his secretary. "No, no, no," I exclaimed, and took the chair from the secretary and asked the millionaire to carry it. He did, but it must have hurt. Mr. K. M. Munshi, former Indian minister of food, launched a movement called, "For Dirty Hands." Recognition of the evil is the first short step to its extirpation. The negative attitude toward work arises from the false values that attach to status, caste, and class, and that belong to the obsolete age which fathered the Orient's decadence. Asia cannot rebuild materially unless it reforms mentally.

One day in April, 1958, I went with Dr. Ralph W. Dunkle, industrial development adviser of the American aid mission, to inspect the Tugas metalworking enterprise in Jakarta. Tugas, which means duty, was launched by a Mr. Sukarna in September, 1953, with 3,500 rupiahs, say $500, borrowed from a bank. Alone the machinery which he had imported by 1956 was worth a quarter of a million rupiahs. Sukarna was born in 1923 in a West Javanese peasant home, the eighth of fourteen children, of whom seven survive. His father owned 5.5 acres of rice fields. Su-karna attended elementary school and from 1938 to 1942 studied in a technical institute on a Dutch governnment stipend. From boyhood he dreamt of owning a factory. His only ambition is to develop Tugas. He arrives at the plant early in the morning and sometimes stays until ten P.M. "Officials," said Sukarno, who speaks fluent English, "go home at one P.M. I would rather work hard and earn my money honestly. Indone-sians want to get rich quickly. Technical school graduates hope to become wealthy and look for jobs with Stanvac [Standard-Vacuum Oil Company] or Caltex [California-Texas Oil Company] that will give them a flashy car and status."

Would he like to study in the U.S.A.?

"No," he replied, "who would run my shop? When I'm sick the workers come to my bedside to ask for directions."

Tugas began with 3 workers. It now employs 71 in the shop I saw and 60 in a branch. Sukarna has a partner, Maman Kasmin, age 36, who is an engineer. In 1957, the two accepted a third partner, Abi Kusnu, age 61, who owns a large building where they soon expect to house both shops.

"I know of no Indonesian," Sukarna said, "who started a shop like this."

Tugas, completely mechanized, uses Czech, West German, Swedish, American, and other foreign equipment for welding, metal cutting, frame making, and other processes. A metal-cutting lathe worker said he was 22, earned 220 rupiahs a month, too little to marry on, and belongs to a trade-union affiliated with the Communist SOBSI but does not subscribe to the program of any political party. Sukarna told us that he has had practically no labor fluidity and no strikes. Average pay, he declared, amounted to 400 rupiahs a month. On the black market that would have been less than $8. The hours of work are from 8 A.M. to noon and from 1 to 4 P.M.

Sukarna himself takes a salary of 4,000 rupiahs a month; Maman 3,500 rupiahs. He pays 2,000 rupiahs a year in taxes on his salary ("You're getting off very light compared to an American or West European," I said) but no tax on profit which amounts to 27 per cent of capital and is plowed back into the business.

"What are your problems?" I inquired.

"Foremen," he replied. "They are hard to find. We have promoted three of our older men to the job. A foreman should understand people and not be made of iron; he needs a sensitive heart."

The biggest bottleneck is credit. Tugas has contracts from the government and private firms, but needs money for expansion and workers' training, and cannot obtain it.

In 1948 Sukarna married a girl from the village next to his. They now have two daughters and three sons. (Maman has seven daughters, no sons.) He drives a secondhand rebuilt baby Austin. The firm owns a two-ton truck but has no telephone. That would cost 25,000 rupiahs to install.

Sukarna is a PNI sympathizer. He fought against the Dutch between 1945 and 1948. President Sukarno is his hero. He admires Premier Djuanda for his interest in economic affairs. "Hatta in office would help the country's business," he said.

I also visited the Klender woodworking establishment in the Djatinegara suburb of the capital. Started in May, 1956, Klender is a government plant directed by the Ministry of Industry through the Institute for Industrial Development. Its chief activity is furniture making. It employs 76 persons, 18 of them on clerical jobs. I noted several expensive-looking machines which were not in use and which, judging from their position behind piles of wood and finished furniture, had not been used for a long time. Some large electric saws and planes were in operation.

Walking through the one-story establishment with the manager and his assistant, I spied an array of trucks in the courtyard and inquired about them. What emerged, after persistent questioning, is a most extraordinary, distressing story:

On October 28, 1957, Klender signed a contract with the police to build "boxes" or wooden bodies for thirty-eight 2- and 2½-ton Dodge trucks designed for hauling and towing and fitted with a winch in front of the radiator. The police department agreed to pay Klender 8,500 rupiahs for each of the 38 boxes, Klender to supply the wood and metal and to pay a Mr. Dunih 650 rupiahs per truck for special services on a sub-contract.

The job seemed simple indeed: the driver's wooden seat; wooden benches, each of three narrow boards, running along the two sides of the trucks; and curved wooden "ribs" over which a canvas roof could be installed; plus a few primitive metal pieces.

The trucks were delivered to Klender fourteen days before the signing of the contract. After the signing, Klender designed a model box or "prototype"—this took two weeks—and then each truck was equipped with a box patterned on the model. The police rejected the design.

The designing of the second model lasted three and a half months. This occurred during the incumbency of a manager who came on the scene in November, 1957, and remained until he was transferred to the head office early in February, 1958. He approved the second model, and supervised the building of 27 finished boxes. At this juncture the police rejected the second design.

A third model was produced on February 10. The new manager from whom I extracted this information came on the job on February 15. The police O.K.'d the third model on February 21. The thirty-eight trucks were fitted with the boxes by March 11. It thus took eighteen calendar days, perhaps fifteen workdays, to do all the work. Yet the trucks, which represented a fortune in capital and potential commercial earnings, had been standing there five months.

Now a new merry-go-round began. The trucks needed painting. The police submitted its own paint mixture but did not like the result when applied to the boxes. A second mixture was sent over. This too failed to please the artistic eye of the police inspector and it was withdrawn. That happened nine days before my visit. Then the police officer in charge went on leave, and everything stood still pending his return.

The waste angered me and I made no secret of my feelings. Mr. Paljono, the manager, on the defensive, assured me that Klender was not losing any money on the transaction. "But your country is," I protested.

Paljono had returned on January 9, 1958, from a year at the University of Syracuse (New York) studying business administration. Did Syracuse teach him how to apply American administrative techniques to a police department that did not know its mind?

Personnel and finance are Indonesia's foremost economic problems. The personnel will become available as an inevitable result of the spread of education. Soon the graduates of schools at all levels will be clamoring for work, and since they cannot all be accommodated behind desks they will have to make their peace with activity in productive enterprises.

In an underdeveloped country the most abundant available capital is underemployed and unemployed labor. At very little expense in materials and wages, this surplus labor could increase the rice yield, expand fisheries (the government should campaign simultaneously for more fish eating), improve and extend irrigation, breed more cattle—a neglected branch of agriculture in Indonesia—build secondary roads between villages and market towns, and erect rural inns, cinemas, youth clubhouses, and other amenities. Of Indonesia's population, 90 per cent live in villages. An active, fully employed village must be the foundation, the floor, of a healthy economy.

In too many new states the rulers build themselves pyramids in the shape of gigantic construction projects which often are, but often are not, urgently necessary and which swallow huge volumes of capital without yielding concrete results for years. A poor country cannot afford this. Wherever possible, it should invest its limited resources so as to bring speedy benefits. The giant factories and dams can wait a little. New states suffer from two aberrations: conspicuous construction, or bigness, and worship of steel.

Steel is the modern god. Steel is of course indispensable to industrial growth. But instead of building a small unprofitable steel mill, Burma would have done better to import steel from India or Japan or Russia or Germany or England. John Scott, assistant to the publisher of *Time* magazine, makes the same point about Egypt. "The Egyptians," he declared in November, 1958, "have no economic business with a steel mill at all. They have no coking coal and their best ore is 33 per cent, and that's 600 miles away up at Aswan, and the domestic market cannot consume the steel which the mill is putting out, namely about 280,000 tons. The mill was put into operation last July. When the first plate was put through the plate mill, a number of the Egyptian workers, carried away with enthusiasm, began a snake dance around the cages of this mill in the course of which one young Egyptian, swept away with emotion, jumped up and on to this hot plate, where he lay sizzling. Two of his comrades jumped up and pulled him off it. Those two lost their feet; the first man, of course, was fried. Here is an example of a ritual sacrifice committed on the altar of a temple of the imagery of the 20th Century, the steel mill, within a stone's throw of the other temples on which other Egyptians committed ritual sacrifice, perhaps with no less enthusiasm, to the symbols and imageries of another millennium."

It would be much wiser to construct a solid village foundation first. An enriched village will increase national production quickly and create savings for investment in industry. "There is good reason to believe," writes Benjamin Higgins of the Massachusetts Institute of Technology in his book, *Indonesia's Economic Stabilization and Development,* "that the most productive use of the small amounts of capital available to Indonesia will continue for some time to be in the improvement of food production."

However, no underdeveloped country is likely to delay industrialization until it can be financed from farming. The two processes of village amelioration and industrialization should proceed simultaneously with maximum concentration, at first, on farming and mining and a gradual increase thereafter of invesment in industry.

Naturally rich though she is, Indonesia will hardly form ample capital soon for rapid, large-scale industrialization. Her priority requirements, rather, are irrigation, flood control, highways, railways, shipping—without which the island empire cannot breathe economically—fertilizer plants, electric power, cottage industries, intensified exploitation of mineral wealth, reforestation in Java, and small factories: textile mills, sugar mills, rubber goods and ceramics plants, fruit canneries, fish canneries; as well as more oil refineries, etc.

In present circumstances the expansion of mining (including oil) and the construction of large industries and hydroelectric power projects would need foreign capital. Having been bitten by Dutch colonialism, many Indonesians are shy of new forms of what they call "economic imperialism." Debates in Parliament have protested against foreign loans and credits which were not being offered. These fears usually stem from an insufficient understanding of the meaning and power of sovereignty. A sovereign country can always get rid of dangerous economic infiltration from the outside.

If Indonesia is afraid of foreign capital, her citizens should get busy and create their own. They have the natural means and the men. Put to work, these would spell money in the pockets of the people and the coffers of the government. But the industrial revolution must be accompanied by a psychological revolution, a new attitude toward labor, leisure, and life. I had the impression, however, that Indonesians cling lovingly to old values. Happiness, beauty, and style are the highest goals; money ranks lower; work near the bottom. This charming way of life would be pleasanter still if it included a longer life, a better diet, enough physicians, no malaria, and all the other benefits of an improved standard of living. Can Indonesia keep what is good in the East and add what is best in the West? That is the question.

Chapter Thirty

THE ROAD TO HAPPINESS

TOMTOM TE TOMTOM; tom te tom te tom; tomtom, tomtom, tomtom. All evening the drumbeats came from across the gorge, from down the hillside, from the village up the road. It was Lebaran, the end of the 30-day Ramadan fast, the Moslem month of abstention.

After the austerity of Ramadan, Lebaran, which Indians call Id al-Fitr, causes an outburst of joy. The holiday is announced by all-night tom-toming. High in the village of Tjilogo, between the Puntjak Pass and Bandung, where I stayed at the weekend house of Michael Harris, Ford Foundation representative, the throb of the drums echoed and re-echoed against the mountains. We heard it at 1 A.M., when our discussion of Indonesian politics tapered off into yawns, and at six when I woke.

In the morning the road below the house was thick with crowded buses, clattering pony carts, private cars, and walking families. Fathers, mothers, and children, bright in new dress, were making calls. Baby rode in mama's slendeng, a scarf suspended from her right shoulder which opens at the left hip to make a safe, deep seat.

On Lebaran, Indonesians visit relatives and the graves of ancestors. It is the holiday of gifts. Just before Lebaran, employers pay their workers a bonus; householders buy their servants new clothing. It is a custom as compulsory as employers' presents to the wives of their male staff members two months before a baby is expected and to a servant's son or daughter at marriage. In effect, the hiring of a servant amounts to the adoption of the servant's family, which sometimes comes to live with him at the master's house. As the master buys new outfits at Lebaran for his own family, so he does for the families of the personnel.

Driving up from Tjilogo to Bandung the cemeteries were full of gaily dressed parties listening to prayers and strewing rose petals on graves. Everybody greets everybody with "Let us this day forgive one another's errors."

Since many relatives have died and many are still alive, Lebaran continues until all visits are ended. A big family may thus celebrate Lebaran for three or four days or even a week. Work would debase the holiday.

The poor give Lebaran gifts, even if it means going into debt to a usurious moneylender till next Lebaran. Neither the Indonesian peasant nor the Indonesian worker, who in most cases is a peasant a few years removed from his village where he may still hold a parcel of land, is providential. "God will provide," he replies when you ask why he doesn't save. Or, "Nature will provide." Man and wife and often teen-age children toil from dawn till dusk thigh-high in the mud of the rice fields and in the heat of the tropical sun. What they produce and earn they spend on day-to-day living or on a circumcision or wedding. To fear the future, to accumulate for it, would show lack of faith in the soil, the rain, and the Almighty. Since nature is usually kind, why worry? If perchance next year brings a bad harvest or a natural catastrophe, it is the will of the Lord. Farmers then pool their meager resources and bow the head to fate. No wonder the minister of finance and the governor of the bank have headaches.

In villages, mutual aid in the agricultural processes and construction of homes for newlyweds and of schools is the rule. This does not preclude "running amuck" (an Indonesian word) in a homicidal-suicidal frenzy, or burning villages and killing villagers in the name of a Darul Islam theocratic state, or launching civil strife. Indonesia is no land of nonviolent saints. Yet normally the people are peaceful, forgiving, loving, and happy. Unhappily, happiness does not conduce to economic effort and progress.

Mr. Sujatmoko, scholar, author, publisher, and Socialist, has written a Cornell University White Book whose very title, *Economic Development as a Cultural Problem,* tells an important story. Industrialization, Sujatmoko finds, and the same would be true of modernized farming, requires "a creative adjustment of our culture." The machine age is more than the importation and installation of machines. "We must completely absorb the machine into our social structure." The peasant, he says, regards the hoe as his natural tool, but a machine is "an alien thing."

The big stumbling block, according to Sujatmoko, is Indonesian society's lack of dynamism. Before Indonesia can get up enough momentum for a "take-off" into capital formation and industrialization she must first achieve social velocity and thereby break free from the gravity grip of social stagnation.

The process has already commenced with "the distintegration of the old social structure" and the dissolution of feudal economy. Many ministries are nevertheless manned by influential members of feudal families who live mentally in the feudal, gentry tradition. Sujatmoko accuses these "circles" of "a lack of desire and determination to proceed with economic development."

He explains why: "In the static feudal-agrarian pattern of society which encompasses a large proportion of the Indonesian population, the essence of life is seen in terms of adjustment and unity of man with the universe and its laws. This is the conception of life by which man fundamentally establishes his place in and his relation to his environment through various rituals and numerical formulae intended to insure his safety and well-being." Here he is referring to magic, mysticism, and animistic rites. "On a higher spiritual level," Sujatmoko continues, "ultimate happiness is regarded as being based on an overcoming of and release from the bonds of his ego and in thus achieving a supreme feeling of one with the universe." Now the kernel: "This outlook excludes any thought of domination of nature by man and of harnessing the natural resources to serve human needs." That would "be un-Indonesian."

But the domination of nature and the use of its resources by man is the key to industrialization and material progress. Is Sujatmoko saying, in effect, that his country must foreswear the joy of identification with nature in order to industrialize? Is he unwittingly damning the West as a world of unhappiness while prodding his country to Westernize? "Man," he asserts, "now has more knowledge on how to defend human dignity against the machine." That reflects a hope. Clearly Sujatmoko, son of a strongly traditional Central Javanese family, is himself worried about the possible evil effects of the machine on Indonesian culture. Yet he will not be deterred. The traditional philosophies, "whatever the nobility of the values these embody," must go. The desire of Indonesians to "possess and to use the products of industrial life" must be stimulated—and speedily. Needs are the motor oil of progress.

Sujatmoko appeals for a "new attitude towards work." To reinforce the appeal, he feels relates the "spirit of progress and the spirit of patriotism." Nationalism is more than fervor, it is labor. Above all, the summit attainment of education should be not a college degree, which merely confers status, but a fitness to play a creative role in society. Status spells stagnation. Creativity brings social change and economic progress. It is the cement of a nation.

Indonesians now know that independence removed the problem of foreign rule but raised the problems of self-rule, many of which are insoluble in the short run. Discontent, confusion, and soul-searching are the expected, legitimate children of freedom from colonialism. But there is scarcely any disagreement in Indonesia on the necessity of industrialization. With their strong yearning for absorbing without discarding, however, some of his countrymen object to Sujatmoko's emphasis. They would take from the West yet keep their own cultural heritage. Phrases like "in search of an Indonesian identity," the title of a speech by Ruslan Abdulgani, and "our own Indonesian personality" frequently recur in private and public utterances. Asian countries are so very different from one another, Indonesia from India, India from Burma, Burma from Indonesia, Indonesia from Japan, from Siam, from Iraq. How much more so from the nations of Europe and the Americas. No Asian people wishes to be, or could be, a carbon copy of the West. It craves individuality and self-expression.

In practice this results in a paradox: while few Indonesians consciously oppose mechanization or industrialization, they insist on retaining that element in their mental equipment—Sujatmoko calls it culture—which makes them content with backwardness. They will work hard for sustenance but no more. Mutual aid in the village has a leveling effect; so has close family life. There is consequently no drive to keep up with the Kromos and the Marhaens, the Joneses and Smiths of the countryside. The machine product to them is not a thing of beauty. Value attaches to hand-painted batiks and wood sculptures. All-night wayang dances and all-night tomtoming, lavish wedding and circumcision feasts which impoverish—these, not possessions, give joy. Perhaps the key to it all is the importance of community living rather than individual material advancement. Community living, where the more fortunate help the deprived, exists in cities too. A village is divided into kampongs, or neighborhoods. The peasant who migrates to town also lives in a kampong with relatives and people from his rural district. He carries with him the custom of mutual aid (Gotong Rojong).

Nevertheless, the changes which Sujatmoko advocates are beginning to begin. New income possibilities bring differentiation and inequality, and hence striving. There never was any dearth of energy. Only the stimuli were lacking. It seems likely, therefore, that development will feed on itself. A little growth (more money and more manufactured consumer goods) will make for additional growth because it will alter culture patterns and social molds. This constant snowballing is the Western formula for economic progress and social change. In America the snowballing of needs and the means of satisfying them have produced so much social change in the past fifty years that, except for a thin layer at the top and a thicker layer at the bottom, the United States has become a largely middle-class and hence almost classless society. The question is whether the breathless rush to the pinnacle of material well-being leaves energy, time, and desire for what Indonesians call culture and what many regard as happiness. Thus the teething problems of the new East are kin to the grown-up problems of the developed West. From the vantage point of Indonesia I often looked homeward, westward.

Chapter Thirty-one

EAST OR WEST

THE ONLY non-Communist Moslem country which has undergone a deep cultural revolution is Turkey, where Kemal Pasha Atatürk abolished the state religion, the Islamic courts, the caliphate, the veil and the harem, and the use of Arabic script, and decreed European dress, a Latin alphabet, public education, votes for women, Sunday Sabbath, and nationalism. None of these reforms is necessary in Indonesia. To that extent Indonesia has already had her Western revolution. The Republic is secular. Though the 1945 and 1950 Constitutions declare that the state is based on belief in God, no government official from the president down is required to be a Moslem or to take an oath of office in the name of God or Mohammed. Freedom "to profess his own religion" is guaranteed by both Constitutions to every citizen.

The non-Islamic, nontheocratic nature of the Indonesian state has antagonized a significant segment of the population and provoked the Republic's longest, most expensive guerrilla war. The usual justification of secularism is the existence of a considerable body of Christians, Hindus, and others. But the big, unspoken reason is the difficulty of conducting a modern government according to the precepts of the Koran, which was ostensibly dictated to the Prophet by the angel Gabriel before A.D. 632. Moreover, if the Koran were the law, the lawyers would be the obscurantist Moslem divines and politics would bear the stamp of their centuries-old ideas. Most of Indonesia's parties, leaders, and intellectuals, however, are

260

enlightened, modern-minded partisans of a secular state, and secularism, for a Moslem country, is Western.

Indonesia erects no barriers against anything Western except power. Whenever foreign policy, be it Western, Russian, or Chinese, conceals power lust it is resisted. Indonesia's attitude toward the world can be summed up as: Independence, Interdependence, but no Dependence. This does not hinder the growing affinity with the West. The tongues of the West are as welcome as its techniques. Paperback books in English enjoy an enormous sale. Now that the Dutch educational system has been discarded, American methods are officially preferred, and the University of Indonesia has contracts with the Universities of Kentucky and California and the Tuskegee Institute to lend professors and give advice. English is spoken by almost all leaders, party politicians, editors, journalists, military men, and scientists, and by numerous teachers and students. The Indonesian language is written in Latin letters. The West is also present with classical music and jazz. Western films would win a popularity contest; Hollywood stars are household names. James Dean is loved by Jakarta youth. An increasing number of young Indonesian women wear Western dresses and most men have abandoned the sarong at work and in the street, often too at home.

Given their desire for oneness, Indonesians are likely to be West as well as East. The literature I read in translation, the painting I saw—much of it good—represents Western treatment of Eastern subject matter, and only the grotesque wayang masks are of the ancient Orient. Ideology and politics reflect a similar dualism. The Moslem goes to Mecca and bows to Marx. The conservative is also a Socialist. A feudal is an industrialist, a nationalist is an internationalist, a democrat wants a dictator as an aid to democracy, military administration offers itself as the medicine of freedom.

In these circumstances it is difficult to disentangle Western strands of thought from Eastern. Is nationalism a Western invention? Most Indonesians who went to study in Holland brought it home in their suitcases, yet the impulse that leads to it is as native and universal as sparrows, crows, and grass. Whatever its origin, nationalism is now the equal sign between Occident and Orient, between white and color. Empire and colonies would always have been twain, but at the right temperature nationalism is the yeast of East-West peace.

So, too, imported Socialism and Marxism are grafted on home-grown ideas to produce a plant uniquely Indonesian. In Indonesia, and generally in the East, I think, the emphasis of Socialism is on the social rather than the ism, on welfare rather than dogma. Indonesian Moslem Socialism vehemently opposes Marxism and of course Communism. The Socialism of the Masjumi, of Hatta, stands for contributions by the community, the co-operative, and the state to individual well-being in the spirit of Gotong Rojong (Mutual Aid).

The 1950 Constitution's Article 38 (Article 14 in the 1945 Constitution) provides that "the national economy shall be organized on a co-operative basis." Branches of production "which vitally affect the life of the people" —including "land and water and the natural riches contained therein"— shall be "controlled" by the state. "Controlled," not necessarily owned or managed; controlled as Western democracies, by myriad means, control the national economy. The Indonesian government puts no restriction on the expansion of native Indonesian, not Chinese, private enterprise and tolerates industrial and trade operations by foreign, not Dutch, companies.

The predominant intellectual bias, however, is anticapitalist. Though today the world's major imperialism is Soviet imperialism, though capitalism in the shape of America and Britain played the major role, as Prime Minister Djuanda and Foreign Minister Subandrio admitted to me, in Indonesia's national liberation capitalism is still, from long habit and mental fog, equated with colonialism and reviled. This lazy-intellectual attitude is reinforced by the prevailing priyayi-gentry prejudice against business and by America's misrepresentation, usually at the hands of her own representatives, as the citadel of conservatism and counterrevolution when in fact a social revolution has made her a middle-class welfare state far less conservative and far more egalitarian than Russia.

In the West capitalism is what you make it. Keynes and the Labor party have revolutionized British capitalism just as wealth, wisdom, and Franklin D. Roosevelt have lifted the face and changed the heart of American capitalism. Similarly, Marxism in West and East is what you make it. If Sukarno, the mystic democrat, Khrushchev, the anti-Tito materialistic dictator, Tito who jails Djilas, Djilas the anti-Tito ex- and anti-Communist, and John Strachey, the democratic Laborite, are all Marxists, then Marxism has no political significance and is merely a cloth cut to national style patterns. Invented by two Western-oriented, anti-Russian Germans, Marxism was adopted as Soviet Russia's theology and impregnated with Slav nationalism and Tsarist imperialism. But during the post-Stalin Khrushchev thaw, when dungeon deaths and 2 A.M. arrests took a vacation, Mao's China, draping a red flag around mechanized Oriental despotism, pressed half a billion peasants into militarized labor camps misnamed communes and allowed the "hundred flowers" to wilt before they bloomed. Sukarno's Marxism, on the other hand, married astrology and bred a gentle populism.

Walking down a country lane Sukarno once encountered a peasant named Marhaen. After that Sukarno called his social philosophy Marhaenism, and since Marhaen is a common Indonesian name, as common as Smith, and a symbol therefore of the common man, I have called it Smithism. Marx sired Marhaenism by Mother Indonesia. Marhaenism is Marxism refracted by independent Indonesia. It is Marxism without materialism. Sukarno rejects the materialism which teaches that there is no God and no idea divorced from matter. A European writer said, "No thinking without phosphorus," in other words, thinking is a chemical process. Sukarno quoted and condemned him. Sukarno's Marhaenism took the materialism out of Marx and thus made Marxism un-Marxist.

Now the credo of the PNI, the party closest to Sukarno, Marhaenism spells uplift for the Smiths, the peasants and workers, hence everybody. Far from being a doctrine, it is not even a policy but rather a sympathy, an intention to start at the bottom and push upward toward village amelioration and industrialization.

Certain tendencies, like industrialization, urbanization, army ascendancy, economic planning, juvenile delinquency, and addiction to jazz, leap across oceans, deserts, and Iron and Bamboo Curtains to achieve a universality which mocks the division of the world into East and West. Military dictatorships in Pakistan, the Sudan, and Burma? During the 1958 crisis which brought de Gaulle to power, Indonesian diplomats in Europe reported copiously on it to Jakarta, where subsequent political decisions were influenced by the Gaullist solution. American obsession with comic strips? A single issue of *Politika,* Communist newspaper in Titoist Belgrade, published the following gems of American capitalist culture: *Flash Gordon, Donald Duck,* Ripley's *Believe It or Not, Popeye the Sailor, The Katzenjammer Kids,* Walt Disney's *Dumbo, Sleeping Beauty, Mickey Mouse,* and *Prince Valiant*—all in color. In Russia Tarzan is a hero imitated by youth. Poles call rock 'n' roll the Dance of Liberation. This is the age of fusion and transfusion.

East and West fuse in individuals as well as in countries, less in Western individuals than one might desire, but to a marked extent in Africa, where tribal chiefs send their sons to American and European universities, and to a greater extent in Asia. Nehru is an East-Westerner, more Western probably than Eastern and unhappy in the resulting unresolved inner conflict. Sukarno, who never saw the West until 1956, is East and West, a kind of republican sultan, democratic in personal relations, aristocratic in the concept of his role in public affairs.

"Sultan" is pure East. Indonesia has two sultans, the Sultan of Solo, who is outside politics, and the Sultan of Jogjakarta, a key figure in Indonesian life. The Sultan Hamengku Buwono IX, comes from a royal line that goes back to the most ancient crowned families of Java. In the presence of his father, Hamengku Buwono VIII, the Dutch Governor General made a deep obeisance and walked backwards to leave the royal chamber. The old Sultan, who died in 1939, never cut his hair, neither did his father, and both held the honorary rank of major general in the Netherlands army. The grandfather, Hamengku Buwono VII, sired eighty children; Hamengku Buwono VIII only forty—from ten or more wives. The present Sultan of Jogjakarta has four wives but refuses to choose one of them as his chief wife, and until he does he is not considered married and has no legal heir. Friends say he may be doing this purposely in order to end the sultanate, which belongs to the dead past. Though peasants and others will prostrate themselves before him, he is completely unpretentious. We talked in the home of an Indonesian acquaintance to which he came at my suggestion, and again when he simply dropped in at the house of Sujatmoko during one of my visits there.

Born in 1912, educated in Holland, the Sultan has traveled in the United States and speaks a fine English. He wears Western clothes and holds Western views. His long, flat, easily remembered face wreathed in a smile, he discussed politics both directly and in "Javanese." The shorter the military action against the rebels the better the chance of successful peace talks with them. He said Hatta had great prestige in Java as well as in the outer islands. While there is so much confusion at the top, the Sultan prefers to stay below it. Immediately after the Second World War, politics were attractive and hope-inspiring. That was no longer the case. When I told him that his name was being mentioned in connection with a Cabinet reshuffle, he said, "As minister of defense?" I had heard, I replied, that he might be offered the Ministry of Economic Affairs.

He shook his head negatively. The Sultan had been minister of defense, but I did not suppose that he wished to return to that post as a vindication, rather his appointment to it would indicate a will to establish peace at the political summit as a preliminary to peace with the rebels. If Hatta returned to office, the Sultan would go with him, I presumed.

Meanwhile the Sultan devoted himself to the practical task of developing sugar and tobacco growing in the Jogjakarta area where he lives and is the government representative. "In my council," he said, "fourteen of the forty-five members are Communists. In the executive committee of the Jogjakarta residency of which I am the chairman we have one Communist. All Communists work very hard and so far we have had no trouble with them." They try to create the impression that they are furthering the general welfare, not feathering their party nest. The PKI won votes in Central Java because it attracted crowds to meetings with wayang dances, gamelan orchestras, and the singing of folk songs and religious hymns. In Semerang, Communist leader Aidit promised there would be no rice shortage if Communists were elected. The non-Communists in office, Aidit added, were corrupt at the people's expense.

I gathered that the Sultan had inner harmony. Highborn, he did not hanker after honor or power. He did not have to prove anything to himself or to others. He wanted to serve. Steeped in Javanese culture, he was devoid of any Javanese chauvinism and felt close to Sjahrir the moderate Socialist, Hatta the conservative Socialist, both Sumatrans. His nationalism took precedence over island patriotism. Though the symbol of traditional Java, he had transcended Java and tradition and was a thorough modern whose prestige and capacity for leadership were not being used by a country in need of both.

When the present Sultans of Jogjakarta and Solo die there may be no more sultans in Indonesia. In the twentieth-century global climate some aspects of the East will disappear. In the Eastern air some importations from the West will find no oxygen, some will take on new shapes.

Chapter Thirty-two

NON-COMMUNISM AND ANTI-COMMUNISM

AT DINNER parties one often had to wear a jacket and necktie in the tropical heat when the best advice always was to keep the body (especially the feet) ventilated. But Ruslan Abdulgani, former foreign minister, now deputy chairman of the National Council, remained consistently informal. After our first evening together we knew we would meet again, and he instructed me to leave my shoes and tie at home the next time. For the second evening I wore trousers, a shirt open at the throat, and Indonesian sandals with no socks. "But I see you have on closed-toe patent leather slippers," I remarked.

"Ah," he exclaimed, "such slippers were worn by feudal chiefs, and my father, a merchant, wore them in defiance of feudal custom."

Ruslan, a brilliant conversationalist, well-read in current political literature and well-informed on world developments (a joy rarely encountered in Jakarta), had fought in East Java against the Dutch and was struck by a bullet at the point of the V between the thumb and index finger of his right hand. The wound still festers.

He reminisced about his father. "My father," he said, "went on a pilgrimage to Mecca and became a haj but didn't take me. I was too young. I went later with President Sukarno."

"Instead of going with your natural father," I commented, "you went with your political father."

"My political brother," he amended.

266

I was being told in "Javanese" not to overstate the distance between them. Ruslan was Sukarno's adviser.

"In many of our towns," Ruslan continued, "there is a central square with a mosque on the west side, a government building on the east side, and giant waringin trees on the north and south sides. We have two political waringins, Sukarno and Hatta, and we play in their shade. The next generation will be exposed to the sun."

"Sukarno-Hatta are your political umbrellas," I interpreted.

"The Hatta waringin is tall and strong," he asserted, "but gives less shade than Sukarno's."

This was more "Javanese." It meant that Ruslan would be happy to see Hatta in the government, but felt closer to Sukarno. He also saw the possibility of a reconciliation between Jakarta and rebel Premier Sjafruddin and Colonel Simbolon, the Sumatran commander, but not with Sumitro: "He's too Western, too clever."

I asked whether Mohammad Natsir, chairman of the Masjumi, the country's strongest party, might likewise return from Sumatra into active national politics. "Natsir and Sukarno," Ruslan replied, "had a controversy in 1940. In a review of Turkey's national revival, Sukarno wrote that if Islam in Indonesia was to find new vigor it must reject traditional interpretations of the Koran and read it rationally in the light of modern life. Natsir differed. Natsir is traditional, Sukarno progressive."

Ruslan supports the secular against the Islamic state. He would, he asserted, bar both extremes, the Darul Islam and the Communists, from the government. He thus departed from Sukarno's Guided Democracy Concept which, as originally formulated, would have brought the Communists into the government. Even that part of the Concept which had been adopted, the National Council, Ruslan said, was already evolving. At first it included only representatives of functional groups: peasants, workers, intellectuals, military, and so forth. Now, he explained, representatives of geographic areas had been added. This was his reply to my advocacy of a Senate for Indonesia. "Sukarno," he stated, "is prepared to expand the National Council into a Senate. But we Indonesians do not always go forward by deciding to advance.

"I am a Dutch child," he said with a laugh. (He meant this only in the cultural sense.) "I translate from the Dutch when I speak. The Dutch have a saying that if you want a pig to go forward you pull his tail and if you want him to back up you push him. Don't worry about us. We will get ahead."

I remarked on the plethora of political parties. "They multiply by fission." (Imron Roshadi, deputy chairman of the Nahdatul Ulama—Moslem Teachers' party—or NU, told me that his party split from the

Masjumi "not for reasons of principle or ideology but because of practical politics." I asked him whether I could translate "practical politics" into "ministerial portfolios and government jobs." He agreed.) Ruslan knew far more about these procedures than I did and deplored them. "Couldn't you," I urged, "introduce something similar to the West German provision which eliminates a party that has less than 5 per cent of the votes?"

"We have discussed that in the National Council. Even 10 per cent."

"You discuss everything," I noted, "but the changes don't come."

"They will come," he said. "Somebody is pulling our tail."

I spent four evenings with Ruslan in his home and also attended a large, delightful, informal buffet dinner party there. I met his devoted wife and on our last evening together I was photographed with him and his two bright-eyed, white-toothed sons. Ruslan always wore a sarong instead of trousers, usually slipped off his slippers, and kept on his black velveteen skullcap. In dress the "Dutch child" was an Eastern priyayi.

"We have no land frontiers," he said to me on one occasion. "Our northern frontier is the United States Seventh Fleet [based in the West Pacific] and our western frontier is British Singapore." That placed Indonesia in a Western lake. The pronouncement was a mirror of Ruslan's realism. "I wish our relations with Holland weren't so bad," he declared in another context. As a keen student of the world, Ruslan Abdulgani knows where his country's interests lie; he was neutrally pro-West in theory and had no illusions about Communist countries. "The Communist states," he found, "necessarily have a dictatorial trait hidden behind whatever name or dogma. This aspect is hard to accept by our people because of the prevalence of the spirit of deliberation, mutual agreement, and mutual assistance in the character of our people's daily life." Moreover, Communism does not "leave enough room for religion."

In 1956 Ruslan joined President Sukarno in Prague and flew with him to Sochi on the beautiful Black Sea riviera of the Soviet Caucasus. "One day, on a porch overlooking the beach," Ruslan recounted, "we met with President Voroshilov, Prime Minister Bulganin, and Foreign Minister Shepilov. Shepilov introduced the subject of China's membership in the UN. Bulganin did most of the talking. They asked us to raise the issue at the next session of the UN General Assembly. I said we favored China's admission and would take it up with the Cabinet on our return to Jakarta. Sukarno promised to do everything possible. Then, after a stopover in Ulan Bator [capital of Outer Mongolia], Sukarno and I arrived in Peking, where we had an audience with Chaiman Mao Tse-tung, Liu Shao-chi, and Chou En-lai. Sukarno mentioned the conversation with the Russians at Sochi. Mao told us China was in no hurry. 'We are already negotiating

with the Americans in Geneva. We can wait six months.' Sukarno recalled the Soviet leaders' sense of urgency. 'Yes,' Mao said, 'we appreciate
that. But it is better not to rush matters. This has time.' When Sukarno
and Ruslan were leaving Peking, Chou En-lai saw them off at the airport
and drew Ruslan aside and in fairly good English declared, 'We know
the situation in Washington. We know the attitude of Walter Robertson
[United States assistant secretary of state] and it is better not to antagonize
anybody by demanding what is not obtainable.' "

Ruslan interpreted this to mean that China did not wish to be under any
political obligations to Moscow. I offered as an additional explanation the
need Mao felt of having an enemy. "China," I suggested, "is squeezing
her people through a red wringer. In times of such stress, a dictatorship
requires an enemy on whom it can pin all its difficulties. 'Rally around
your government,' it proclaims. 'Submit to sacrifices. The American imperialists are upon us.' China does not want good relations with the United
States."

(Recently, a high Polish Communist who had visited China told me
that the Chinese asked him why the Poles were not anti-American. "Our
'America' is Germany," he answered. Poland's enemy and scapegoat was
Germany. "Not Russia?" I wondered. "No," he protested. I had not expected a yes from an official. But millions of Polish citizens undoubtedly
abhor Moscow and accept Gomulka as the best temporary alternative to
worse Kremlin domination or a Hungarian bloodbath. Their "America"
is Russia. Hence their pro-Americanism.)

Ruslan was cynical about Communist foreign policies. His attitude to
American foreign policy, however, could not be characterized as un-
critical. "You know," he wrote me after I left for Europe, "that Indonesia
is far from being Communist and that many social and cultural forces
are tending to maintain that non-Communist position. However, we
wonder what kind of profit this gives our underprivileged people. What
is anti-Communism when it supports and aids Yugoslav Communism but
denies that aid to a non-Communist society striving to maintain its non-
Communism?"

I had no reply. I could only hope that the Eisenhower-Dulles administration would stop expecting the Sumatran rebels to achieve by Javanese
magic a victory which they could never win by material means.

I noticed that Ruslan always used "non-Communist" and "non-Communism." He was what Arthur Koestler calls "an anti-anti-Communist."
"Anti-Communism," Ruslan wrote, "like anticapitalism and anticolonialism and so on, in itself is empty. I mean that any form of aid should represent a flowering of friendship and good will. . . . If it is offered in a Cold

War context, it is hardly honest, and will certainly, sooner or later, be seen by the recipient as being hardly honest." This applied to both sides. "All gift horses now have a thorough dental examination."

These are wise words. Most of the newly independent countries have regarded the Cold War as a great-power struggle for world supremacy which does not concern them or, at least, from which they wish to stay aloof lest they get hurt. The Cold War is, in essence, a power struggle. That, however, does not explain the nonalignment or neutralism of Afro-Asian countries which oscillate between being pro-West and pro-Soviet according to their understanding of self-interest. Morality has little to do with it. In a discussion on this subject with an official who made a major Asian country's foreign policy during the 1956 Hungarian revolution, he said explosively, "You have it easy. You are a free man. You can have ideas. We are politicians. We want to be on good terms with both the United States and the Soviet Union." This comes nearer the truth without being the whole truth. As far as we know, little Burma did not suffer by condemning Russian conduct in Hungary although her frontier runs for a thousand miles with that of Communist China. Yet neutralism or nonalignment is usually justified by fear of a Communist neighbor or by fear of a strong Communist party at home. It serves only futility for Westerners to contend that the best refuge from possible Communist aggression is under the wing of the Western bloc; Afro-Asian nations already enjoy that protection through NATO, without which Europe, Asia, and Africa would be at Russia and China's mercies. Equally it serves no useful purpose to argue that the best way to fight a strong Communist party is by being anti-Communist. Asians will have to make the discovery themselves. If the West pulls them, they will back away.

For years Indians and Indonesians said they were not afraid of Communism and thought the Cold War ought to cease. Though India had not been able to settle her minor cold war with Pakistan, she cavalierly dismissed the far-flung Soviet-West problems as easily soluble and irrelevant. Of late, however, the official New Delhi line has changed. Now, we hear, India is engaged in an economic race with China and if China proves that her methods bring greater good then democracy in Asia will go under. This new approach reflects fear of Communism and makes India a Cold War battlefield. It is India's own decision.

"We have suddenly arrived at a stage," Prime Minister Nehru told the Lucknow conference of the Institute of Pacific Relations in 1950, "when we have to run. Walking is not enough, and in running we stumble and fall and we try to get up again. It is no good anybody telling us to walk slowly. . . . It involves risks and dangers but there is no help and no choice for it, for there is torment in our minds."

Though mental torment has not always been Nehru's best counselor, a person like myself, born to poverty, who has seen the filthy misery of Bombay tenements and the animal existence of Indian peasants, grasps Nehru's sentiments fully. Ruslan Abdulgani made somewhat the same point. "Louis," he wrote, "do not underestimate the explosive power of economic discontent. It contains more potential energy than a hydrogen bomb. Unless channels are prepared for it into which it can flow, then that discontent can destroy, just as in other circumstances it can irrigate the nation's future."

We had discussed this matter in his home and he knew that my emphasis was different. The primary problem, I said to him, is not the economy but the administration. The smooth functioning of a government apparatus is more basic even than economy, in fact economic progress is impossible, certainly impeded, without an effective executive branch. I told him that the strength of the Indonesian Communist party (PKI) derived, first, from the country's administrative mess, which includes guerrilla war, corruption, and unstable governments; secondly, from being allowed to masquerade in nationalist garb, which Sukarno could rip off as Nehru was doing in India; and thirdly, from economic stresses.

Ruslan disagreed. "I certainly do not agree," he wrote, "that bad administration is the first cause of Communist strength. In my view the repeated follies of Washington take that place." This opinion cannot be dismissed as implausible. It must be judged against the background of events. Indonesians, forgetting their refusal to side with India or Pakistan in the Kashmir dispute, are angered by America's failure to take an anti-Dutch position on the West Irian dispute. Moreover, Indonesian sentiment in 1958 assumed that the United States had intervened in favor of the rebels, and the Communists made the most of this—with much assistance from non-Communist officials.

It is human to repulse guilt and foist it on outsiders, especially if they are not wholly blameless. Neverless, Indonesians themselves are beginning to say it is time to put their own house in order. Foreign Minister Subandrio declared on February 27, 1959, that the success of Indonesia's struggle for New Guinea depended "on the consolidation of her domestic strength." Prime Minister Djuanda made a similar statement to me. Djuanda, in fact, said, "My chief interest is administration." He told me of a conversation he had had in The Hague, on the eve of the Dutch transfer of sovereignty, with a representative of the *Christian Science Monitor* who asked, "How are you going to manage?"

"I always recall that," Djuanda said.

Djuanda was outspoken about very important matters. "At any moment," he admitted, "the government could be replaced by an antidemocratic regime under army domination. Therefore, we must save Parliament. The army now supports my Cabinet fully. That is good and bad. The support of the PKI is also good and bad. We have accepted it but did not ask for it. The good about our army support is that we could use it against the PKI. There are few Communists in the army. Sukarno is opposed to a Fascist regime either by the army or the PKI.

"The error of our right-wing parties," Djuanda continued, "was to withdraw their backing from Sukarno. That made him more dependent on the Communists. The U.S. government is wrong in underestimating Sukarno's strength. During the last few months the U.S.A. had favored Hatta only. You must not do it that way. [American] Ambassador Allison was beginning to favor a Sukarno-Hatta reconciliation. Your State Department thereupon transferred him because he was too friendly to Sukarno. Nothing would be gained by getting rid of Sukarno. A Sukarno-Hatta combination cannot solve all problems but it would solve many. Otherwise the PKI will be strengthened."

I liked Djuanda for his crystal honesty and frankness. In one interview with him I charged that members of the government were enhancing the power of the PKI by giving the public the impression of being anti-American. "Why," I asked, "should a minister enter into a public controversy with American newspapers? The other day, at your press conference, you attacked *Time* magazine. In some respects what *Time* wrote about Sukarno was unfortunate, but *Time* is a privately owned publication and a prime minister should not argue with it."

He hesitated and then said, "I am glad you told me this. I was of two minds about doing it. It is the first time I have done it."

Would he talk to me about his views?

"In thought," he asserted, "I am close to the Socialists. But I search for an Indonesian way. I, as well as some leaders of the PNI, dislike certain Socialist personalities."

How would they end the civil war?

"Reduce the rebels to the status of guerrillas and deal with the political causes of the revolt," he replied. After the fighting it should be possible to reconcile Hatta and Sukarno. The army had learned a lesson from the Sumatran and Celebes insurrections: it would never be united, and any attempt, therefore, at a military coup must split the country and the army. "When Colonel Zulkifli Lubis was planning to overthrow the government in 1955," Djuanda recalled, "he sent me a message saying, 'Join us and we will seize power and let you administer the government without political parties.' I refused. 'If the army were unified,' I replied, 'I might consider it.

But no, thank you, there are so many groups in the army that it is really an assemblage of political parties.' "

Djuanda had a loyalty to Parliament and told me he spent much time listening to its debates. Nevertheless, his experiences as prime minister were leading him to the conclusion that Indonesia needed a Presidential Cabinet. "Meanwhile," he declared, "I work closely with the army."

In 1958, 80 per cent of the routine administration of Indonesia was in the hands of the military. The Djuanda-Nasution-Sukarno triumvirate exercised effective control. "The decision against deputations to foreign embassies," Djuanda said, "was made by me and announced by Nasution."

Late one afternoon I was sitting with U.S. Councillor of Embassy Sterling J. Cottrell on his airy, ground-level porch facing Suropati Square, when the ambassador's car came up the path and the chauffeur said there was a hostile demonstration at the ambassador's residence. "Cott" and I walked across the square toward the Jones home. As we approached we saw a crowd of white-clad young men, some on foot, some on bicycles, yelling "To hell with SEATO" and similar slogans. We walked through the group into the grounds and up the driveway to the broad terrace where Mr. and Mrs. Howard P. Jones greeted us. The ambassador said they had just been invaded by a student delegation. He asked us to sit down, ordered drinks, and told the story. Some fifty young people, obviously Communist-led, had come up the driveway. He walked out to meet them. They were shouting denunciations of SEATO and of American intervention in Sumatra. The ambassador allowed himself to be encircled by the students, shook hands with each, and listened to their English-speaking spokesman. In reply, Jones declared that there had been no U.S. intervention in Indonesia and that the South East Asian Treaty Organization was a defensive arrangement which meant no harm to anybody but an aggressor. The Philippines was a member of SEATO. Did they fear an invasion from the Philippines? Some students laughed, others waited for the translation and swore at the translator as though he were presenting his own arguments. At times Communist agitators led the group in a kind of college cheering. It was all amicable, and the ambassador ended the confrontation by warning them, with a smile, against Communist propaganda and shaking hands again with each one of them. "My only regret now," Mr. Jones concluded, "was that I didn't invite them in for a cold soft drink."

At this point Australian Ambassador McIntyre arrived wearing a short-sleeve, open-neck shirt and short shorts, showing his hairy legs, and we heard the story repeated. Jones would be seeing Foreign Minister Subandrio that evening at a diplomatic dinner and planned to discuss the demonstration with him.

During the next week the American, Australian, and Philippine embassies and residences, especially the American, were deluged with delegations voicing carbon-copy protests. They were heard patiently, answered politely, cautioned against Communist lies, and given a mimeographed statement on American policy to take home. But these visitations became tiresome, and one could never know when they might become troublesome. If someone threw a stone or fired a shot, tempers might flare and lead to disaster. Moreover, prolonged toleration of these demonstrations would be wind in the sails of the Communists and create the impression that they, by attacking America for intervening, were patriotically defending Indonesia's national interests against "Western imperialism."

One morning Major General Nasution made a statement, announced by press and radio, that it was not dignified for Indonesian citizens to complain to foreign governments. If they had views to express they could do so through their own officials. There were no further delegations.

This was one of a series of anti-Communist measures. On March 31, 1958, Nasution announced through Lieutenant Colonel Rudy Pirngadie, his information chief, that May Day celebrations required army permits. The exact text of speeches at such celebrations must be submitted in advance for approval by the Military War Administrator. Public meetings were to be held at previously assigned locations without parades before or after. Only the red-and-white national flag of Indonesia would be displayed.

On May 1 my student friend Sarwono and I went by betjak to a large park in Jakarta to see the Communist May Day celebration. The crowd numbered perhaps 5,000. Sar said it was but a fraction of last year's crowd. Instead of delivering the usual free-wheeling, emotional harangues with expressive gestures, orators held papers in front of them and read the texts which the army had O.K.'d. The small audience of young people looked bored. In one city where a Communist speaker deviated from the approved wording an army officer stopped him.

Another of Nasution's anti-Communist acts was the ban on "the printing, publication, delivery, distribution, and sale of newspapers and magazines not using Latin, Arabic, or regional Indonesian scripts." This decree proscribed one kind of publications: those in Chinese characters.

In Makassar on Celebes island I had inspected a Chinese school full of charming children and staffed by Chinese teachers. Most of the textbooks were imported from Red China. In the first-grade classroom I saw on the walls a colored poster divided into three panels. The topmost panel showed an emaciated, listless, ragged peasant plowing with two bony, sluggish oxen. The next panel down depicted the same peasant, now cheerful and well-dressed and wearing a red neckerchief, guiding two fat, energetic oxen with red ribbons tied to their horns. In the bottom panel the same peasant was driving a tractor decorated with red bunting. The poster came from Communist China. Nasution's decree would bar such literature along with Chinese propaganda domestically produced.

In the same period PKI General Secretary Aidit, who is part Chinese, part Arab, and chiefly Sumatran, sent a telegram to U.S. Ambassador Jones threatening action against the American-run oil fields in Indonesia unless American aid to the Sumatran and Celebes rebels ceased. Nasution thereupon issued a calm statement that "interference by whatever quarter in the operation of fuel installations is not allowed." Aidit did nothing. The oil fields remained safe. What is more, at the end of June, 1958, the Indonesian government invited the Royal Dutch-Shell Company to resume work in the East Borneo field.

Prime Minister Djuanda told me that all these anti-Communist decisions were taken by him and Nasution with Sukarno's approval. They marked a change of the tide. The Communist party's mounting strength had made it too aggressive. Aidit was more interested in the Cold War than in the class war. The party's intensified anti-American campaign during the outer-island revolts revealed a clear intent to divert Indonesia's foreign policy into pro-Soviet, anti-Western channels. The result, inevitably, would have been a further expansion of PKI power, which already threatened to rival the army's and make Sukarno a political prisoner of the Communists. The situation had become intolerable. The PKI, as usual, was crude, brutal, unrestrained, and impatient. It overreached itself. Aidit's telegram to Ambassador Jones was a museum piece of stupidity; he might have known that the Indonesian government could not permit it to go unanswered.

Perhaps the Communists believed that the army's preoccupation with the rebels gave them immunity. Nasution disillusioned them by his anti-Communist measures. One alternative remained to Aidit: take up arms or behave. The army would easily have crushed a Communist revolt. Aidit behaved.

Non-Communism would not have been enough.

Chapter Thirty-three

AMERICAN POLICY IN ASIA

NEITHER IS American anti-Communism enough. Time has helped Washington achieve better understanding of Afro-Asian mentality, but it still comes hard. The State Department tends to see the world in black and white, or perhaps one should say in red and red-white-and-blue. If you are not with us you are against us. When President Sukarno went from a triumphal tour through the United States, where he was hailed as the "George Washington of Indonesia," to triumphal tours through Russia and China, the Eisenhower-Dulles administration acted as though it had been betrayed. Sukarno's Guided Democracy speech of February 21, 1957, convinced American policy makers that he had indeed sold out to the Communists. "As you know," Secretary Dulles said at his press conference on January 11, 1958, "there is a kind of a 'guided democracy' trend there now which is an evolution which may not quite conform with the provisional constitution and apparently does not satisfy large segments of the population."

Should a secretary of state accuse a foreign government of a breach of its own constitution? Should he, knowing the rebel colonels had set up a rival government in Sumatra, suggest that many Indonesians would oppose Sukarno's proposal? Is this not interference in the domestic affairs of another country?

"We doubt very much," Dulles continued, "that the people of Indonesia will ever want a Communist-type or a Communist-dominated government, and they would not want, I think, to be subjected to a type of

276

government which . . . maintains itself by coercive methods and does not respond to the will of the people."

In view of conditions in Indonesia at the time, these words hinted broadly that resistance to Sukarno's proposal was in order and might be welcomed by America. This is how it was read in Indonesia. Above all, the Dulles statement, to which Indonesians on both sides of the barricades attached great significance, assumed—falsely, as events showed—that the admission of Communists into the government was inevitable or so probable that he had to take a public stand against it. Mr. Dulles might have known that overt foreign pressure against a policy makes Asian leaders adhere more stubbornly to it in order to prove their independence. A subtle, private inquiry by the U.S. ambassador in Jakarta or to the Indonesian ambassador in Washington would have been more effective. Had the Indonesian government been in real danger of going Communist, Mr. Dulles' use of the sledge hammer would only have hastened the consummation.

In the subsequent months the Indonesian government's chief fear was American intervention on the side of the rebels; this may have hastened Sukarno's February, 1958, decision to extirpate the rebels by force before foreign aid reached them. In any event, the stress of Jakarta's propaganda against the Sumatran and Celebes insurgents was their possession of American weapons. One argued in vain that anybody with dollars in his pocket could buy U.S. arms in Singapore and many other places. "Tito, Mao, Moscow, Siam, Greece, Turkey—who hasn't got American munitions, including planes?" I said to high officials in Jakarta. "You have too."

"Our cities and ships," came the unvarying answer, "are being bombed by planes based on Formosa and Clark Field in the Philippines."

"Proof?"

Evidence is not needed when tempers are hot. Or agents supply it. Or the allegations were at least partially correct. When the Sumatran rebels were repulsed, their captured American weapons were publicly exhibited in Jakarta. Crowds saw them. I asked Foreign Minister Subandrio why this was done; would it not help the Communists and obstruct a rapprochement with the United States?

"The army wants to show that it has won victories," he replied.

The government's wish to demonstrate the truth of its propaganda was probably a supplementary motive.

One day Mr. Allan Lawrence Pope of Miami, Florida, flying an American-made bomber, was shot down during a rebel raid on government territory and captured. No country can control all the actions of its citizens abroad. Had not the Republic hired American aviators who helped fight the Dutch? But logic did not convince politicians apprehensive of America's alignment with the rebels.

Dulles told the House Foreign Affairs Committee in testimony released early in March, 1958, that, "We would be very happy to see the non-Communist elements who are really in the majority there . . . [security deletion] exert a greater influence in the affairs of Indonesia than has been the case in the past where Sukarno has moved toward the so-called guided democracy theory, which is a nice-sounding name for what I fear would end up to be Communist despotism."

Congresswoman Marguerite Church, of Illinois, thereupon asked the Secretary, "Is there any chance for these people [the rebels] if they have no air umbrella and if Sukarno continues to use American-bought planes to bomb them?"

"I think there is a fair chance," Dulles replied, "that out of this will come a curtailment of the trend toward Communism. I do not want to be more precisely detailed at the moment than that."

The Dulles testimony received front-page headlines in the Indonesian press and was taken to foreshadow American military aid to the rebels.

Through this dark cloud Mr. Howard P. Jones flew into Jakarta to take up his assignment as ambassador. He was not new in Indonesia. He had served some years before as head of the American aid program and left behind a reputation for understanding and warmth which awaited him upon his return. I first saw him early in March, up at Bill Palmer's mountain haven. He had been expected Saturday, but frequent telephone calls on a bad line elicited the information that urgent business held him in Jakarta. Had the rebels bombed the Sumatran oil fields managed by Stanvac and Caltex? Had there been further protests by the Indonesian government against "U.S. intervention"? We listened to Australian broadcasts about Indonesia and speculated. More telephone calls Sunday morning. Jones hoped to come to lunch. The fifty Americans, Indonesians, and European and Asian diplomats invited for the meal were beginning to arrive. Smells from the kitchen made my mouth taste turkey while we talked Indonesia. Tranquil music from Palmer's village gamelan orchestra failed to dispel the sense of crisis. United States-Indonesian relations had to improve quickly or they would deteriorate seriously. When the ambassador and his wife finally appeared, the American newspapermen surrounded him. What new policy had he brought from Washington? I stood in the group for a while and listened, but it was soon evident that he intended to say nothing and I retreated to the bridge table where several of us had been working through the weekend on a jigsaw puzzle of an Austrian Alpine scene that was good practice for fitting together the myriad pieces of Indonesia's complicated political mosaic.

An ambassador, even the American ambassador in Moscow or the Soviet ambassador in West Germany, naturally strives for better relations with the country to which he is accredited. It makes his life pleasanter. Also, diplomatic laurels do not grow on a downward slope. Above all, Jones recognized that the rebels must lose.

Washington recognized this too. On March 30 Jack Raymond, the ear of the *New York Times* at the Pentagon, reported that "United States military officials are worried about the continuation of hostilities in Indonesia." A growing amount of Soviet military supplies, he heard, had reached Jakarta. "United States sources at the Pentagon and the State Department made no secret of their inclination toward the rebels' anti-Communist aims and their distrust of President Sukarno's liaison with the Communists." However, the rebel outlook seemed gloomy and "many officials here" accordingly believed that the "best solution would be a reconciliation between the government and the Sumatran-Celebes insurgents."

"The stakes in Indonesia," wrote Mr. Hanson W. Baldwin, competent military commentator of the *New York Times,* "are high enough to warrant strong action by the United States and the Western world to prevent the wholesale triumph of Communism in the archipelago."

Did the Eisenhower-Dulles administration intend to intervene forcibly and reverse the tide? Having decided that Sukarno meant to lead Indonesia down the Red path, having decided, too, that his influence had ebbed, Washington assumed an anti-Jakarta stance and saw disaster loom if the government defeated the rebels. It might have occurred to Mr. Dulles that the strongest factors in the Indonesian government were as opposed to a Red Indonesia as he was. Sukarno's "liaison with the Communists" was intricate domestic politics, but not the politics of surrender. Moreover, it is doubtful whether the President could have given power to the Communists if he had wished. The fact is that he could not even bring the Communist party into a Cabinet in which it would have been a minority. The opponents of such a move blocked it.

Far too often fanatical abhorrence of Communism leads to policies which reflect agreement with the Kremlin that Communism is the irresistible wave of the future. Prejudice obstructs vision. Indonesian developments demonstrated that Washington misjudged the rebels' prospects and the government's politics.

Betting on the rebel card was a poor gamble. In April, 1958, Padang, Bukittinggi, and all other important rebel cities were seized with ease by government troops, thereby reducing the insurrection to enervating but politically hopeless guerrilla warfare. The stupidity and frivolity of basing a great power's policy on the Sumatran revolt is evident from the conduct of the rebel leaders. They were asleep, the day Padang fell, in Bukittinggi.

Awakened by a platoon of foreign journalists who covered the "war" and told the bad news, they refused to believe it.

"But government airborne troops have taken the Padang airfield," a correspondent insisted.

"They're dummies," the ministers retorted.

"Do dummies move their arms and legs?" a journalist argued.

"Do dummies have supplies dropped to them?" another demanded.

"Slowly, unwillingly," said the London *Times* special correspondent, "the rebels began to grasp what was happening to them. That was the climax to the war in Sumatra, the sorry finale to the hopes and delusions of the rebels there. Most Indonesians cannot come to terms with reality in politics, and the rebel politicians could not believe that their soldiers would not fight."

The nadir of American-Indonesian relations in February and March became the genesis of their improvement. Hesitatingly yet persistently Ambassador Jones probed for an alternative policy. Others in the U.S. embassy commenced to speculate in private on the desirability of reversing Washington's attitude—provided Jakarta gave proof of anti-Communism. What proof? "The suppressing of the Communist party." Wasn't that impossible at the moment? "Then peace negotiations with the rebels." The ambassador actually made this latter suggestion, only to be rebuffed decisively. After all the manifestations of America's hostility to him, it was too much to ask a proud Asian like Sukarno to court America's favor. Washington would first have to court him. Courtship proved infinitely more creative than pressure and superfluous transoceanic criticism.

The rebel defeat was the decisive reality. Ambassador Jones, meanwhile, had accumulated impressive evidence of the Sukarno government's eagerness for good relations with the United States and its readiness to curb Communists who grew obstreperous. Washington accordingly executed an unblushing *volte-face*. On April 30 President Eisenhower said it was America's intention to observe careful neutrality in the Indonesian situation. On May 23 the editor of the *Times of Indonesia,* the *enfant terrible* of Jakarta journalism, wrote: "Mr. John Dulles, with unwonted yet admirable dexterity managed to keep his foot out of his mouth when commenting on matters Indonesian at his latest press conference. Even Foreign Minister Subandrio, hardly to be classed as a pro-Dulles votary, cautiously welcomed the American Secretary of State's statement that there would be no intervention in Indonesia's present troubles." The State Department also announced that export licenses would be granted for a small shipment of small arms to Indonesia. Mr. J. H. van Royen, the Dutch ambassador in Washington, called on Secretary Dulles to protest the arms sale. After the confrontation, Assistant Secretary of State Walter

S. Robertson, who was present, escorted the ambassador to the private elevator and they rode up and down, Robertson saying, "This is an impertinence," and the Hollander insisting it wasn't, he had a perfect right to intervene in the matter because the arms might be used to seize West Irian.

But having reversed itself, the U.S. government could not be deterred. From then to now relations with Indonesia have improved concretely as well as atmospherically. Washington's high prophets of Red doom threw their crystal ball into the mothballs and put on silencers. An impressive array of American topmost admirals and generals visited Indonesia to see for themselves. Deputy Army Chief of Staff Brigadier General Gatot Subroto and other Indonesian officers joined the U.S. Seventh Fleet as observers during maneuvers in the Pacific. General Nasution declared that, despite documentary proof of American intervention "not officially but in fact" on behalf of the rebels, he wanted bygones to be bygones in the new day of better relations. Beginning August 15, 1958, a giant U.S. Air Force Globemaster flew fourteen heavy loads of American arms into Indonesia—one flight a day—and after the entire arsenal had been delivered, President Sukarno took an 80-minute joyride in the mammoth plane together with his young wife, Foreign Minister Subandrio, and Ambassador Jones. More American war material came by ship. On October 5 Indonesia displayed the foreign planes of its air force: nine Soviet MIG-15's, six Ilyushin-28 jet bombers, six Avia-14 transports, but also British Vampire jet trainers and American Grumman Albatross amphibians cavorted over Jakarta.

The year 1959 began with the arrival on January 2 of the first of six U.S. patrol boats for the Indonesian navy. In February the U.S. government agreed to make available to Indonesia additional arms for the equipment of twenty army battalions. The *Times of Indonesia* greeted this measure with an editorial entitled "Thank You, Uncle Sam." Some Asian countries find it difficult to say thanks. Indonesians have fewer inferiority complexes. But the whole matter of gratitude is of negligible significance. Aid should be given not to purchase friendship, allies, or pats on the back, or as a reward or an inducement to a pro-American or anti-Communist policy. No Asian country likes to feel that its sympathies are for sale or that its independence had been pawned. Governments, to be sure, are not in the business of global charity. America's giving, unprecedented in history—over $60 billion since 1945—has been motivated by generosity and self-interest. Most of the treasure went to democratic nations. A good deal went and is going to dictators. Political sermons about "the preservation of human freedom" therefore sound hollow. It should be left to others to know or discover where their interest lies.

The United States has given Indonesia not only arms. Even in the trough of relations between the two countries the work of helping Indonesia's economy marched on under the guidance of Americans whose devotion to the people among whom they were living spoke louder than any words of Bahasa (the language of Indonesia) learned from a book. Too much has been made of the need of mastering foreign tongues, too little of speaking to the heart. An agriculturist who gets down on his knees in a rice field and shows the peasant how to transplant rice can dispense with a dictionary. If necessary the specialist can travel with an interpreter. Knowledge of language is good. The universal language of kindness, understanding, and technology is better. The Indonesians knew they had a friend in James C. Baird, Jr., director of the International Co-operation Administration (ICA), even though his Bahasa vocabulary was primitive.

Through political gloom and sunshine, United States assistance to Indonesia has included everything from 300,000 tons of rice during 1957, 1958, and 1959 to 30,000 books on the physical, social, and medical sciences for the Gadja Mada University in Jogjakarta, to diesel-power generators for 25 communities in Sumatra, 19 in Borneo, 14 in the islands of East Indonesia, and 3 in Java.

Joseph Goyette's father made shoes by hand in Haverhill, Massachusetts. Joseph became his father's apprentice in 1898 at the age of fourteen. Later he worked in shoe factories and joined the United Shoeworkers' Union (AFL-CIO), first as an ordinary member, subsequently as a specialist in job evaluation and motion studies preparatory to contract negotiations with shoe manufacturers. Since 1949 he has been going from country to country on behalf of American economic and technical aid missions. The year 1959 found him in Bandung helping to install shoe machinery worth $73,000 provided by ICA and training the machinists in a new plant established by the Railroad Central Social Welfare Organization to produce 500 pairs of shoes a day for railway employees and their families. Hundreds of Joe Goyettes far from home are rendering great services to mankind in all continents. The participants in these programs and the taxpayers who pay for them little realize how valuable is this practical demonstration of globe-girdling brotherhood. There should be more of it between governments, between professional groups, cities, students, and other individuals. If words about building a better world have any reality this is it.

Total American economic aid to independent Indonesia from 1950 to 1959 amounted to $335,150,000—a large sum, but not nearly large enough to meet the problems. Millikan and Rostow estimate in their book, *A Proposal—Key to an Effective Foreign Policy,* that Indonesia could profitably absorb between $400 and $600 million each year.

In addition to American aid, Indonesia has received scores of millions of dollars from Commonwealth countries under the Colombo Plan, as well as advances from Japan and West Germany, and in 1956 a $100 million credit from the Soviet government now being used. Supplementing this government-to-government assistance, the Soviets in 1958 gave $795,200 in credit on easy terms to private Indonesian firms.

Does economic aid conduce to contentment which acts as a brake on Communism? One would think, then, that the Soviet Union would withhold it from non-Communist countries. Or is Soviet aid designed to win friends rather than make Communists? Probably it does make some Communists, for everybody knows that America is rich and therefore why doesn't she help more? But the fact that Russia can help even a little is presented as proof of Communist success which should be imitated locally. The ballyhoo accompanying Russian gifts or loans drives Americans mad with envy; they hate to see the Kremlin out-Madison Avenueing Madison Avenue. But in the long run such propaganda virtuosity can only prove that self-aggrandizement is a priority objective. The best way to make a friend is to be a friend. And a friend does not boast of his munificence. Asia gained understanding of the strategy of Soviet aid when Mr. Khrushchev abruptly canceled a £200 million sterling credit to Yugoslavia after Tito refused to bend the knee to Soviet imperialism in 1958. Nor are Asians entirely unaware that Soviet loans and gifts of stadiums, hospitals, hotels, and food, welcome though they be, derive not from surpluses but from the Soviet citizens' daily necessities.

The leaders of less-developed countries have learned to benefit from great-power competitiveness. They are too poor to refuse help from any source. They are too mindful of past attachments to one European nation to reject double courtship now. They seek safety in promiscuity. It is best to accept this as one of the facts of life. Any attempt at leadership or pressure, whether from Moscow or from Washington, is sure to bring hostile reactions. History has taught Asians to suspect gift horses and to inspect them for hooks and strings.

United States diplomacy sometimes sulks or balks when the underdeveloped countries take with both hands from both Cold War camps. If Communist giving is harmful to them, they will learn it; they will learn it sooner if the non-Communists ask no reward except the welfare of the recipient. His improved living standard should be reward enough without asking him to hoist an anti-red or red-white-and-blue flag.

The only condition the United States can legitimately make is that its aid contribute to the general welfare rather than to political power of a clique that is not, judging by performance, effectively engaged in national uplift. It is foolish for America to share the unpopularity of ruling oligarchs by propping them up with arms and dollars.

A discriminating assistance program is easier to carry out with economic aid than with military aid. Weapons must go to the government. Food, machinery, raw materials, and technical help can be assigned to projects and plans whose benefits must, by their very nature, be widespread.

Roads and railways for Sumatra, for instance, are economic enterprises with predictable healthy political results. Harbor development and shipping will bring the Indonesian archipelago more internal unity and peace. Aid can also promote general literacy, technical know-how, and the growth of a middle class which gives greater stability to society.

In Indonesia the United States cannot properly make a peaceful settlement with dissident groups the condition of expanded assistance. But it can indicate, diplomatically, that it does not wish its treasure to go down the drain in waste because the country is in political turmoil. The foreign government willing, aid can even be concentrated in areas most affected by unrest and most in need therefore of an economic push.

President Sukarno, who usually addresses himself to questions of national unity and West Irian, has of late been stressing the production aspects of Indonesia's resurgence. The true nationalism is work. Intensified economic effort by all would be the real revolution. Once the mood to labor succeeds the wish to bicker, America should supply the tools. The United States, in co-operation perhaps with the Colombo Powers, Japan, West Germany, and the United Nations, can become a major factor in the quick emergence of a prosperous Indonesia—provided Indonesians put their politics in order by stopping the squabbling.

Chapter Thirty-four

THE MAN WHO IS HATTA

THIS TIME Hatta was dressed less formally in white trousers and an open-neck white shirt. I waited and said nothing. "Our parties," he began spontaneously, "have neglected the political education of the people. They have thought only of party advantage. The Communists have profited. We must take another road. We must create a sense of political responsibility. We need a period of education, perhaps five years."

"Have you got the time?" I asked. "The situation is critical."

"We must immediately introduce a Presidential Cabinet," he proposed. "In it, the Chief of State will be responsible for governing the country."

"But Sukarno doesn't want this."

"It will be difficult to persuade Sukarno to do it," Hatta agreed. "Our political parties prefer not to apply the principles of Western democracy. The parties are oligarchies. Now we are in turmoil."

"How can you get out of it?"

"I don't know," Hatta confessed. "Maybe it will come when everybody is conscious of his responsibility. Anyway, at present we are in the wrong path. The military are thinking in terms of abolishing parties. But there are no able political leaders in the army."

"You mean there is no Kemal Pasha Atatürk or Nasser in the army."

"Perhaps," he mused, "Sukarno and the army could govern."

"And you?"

"I would first ask agreement on a program," he asserted.

"That will be difficult," I suggested. "You want guarantees on future government policies. We have an expression, 'Boring from within.' If you were in the government, and given your prestige, given Sukarno's disinclination to engage in daily routine and Djuanda's readiness to defer to you, you could make policy without previous guarantees or programs."

"No," he said firmly, "I do not wish to return and then expand my powers. At present, the National Council behaves sentimentally." I presumed he meant it followed Sukarno's lead. "The Planning Board which I am expected to head would have no official relation to the National Council or to Parliament. Parliament might refuse to approve new taxation urged by the board or an American loan. There would be conflicts between Prime Minister Djuanda and Parliament even if he deferred to me."

"Civil wars divide nations for generations," I said. "That was so in the United States and it is so in Spain. You must prevent that happening here. You could help reunite the country."

"I can't do it by running a Planning Board," Hatta retorted. "The rebels demand a strong central government. They want Jakarta to do more, not less." (They wanted states' rights but also more aid from the federal authorities.) "They demand a Cabinet with Hatta as prime minister and the Sultan as deputy prime minister. I proposed a compromise: Sukarno to head a responsible government."

"He refused," I probed.

"He did not refuse, but those around him refused, and then he encouraged the military to fight in Sumatra. The alternatives were: to fight or negotiate. If you fight, there follows a long period of guerrilla combat. I prefer the way of statesmanship."

"In all things," I ventured, "you are constitutional and legal. Yet you want to negotiate with rebels who have defied the Constitution and set up a rival government."

This gave him pause. He thought, then said, "My way is political, not legalistic. We must recognize that discontent exists. All sides must return to the Constitution. The Sumatran government must be scrapped and a Presidential Cabinet established in Jakarta. No shooting, and no radio controversies. Fighting might lead to foreign intervention and then we would be divided for a long time."

"Won't it be difficult," I asked, "to negotiate with the rebels? If you now concede their demands, the country will ask why you didn't do it earlier and prevent the bloodshed."

"The rebels will not lay down their arms," he affirmed, "unless some of their demands are accepted. But even if the government agrees to this the army won't."

"You can return and bore from within."

"The parties won't let me," he emphasized. "I couldn't do anything if I re-entered the government. I left the government because I was powerless to resist the regime of parties."

"As you know," I said, "Indonesia's relations with the United States have improved in recent weeks. You may get a loan from America. The rebels will grow weaker. A better mood might prevail. Then you could work. I should think it better to be inside."

"Sukarno would quarrel with me," he replied, "and the army would divide, one faction for, the other against me. The PNI wants me back to use my prestige. But I will do nothing unconstitutional. I must not pave the way to totalitarianism. I won't accept a post with power to impose my will on Parliament. I could not carry out an economic plan with pink-tinted ministers like Chairul Saleh, Hanafi, and Prijono in the Cabinet. It's all nonsense. They are protégés of Sukarno."

"What about the Sultan?" I inquired. "I hear he has been offered the Ministry of Economic Affairs in a Cabinet reshuffle which would get rid of some of those you object to. With you and the Sultan in, and those out, you could move forward with your economic plans."

"I don't believe Djuanda could persuade Sukarno to make a drastic reshuffle. We need a strong government, the right man in the right place."

"Did you talk with Djuanda in Bandung?" I asked.

"Not about essentials. I cannot discuss with Djuanda while fighting is in progress in Sumatra and the Celebes. We must negotiate with the rebels."

"If you and the Sultan joined the government," I urged, "the fighting would stop."

"I don't believe that. I want a completely new Cabinet accepted by the political parties. But the time is not ripe for a change of policy acceptable to the parties."

"You are asking for a perfect solution," I said, "but, as you know better than I, in politics there are no perfect solutions. You ask for things that are impossible. That is hardly a policy."

"If a Presidential Cabinet is impossible because of Sukarno's opposition, then a caretaker government presided over by me."

"But isn't that impossible?" I objected.

"It *is* impossible. But I don't wish to be the prisoner of other men's policies," he said vehemently, almost with anger. Then raising his voice,

"I have known Sukarno for decades. He won't change. He will always start mass demonstrations for West Irian."

"I'm sorry," I whispered. "You may sit here for years."

"There will be changes," he declared with quiet assurance.

We shook hands firmly, and he smiled in a friendly manner.

It had been a fruitful interview. He had revealed not only himself but much of the country's situation.

Chapter Thirty-five

NASUTION TALKS

"WELL-BUILT, tight body; bright face; short black hair, sort of crew cut," my notes read. "Walks in with a smile, wearing slacks and a white, open-collar shirt. Forty years old." This was Army Chief of Staff Major General Abdul Haris Nasution. This was the first interview he had ever given a foreign journalist.

"How is it," I began after greetings, "that today, the Day of Ascension, a Christian holy day, is a legal holiday in Moslem Indonesia?"

"It shows we have a tolerant philosophy," he explained. Without any transition, and apparently feeling that he needed none, he started to talk about the rebellion. "I know the rebel colonels," he said, "I know what rebellion is. October 17, 1952, was half a coup. It split the army into two camps. The officers who took this action were divided, and before the coup commenced they were already quarreling about jobs. It was not a Communist versus anti-Communist affair. Since then I have not believed in coups, I believe in loyalty to the Constitution. But the Constitution gives the military an important influence in politics. Eighty per cent of the administration of the country is being carried out by the army."

"One of the major benefits obtained from membership in any dominant political party," wrote the *Times of Indonesia,* "is the opportunity it has provided businessmen, members of that party, to obtain loans from the government. As a result, successive governments have lent some 250 million rupiahs . . . on the lightest of terms. And till recently the borrowers thought they could get away with the problem of repayment."

Now the army stepped in "and there has been much weeping and wailing and gnashing of teeth." The army had so far collected 56 million rupiahs from 119 business enterprises, and it intended to get back the last rupiah.

This was only one of the multifarious duties the army, under Nasution, had taken upon itself. It suppressed newspapers, censored the press, put editors under house arrest, managed plantations, ran ships, watched banking, curbed Communist agitation, and so on.

"President Sukarno and Parliament," General Nasution said to me, "understand that we must play a role in political affairs. The military are represented in the National Council and other government bodies. This is the chief difference between me and the rebel colonels. I refused to participate in the Lubis attempt to overthrow the government in June, 1955. I was the last officer visited by Lubis, but I refused to help him. Lubis wanted to take over the government because the political parties had failed. But the army would have been divided. If Colonel Kawilarang, then commander of West Java, had joined the rebels, half his officers would have opposed him. I have learned this. Therefore we participate in the government. But the rebel colonels are still striving to overthrow it.

"The colonels," Nasution continued, "disliked the Cabinet of Dr. Ali Sastroamijojo, and Lubis brought around a list of ministers in a new government. Deputy Prime Minister Leimena's name was on the list. No politician had the courage to refuse Lubis. Then I ordered Lubis arrested. That precipitated a coup in Bandung, where an attempt was made to arrest me. The same thing happened in Makassar. We did not want the people to know all this."

General Nasution was speaking a good English. Colonel Rudy Pirngadie, chief of Army Information Service, Mr. Rudy Gontha, of the Foreign Office press department, and I were taking notes. We sat on soft chairs in the Nasution ground-floor parlor. There was no need for me to ask questions—until later.

Nasution came to the subject of corruption. "I initiated steps against corruption," he said. "But the colonels opposed anticorruption measures in Menado [the biggest city in northeast Celebes]. The rebel colonels have another issue in regional autonomy. I am assisting the regions in building harbors, etc. The government wanted to halt this activity. I persuaded the ministers to continue it.

"The rebels then seized on anti-Communism," Nasution asserted. "But [Colonel Joop F.] Warouw and his friends collaborated with the Communists in East Java before 1952. They are calling themselves anti-Communists in the hope of obtaining aid from the West.

"Our army is not a South American army," he went on without any prodding. "But neither are we a politically inert European army. President Sukarno understands this. Sukarno says our army was in the revolution, it was an army of partisans.

"Indonesia," he said, "has been independent a short time. Our nationalism is very sensitive. Religion is another key to our politics. Emotionally if not intellectually the Socialists and Communists are materialistic. This conflicts with the feelings in the hearts of our people. If materialism intruded into our revolution, there would be civil war. On the other hand, the Darul Islam and some forces in the Masjumi party want an Islamic state. That too would split the country."

Nasution was putting himself in the moderate secular center of Pantjasila: Nationalism, Internationalism, Representative Government, Social Justice, and Faith in God. Sukarno enunciated these five principles. Nasution believed in them. "The Pantjasila," he declared, "are very important to our people."

No intrusion of materialism meant no Communists in the government. Pantjasila meant no religious reactionaries in the government. Nasution and the army had a clear policy.

Next the young general referred to the party system. Here, for the first time, I intervened by saying that Western democracy had never been tried in Indonesia: twenty-nine squabbling parties playing irresponsibly with the national interest was not democracy of any kind; vast constituencies with millions of voters were a travesty of democracy—the voter did not know his member of Parliament. Finally, the country needed a Senate.

"The President and Dr. Hatta," Nasution replied, "do not believe in our present electoral system. It is based on parties, not on policies or men. I agree with Sukarno and Hatta that democracy must be based on persons not parties. Politicians cannot solve our problems."

I asked who could solve Indonesia's problems.

"Separate areas of activity," he proposed, "must be marked out for the military, economic, and political organs. Now we are moving in a vicious circle, each authority is waiting for the other. I begin with the views of the army. I agree with you that Indonesia should have small electoral constituencies and a Senate. I believe in the 1945 Constitution and never understood why it was scrapped."

Later I realized that this was the most important political statement he or any other Indonesian had made to me on domestic affairs. The 1945 Constitution, the Republic's first, differs in fundamentals from the 1950 temporary Constitution. Since 1956 the Constituent Assembly, sitting in Bandung at intervals, had tried to draft a new permanent constitution, but all its endeavors were in vain because it and the top Jakarta leaders were undecided on the central issues: Secular state or church-state? Presidential

Cabinet with fixed tenure for five years or a Parliamentary Cabinet dismissible by a majority in Parliament? Small single-member election districts or vast multimember constituencies which arm party leaders with dictatorial powers over their followers? A House of Representatives elected according to population or a House and a Senate?

Now Nasution was saying, Return to 1945. Instead of writing a new constitution, a complicated task requiring years of haggling, readopt the old one which is known and ready-made and under which Indonesia made the revolution and won freedom from Holland. This had emotional appeal and practical advantage. The 1945 document is linked with the Jakarta Charter, signed on June 22, 1945, by Sukarno, Hatta, Haji Agus Salim, Yamin, and a number of Moslem notables, which asserts that the Indonesian Republic is founded on "the obligation of its followers to follow the rules of Islam." This formula might placate the advocates of an Islamic state.

The 1945 Constitution provides that "the State shall be based upon the belief in the God of mankind." It provides for a Presidential Cabinet under a president and vice-president. They hold office for five years and may be re-elected. They may take the oath of office "In the name of God" or "affirm" without reference to the Deity.

This is the heart of the 1945 document. In addition, Parliament shall consist of a House of Representatives "augmented by deputies from the provinces"—in other words, a House that includes a Senate—and, in addition, by deputies from various social and professional groups.

Apparently Nasution's opinion carried great weight, for on February 20, 1959, the Cabinet of Prime Minister Djuanda resolved to return to the 1945 Constitution "in its entirety." The new system would be called not "Guided Democracy," which connoted Communist participation in the government, but "Democracy with Leadership." The army would play a role in that leadership, the Communists would not.

Nasution spelled this out in my interview with him. "We need a Parliament," he said, "consisting of a body directly representing the electors and another body representing the regions and functional groups. A conference of both would choose the president and vice-president and outline a five-year national program.

"This," he emphasized, "is what we had after 1945, but Sjahrir changed all that to prove that we were democratic. Dr. Hatta restored the 1945 system in 1948; then we dropped it in 1950. I would put it back again. But I haven't the power. The army has no power to make such a change and the Constituent Assembly will not consent."

He underestimated himself and the agreement he would find.

(On June 2, 1959, however, when the readoption of the 1945 Constitution failed, by a few votes, to win a two-thirds majority in the Constituent Assembly, Nasution prohibited all activity by political parties until the document became the law of the land.)

Nasution now passed to practical implementation. "Sukarno, Hatta, Djuanda, and the Army Chief of Staff," he suggested, "should get together and propose solutions of current problems. The President would be chief of state and prime minister, but the Vice-President would be the active head of the executive branch, the day-to-day working chairman of the Cabinet.

"I have never been able to carry out this plan," he continued, "and now, owing to Hatta's position toward the Sumatran and Celebes fighting, it is impossible. Besides, Sukarno and Hatta might clash and I would be in between."

"What about the unitary state?" I queried. "Shouldn't an archipelago like Indonesia have a federal state as in the United States of America?"

"That is what the Dutch introduced," he retorted.

"I know van Mook was setting up a federal state of puppets," I said. "Still, that should not forever rule out the federalism you need. Why not have a federal state and call it nonfederal?"

"I am in favor of that," Nasution asserted, amid the laughter of all of us. "We have come to this idea ourselves. I am instructing the war administrators of the outer islands to given them a considerable percentage of their income from exports."

I asked about Colonel Kawilarang, who had left his post as military attaché in Washington and was at that moment in Manila en route to rebel territory in northern Celebes. "How could you prevent him from joining the rebellion?"

"Kawilarang," Nasution explained, "has a personal problem. He is hostile to Sukarno and to me. He used to be the commander of our Siliwangi Division. I have sent Siliwangi officers to see him and try to divert him from his present course. So far," he added with a smile, "they haven't failed."

"Wouldn't a letter to him from Sukarno help?"

Nasution and Pirngadie laughed. "It would make matters worse," the general stated.

"And a letter from Hatta?"

"Hatta refuses to participate in mediation. Besides, he is opposed to the President's Concept. He wants no Communists in the government. But the prospect of that is remote and the problem does not trouble me."

I mentioned the recent arrest of *New York Times* correspondent Bernard Kalb and blamed it on Major Marsudi, chief of staff of the Jakarta Garrison, who had signed the warrant for the arrest and who,

I said, was, according to rumor, under Communist influence. Pirngadie declared that Marsudi was not a Communist.

"If I followed the dictates of my heart," Nasution confessed, "I'd suppress all political parties."

The interview had lasted an hour and half and I knew I must not keep the general much longer. But I still wanted to draw him out on foreign policy. Indonesia had been receiving Soviet war material and I did not blame the defense forces for taking it. They needed it. Yet I knew they were asking the United States for weapons and that some high military men had publicly stated a preference for American weapons. "Why," I asked, "do you prefer American arms to Russian arms?"

"We have been receiving Czechoslovak munitions," he replied. "Czechoslovakia has good industries."

He was evading my question. "In 1955," I recalled, "Egypt received arms and they were officially called Czechoslovak. But Soviet Foreign Minister Molotov, speaking Russian to Israeli Foreign Minister Moshe Sharett in Geneva in October, 1955, said: 'We have supplied arms to Egypt.' So it doesn't really matter whether you regard the supplies as Russian or Czechoslovak. Why do you prefer American arms?"

"It's a matter of logistics," Nasution replied.

"I don't understand military lingo."

Nasution: "Indonesia is on the American side of the line of demarcation which separates the two blocs. If there were a major war we would be cut off from Soviet arms sources."

"I had hoped you would also say," I remarked, "that the receipt of Soviet arms would strengthen the Communist party just as it did in Spain during the 1936-39 civil war there."

"The trouble is," he complained, "that we cannot even get spare parts for the American military equipment we already have. Our soldiers know this. We asked for several places at the advanced officers' training school in Fort Leavenworth and received a refusal. Can't they make room for two or three more men?"

As an afterthought, while I was making a note, he added. "The reason we ask for American arms is because it would be confusing to have Russian and American weapons."

In parting I inquired whether he was a good Moslem. I had put that question to one member of the government and he replied, "What do you mean?" and I said, "That's the answer," and he laughed. I asked an Indonesian ambassador, and his answer was a negative shake of the head. Nasution said, "I pray five times a day at home; twice in the morning before going to the office, once in the lunch break, and twice after working hours. Friday I attend services in the mosque."

As I was leaving he went to his study and brought out his Indonesian-language book, *The Principles of Guerrilla Warfare,* which he autographed to me and wrote in English, "I hope you have pleasant memories in Indonesia," and signed that too.

Colonel Pirngadie gave me his card, printed in English on one side and Chinese on the other.

On the front lawn, Janti, Nasution's only child, a girl of about nine, was playing. Shyly she shook my hand and allowed me to pat her head.

(In the latter half of 1958 Sukarno promoted Nasution to the rank of lieutenant general.)

Chapter Thirty-six

INTERVIEW WITH SUKARNO

FIVE MINUTES after the beginning of a private discussion of politics in India it becomes a discussion about Prime Minister Nehru. Five minutes after the beginning of such a discussion in Indonesia it becomes a discussion about President Sukarno. The new states of Asia and Africa were born in dreams and live on hope. Their people pine for a savior. They are hero-worshipers. They worship yet criticize. Imperfections in their idol make them bitter. He is a god who must produce miracles—or else. Asians are both impatient and impassive, and one can never know when impatience will take the upper hand. Everything depends on the leader's appeal to mass imagination. This one-man eminence may turn his head or break it. It is a tremendous responsibility, a great opportunity, and in the final analysis an impossibility. No single individual can achieve what a poor, underdeveloped country expects of him. He inevitably disappoints. His pink charm grows tarnished.

From highest to lowest, Indonesians are frank. The less they can say about Sukarno in public—because he is chief of state and dislikes criticism —the more they dissect him in private. "Bung Karno," a Bandung professor said to me, "is not a statesman, he's an artist. But then we are a nation of artists. We understand beauty better than politics."

"True," his colleague commented, "but politics are rice and housing and an end to Darul Islam guerrillas. Any teen-ager understands such things."

"Sukarno is our greatest asset and greatest problem," a newspaper editor said.

"The President," a member of the federal Cabinet asserted after warning me not to quote him, "has a tongue but no ears. He doesn't listen to us."

Occasionally, in my conversations with top officials about current events in Indonesia and abroad, they would say, "Tell Sukarno that. He'll take it from you." (I thought of suppressing this as immodest, but it is part of the political scene that I am describing.) They knew that I had differed with him and that he at least listened, and perhaps agreed, because I was obviously very fond of him. I liked President Sukarno for his warmth, informality, vivacity, versatility, artistic temperament, love of women, absence of hypocrisy about it, absence of arrogance, absence of color prejudice, wide reading, encouragement to painters and writers, resilience after defeats, dedication to Indonesia, sense of mission and kindness. I do not think he could ever be cruel. I liked him despite his faults.

He wanted power. To some, power is the possibility of compelling obedience, of subjecting others to one's will. There must be elements of this in Sukarno's desire for power, but I do not believe that it is the essence. Rather it is the possibility to stage-manage, rearrange, sway masses, express his personality, exert influence, display showmanship. His power is for pleasure, like the pleasure of winning a woman, of driving a good car, the pleasure of demonstrating skill, not the pleasure of crushing, punishing, or dominating. It is power for the joy of a theater producer, of an editor who puts out a newspaper, of an architect who sees a building rise from his blueprint, of a city planner who watches a city grow from his sketches.

Sukarno wanted power without the routine of executive office. He scorned the paper work that accompanies governing. He loved the peak of the pyramid. In youth he climbed the highest trees, and his playmates called him "djago," or rooster. His politics were personal. He took support where he found it. His first criterion was, Are they for me? That, rather than ideological affinity, explains his flirtation with the Communists, that and their making him the object of a copied-from-Moscow "cult of personality."

Like Nehru, Sukarno yearned to be loved. Unlike Nehru, he exuded happiness. But his joys, I felt, were not unalloyed. He knew the tragedy of fear, the fear of growing old, for instance. Surrounded by people he knew loneliness. The mountain peak is a windy, wintry, solitary spot. In Indonesia—and this probably applies to most new states (and some old ones)—the man on the pinnacle cannot be sure whom to trust or in whom he can safely confide. Hence his reticence except on the public rostrum. Stalin shot opponents, suspects, and independent spirits. Khrushchev purged his rivals and transferred them to minor jobs far from the center of power. Sukarno was neither politically equipped nor personally inclined to adopt such drastic measures; he had to maneuver, play to the gallery, and keep everybody off balance and guessing. He held his cards close to his chest. He could bare his heart to no one. For a person as outgoing, expansive, and extravert as Sukarno this is difficult. Friends of the President said he missed Fatmawati; probably they thought it would be good for him to have her back again as a sympathetic ear.

Fatmawati was Sukarno's third wife. At the age of fourteen, Sukarno left the home of his father, who was a schoolteacher, and went to live, as a foster son, with Tjokro Aminoto, a Surabaya businessman, chairman of the nationalistic Sarekat Islam and often regarded as the grandfather of Indonesian independence. In time, Sukarno married Siti, Tjokro Aminoto's daughter; the marriage, however, was never consummated and ended in a formal divorce. Later, while studying in Bandung, Sukarno met a rich widow and lived happily with her in a childless marriage for twenty years or more. Fatmawati followed. She was a village girl; simple, unspoiled, beautiful, and intelligent. Catapulted into the highest society by her marriage, Fatmawati developed all the talents expected of a First Lady—grace, poise, political discrimination, and devotion to social obligations. On the other hand, the friends said, she neglected Sukarno as a husband and he resented it. Hartini, his beautiful new wife, they told me, cooks little delicacies for him, humors him. Fatmawati didn't. But he still loves and needs her, they declared, and that is why he refused her a divorce. It would have been the acceptance of final loss and failure. Also, she is the mother of five of his children.

Power has its minuses as well as its pluses. Once, on a trip, Sukarno referred to a certain country and said, "I wonder why old men struggle so hard to retain power." I wondered why anybody does. Sukarno's power seemed real. Yet it rested on intangibles like oratory, appearance, and past—on his public appeal. At least a few rivals would have been glad to replace him, and many were ready to support them. Sukarno, therefore, had to perform a complicated balancing act, and his skill at it was a sight to see and study. Watching a political tightrope walker is a pleasure to the beholder.

At an evening party the palace press secretary whispered, "The President said to me today, 'Why does Louis want to talk with me so often?' "

"Tell him I enjoy it," I replied.

Shortly thereafter a telephone message, confirmed later, brought the information that the President would receive me Sunday morning at ten in the Bogor Palace. I spent Saturday at William E. Palmer's mountain retreat and borrowed his car and driver to descend to Bogor. I arrived ten minutes ahead of time and was met by an adjutant who offered tea, cigarettes, and small talk. The President would be a little late, he said.

I walked to and fro in the huge white-marble foyer and went out to the palace steps to look at the great green gardens. An officer approached and greeted me. He was the pilot of the President's two-seater helicopter which stood at the bottom of the steps, just like an automobile, ready to take off. He had trained for eighteen months in Bakersfield, California. He loved California. He told me how much the helicopter cost, how high it flew, and how fast. He regularly piloted Sukarno from here to the lawn of Merdeka Palace in Jakarta and back. The trip took twenty-five minutes instead of one hour or more by car and obviated the security arrangements, sirens, and traffic stoppages connected with the President's travel on the crowded road. They had two helicopters and were about to buy two bigger ones.

At 10:45, fifty-five minutes after my arrival, Sukarno came out into the foyer with Prime Minister Djuanda and Third Deputy Prime Minister Leimena. We chatted at the top of the steps for a moment and then the President bade them farewell and led me into the chamber where they had been discussing, I surmised, a Cabinet reshuffle. A waiter served coffee and sweet Indonesian cakes and left us. I opened a large notebook. "Oh," Sukarno exclaimed.

I smiled and said, "Don't be afraid. I won't misquote you."

He immediately took the offensive. "Tell me," he began, "is Dulles a Christian?"

"I know only," I replied, "that a few of his statements and acts have been unchristian."

"But in my front office in Jakarta," Sukarno said, "you will find a picture of Christ, and there's another in my back office."

"So you are a Christian, a Moslem, and a Hindu?"

"Yes," he agreed.

"I spoke to Minister Prijono about this, and he mentioned the layers upon layers in Indonesian culture."

"Prijono knows," Sukarno stated, "he has studied these matters. Do you think Prijono is a Communist?"

"Some of my fellow Americans do because he accepted the Stalin Prize and belongs to the Murba party. I have spoken with Murba leaders. They say they are Titoists. Some call them Trotskyites. I call them fuzzy. Prijono told me Indonesia needs a Kemal Pasha Atatürk, who was anti-Communist. In thirty-six years of journalism I think I have developed a sense of smell for Communists and I don't think Prijono is one."

"Good," Sukarno approved. "Yet the world seems divided into Communists and anti-Communists and we are drifting toward a third world war."

"I am convinced," I argued, "that there is not going to be a third world war because both sides have the H and A bombs and could annihilate one another. What would they gain?"

"But the first and second world wars were not premeditated either," Sukarno remarked.

"The first world war was the result, primarily, of Austro-Hungarian, German, and Russian urges and intrigues for imperialist expansion. The second was certainly premeditated and deliberately launched by Hitler after he had neutralized Russia through the Molotov-Ribbentrop pact. Clearly, the Japanese attack on Pearl Harbor was planned. But today both camps are avoiding war and even incidents that might lead to war. The Cold War is a substitute for hot war, a new way of adjusting the international balance of power without war. Soviet expansion into Europe has been blocked by NATO and in Asia by China. Russia is worried by China."

Sukarno: "That is true. I have heard of this. Nevertheless, there are unpredictable factors in the Cold War."

L.F.: "But they won't lead to a hot war."

Sukarno: "In any case, Indonesia occupies an important strategic position and we wish to avoid involvement in the two-camp struggle."

L.F.: "By all means do. But when you said in your speech at Bandung that the Sumatran and Celebes revolts might lead to a third world war I could not agree. Not even the Korean War or the Berlin Airlift of 1948-49 led to such a war though America and Russia were intimately involved in both. The Soviets are not coming down here from Vladivostok to fight in an area remote from their central base."

I took a breath and waited, and when he waited too, I continued: "You say you wish to remain nonaligned, and that is fine with me. But your most active political party, the Communist party, is trying to embroil you." I mentioned the confiscation, under Communist inspiration, of Dutch businesses late in 1957.

"No," Sukarno interrupted. "In 1950 I urged the confiscation of Dutch properties but Prime Minister Natsir and his Cabinet were opposed. It was I who ordered the seizure of Dutch enterprises in 1957. I decided that the fate of West Irian would not be decided at the UN, or in Moscow or Amsterdam, but here. That is why I moved against the Dutch in 1957."

L.F.: "You wanted the government to take over the Dutch plants and plantations, but the Communist-led trade unions [SOBSI] forced your hand."

Sukarno: "No, it was not only the SOBSI who seized the properties. The Pemuda [Youth] did too."

L.F.: "Well, may I state my point? I see clearly that the PKI is trying to make Indonesia economically dependent on Russia. First, the Communists wished to destroy Dutch business. Now they are agitating against the Chinese merchants of Indonesia. Aidit sends a telegram to Ambassador Jones threatening to interfere with American operations on your oil fields. He is trying to stop the importation of American films. All this fits into Aidit's statement to the PKI plenum in April, 1958, that America is economically unreliable because of the recession and Indonesia should therefore rely for trade and aid on the Soviet bloc."

Sukarno: "I will not insist that you are wrong about Aidit's intentions. But American blunders help him. When I was in the United States [in 1956] I told Nixon, President Eisenhower, Justice Douglas, and others that America's attitude toward our process of nation-building had been full of mistakes."

L.F.: "But in the last few weeks I have noticed an improvement in Indo-U.S. relations."

Sukarno: "To my great joy. But why can't Washington stop the intervention of Taiwan and the Philippines on the side of the rebels?"

L.F.: "I hope we will. But you know more about governments than I do. A change of policy takes time. Jones succeeded John Allison and that made his mission difficult. It was not easy for Jones to be friendly to you after Allison had been transferred for being friendly."

"Of all the American ambassadors here: Cochran, Cumming, Allison, Jones," Sukarno remarked, "I like Jones best. I like Nixon, Douglas, Eisenhower. But what about Bohlen? He is the spearhead of your intervention on the side of the rebels." (This was a reference to Charles Bohlen, former U.S. ambassador in Moscow, then ambassador in Manila, the base, according to Indonesians, for the planes that had bombed Indonesia in the interests of the rebels.)

"Please," I begged, "don't blame Bohlen. I don't know what is happening. He may be carrying out orders. But Bohlen is a liberal. He opposed MacArthur's advance to the Yalu River. He has disagreed with Dulles on a number of issues. You know governments. It is impossible to speak of a Sukarno government or an Eisenhower government. Governments are made up of discordant elements and it will take time to straighten out America's new policy toward Indonesia. What do you want?"

Sukarno: "I want you to understand the Indonesian mind. Understand our neutralism. Don't be prejudiced against nonalignment. We asked your country to sell us arms. You refused, at first politely."

L.F.: "You are getting American arms now."

Sukarno: "After long and bitter experiences."

L.F.: "The U.S. is growing wiser."

Sukarno: "To my great joy. But I hope this is not merely a tactical and temporary change. I hope America is embarked on a definite course of understanding and help. Help comes from understanding. I am a lover who has been disappointed." He had fallen in love with America. He spoke of his favorable impressions of the United States during his 1956 tour.

L.F.: "You know about love. Lovers quarrel and are reconciled."

Sukarno: "If I see that my girl is behaving better I return to her. But don't let my quarrel with America last till it affects the sentiments of my people. After the bombings of our islands by U.S. planes I exploded. I even spat anger at the United States in my Bandung speech which you heard. I am anticolonial. We suffered from colonialism for three hundred fifty years."

L.F.: "You are anti-imperialist because your country suffered. I am anti-imperialist though America has not suffered. But you are not fair in your anti-imperialist attitude."

"How?" Sukarno demanded.

"In all the speeches I have heard you make on our trips together, and in your palace lecture, you attack only Western imperialism. That is not being neutral."

"What do you mean I am not neutral?" Sukarno objected, unbuttoning his military tunic and revealing a mustard-colored shirt.

"Western imperialism is in retreat. India, Pakistan, Burma, Ceylon, Vietnam, Ghana, Malaya, Tunis, Morocco are free. Indonesia is free. It is only a matter of time before the West abandons the remnants of empire in Asia: West Irian, Goa, etc. But before our eyes, in the past nineteen years, Russia has built a new empire consisting of annexed territory and satellites, yet you overlook that."

Sukarno: "I have visited Czechoslovakia and Outer Mongolia, which are considered satellites, and nobody there told me they were not free."

L.F.: "You meet only officials."

Sukarno: "I know Rashid in Uzbekistan. I spent four days with him."

L.F.: "He would not talk frankly to you. Wherever President Sukarno goes in a Communist country there's a microphone."

Sukarno: "How do you know?"

L.F.: "I lived in the Soviet Union fourteen years." I told him about the experience of the American embassy in Moscow, which found microphones hidden in its new building.

Sukarno: "That's because they're worried about America."

L.F.: "No. I visited an Asian ambassador in Moscow in 1956, and when we started talking politics, he said to me, 'Do you know our garden?' and he led me out into the garden because he suspected there was a Soviet microphone in his own home. That's the Soviet way and that's why no one will speak the truth to you in Russia or her satellites."

Sukarno: "How can I know the truth? I read twenty American magazines. I read *U.S. News and World Report*. They give a biased view."

L.F.: "You have the objective truth in the Polish and Hungarian revolutions of October, 1956."

Sukarno: "I told you in the plane that I had heard in Vienna, months before the Hungarian revolt, that a revolution was being prepared."

L.F.: "You can't go by a chance report. You can hear anything in Vienna. The fact is that the Hungarian revolution was a nationwide nationalist uprising against Russia which thousands of Soviet tanks suppressed in blood. This has worked havoc with European Communist parties. Intellectual fellow travelers were shocked and withdrew from collaboration with Communists after Hungary. There can be no doubt that Hungary was a case of an imperial power crushing a colonial revolt. And Poland. Ask any Pole. You have talked with Tito. Why did he break with Russia? I interviewed him twice in 1952, and he told me the rupture came because he refused to toe the Kremlin line."

Sukarno rocked his head from side to side. "Americans," I continued, "tell one another that Dulles would often do better to keep quiet. Remember his unfortunate statement on Goa. Statesmen talk too much. But if you are going to talk against imperialism you should include them all: French, British, Dutch, Portuguese, *and* Russian. You may condemn American action in Guatemala. But if you censure only the West for imperialist acts, the world must conclude that you are not neutral, that you are pro-Communist."

Sukarno: "At the Afro-Asian Bandung conference in 1955 I was the one who proposed the words 'against colonialism in all its manifestations' in a resolution."

L.F.: "Fine. Will you hereafter use that formula instead of attacking the West alone?"

He laughed. "Yes, I shall," he promised. "But why does the United States support the Western colonial powers?"

L.F.: "You know it was America that got the Dutch out of Indonesia."

"No," Sukarno protested. "We fought the Dutch."

L.F.: "You fought the Dutch, true, yet you didn't drive them out. It was because the Republic resisted the Dutch that America forced them out of here."

Sukarno: "Correct. But since 1950 America has changed her policy."

L.F.: "You know why. On account of NATO. It's wrong of Washington to consider Dutch wishes in regard to Indonesia. Holland isn't going to join the Soviet bloc. But NATO is important, and Dulles wants it to work smoothly, without U.S.-Dutch friction. I agree with your young-sters who yell, 'To hell with SEATO!' SEATO is not worth much. NATO, however, is the defense of Europe *and* of Asia. If American forces left Europe, all of Asia would be exposed to conquest by Russia or China. In India I tell my friends that NATO defends them. They don't like it, but I am convinced it's so."

Sukarno: "Then why does the United States support Holland on the West Irian issue?"

L.F.: "Because of your failure to condemn Soviet suppression in Hungary."

Sukarno: "But your country was against us on West Irian before Hungary."

L.F.: "That was because of an attitude which existed here before Hungary. I said to [Prime Minister] Djuanda recently, 'Why should an American in Maine or Kansas care about the liberation of West Irian when you don't care about the liberation of Hungary?'"

"What was Djuanda's reaction to that?" Sukarno inquired.

"Djuanda said he had never seen it in that light. Mahatma Gandhi always urged people to 'Turn the searchlight inward.' You ask Americans to understand the Indonesian mind and I agree that we should. But you must understand the American mind. If you don't take an anti-imperialist stand on Russia's colonies, Americans may think you are anticolonial only because you want the Dutch out of West Irian and not because you are anticolonial in principle."

Sukarno: "You say that my speeches are anti-West. I am not anti-West. I am not antiwhite. Two Dutchmen are among my best friends."

L.F.: "I would be ashamed if you were antiwhite. I know you are not. And as for me, I'm color-blind. I don't understand distinctions based on skin color."

Sukarno: "I am neither anti-West nor antiwhite. I want America as a friend. Give me something to say to my people and I will change their sentiments overnight."

L.F.: "I'm sure you could. I've heard the magic of your speeches. I told you in Bandung last week that except for your reference to a third world war arising out of the Indonesian situation it was the speech of a statesman. But in your two-hour and twenty-minute speech in the palace . . ."

Sukarno: "I saw you from the platform."

L.F.: "Any Communist there could have said, 'Sukarno is talking like a Communist.' And a non-Communist would have said the same. Every time you attack only Western imperialism and capitalism you make Com-munists even though you are not a Communist."

Sukarno, with a smile: "All right. I have promised you to use the formula 'Colonialism in all its manifestations.' "

L.F.: "You assume that capitalism is responsible for imperialism?"

Sukarno: "Yes."

"At a certain stage," I began, "capitalism does create imperialism. That is why Russia is now imperialistic—because she's capitalistic. There is no qualitative difference between Western capitalism and Soviet state capitalism. It's all capitalism. There is no Communism in Russia. Only in India and Israel do some thousands of people live in free communes where everything is shared alike. Otherwise the world knows only capitalism in various phases or precapitalism as in less-developed countries."

Sukarno: "Then why all the excitement about Communism? Why am I called a Communist? My Guided Democracy Concept has nothing in common with Communism."

L.F.: "I am not responsible for the name-calling or for the names the so-called Communists give themselves."

"Louis," Sukarno exclaimed, "what are you doing to me? You're confusing me."

L.F.: "I think we think in antiquated terms. Up to about 1900 the emphasis of American capitalists was on production. They accumulated capital in order to enrich themselves and to make America rich. But in the past fifty years or so we have seen a social revolution in America. The emphasis now is on distribution and welfare. Therefore nineteenth-century exploitation is gone and the poor have become richer. Russia is still in the period of capital accumulation and of exploitation. Someone has to pay for all those new industries. The Soviet people pay. It's Russia that is the exploiting capitalist country. England is not capitalistic."

Sukarno: "No, it's partly Socialist."

L.F.: "Yes. England has got rid of most of its empire. But you never mentioned that in your palace lecture. So it appeared that you stood behind the PKI. When an Indonesian looks he sees the PKI and you behind it."

"What do you expect me to do," Sukarno protested, "support the PNI? I am head of state. I belong to no party."

L.F.: "I understand. But everything that Nehru achieved is booked to the credit of his Congress party. Eisenhower is chief of state and a Republican, and his party benefited from his popularity. Here, a party which is not yours gains by supporting you. In his last speech to the PKI plenum, Aidit predicted that in two years the PKI would be the largest party in Indonesia."

Sukarno, vehemently: "That is due to America's blunders. I will not call them mistakes, they are worse, they are blunders."

L.F.: "May I repeat Gandhi's injunction, 'Turn the searchlight inward'?" If something goes wrong, find out where you, not the outsiders, are to blame."

Sukarno: "Yes, we have our faults. But America has made them worse."

L.F.: "What would you have America do?"

Sukarno: "I will tell you. My short-term wishes are: First, stop foreign intervention in our civil strife. Washington can do that. Second, stop the verbal attacks on us. Third, aid without strings. Fourth, confidence in our neutralism."

L.F.: "I agree with the first three. I hope the bombers cease bombing you, and that you get arms."

Sukarno: "It would fill my heart with joy."

L.F.: "But there is a party here which is pulling you toward Russia."

"Louis," Sukarno exclaimed, "you have an obsession about Russia."

"Bung Karno, if you had known me in 1942 you would have said I had an obsession about British imperialism in India. Had you known me in 1936-1939 in Spain you would have said Franco was my obsession. I am a fighter."

Sukarno: "I know you are a fighter. That's why I like you."

L.F.: "Thanks. Let me talk to you about Bernard Kalb of the *New York Times*."

Sukarno: "He was summoned for questioning because he wrote more than Djuanda told him." (Kalb had had an interview with the Prime Minister about arms shipments.)

L.F.: "He could have been summoned without being arrested. He was arrested, fingerprinted, and put in a cell."

Sukarno: "I didn't know that."

L.F.: "You ask about it."

Sukarno: "I will ask."

L.F.: "That is the personal side. The political side is more interesting. He was arrested by the Jakarta garrison and liberated by the Army General Staff as soon as Colonel Ibnu heard of it. This seems to reflect a policy discrepancy. Don't you think that the Communist party, aware of the emerging Indonesian-American rapprochement which your army supports and knowing what a bad effect the arrest of a *New York Times* staff correspondent would have in America, did it to spoil your friendship with the United States? Wasn't this the work of Major Marsudi, Jakarta garrison chief of staff?"

Sukarno: "Marsudi is not a Communist. He is a revolutionary nationalist."

L.F.: "He might have been acting under Communist inspiration to alter your foreign policy."

Sukarno: "I have no proof that this was involved in the Kalb case."

L.F.: "Then why would the Army General Staff have released him immediately?"

Sukarno, firmly: "I will investigate that."

(In February, 1959, Marsudi joined a military attaché course in preparation, presumably, for an appointment abroad. On January 31, 1959, Lieutenant Colonel Dachjar, commander of the Jakarta garrison, was transferred to a post in army headquarters.)

L.F.: "I hear that Colonel Sugandhy is to be appointed commander of the Jakarta garrison."

Sukarno smiled and shook his head. "No," he said, "I need him here."

L.F.: "And is Major Sudarto going to America to study?"

Sukarno: "I don't know yet. I can't spare him now."

L.F.: "The term would begin later this year."

Sukarno: "I don't know yet."

I asked the President about other persons, and then said, "What about Hatta?"

"I want Dr. Hatta in the government," Sukarno stated. "I offered him the chairmanship of the State Planning Board."

L.F.: "And would he be vice-president too?"

Sukarno: "Yes. But it is impossible to give up the fight against the rebels. When I returned from my recent visit to Tokyo I gave the order to attack the Padang gang and I cannot withdraw that order. . . . I cannot say, 'Father, forgive them, for they know not what they do.'"

L.F.: "Why not? To forgive is the best way to overcome misunderstanding. I thought that was the Indonesian way."

The President explained his viewpoint: there must be discipline in the army and unity in the country. Separatism could not be tolerated. We then discussed the American magazines he read, the Communist jamming of broadcasts, freedom of the press in democracies, and so on.

Sukarno looked at his watch. "It's one o'clock," he said. "Will you have lunch with us?"

"Of course," I agreed.

We walked across the vast, green, carefully kept park where deer grazed beneath huge spreading trees. The palace is reserved for receptions and conferences. The President lives in a small house on the grounds.

We passed two men, gardeners perhaps, who were trying to make two cocks fight. (Cockfighting is a favorite Bali sport.) "Terrible," Sukarno said to me. He made no attempt to stop them.

"Before I go I'd like to take some photographs," I told the President. "Better do it before we are full of food," he suggested.

At the house Hartini came out to the steps with Dr. Lauw, the President's Chinese-born physician, and Mrs. Lauw. Hartini and Sukarno posed for me, and then Colonel Sabur took snapshots with my camera of the Sukarnos and me. Alas, I had done something wrong with the film and the photography was a dismal failure.

Inside, the President asked whether I wished to wash and led me to "the small room" where I found the U.S. *News and World Report* on a reading rack.

Three oil paintings of Hartini, several landscapes, and one of two bare-breasted Balinese damsels hung in the sitting room, which merged into a dining alcove.

"We have Western food for you," Sukarno announced as we sat down to the table.

"Fine," I said, "I like Western imperialist food."

"And we shall eat colonial food," Sukarno declared amid laughter. He had taken off his tunic (displaying suspenders), loosened his tie, and turned up his shirtsleeves to the elbows. "You don't mind if we eat with our fingers?" Sukarno asked.

"No," I replied, "I've often seen my Indian friends do it."

A battery of vitamin bottles stood before Sukarno. As he opened them he invited me to partake. "They'll keep you young," he suggested. "How old are you?"

I told him I was sixty-two. "I'm fifty-seven," he said. "Guess Hartini's age."

I guessed she was twenty-five.

"No," Sukarno corrected, "she's thirty-three." A very young thirty-three.

"Louis," Sukarno said, "when did you begin getting gray around the ears?"

"Three or four years ago."

After a pause, while we consumed good food busily, Sukarno looked at me and asked, "Louis, why don't you deliver a public lecture here on international politics?"

"No," I rejoined, "I didn't come here to talk." After the lectures I had hurled at him all morning I thought the question revealing.

Sukarno extended a plateful of small chilis. I refused. "Didn't you eat them in Spain?" he asked.

"No," I explained, "they're too hot."

He asked about conditions in Spain. I said the Spanish Civil War was still on; not that there was any shooting, but Franco had tried to unite the country and failed, and the two camps were glowering angrily at one another. "A civil war," I continued, "lives on long after the firing stops. The American Civil War did for decades." He said nothing. I hoped he was thinking of Indonesia.

"Do you believe in djamu?" I asked Dr. Lauw.

"Oh, yes," he replied, "for certain illnesses."

"Do you take them?" I asked Hartini.

"Yes," she said, "I took the ten after each childbirth, and others at other times."

"Dr. Grunek of Bandung," I volunteered, "believes in spiritual healing. Do you, Dr. Lauw?"

"Sometimes," he answered.

"There is psychosomatic medicine," Sukarno affirmed. "Recently a woman came to me who hadn't menstruated for six months and wanted me to cure her. I promised to pray for her. The next day she menstruated."

"It's true," Hartini interjected.

"When I was in prison some people swore they saw me in the street," Sukarno stated. "There are people who believe I can be in two places at the same time. That worries Hartini. I may go off with another woman." (General hilarity.)

I gave Sukarno and Hartini regards from Bill Palmer. "Yes," Sukarno said, "thanks. Has he any new American films? Who is your favorite cinema actress?"

"His is Sophia Loren," Hartini interjected. (We discussed films and Hollywood.)

I asked the doctor how widespread was circumcision. "Very," he replied.

"At what age?"

"It is best before the boy has erections."

"Oh," Sukarno exclaimed, "I was circumcised at fifteen when I already had them."

"Did they give you whisky or an anesthetic?" I wondered.

"No," Sukarno recalled, "my father held me down and I gripped the arms of the chair." He presented further intimate data. (General amusement.)

"We must have it done to Guntur next year," Sukarno said, turning to Hartini.

Guntur, Fatmawati's child by Sukarno, was fourteen.

"The Jews," I said, "circumcise when the boy is eight days old. But the Bible states that Ishmael, Abraham's son by Hagar, the housemaid, was thirteen at the time of circumcision." Tradition makes Ishmael the ancestor of the Moslems.

"Girls are circumcised too," Dr. Lauw said, "but it is merely a slight token cut, at the age of three or four."

"What was the reason for those demonstrations against Nixon in South America?" Sukarno asked after a pause. I offered one or two explanations. "I like Nixon," Sukarno said. "We went to a village and fried potatoes together." Then he mentioned Eric Johnston. "I put to him the question why American films are segregated. Whenever Americans and Asians love it always ends badly."

I remarked that in *Sayonara* both American-Japanese couples married for love; and one ends tragically, the other, Marlon Brando's, happily.

Sukarno said President Eisenhower named Randolph Scott, who acts in Westerns, as his favorite movie star. "The more shooting in a film the more Eisenhower likes it," Sukarno commented. "We enjoyed the West," he added. "Remember the waitress at the Grand Canyon?" he said, turning to Hartini. "What was her name?"

"Gloria," Hartini helped.

"She was proud of being an Indian," Sukarno recalled. "Her name sign read, 'Your waitress is Gloria.' I changed the 'your' to 'my' and autographed it."

"You remember," Hartini reminisced, "how embarrassed John Simmons [chief of protocol] was in San Francisco when a woman yelled to him as we drove by?"

"Yes," Sukarno agreed. "We called him 'Jack.' I said to him, 'Don't be embarrassed. I'm sorry she didn't call to me.'"

Sukarno cut a banana in half. "Take one half," Sukarno offered. "It means friendship."

I asked to see the children. A beautiful child of three, in shirt and shorts, eyes slightly open, was having his afternoon nap. In another room two young girls were cooing over the latest arrival, a boy three months old.

We said warm farewells and I drove off in a palace car to hot Jakarta.

Chapter Thirty-seven

THE FUTURE OF ASIA AND AFRICA

"Is INDONESIA going Communist?" a United Press correspondent asked Sukarno in 1957. The President offered arguments to prove the negative. "But apart from that," he continued, "let me express a firm warning . . . that it would not be wise to ascribe every deviation from Western thought in Asia to Communism or Communist influence. . . . All Asian problems cannot be solved by Western formulas."

Foreign ministries in Europe and America might hang this statement over their desks.

The newly independent countries of Asia and Africa—there are now some thirty—face grave problems. They get help from the Communist world and the West but not much light. Each side beckons. Neither holds up a beacon.

In October, 1958, the Congress for Cultural Freedom, with headquarters in Paris, convened a conference on the Greek island of Rhodes attended by about fifty men and women from Asia, Africa, Europe, and America. The topic of the eight-day seminar read: "Representative Government and Public Liberties in the New States." The abused word "democracy" was avoided.

All these new states are non-Communist and, together with Franco Spain, Latin-American dictatorships, Syngman Rhee's South Korean democracy, Chiang Kai-shek's regime in Formosa, and Turkey, which has arrested dozens of opposition editors, journalists, and members of Parliament, they therefore belong to what is called the Free World. But of the new states only India and Israel implement parliamentary democracy. In India this has been possible because one party, the Congress party dominated by Nehru, rules. In Israel it has been possible because one party, the moderate Socialist Mapai dominated by Prime Minister Ben-Gurion, is the indispensable keystone of every coalition. The rest of the new Afro-Asian states run the gamut from avowed military dictatorships to disguised personal totalitarianisms to countries like Indonesia where, Sukarno said, "We suffer from overdemocracy," and which is heading for a political-military oligarchy. With few exceptions, like Pakistan whose ruling general announced the temporary suspension of the constitution and its democratic devices, all the dictatorships, semidictatorships, twilight democracies, and dawn democracies have parties and parliaments, but these are not synonymous with representative government or public liberties. The definition of a democracy as a multi-party political system operating through an elected legislative assembly is ripe for the museum shelf.

At Rhodes, Prince Kukrit Pramoj, editor, publisher, novelist, and wit, described how the army dictatorship of his native Thailand won the assent of a puppet parliament by either buying or browbeating its members. Parliament there is an expensive fig leaf. An expert on Pakistan told how the parties and individual members of the national parliament, which had never been elected, moved from the progovernment side to the opposition and back depending on the material benefits deriving from these gyrations. When General Ayub Khan, in an effort to reduce food prices, warned hoarders to make public avowal of their hoards or be jailed, the former Prime Minister revealed that he was hoarding 3,000 tons of grain. Other high officials did likewise, and an ex-minister of defense got a prison sentence for making money from the purchase of military equipment. Did Ayub Khan, in disbanding Pakistan's parties and parliament, suppress democracy or a baleful burlesque of it?

Pakistan needs a land reform. Without it the country's economics and politics face a grim future. But can one expect a parliament, whose parties are financed and dominated by landlords, to pass a land reform act? General Ayub Khan erased the fiction of parliamentary government and decreed a land reform. If this measure is not only initiated to propitiate the masses, as in other Afro-Asian countries, but carried to a successful conclusion, it could lay the foundation of a democracy in which a free peasant will vote according to his wishes, not according to the landlord's whip. General Ayub Khan declared on January 27, 1959, that it would take "a couple of years" to restore "representative government." The "ground" had to be prepared. When "representative government is returned," he added, "it should be headed by a de Gaulle-type presidency."

Then significantly: "We need a nonpartisan president elected by sensible elements of the country. The President must have a free run for five years."

This solution has been adopted by Indonesia.

How real are parliamentary elections for the literate and illiterate Marhaens of Indonesia, the Mohans and Anands of India, and the Ibrahims and Abduls of Arab lands? Can one who has never been outside his village envisage the workings of parties and parliaments? An election campaign could be an education if the propaganda were honest. Where is it so? Often a dazed Indian peasant arrives at the polls and says, "I want to vote for Nehru," or, "Can I cast my ballot for Jayaprakash." Nehru is not a candidate in that constituency and Jayaprakash is not up for election anywhere.

"Jayaprakash is a future prime minister of India," Nehru once said to me. But now Jayaprakash Narayan has withdrawn from politics. He was the leader of the Socialist party. In 1946 I sat with him on the earth at the feet of Mahatma Gandhi when he justified his anti-British violence during the war while Gandhi preached nonviolence in all circumstances. J.P., as India calls him, remained unconvinced. Gandhi died in 1948. In 1952 Jayaprakash went on a three-week penance fast and while recuperating in Dr. Dinshah Mehta's Nature Cure Clinic in Poona he said, "For years I worshiped at the shrine of the goddess of Dialectical Materialism; now I have discovered goodness." He became a Gandhian. "My regret is," he wrote, "that I did not reach this point in my life's journey while Gandhiji was still in our midst." But he did the next best thing and joined Gandhi's spiritual heir, Vinoba Bhave, who has been walking for ten years from village to village, ten miles every day under the broiling sun, collecting millions of acres from those who have land for distribution among those who haven't. This now is Jayaprakash's politics, although occasionally, as when he condemned Soviet suppression of the Hungarian revolution, the political world of India listens and reacts.

"Is Jayaprakash out of politics permanently?" the skeptics wonder.

The answer probably is, out of today's politics.

Here are the words of Vinoba Bhave, J.P.'s political mentor, perhaps after Nehru the most influential person in India: "Political parties, whether in our country or outside, which subscribe to narrow ideals and loyalties, are out of date in this Age of Science." Vinoba's reasoning stems from his philosophy of nonviolence and the political thesis that "that government governs best which governs least." But now, he complains, "People are taught to look to the state for every little thing. All this is being done in the name of democracy. Everyone says, 'You vote our party to power and we will do the rest.' People thus elect their representatives,

but when the latter are unable to fulfill their promises, people become dis-
satisfied. . . . Under these circumstances it becomes very easy for the army
to step in and take power in its own hands."

Sometimes, one might add, the people's distress makes it a race between the army and the Communists. At the Rhodes conference, a Burmese, taunted by an Indian colleague because Burma had succumbed to
an army dictatorship, exclaimed, "You are next." He is not the only one
who has given this speculative reply to the difficult question, "After
Nehru, what?"

Jayaprakash Narayan takes this analysis several steps further and pro-
pounds a cure for all Asia. He ascribes the Stalinist terror in Russia not
merely to Stalin (that would be the cult of personality in reverse) but to
the speed of industrialization. "This incidentally," he writes, "has a great
lesson for India and indeed, for all the industrially backward countries
of Asia. . . . Russia and the other Communist countries warn us of what
happens when the pace is forced too hard. . . . It would be an illusion
to think that the pace of industrialization does not matter if the process
were carried out under democratic aegis; beyond a certain limit the pace
itself would give rise necessarily to conditions of dictatorship."

The tempo of planned industrial progress is not the main factor, but it
is one factor in the Asian trend toward oligarchic or dictatorial rule. The
dictatorships are an open, as the oligarchies are a concealed, disregard of
the party system and parliament. Jayaprakash recognized the trend. "The
party system as I saw it was emasculating the people," he declared. "It
did not function so as to develop their strength and initiative, nor to
help them establish self-rule and to manage their affairs themselves. All
the parties were concerned with was to capture power." The people
seemed destined to become political sheep "whose only function of
sovereignty would be to choose periodically the shepherds who would
look after their welfare."

"It is a fact that the regime of parties has not solved, is not solving,
and will not solve the enormous problems with which we are confronted,"
General de Gaulle said on May 19, 1958. Worlds apart in character and
career, the general and the Gandhian agree on this basic question.

Jayaprakash proposes for India what Gandhi called village republics
in which an agrarian community, pooling its land and labor voluntarily,
will strive for the highest possible degree of economic and political self-
sufficiency. The village, where everybody knows everybody else, will
conduct direct elections for a governing council (the five-man Panchayat,
as it is called in India). Votes will be cast not on the basis of unread
party programs, or dishonest slogans, or propaganda promises, or remote
international issues, or national-personality contests, but of known ability

and devotion to the community. At present, villages are often split into feuding factions by party-type elections which have no significance in their daily, difficult lives.

The Jayaprakash method would eminently suit Indonesia which, in contrast to some other Asian and African countries, is happy in her peaceful villages devoid of castes, outcastes, and landlords. More than 80 per cent of Indonesia's village land is owned by smallholders, and the rest as commons by the community. The ancient democratic tradition of mutual aid and rule by discussion and consensus also fits Jayaprakash's village republic.

Jayaprakash proposes that the village councils of an area elect the next highest authority—say a county council. The county councils elect a state council, and the state councils a national parliament which would interfere as little as needed with the village republics. Ideally, Jayaprakash, in the Gandhian ethic, hopes to abolish the national state. As a student of politics, he realizes that this is now impossible.

If Jayaprakash ever becomes prime minister it will be of an India that has abandoned the present party system for nonpartisan village elections and indirect other elections. Meanwhile, he and, in particular, Vinoba Bhave have organized thousands of Bhoodan (Land Gift) and Gramdan (Village Gift) rural areas on the twin pillars of economic co-operation and social service to which Gandhi gave the name Sarvodaya, or Community Good.

As parliaments flounder and violence flares in Afro-Asia, and in the world, Gandhi gains in relevance to today's living. His economics of hand spinning, cottage industries, and antimechanization have been misunderstood and laughed to scorn. He never rejected the machine. "Machinery has its place; it has come to stay," he said. He warned, however, against the rule of the machine over man. Stalin, like Hitler, was a psychopath, but that he could maintain his autocracy for two and a half decades may be ascribed to the Hegelian principle of State First, to the Leninist principle of Party Ueber Alles, and above all to the rapid industrialization and mechanization, the gods on whose altars he sacrificed millions of human beings. This has a moral for Indonesia, for Asia, for others. Progress yes, but eyes to the village first. On March 22, 1959, Colonel Nasser revealed that the United Arab Republic was manufacturing tens of thousands of submachine guns. What joy for the land-hungry, undernourished, trachoma-ridden, bilharzia-ridden Egyptian peasant!

The Gandhi-Bhave-Jayaprakash plan for moderate industrialization balanced by maximum emphasis on village economy would avert lopsided urban development with all the city's social evils. Intensified industrialization, in conditions of state capitalism, must enhance the

power of the rulers and sow the seeds of one or another form of dictatorship, especially in countries with no deeply rooted, national system of
representative government. In Indonesia, moreover, the fragmented nature
of an archipelago is likely to make a further contribution to the power of
the central government which, even if it wisely grants island autonomy,
will hold the purse, make the plan, and control foreign trade.

Are the newly independent states to substitute their own dictatorship
for the foreign dictatorship from which they so recently liberated themselves? This is the choice they face unless, as Jayaprakash suggests, they
turn from urban-centered planning to "a decentralized village-centered
society."

Gandhi's goal was more than the replacement of British rulers by native
rulers. He wanted a free Indian as much as he wanted a free India.
Vinoba Bhave too makes personal liberty the test of national independence, and since India, like Indonesia and all other Afro-Asian countries, is agrarian, he wants a free village. "Today our country is free," he
wrote on February 11, 1959, "tomorrow this freedom must extend to the
village." His aim is a village free from the domination of the government
of free India. I find this the most creative thought coming out of the
East. Freedom for the village is creative because it implies that nationalism is a means, not an end, that the individual's importance is higher
than the state's, and that in this age of obsession with big-project super-
structure industrialization, village uplift is the best economics and village
democracy the best politics. The rest is a poor imitation of the West.
Sukarno's "All Asian problems cannot be solved by Western formulas"
is being ignored by Asians.

The Western powers and Russia are running a military-economic race
in which, Mr. Adlai Stevenson declares, the West might get "licked."
In a hydrogen-atomic war both would get "licked." Mr. Khrushchev, the
twentieth century's greatest butter-and-egg man, stirs his subjects to catch
up with America in butter, milk, meat, oil, steel, and machine production, and Americans aim to put as many sputniks into the air and manufacture as many technicians as Russia. The Kremlin's ideal is America;
America's ideal becomes Russia. Where will this militaristic-materialistic
contest lead? Even if the Western democracies win it they lose. Free
nations are allowing a dictatorship to dictate their standards and subvert
their independence of action. What a victory for totalitarianism!

In any case, Asia and Africa must have no part of this. Here they
should remain truly nonaligned and keep their own tempo, retain their
own personality. Neither madman industrialization nor the submergence
of the village by the city should be their object. China is a lesson in what

to avoid. Recently a prominent Indian sociologist, Dr. Sripati Chandrasekhar, visited China, studied the communes, and described their life for Indian readers. "This is the commune," his report concluded, "where human beings are reduced to the level of inmates in a zoo. But there is a difference. The animals in a zoo do not have to work hard, and, what is more, they do not have to listen to the quasi-compulsory radio. The lack of peace and quiet in the countryside, where one can retire and reflect, and the lack of privacy and solitude are to me more terrifying than all the hells put together." Mao's communes are the inevitable concomitant of industrialization. Stalin did it too. To industrialize he collectivized. No dictatorship can endure half-slave and half-free. All must be slaves. This was Stalin's last testament, written in October, 1952, for Mao.

Such are the pitfalls for countries in a hurry. They stumble. Asia and Africa need neither move like a snail nor zoom like a jet. The tropics can probably be more temperate than the nations of the Temperate Zone. Especially Indonesia, I believe, has the mental health to elude the push into Western civilization.

Another major cause of the descent to dictatorship of young states is their insecurity. An army dictatorship offers security against inner and outer enemies. Communists offer security from Communist aggression by submitting to it in advance. Syria's merger with Egypt was due to the fear of a Communist coup against the weak army. Pakistan fears her divided geography and India. Burma fears her Communist insurgents. Indonesia fears her rebels. Iraq feared Nasser and Moscow and had to choose one. An unsettled world is not conducive to liberty. Two world wars and little wars between and after, and now armaments to prevent a third world war, do not make for human freedom.

Some new states, confronted with the complicated international situation, decide on neutrality, or noncommitment or noninvolvement. This noninvolvement, however, is a superficial thing and illusory; it merely enables the governments to avoid uncomfortable moral judgments but not to escape what is really dangerous: involvement in the modern race for state strength, heavy industries, armaments, and the threat, therefore, of dictatorship. The Western nations and some others are already involved. The new states are not yet fully committed. They still have a possibility of being themselves instead of photostats of this or that foreign system.

India still reacts to the spell of Gandhi and his disciples. Indonesia is uniquely qualified to go her own way. She is richly endowed by nature. Her peasants are industrious. Thousands of trained persons are graduating from her schools. The habit of co-operative labor and community discussion and decision runs deep. Her leaders harbor no illusions of national grandeur or glory or power. The Indonesians are a modest, sensible, lovable people without envy, sickly arrogance, or ambitions. The country has no troublesome neighbors. In freedom and peace, with science and work, this could indeed be a paradise. Racially homogeneous, being largely Malay and Polynesian, possessing a language which in a decade will be, if it is not already, the tongue of the entire nation, tolerant in religion, not yet spoiled by politics, the problems of government would not be insuperable if politics ceased to be an unprincipled joust between those in office and those out of office. At the least, the ins should enjoy a few years of surcease from combat during which they can attend to business.

Such administrative stability is essential but not sufficient. With it must come maximum economic development with minimum bureaucratic controls. This can be achieved by small irrigation schemes, small hydro-electric power stations, and small processing plants like sugar mills, rice mills, fish canneries built, where necessary, with central government loans but owned and managed locally in villages or counties. Size of enterprises should be determined by technological and financial considerations, not by the mania for bigness. A fertilizer plant may have to be big and operated by Jakarta. Likewise a tin smelter on Bangka island. But tobacco curing can be left to the free co-operatives which Hatta has fostered. In avoiding the embrace of private capitalism Indonesia ought not rush into the arms of state capitalism whose squeeze smothers the personal freedom for which national freedom was won. The national government can prime the pump of industrialization without retaining the power over industries. Wherever it is scientifically feasible it will always be politically and economically desirable to let the islands roll their own. Through taxation, the issuing of currency, and other legitimate devices, a veto remains in the hands of the federal government.

Indonesia's fight for independence was a volcanic explosion of popular energy and enthusiasm because it spelled hope and involved millions of people. The *élan* has vanished and the hope is dimmed not so much on account of civil strife as of the crushing of individual initiative. The Dutch were never fought in big pitched battles; the Indonesians waged a guerrilla war in which the group commander and even the single soldier had to act on his own. That suited the Indonesian personality. It can be translated into economics and politics. The best industrial manager does least himself and allows others to do most. This is also the essence of national leadership. Government officials need not keep a finger in every pie. The important thing is that the pies be baked and that the people eat them when and as they wish. Indonesians, on the good earth of Indonesia, moreover, should not be asked to wait for pie in the sky or in the next generation. The living have paid heavily for the past. Must they pay for the unborn future too?

Asia and Africa will soon discover that nationalism is not enough and that no ism satisfies. The proper purpose of politics is man.

AUTHOR TO READER

       I HAVE simplified the spelling of some Indonesian names. For instance: the Indonesians and Dutch write Djakarta and pronounce it Jakarta. So I have written it Jakarta. The "d" before the "j" has been retained in a few cases like "Djamu," which is a technical term, and at the beginning of some surnames. . . . Mohammadijah is pronounced Mohammadiya, and that is how I have spelled it . . . Sukarno writes Sukarno and Soekarno. On the personal stationery of the former Indonesian Foreign Minister, Ruslan Abdulgani, his name is printed "Ruslan Abdulgani"; on the same paper he signs "Roeslan." I have used only the "u" except in book titles in the bibliography. The pronunciation of the "u" is the same as of the "oe."

I wish to thank the hundreds of persons who helped me in the preparation of this book. In Indonesia, my researchers were aided by Indonesians, Indians, Chinese, Americans, British, Australians, French, Dutch, and other officials and nonofficials. They made my stay in the country fruitful and pleasant. . . . In The Hague the librarians of the Royal Library and in Amsterdam the authorities at the Royal Tropical Institute gave me the finest service. One Dutch lady kindly made numerous appointments for me with former colonial administrators and present high Netherlands officials, as well as with Dutch historians and businessmen. Another Dutch lady volunteered to check dozens of facts, dates, and names in her country's rich history. That I am anticolonialist did not interfere with their will to help. . . . At Cornell University in Ithaca, New York, Professor George McTurnan Kahin, director of the Modern Indonesia Project, put his own knowledge and that of his learned associates, as well as the resources of his institution at my disposal. . . . In New York, I enjoyed the valuable assistance of J. Hubertus van Mook, former Dutch Governor of the East Indies, of several former State Department officials, of Dr. Frank P. Graham, of Asian diplomats at the United Nations, and of the librarians of the Council on Foreign Relations. . . . I am also most grateful to Marguerite Hoyle Munson and Julie Eidesheim for meticulous editing and copyreading.

LOUIS FISCHER

BIBLIOGRAPHY

AMBLER, ERIC. *State of Siege.* New York: Alfred A. Knopf, Inc., 1956. (Printed in Great Britain under the title *The Night Comers* by William Heinemann, Ltd.)

ATTENBOROUGH, DAVID. *Zoo Quest for a Dragon.* London: Lutterworth Press, 1957.

BANNER, HUBERT S. *Romantic Java as It Was and Is.* London, 1927.

BASTIN, JOHN. *The Native Policies of Sir Stamford Raffles in Java and Sumatra—an Economic Interpretation.* Oxford: The Clarendon Press, 1957.

BEAUMONT, JOHN. *Dutch Alliances: or, a plain proof of their observance of treaties; exemplified in the particulars of their inhuman treatment of their friends and confederates, the English, at Amboyna.* London, 1712.

BEMMELEN, J. F. VAN, and G. B. HOOYER. *Guide Through Netherlands India.* Compiled by order of the Koninklijke Paketvaart Maatschappij (Royal Packet Company). London: Thomas Cook & Co., 1903.

BENDA, HARRY J. *The Crescent and the Rising Sun.—Indonesian Islam under the Japanese Occupation 1942-1945.* The Hague and Bandung: W. van Hoeve, Ltd., 1958. Distributed in the U.S.A. by the Institute of Pacific Relations, New York.

BOEKE, DR. J.H. *Economics and Economic Policy of Dual Societies.* Haarlem: H.D. Tjeenk Willink & Zoon N. V. 1953.

BONE, ROBERT C. JR. *The Dynamics of the Western New Guinea (Irian Barat) Problem.* Cornell University: Modern Indonesia Project Southeast Asia Program, Dept. of Far Eastern Studies, 1958.

BOULGER, DEMETRIUS CHARLES. *The Life of Sir Stamford Raffles.* London: Horace Marshall & Son, 1897.

BOUSQUET, G. H. *A French View of the Netherlands Indies.* (Translated from the French by Philip E. Lilienthal, Secretariat, Institute of Pacific Relations.) London and New York: Oxford University Press, 1940. (Issued under the auspices of the Secretariat, Institute of Pacific Relations.)

BOUSQUET, G. H., and J. SCHACHS (Editors). *Selected Works of C. Snouck Hurgronje.* Leiden, 1957. Edited in English and in French.

BOWERS, FAUBION. *Theatre in the East—A Survey of Asian Dance and Drama.* London: Thomas Nelson & Sons, Ltd., 1956.

BRO, MARGUERITTE HARMON. *Indonesia: Land of Challenge.* New York: Harper & Brothers, 1954.

BROUWER, DR. B.J. *De Houding van Idenburg en Coljin Tegenover de Indonesische Beweging.*

BROWN, J. MACMILLAN. *The Dutch East—Sketches and Pictures.* London: Kegan Paul, Trench, Truebner & Co., Ltd., 1914.

Civil wars of Bantam. or An Impartial Relation of all the Battels, [sic] Sieges, and other Remarkable Transactions, Revolutions and Accidents that happened in the late Civil Wars Between that King and His Eldest Son, Commonly called By Them The Young King, Giving A Particular Account of the Circumstances and Manner of the Siege and taking of the City of Bantam and the English Factory There by the Young King, with the help and Alliances of the Dutch in several Letters from a Gentleman Residing for the East-India Company at Bantam, to a Merchant in London. London: Printed by H.C. for Tho. Malthus at the Sign of the *Sun* in the Poultrey, 1683.

COAST, JOHN. *Recruit to Revolution—Adventure and Politics in Indonesia.* London: Christophers, 1952.

COLLINS, J. FOSTER. *The United Nations and Indonesia.* (*International Conciliation,* March, 1950, No. 459.) Published by the Carnegie Endowment for International Peace, New York. (Pamphlet)

COUPLAND, R. *Raffles, 1781-1826.* Oxford University Press, 1926.

COVARRUBIAS, MIGUEL. *Island of Bali.* New York: Alfred A. Knopf, 1937.

CRAWFURD, JOHN. *History of the Indian Archipelago. Containing An Account of the Manners, Arts, Languages, Religions, Institutions And Commerce of Its Inhabitants.* Edinburgh, 1820. Three volumes with maps and engravings.

DAENDELS, H.W. *Correspondance de Son Excellence le Marechal Daendels, Gouverneur General des Possessions Hollandais dans l'Inde, etc., avec leurs Majestés le Roi de Hollande et L'Empereur des Français depuis le 9 Janvier 1808 Jusqu'a ce Jour.* (Manuscript)

DAY, CLIVE. *The Policy and Administration of the Dutch in Java.* New York, 1904.

DEKKER, EDUARD DOUWES. *Once More Free Labor.* (Pamphlet)

DENNETT, RAYMOND, and ROBERT K. TURNER (Editors). *Documents on American Foreign Relations.* Vol. XI. Princeton University Press, 1950.

DIJKMAN, M.J. *Hevea: Thirty Years of Research.* Coral Gables, Fla.: University of Miami Press, 1951.

DJAJADININGRAT, IDRUS NASIR. *The Beginnings of the Indonesian-Dutch Negotiations and the Hoge Veluwe Talks.* Ithaca, N.Y.: Cornell University Department of Far Eastern Studies, Southeast Asia Program, *Monograph Series,* Modern Indonesia Project, 1958.

ELLIS, HENRY. *Journal of the Proceedings of the Late Embassy to China, Comprising a correct Narrative of the Public Transactions of the Embassy, on the Voyage to and from China, and of the Journey from the Mouth of the Pei-ho to the Return to Canton.* London: John Murray, 1818.

ELSBREE, WILLARD H. *Japan's Role in Southeast Asian Nationalist Movements, 1940 to 1945.* Cambridge, Mass.: Harvard University Press, 1953.

ENCYCLOPAEDIE VON NEDERLANSCH-INDIE. The Hague, 1918.

FEITH, HERBERT. *Indonesian Elections of 1955.* Ithaca, N.Y.: Cornell University Modern Indonesian Project Southeast Asia Program, 1957.

———— *The Wilopo Cabinet, 1952-53; A Turning Point In Post-Revolutionary Indonesia.* Ithaca, N.Y.: Cornell University Modern Indonesian Project Southeast Asia Program, 1958.

First voyage Around the World by Magellan. Translated from the Accounts of Pigafetta and Other Contemporary Writers, Accompanied by Original Documents with Notes and an Introduction by Lord Stanley of Alderley. (Printed for the Haklukt Society) London, 1874.

FISCHER, LOUIS. *The Life of Mahatma Gandhi.* New York: Harper & Brothers, 1950.

———— *This Is Our World.* New York: Harper & Brothers, 1956.

FISHER, H.A.L. *A History of Europe.* London: Edward Arnold & Co., 1936.

FORBES, HENRY O. *A Naturalist's Wanderings in the Eastern Archipelago—A narrative, of Travel and Exploration from 1878 to 1883.* London, 1885.

FRYKE, CHRISTOPHER AND CHRISTOPHER SCHWEITZER. *Voyages to the East Indies.* London: Cassell and Co., Ltd., 1700.

FURNIVALL, J.S. *Colonial Policy and Practice—a Comparative Study of Burma and Netherlands India.* New York University Press, 1956. (First published by Cambridge University Press, 1948.)

———— *Netherlands India—A Study of Plural Economy.* With an Introduction by Jonkheer Mr. A.C.D. de Graeff (Governor-General of Netherlands India 1926-31) Cambridge University Press: 1944; (Reprinted.) First Edition, 1939.

GERBRANDY, P.S. *Indonesia.* London: Hutchinson & Co. Ltd., 1950. With 28 illustrations.

GROENEVELDT, W.P. (Editor.) *Notes on the Malay Archipelago and Malacca Compiled from Chinese Sources.* Batavia-The Hague, 1880.

HAAR, B. TER. *Adat Law in Indonesia.* (Translated from the Dutch.) New York: Institute of Pacific Relations, 1948.

HAHN, EMILY. *Raffles of Singapore.* Garden City, N.Y. Doubleday & Co., 1946.

HALL, R. *The History of the Barbarous Cruelties and Massacres Committed by the Dutch in the East Indies.* London and Westminster, 1712.

HATTA, MOHAMMAD. *The Co-operative Movement in Indonesia.* Edited by George McT. Kahin, with an introduction by Roesli Rahim. Ithaca, N.Y.: Cornell University Press, 1957. (Published under the auspices of the Modern Indonesia Project Southeast Asia Program, Cornell University.)

HELSDINGDEN, DR. W.H. VAN and DR. H. HOOGENBERG (Editors). *Mission Interrupted. The Dutch in the East Indies and Their Work in the Twentieth Century, A Symposium.* Amsterdam, 1945.

HENDERSON, WILLIAM. *Pacific Settlement of Disputes.* New York: Woodrow Wilson Foundation, Sept., 1954. (Pamphlet.)

HIGGINS, BENJAMIN. *Indonesia's Economic Stabilization and Development.* New York: Institute of Pacific Relations, 1957.

HORSFIELD, THOMAS. *Zoological Researches in Java and the Neighboring Islands.* London, 1874.

INDONESIA, GOVERNMENT OF, MINISTRY OF INFORMATION. *Illustrations of the Revolution —From a Unitary State to a Unitary State, 1945-1950.* Jakarta: 1954, Second Edition.

Investment in Indonesia—Basic Information for United States Businessmen. U.S. Department of Commerce, Bureau of Foreign Commerce. Washington, D.C., February, 1956.

IQBAL, SIR MOHAMMAD. *The Reconstruction of Religious Thought in Islam.* Lahore: Shaikh Muhammad Ashraf. Reprinted, 1951.

JANE, CECIL, (Editor and translator). *The Voyages of Christopher Columbus. Being the Journal of His First and Third, and the Letters Concerning His First and Last Voyages, to which Is Added the Account of His Second Voyage Written by Andres Bernaldez.* (With an introduction and notes by Cecil Jane.) London: The Argonaut Press, 1930.

KAHIN, GEORGE McTURNAN (Editor). *Major Governments of Asia.* (By Harold C. Hinton, "China"; Nobutaka Ike, "Japan"; Norman D. Palmer, "India"; Keith Callard, "Pakistan"; and George McTurnan Kahin, "Indonesia.") Ithaca, N.Y.: Cornell University Press, 1958.

——— *Nationalism and Revolution in Indonesia.* Ithaca, N.Y.: Cornell University Press, 1952.

KAT ANGELINO, DR. A.D.A. DE. *Colonial Policy.* Chicago: University of Chicago Press, 1931.

KEESING, FELIX M. *Native Peoples of the Pacific World.* New York: The Macmillan Co., 1947.

KENNEDY, RAYMOND. *The Ageless Indies.* New York: John Day Co., 1942.

KEPPEL, CAPTAIN THE HON. HENRY, R.N. *A Visit to the Indian Archipelago in H.M. Ship Maeander with Portions of the Private Journal of Sir Francis James Brooke, K.C.B.* London: Richard Bentley, 1853. Two volumes.

KING, JOHN KERRY. *South East Asia in Perspective.* New York: The Macmillan Co., 1956.

KLERCK, E.S. DE. *History of the Netherlands East Indies.* Rotterdam: W.L. & J. Brusse N.V., 1938. Two volumes.

KOOT, TON. *Spell of the Netherlands.* (Preface by His Royal Highness the Prince of the Netherlands.) Haarlem, Holland, 1952.

KROEF, DR. J.M. VAN DER. *Indonesia in the Modern World.* Bandung, Indonesia: Masa Baru, 1954. Two volumes.

LEUR, J. C. VAN. *Indonesian Trade and Society—Essays in Asian Social and Economic History.* (Written between 1934 and 1942.) The Hague-Bandung: M. Van Hoeve, Ltd., 1955.

MAJOR, R.H., ESQ. (Editor and translator). *Selected Letters of Christopher Columbus. With Other original Documents Relating to His Four Voyages to the New World.* London, 1847.

MALINOWSKY, BRONISLAW. *Argonauts of the Western Pacific—An Account of Native Enterprise and Adventure in the Archipelagoes of Melanesian New Guinea.* London: Routledge and Kegan Paul, Ltd., 1922.

MANGKUNAGORO VII, K.G.P.A.A. of Surakarta. *On the Wayang Kulit (Purwa) and Its Symbolic and Mystical Elements.* (Translated from the Dutch by Claire Holt). Ithaca, N.Y.: Cornell University Press, 1957. (Pamphlet, original text published in *Djawa,* Vol. XIII, 1933.)

MARSDEN, W. *The History of Sumatra*. London, 1783.

MARYANOV, GERALD S. *Decentralization in Indonesia as a Political Problem*. Cornell University: Modern Indonesia Project Southeast Asia Program Dept. of Far Eastern Studies (Interim Reports Series), 1958.

MILLIKAN, MAX F., and W.W. ROSTOW. *A Proposal—Key to an Effective Foreign Policy*. New York: Harper & Brothers, 1957.

MOOK, HUBERTUS J. VAN. *The Netherlands Indies and Japan—Battle on Paper, 1940-1941*. New York: W.W. Norton & Co, 1944.

———— *Past and Future in the Netherlands Indies*. (An address delivered before members of the Institute of Pacific Relations at San Francisco, May 18, 1945.) New York: The Netherlands Information Bureau.

MULTATULI (Eduard Douwes Dekker). *Max Havelaar or the Coffee Auctions of the Dutch Trading Company*. (Translated by Baron Alphonse Nahuys.) Edinburgh: Edmonston & Douglas, 1868.

MYRDAL, GUNNAR. *Rich Lands and Poor*. New York: Harper & Brothers, 1957.

NARAYAN, JAYAPRAKASH. *From Socialism to Sarvodaya*. Rajghat, Kashi: Akhil Bharat Sarva Seva Sangh Prakashan, 1958.

NIEL, ROBERT VAN. *Development of the Indonesian Elite in the Early Twentieth Century*. Cornell University Thesis, 1954.

PALTHE, PROF. DR. P.M. VAN WULFFTEN. *Psychological Aspects of the Indonesian Problem*. Leiden: E.J. Brill, 1949. (Pamphlet)

Perspective of Indonesia, An *Atlantic Monthly* Supplement. (1956)

Political Events in the Republic of Indonesia—A Review of the Developments in the Indonesian Republic (Java and Sumatra) Since the Japanese Surrender, Together with Statements by the Netherlands and Netherlands Indies Governments, and Complete Text of the Linggadjati Agreement. New York: Netherlands Information Bureau, 1947.

RAFFLES, LADY SOPHIA. *Memoir, Life and Public Services with some of the Correspondence, of Sir Thomas Stamford Raffles, Particularly in the Government of Java, 1811-1816, and of Bencoolen and its Dependencies, 1817-1824; with Details of the Commerce and Resources of the Eastern Archipelago and Selections from His Correspondence; By His Widow*. London, 1830.

RAFFLES, THOMAS. *Letters During a Tour Through Some Parts of France, Savoy, Switzerland, Germany, and the Netherlands in the Summer of 1817*. (Letters sent to and dedicated to Sir Stamford Raffles.) Liverpool, 1820, Third Edition.

RAFFLES, SIR THOMAS STAMFORD. "Copies of the ancient inscriptions on copper plates dug up in the vicinity of Surabaja, and now deposited in the Museum of the Society of Batavia, rendered from the ancient Kawi characters to the Roman and communicated by the President."

———— *The History of Java*. London, 1817. Two volumes with a map and plates.

———— *Substance of a Minute recorded on the 11th February, 1814, on the introduction of an improved system of internal management and the establishment of a land rental on the island of Java*. London, 1814. With documents.

SASTROAMIDJOJO, DR. ALI, and ROBERT DELSON. *The Status of the Republic of*

Indonesia in International Law. Reprinted from *Columbia Law Review,* Vol. 49, (March, 1949), p. 344. (Pamphlet)

SCHILLER, A. ARTHUR. *The Formation of Federal Indonesia 1945-1949.* The Hague-Bandung: W. van Hoeve Ltd., 1955.

SCHRIEKE, B. *Indonesian Sociological Studies—Selected Writings.* The Hague-Bandung: W. van Hoeve, Ltd., 1955. Part One.

SJAHRIR, SOETAN. *Our Struggle.* Amsterdam, 1946. (Pamphlet)

———— *Out of Exile.* (Based upon letters by Soetan Sjahrir rewritten and edited in Dutch by Maria Duchateau-Sjahrir; translated, with an introduction by Charles Wolf, Jr.) New York: John Day Co., 1949.

SMAIL, J.R.W. *The 27th June Affair.* Unpublished paper, Modern Indonesia Project, Cornell University Project, Cornell University, Ithaca, N.Y., 1957.

SOEDJATMOKO. *Economic Development as a Cultural Problem.* Ithaca, N.Y.: Cornell University Modern Indonesia Project, Southeast Asia Program, 1958.

STEVENS, BENJAMIN FRANKLIN. (Editor and compiler). *Christopher Columbus, His Own Book of Privileges, 1502. Photographic Facsimile of the Manuscript in the Archives of the Foreign Office in Paris, Now For the First Time Published, With Expanded Text Translation into English and an Historical Introduction.* Transliteration and Translation by George F. Barwick, B.A., of the British Museum. Introduction by Henry Harrisse. London: B. F. Stevens, 1893.

THOMSON, J.T. *Translations from the Hakayit Abdulla (Bin Abdulkadar,) Munshi.* London: Henry S. King & Co., 1874. Second Edition.

UNITED NATIONS, DEPARTMENT OF PUBLIC INFORMATION. *Peaceful Settlement in Indonesia.* (Pamphlet)

United Nations Demographic Yearbook, 1957.

VANDENBOSCH, AMRY. *The Dutch East Indies—Its Government, Problems, and Politics.* Berkeley: University of California Press, 1941.

VETH, PROF. P.J. *Java Geographisch, Ethnologisch, Historisch.* Haarlem, 1907.

VLEKKE, BERNARD H.M. *Evolution of the Dutch Nation.* New York: Roy Publishers, 1945.

———— *Nusantara* (Empire of the Islands)—*A History of the East Indian Archipelago.* Cambridge, Mass.: Harvard University Press, 1943.

———— *The Story of the Dutch East Indies.* Cambridge, Mass.: Harvard University Press, 1945.

WALLACE, ALFRED RUSSEL. *The Malay Archipelago—The Land of the Urang-Utan, and the Bird of Paradise. A Narrative of Travel, with Studies* of *Man and Nature.* London: Macmillan and Co., 1869. Two volumes.

WEHL, DAVID. *The Birth of Indonesia.* London: George Allen & Unwin, Ltd., 1948.

———— *The Moon Upside Down.* London: James Barrie, 1948.

WERTHEIM, W.F. *Indonesian Society in Transition—A Study of Social Change.* The Hague and Bandung: W. van Hoeve Ltd., 1956.

WILCOX, FRANCIS O., and THORSTEN V. KALIJARVI. *Recent American Foreign Policy.* New York: Appleton-Crofts, 1952.

WIT, AUGUSTA DE. *Java: Facts and Fancies.* London: Chapman and Hall, Ltd., 1905.

WOLF, CHARLES JR. *The Indonesian Story—The Birth, Growth, and Structure of the*

Indonesian Republic. (Issued under the Auspices of the American Institute of Pacific Relations.) New York: John Day Co., 1948.

WOODMAN, DOROTHY. *The Republic of Indonesia.* New York: Philosophical Library, 1955.

WRIGHT, ARNOLD, and OLIVER T. BREAKSPEAR (Editors). *Twentieth Century Impressions of Netherlands India—Its History, People, Commerce, Industries and Resources.* London: Lloyd's Great Britain Publishing Co., Ltd., 1909.

YULE, COL. SIR FRANCIS (Editor and translator). *The Book of Sir Marco Polo, the Venetian, Concerning the Kingdoms and Marvels of the East.* London: John Murray, 1903. Two volumes with maps and illustrations.

INDEX

331